Collected Works of Northrop Frye

VOLUME 2

The Correspondence of
Northrop Frye and Helen Kemp,
1932–1939

The Collected Edition of the Works of Northrop Frye has been planned and is being directed by an editorial committee under the aegis of Victoria University, through its Northrop Frye Centre. The purpose of the edition is to make available authoritative texts of both published and unpublished works, based on analysis and comparison of all available materials, and supported by scholarly apparatus, including annotation and introductions.

The Correspondence of Northrop Frye and Helen Kemp 1932–1939

VOLUME 2

1936–1939

Edited by Robert D. Denham

UNIVERSITY OF TORONTO PRESS
Toronto Buffalo London

Toronto Buffalo London

Printed in Canada

ISBN 0-8020-0772-4 (Volume 1)
ISBN 0-8020-0773-2 (Volume 2)

Printed on acid-free paper

Canadian Cataloguing in Publication Data

Frye, Northrop, 1912–1991
The correspondence of Northrop Frye and Helen Kemp,
1932–1939

(Collected works of Northrop Frye ; v. 1–2)
Includes index.
ISBN 0-8020-0772-4 (v. 1)   ISBN 0-8020-0773-2 (v. 2)

1. Frye, Northrop, 1912–1991 – Correspondence.
2. Frye, Helen Kemp, 1910–1986 – Correspondence.
3. Critics – Canada – Correspondence.   I. Frye, Helen Kemp,
1910–1986.   II. Denham, Robert D.   III. Title.

PN75.F7A44 1996   801'.95'092   C96-930390-4

University of Toronto Press acknowledges the financial assistance to its publishing program of the Canada Council and the Ontario Arts Council.

Contents

Abbreviations

AGO	Art Gallery of Ontario
AGT	Art Gallery of Toronto
AHCM	Associate diploma, Hambourg Conservatory of Music
ATCM	Associate diploma, Toronto Conservatory of Music
Ayre	John Ayre, *Northrop Frye: A Biography* (Toronto: Random House, 1989)
BBC	British Broadcasting Corporation
BM	British Museum
Bob	the annual skit put on for the first-year students at Victoria College, named after Cobourg campus custodian Robert Beare
CCF	Co-operative Commonwealth Federation
CGIT	Canadian Girls in Training
CNE	Canadian National Exhibition
CNR	Canadian National Railway
CPR	Canadian Pacific Railway
E	The letter E between two numbers represents the year of graduation from Emmanuel College (e.g., 3E7).
EC	Emmanuel College
HCM	Hambourg Conservatory of Music
HFF	Helen Frye Fonds, Northrop Frye Papers, Victoria University Library, Toronto
HGK	Helen Gertrude Kemp
HK	Helen Kemp
HKF	Helen Kemp Frye
HNF	Herman Northrop Frye
illus.	Illustration
IODE	Imperial Order Daughters of the Empire

JCR	Junior Common Room
LCC	London County Council
LSR	League of Social Reconstruction
MPP	Member of Provincial Parliament
NF	Northrop Frye
NFF	Northrop Frye Fonds, Northrop Frye Papers, Victoria University Library, Toronto
NGC	National Gallery of Canada
NGCA	National Gallery of Canada Archives, Ottawa; File 7.4C, Outside Organizations, Carnegie Corporation, Individuals: Kemp, Helen G.
NRA	National Recovery Administration
OCA	Ontario College of Art
OCE	Ontario College of Education
OEA	Ontario Education Association
OSA	Ontario Society of Artists
OUDS	Oxford University Drama Society
OUP	Oxford University Press
PLS	Picture Loan Society
PLT	Postal Telegram
PT	Physical Training
RAF	Royal Air Force
RCA	Royal Canadian Academy of Arts
RCM	Royal Conservatory of Music
RDD	Robert D. Denham
RDF	Roy Daniells Fonds, Special Collections and Archives, University of British Columbia
ROM	Royal Ontario Museum
SCM	Student Christian Movement
SCR	Senior Common Room
SPS	School of Practical Science, University of Toronto; later, the Faculty of Engineering
T	The letter T between two numbers represents the year of graduation from the University of Toronto (e.g., 3T2).
TCM	Toronto Conservatory of Music
TPL	Toronto Public Library
TSO	Toronto Symphony Orchestra
UBC	University of British Columbia

UC	University College, University of Toronto
UCC/VAU	United Church of Canada / Victoria University Archives, Toronto
UNB	University of New Brunswick
U of T	University of Toronto
V & A	Victoria and Albert Museum
VC	Victoria College
VU	Victoria University
VUA	Victoria University Archives
WMS	Women's Missionary Society

Frye and Kemp often use periods with abbreviations, which are reproduced in the text of the letters as they have written them.

The Correspondence of
Northrop Frye
and Helen Kemp

VOLUME 2

1936–1937

From the time of Kemp's return from England in October of 1935 until August of 1936, no letters pass between the two correspondents. During these ten months Kemp seems to have been renting a flat, having moved out of her parents' home, and Frye was living, at least officially, in the Emmanuel College residences. Ayre traces what little we know about their lives during this period. Kemp busied herself with the educational projects of the art gallery, arranging lectures and study groups, and Frye, having set aside his Blake thesis, threw himself into his teaching, assisted E.J. Pratt in reviewing poems submitted to the *Canadian Poetry Magazine*, and wrote a half-dozen reviews on opera, ballet, and music for *Acta Victoriana*, the *Canadian Forum*, and *Saturday Night*. Toward the end of the year he tried his hand at fiction-writing, producing the first two of his several "fables," and he published his first essay, "Wyndham Lewis: Anti-Spenglerian," in the *Canadian Forum*. Several stories he sent to the *Atlantic Monthly* were rejected. He naturally spent a number of hours at the art gallery, attending the lectures Kemp had organized and using the collection of art books in the gallery's library. After his ordination in the United Church in June, he spent a month at the Kemps' Gordon Bay cottage working on his Blake manuscript. Meanwhile, Pelham Edgar, who wanted to see Frye become a permanent member of the English staff at Victoria, promoted his case for a Royal Society fellowship that would support a year's work at Oxford. Frye received the award—$1,500 to study the symbolism of Blake's prophecies—and so planned to set out for Merton College in the fall (Ayre, 118–23).

Following that year's hiatus, the letters resume after Frye has left Gordon Bay for Moncton, where he spends a month before sailing for England. This is the first trip home he has made since the summer of

1933, and the visit produces little comfort. He is distressed that he will not see Kemp for a year. His mother, now sixty-five, has aged considerably, and his father is barely managing to eke out a living. Frye arranges his passage to England from Montreal, rather than Halifax, with the hope that Kemp might meet him there before he sails. "I want to see you," he writes. Kemp replies sometime during the third week of August (the letter is missing from the files), saying that she is ill. Frye quickly advises her to see a doctor when she returns to Toronto from Gordon Bay, adding that she shouldn't "jump to conclusions quite so quickly this time—I've been away two weeks, remember." Kemp writes again from Gordon Bay with the news that she "may have to have some kind of treatment" for she seems "to have missed a month," and the subsequent letters confirm what they both suspect—that Kemp is pregnant, apparently for the second time. "I keep telling myself," Frye says in his next letter, "that I can't have caused it both times, that there must be something else the matter, but that doesn't work." On 27 August, Kemp, having gone back to Toronto with her mother, sends Frye the news that she has had an abortion, performed by a doctor who has learned a new method in Germany. Abortion was illegal at the time, but Kemp's mother, working through a nurse who was "very competent, experienced and sympathetic," is able to make the necessary arrangements.

Throughout their correspondence in late August Frye is distressed that Kemp may be moving back home to live with her parents and not, as she had planned, sharing an apartment for the year with her friend Barbara Sturgis. He is also troubled that Kemp is being "stampeded" by her family to abandon her plans for "living independently" in order to help with the family's expenses, particularly the fees for her brother Harold's music lessons and college tuition for her other brother, Roy. Consequently, he gives her a rather stern lecture at a time when she needs empathy. Although he shortly apologizes for his "rather unnecessary outburst" and sends $15 to help pay for the operation, on the whole he seems somewhat insensitive to Kemp's plight.

One of the ironies of this unhappy episode is that Kemp's father was engaged in making birth control information available in Canada. When Kemp was in England two years before, he had requested that she send him Marie Stopes's books on birth control, which were considered contraband in Canada; and he circulated these books, as well as others already in his possession, to a number of friends and acquaintances.[1]

The same year, Kemp herself had given the promiscuous and somewhat naive Millicent Rose one of Stopes's books to read.

After her recovery, Kemp returns to work at the Art Gallery of Toronto on 1 September, and on the same day she receives a telegram from Frye, asking her to meet him at the Bonaventure Station in Montreal. Though strapped for money, Kemp does take on the train to Montreal, where they have a day together before Frye boards the *Alaunia* for London on 4 September. In mid-September she rents an apartment with Barbara Sturgis at 24 St. Joseph Street, but stays there for only a week or so because Jessie Macpherson, the dean of women at Victoria College, taps her to become a don in one of the women's residences. Thus, in late September she ends her arrangement with Sturgis and moves into Wymilwood at 84 Queen's Park Crescent. Her first letters abroad contain advice to Frye about room and board in London, news of their Victoria College circle of friends and the art gallery staff, and family gossip. She also sketches the first chapters in the saga of Robert K. Arnold, a member of the German department at Victoria, and Magda, his wife—a continuing melodrama in which Kemp is confidante to both parties. In early October she attends an art conference in Cleveland with three members of the art gallery staff, and she occupies herself with a flurry of chores for a show of Soviet art and a Van Gogh exhibition.

Meanwhile, Frye, after an uneventful voyage, arrives in London on 14 September, and sets himself up in Bloomsbury, just off Russell Square, at 90–92 Guilford Street, the same boarding house where Kemp had stayed when she returned from Italy in April 1935. He looks up Cameron Caesar and Don Stuart, Victoria and Emmanuel classmates respectively, visits Veronica Wedgwood on two occasions, records his impressions of England, and manages all the while to take advantage of London's bookshops, concert halls, and galleries. He also travels to Cheltenham to visit W.F. Jackson Knight, a classics scholar and brother of University of Toronto professor G. Wilson Knight. The trip to Cheltenham, Frye writes, "was fascinating—it was like being dragged through one Constable painting after another." He gets along well with Knight in spite of Knight's Fascist sympathies because they speak "the same language." On 9 October Frye leaves London for Oxford, but not before he sends Kemp birthday greetings and another earnest declaration of love. He is promptly introduced to his tutor, Edmund Blunden, and launches immediately into his first paper—an essay on Chaucer's early poems. "Blunden said very flattering things about it," Frye reports, "but he obviously isn't very fresh on Chaucer."

At this time, there were three courses in English literature at Oxford, which were, as Frye described them later, "arranged in order of prestige. Course I consisted largely of Gothic and Old Norse. Course II embraced English literature, but embraced it only as far as the year 1500. Course III, which was strictly for the birds and Rhodes scholars, went on until 1830. . . . I decided to read the third course, but even so I found myself doing most of my work on the earlier period, Old and Middle English, largely because it was new to me."[2]

On arriving at Oxford Frye says, "I am completely surrounded by shell: I have no curiosity: don't want to go see anybody, or go for a walk: just want to sit in my room, devour books nervously and feverishly." Still, he appears to involve himself in Merton College life rather quickly, having tea with fellow Canadian Douglas LePan, joining the Oxford Union, and making friends with Joseph Reid, a Rhodes scholar from Manitoba, and two Rhodes scholars from the United States, Rodney Baine and Alba Warren.

In mid-October Frye has a chance encounter with Elizabeth Fraser, a Canadian graphic artist with whom he and Kemp had had a passing acquaintance in Toronto. "We parted with expressions of esteem," he writes, "and promises to come together later. I may give a tea for her and LePan soon. She looks interesting." But before he can send an invitation, Fraser asks him over for a meal, which he accepts, showing up at her place two weeks later. Thus begins the most intriguing relationship Frye has during the year. Fraser, a pipe-smoking free spirit who is twelve years older than Frye, is trying to survive in Oxford by illustrating books. One of her projects, described in some detail in Frye's letter of 3 November, mystifies him because he cannot imagine why she is drawn to the turgid prose of the text. But he says she is "a very remarkable girl" and is attracted to her ideas, which he says "have been gradually developing the way mine have on Blake, into a more and more objective unity all the time," as well as to her drawings, which he sees "as sincere as the book is faked, and as concrete as the book is vague."·

Frye and Elizabeth Fraser share each other's company on a number of occasions during November and December, having tea together, going on a "pub-crawl," hiking to the countryside and surrounding villages on numerous occasions, and seeing plays and movies together. "God knows what one can make of the girl," Frye writes. "Her relief at finding

someone who wouldn't blush and look the other way when she powdered her nose and who wouldn't think she was a fallen woman if she
wanted to go find a bush in the course of the walk suggested that she
had been making rather a fool of herself in front of Englishmen
recently—I suspect she has a genius for that." They continue to see each
other frequently throughout the 1937 Easter term. Toward the end of the
term Frye writes to Kemp that Elizabeth is "a lonely girl with lots of
courage, pride and sensitiveness, but she is a swell girl. She hits hard
and rubs people the wrong way, in a way I think you understand, after
six years of me, but she's more honest and straightforward than I am
and has more guts. You'll love her when you meet her." Both Frye and
Fraser teeter on the brink of insolvency, frequently borrowing money
from each other, and each is attracted to the other's creative bent, even
though Frye hardly knows how to respond to some of her illustrations
and designs. John Ayre describes their relationship as a "lonely hearts"
one that "centred on discussions of art and the damnation of poverty"
(133). It is certainly that, but, as Fraser's letters to Frye suggest, there
may have been a romantic involvement as well.[3]

Back in Toronto Kemp is fully engaged in the bustle of Victoria College social life, in the educational programs for teachers at the art gallery, and in the duties of her donship at Wymilwood. She also finds time
to lecture at the Royal Ontario Museum, first on French Rococo and then
on classicism, and to write an occasional article. Like Frye, she has to
watch her finances carefully, especially since she has borrowed money
for her brother Roy's tuition. Her time is divided between two new
groups of colleagues—the dons in the women's residences and the art
gallery staff—and she keeps Frye apprised of the agonies and the occasional ecstasies of both. In her work at the art gallery she rubs elbows
with a number of prominent figures in the Toronto art scene, including
Yvonne Williams, Gordon MacNamara, Charles Comfort, Douglas Duncan, Gordon Webber, and Harold Stacey. She initially intends to return
to the Courtauld Institute in June to retake her examinations, but the
prospect for this dims as the year progresses. She has her own "lonely
hearts" relationship with Douglas MacAgy, a bright young art student
who plans to study the next fall at the famous Barnes collection in
Merion, Pennsylvania. Twice she tells Frye she is quite fond of MacAgy,
but this sentiment never elicits a response from Oxford.

Frye has his moments of loneliness. "Here I am," he writes in November, "in the greatest university in the world, studying the only subject I

care a damn for, and still all I can think of is how much I want you, and how much more I want you. Seven months to keep telling you I love you without proving it." He speaks of his "invincible shyness," but he is hardly a recluse. He is elected to membership in the prestigious Bodley Club, and he tells Kemp a great deal more about his social life than about his studies. Blunden does not want to see Frye's papers, so he forgoes the purchase of a typewriter in favour of a piano. He strengthens his ties with Rodney Baine and Alba Warren, and develops a new friend in Mike Joseph, a New Zealander studying at Oxford. Once the piano is delivered to his Merton room, his circle of companions widens.

Frye's reports on his Monday evening tutorials with Blunden are sketchy at best. His first three papers are on Chaucer, and for each Blunden does little more than flatter Frye with approval. Regarding the third paper Frye says, "Blunden threw flowers at my feet yesterday, I think because my paper was clever, vague and short—Canterbury Tales. Told me I'd made a real contribution to criticism, etc. etc., and then talked about Blake for the rest of the hour." The topic for the fourth session is not named, though they do discuss Skelton, and Frye follows this with a paper on Wyatt. Then, for his 30 November tutorial Frye decides he is not going to write a paper, saying instead, "I'm going to go in and twist his neck with my bare hands. I've scared the shit out of him, in the Burwash phrase, and I'm just beginning to realize it, and to comprehend why he gives me that dying-duck reproachful stare every time I finish reading a paper to him. He returned the Blake with the remark that it was pretty stiff going for him, as he wasn't much accustomed to thinking in philosophical terms." Frye had taken his Blake manuscript to Blunden two weeks before, wanting him to read it and send a favourable report to the Royal Society committee in Ottawa before the end of the term. On 17 December 1937, Frye writes, "I don't think Blunden liked my thesis much—he said something vague about all the sentences being the same length—what I think he really resents is the irrefutable proof that Blake had a brain. I am afraid I shall have to ignore him and just go ahead."

Frye is examined on the last day of the term by the dons and warden of Merton. The examination "lasted ninety seconds, & consisted of a speech by Blunden and a purr from the warden." By this time Frye is miserable and penniless, waiting to receive the next instalment of his Royal Society grant so he can go to London for the Christmas vacation. But his spirits are lifted by the arrival of £50 from the Royal Society and by "a fairly concentrated dose" of Elizabeth Fraser. On 19 December he escapes to London for the holidays, staying with Edith and Stephen Burnett, friends of Kemp through Norah McCullough, the educational supervisor at the Art Gallery of Toronto. Elizabeth Fraser shows up in London on 26 December for a five-day visit, and she and Frye attend two performances of *Murder in the Cathedral* (Fraser gets sick at the first performance and has to be hauled home in a taxi). They also wander out to Hampton Court to see a painting by Mantegna, a German edition of whose work Frye has already sent Kemp as a Christmas present. Mantegna, he says, "must be the very greatest painter who ever lived."

Meanwhile, Kemp, whose salary at the art gallery has been raised from $750 to $900 a year, spends most of the holidays preparing a lecture on Greek sculpture for one of her study groups and shuffling among the women's residences to fill in for vacationing dons. She still worries about returning to London to retake her exams, but in mid-January both John Alford, professor of fine arts at Toronto, and Martin Baldwin, director of the art gallery, discourage her from trying for the diploma. Her busy schedule at the art gallery actually precludes devoting the time required for serious preparation, and in February Peter Brieger, who has left the Courtauld to join the art department at Toronto, gives her the same advice. Eventually, H.O. McCurry sends word from the National Gallery in Ottawa that she is "under no obligation" to try the exam again. In the fall Kemp had resolved to learn German and had four lessons from Magda Arnold, but her enthusiasm wanes during the course of the year, and after February she says no more about it, having apparently abandoned the project. On 20 January she reveals that she has begun to "feel at home in the job" in Wymilwood, but by the end of the month she complains about the "don racket," with its "internal politics and small feminine rivalries." She regularly mails Frye a packet of *New Yorker*s and provides him a steady stream of news about family and residence hall life, pregnancies, romantic entanglements, marriages, and deaths.

During his last week in London Frye tracks down several Toronto friends and lunches with Veronica Wedgwood, and on 15 January he returns to Oxford, where the next day he writes Blunden's term exam. He reports that he was "disgusted" with his exam but that "Blunden was very pleased . . . and said nice things." His tutor in Anglo-Saxon from Balliol, J.N. Bryson, had announced a *Beowulf* exam, and Frye spends six days of his vacation reading the "stupid dreary story," only to discover on his return that Bryson had cancelled the exam.

Early in the new year Frye and Kemp begin to question each other about their plans for the summer, but he decides to postpone any decision until the Easter vacation, when he will know whether he can afford to remain in Europe for the entire summer. For her part, Kemp does not seem particularly eager to meet Frye in London, and although she says in her letter of 19 February that her family is urging her to go abroad if she can manage it, she lists a number of reasons why planning such a trip would not be wise: her family may not be able to pay back the money she has lent them, it would be easier for Frye to travel on the continent with a male companion, he could see more if she were not along, he might be able to get a job as a tutor in Danzig, she does not want to get too deeply in debt, and the coronation of George VI will make for "a very bad summer." Frye hints that he might like to come to Gordon Bay after the term is over; yet he tells a Victoria classmate, Doris Moggridge, that Kemp might be making the trip. Kemp then changes her mind, writing on 3 March that she has begun to arrange her vacation schedule just in case she "can afford a summer in Europe." Frye finally concludes that he cannot make a decision until he gets a report from Geoffrey Keynes on his Blake manuscript and hears from Victoria whether the college will support his staying through the summer. By the end of March Kemp is making plans to take a freighter to England, travelling with Peggy Kidder, a secretary at the art gallery.

In March Kemp begins another art gallery project, writing and presenting talks for CBC radio, all the while supervising the teas and cocoa parties at Wymilwood. In April Eric Havelock offers her the job as art editor for the *Canadian Forum*, a position that Frye mildly encourages her to accept. Throughout the spring she seems particularly intent on keeping Frye posted on the lives and loves of Roy Daniells, whom she had first met when he came to London toward the end of her year there, and of Dorothy Drever, one of the members of the Frye–Kemp inner circle from the class of 1933 at Victoria. Frye was attracted to Daniells the first time they met (they had been junior instructors together at Victoria), and they developed into lifelong friends. Kemp sees Daniells regularly throughout the year. He is a don at Victoria's Middle House, and they frequently chaperone with each other at the various social functions of their residence halls. But Kemp's attitude toward Daniells cools somewhat as the year progresses. She is particularly annoyed by his doting regard for Ev Stewart, a 1935 Victoria graduate, and as the year progresses she becomes increasingly disturbed by his fussiness and lack of manners. Frye interprets Daniells's behaviour as being "scrupulously honourable" toward Kemp, but she still maintains that he is rude and ignores her. As for Dot Drever, Frye says, "I'd rather like to keep in touch with [her] a bit this year," and Kemp obliges by sending frequent bulletins about Drever, especially her Communist activities. The more Drever becomes a convert to party propaganda, the more Kemp distances herself.

Frye declares at the beginning of the Easter term that he and Blunden "are definitely going to get along well this term." But he provides even fewer details than he did the first term about his tutorials. After writing an essay on Fulke Greville, he boasts, "These essays I'm doing are mostly publishable, I should imagine: certainly I've collected a lot of material for future books." On 8 February he reads Blunden his anatomy paper—a paper that would develop six years later into one of his first major published essays—"The Anatomy in Prose Fiction."[4] In late February he spends a week preparing a paper on T.S. Eliot for the Bodley Club in lieu of writing one for Blunden, and two weeks later he announces that he has stopped writing papers altogether.

In mid-March Frye heads down to London again for a brief visit with Edith and Stephen Burnett before setting off on 18 March with Mike Joseph for a month's tour of Italy. After spending the night in Paris, they proceed to Genoa, Pisa, Siena, and Orvieto, arriving in Rome on the evening of 22 March. Frye wishes he had stayed in North Italy. In his second letter from Rome he registers his categorical aversion to almost everything Roman, his invective extending for several pages.

Frye and Joseph meet Rodney Baine in Rome, as well as the two Americans—Lou Palmer and Charles Bell, both studying at Exeter College. Palmer and Bell travel on to Assisi, Perugia, Arezzo, and Florence with Frye and Joseph, and they meet up again with Baine in Venice, as well as with Lou Palmer's mother and sister. In his second letter from Italy—a combination of a Baedeker and a gallery guide—Frye takes Kemp on a breakneck tour of some two dozen churches, museums, and palaces. She refers to his "onslaught" of Rome as "breath-taking," but it is hardly a match for his travelogue of Florence ("the best town in the world"), San Gemignano, Ravenna, Venice, Verona, and Mantua—a 5,300-word letter that Kemp says she "nearly had to take a half-holiday to finish reading." "I know so little of painting," Frye says, and he worries that without field-glasses he is missing much of what he should be seeing; yet he does have an extraordinary eye, and his witty and sometimes irreverent accounts of Masaccio and Bartolo di Fredi, for example, make for lively art criticism. Just as lively are his stories, which have a good measure of the wit that was to become his trademark.

Kemp announces in late April that she indeed will be coming to England, sailing on the *Empress of Britain* on 12 June. Frye, meanwhile, has still heard nothing from Victoria, mostly because the college has heard nothing from him. Since January Frye has hinted that the only thing standing in the way of their getting married on his return would be his winning an IODE grant—an $1800 scholarship offered by the Imperial Order Daughters of the Empire. That would enable him to stay at Oxford for another year. But throughout the year he makes no effort to apply, and he waits until late April to ask Kemp to inquire about the application procedures. She does write to the IODE committee on 31 May, saying that Frye needs financial assistance, but nothing comes of the inquiry. Frye apparently is not altogether serious about staying in England for another year—or else the whole episode is an example of his general ineptitude in dealing with practical matters.

On 1 June Frye cables Kemp, saying that he must come home and ask-ing for money. She has already passed on second-hand information (what Roy Daniells has heard from Principal Walter Brown) that Victo-ria might have a $600 scholarship for him. But Frye remains quite mud-dled about his own plans. He thinks that Principal Brown had promised him that the college would finance his second year. But when Brown's letter finally arrives, it contains no such news. Frye proposes two possi-bilities: "One is to grab Brown's six hundred, trust to God for the IODE or something, and hang on. The other is to propose that if he has any-thing for me next year and will take me without a degree, I'll grab it. I feel nervous now that Brown has started to welsh, and I'd like to have that job cinched. I'm not getting enough out of Oxford to make sacrifices worthwhile to finish my course here." It takes Frye three days to realize that the first option is ill-advised, so he asks Kemp to send him $100 so he can come home. "I'm sorry to spoil your trip," he writes, "but the only excuse I have for staying here—getting the Blake published— would keep my nose in the B.M. all day while you were cooling your heels somewhere else."

In the seven letters that pass between them in May, they appear to be talking past each other: Kemp is planning to come to Oxford; Frye is planning to come home. She is convinced that he would not be in such dire straits if he had kept in touch with authorities at Victoria, and she scolds him for not writing to Principal Brown, Pelham Edgar, and other members of the English department: "Really—*I* can't write reports to these people about you. If only you'd write them a short note from time to time and keep them mollified. But there you are, and you send Brown a letter at last from Italy, after Roy [Daniells] has tipped you off—to say nothing of what I've poured forth by way of invective. Really, Frye, you *are* an idiot." Frye replies, rather lamely, that he has sent Edgar four of his essays, telling Edgar he had been in bad health all year. At this point Kemp takes matters into her own hands and goes to see Principal Brown. On 29 May she dispatches the facts of the case as Brown outlined them to her: "You have not kept in touch with the English Department, you have not made any request for money. The only thing that might have been done, which evidently could have been arranged quite easily, was a renewal of the Royal Society award for a second year. But Pelham Edgar has been very much hurt at your lack of courtesy (Brown) in not keeping in touch with him and has done nothing about it. The word is the same all along the line: you haven't written to any of them but Brown and he knows that that was because [Roy] Daniells told you to, and then you didn't even drop a line to Daniells. It is a bit thick, you know." In the meantime Kemp cancels her passage to England and sends Frye $100. He shortly confesses that "it's perhaps as well that somebody has some idea of how to manage my affairs, as I obviously haven't much idea of it myself," adding that he has been "a complete fool with Edgar." To make amends he posts the first chapter of his Blake manuscript to Edgar.

After announcing in February that he was "going to get a lot of Blake done," Frye has not produced as much as he had hoped. In March Kemp asks, "How is the Blake anyway?" Frye had expected to finish the manuscript in Italy, with the help of Mike Joseph, who was "interested in literary symbolism," and this leads Kemp to report to Principal Brown that "the Blake was nearly finished." But Frye does little work on it in Italy, and when he arrives in Padua his bag, with the Blake thesis in it, is mistakenly left on the train by Charles Bell and sent on to Venice. Frye intends to get the manuscript into the hands of Geoffrey Keynes and to send a copy to a publisher before he leaves for Canada. He writes Kemp that "the Blake is the only thing I can do now to recoup myself. I am sure it will be published, and that it will attract a lot of attention when it is published. Things will look different then. The whole story looks very different to me than it does to you, but you'll understand much quicker if I don't go into explanations or excuses. I'm damned sorry about spoiling your trip this summer, much more grateful than I can possibly say for what you are doing, and I concede that I have spent the year sleepwalking, oblivious to everything, with my sense of proportion, perspective, good manners and common sense totally atrophied."

Blunden has suggested Faber & Faber as a publisher, and a day or so before he returns to Canada in late June Frye does send off his manuscript, which he has called *The Blake Prophecies*, to R.E. Stoneman at Faber & Faber. What Frye submits is actually only the first two chapters; he takes chapters three and four, which are twice as long as the first two, back to Canada with him, where he intends to make a final revision. Elizabeth Fraser serves as his intermediary, the correspondence with Faber & Faber being directed through her. On 6 July Stoneman rejects the manuscript because he "cannot foresee a wide enough sale."[5] Fraser mails the rejection letter to Frye at Gordon Bay, but holds on to the manuscript so it can be sent out again, asking him to forward to her "a series of fresh & inspired letters to all the publishers." Frye obliges in late July with a letter to Cambridge University Press.

At this point Fraser seeks Blunden's advice, which is to send the manuscript to Jonathan Cape if Cambridge rejects it. "Blunden," Fraser reports, "thinks it is a good book, but he wishes it was more freely supplied with breaks, of the sort he describes as 'landing-stages.' He would like you every now and then to get off from your subject & sidle up to it. He wants in other words bits of relief. The pictures will supply this to some extent, & if the selection is right I myself feel that they will supply it all."[6] Blunden also advises Frye to inform Geoffrey Keynes that the manuscript has been sent to Cambridge. Fraser, now acting more or less as Frye's agent, does send the manuscript to Cambridge on 31 July, saying that the other two-thirds of the book will follow in September; Cambridge replies, not unexpectedly, that it will consider the manuscript, but only after it has the complete text in hand.[7] Frye does send the manuscript back in the fall, but in November Cambridge rejects it, and Fraser posts it back to Frye, thus bringing to an unsuccessful close Frye's first effort to have his Blake book published. It will be ten more years before it finds its way into print.

After Frye arrives back in Canada on 1 July, he travels immediately to the Kemps' cottage at Gordon Bay. Three weeks later he takes the train to Toronto to negotiate the terms of his contract for the next academic year with Chancellor Edward Wallace. But as Frye has very little to

show for his year in Oxford—no book and no degree—he is in no position to negotiate. Chancellor Wallace indicates that he will recommend a
salary of $1500 to the board, which is $300 less than a lecturer's salary,
and tells Frye that he cannot become a member of the permanent staff
until he has had "at least two years' training abroad." Frye believes he
will inherit the courses of Roy Daniells, who has just accepted a position
at the University of Manitoba, and in his last letter from 1937 he tells
Kemp his probable teaching schedule: a first-year course in the sixteenth
century, a third-year course in Milton, and a fourth-year course in nineteenth-century thought. "They sure picked up a bargain," he writes. "I
shall remember it when the time comes to discuss my 'obligations' to
Victoria College." On 23 July he heads back to Gordon Bay, bringing to a
close this chapter of the Frye–Kemp correspondence.

1 Shortly after she arrived in London in 1934, HK sent her father a copy of
   Marie Stopes's *Birth Control Today*. Replying to her after he had received the
   parcel, he said, "Later on, when I can send you a little money to cover the
   price, I am going to ask you to try the same plan & wrap up separately like
   you did this one, two or three others I see advertised in the back cover of this
   book, such as *Enduring Passion, Roman Catholic Methods of Birth Control, Mother
   England*, and even maybe *Contraception*, all by Marie Stopes. . . . The new book
   is very wonderful, going straight to the point. Very very wonderful. . . . I may
   want to get one or two more copies of the one you sent me. My, I think if some
   philanthropist could only spread a few thousand of them all over the country,
   how wonderful it would be, away and above the very problematical benefits
   derived from such things as 'missions.' But then I have always had the subject
   very much at heart." S.H.F. Kemp to HK, 9 November 1934, HFF, 1992, box 2,
   file 3. In his weekly letters to HK in 1935, S.H.F. Kemp frequently speaks of his
   crusade to make birth control information readily available. He even toys
   with the idea of writing a book on the subject himself (19 March 1935, HFF,
   1992, box 2, file 3).
2 "Literature and Society," *Reading the World: Selected Writings, 1935–1976*, ed.
   Robert D. Denham (New York: Peter Lang, 1990), 183.
3 See Elizabeth Fraser's letters to NF in the HFF, 1991, box 3, file 1.
4 *Manitoba Arts Review*, 3 (Spring 1942), 35–47.
5 R.E. Stoneman to NF, 6 July 1937, HFF, 1991, box 3, file 1.
6 Elizabeth Fraser to NF, 30 July 1937. The material in this and the preceding
   paragraph about Fraser's role in getting Frye's manuscript to the printers
   comes from her letters to him dated 24 June, 8 July, 26 July, 5 August, and 11
   November 1937, HFF, 1991, box 3, file 1.
7 J.C. Roberts to Elizabeth Fraser, 4 August 1937. Fraser forwarded Roberts's

letter to Frye on 5 August 1937, along with a copy of her reply to Roberts, saying "I shall get the second part [of NF's manuscript] to you as quickly as possible." HFF, 1991, box 3, file 1.

130. NF to HK   Moncton, N.B.
                                              Monday morning. [*10 August 1936*]

Postmarked 10 August 1936; addressed to HK at Gordon Bay, Lake Joseph,
Ontario.

My dearest girl:

The minute I left you I got into a large but sweaty crowd waiting for
the Montreal train, which was late. The trip to Montreal was pretty
bloody—I got the last seat in the carriage, between an open door behind
and an oxygen-and-cinders addict in front with an open window, so I
caught a hay feverish cold which kept me sneezing like a threshing
machine for a day or two—I've got it under control now, I think. The
day was hot and the train hotter, with a fretful two-year-old across the
aisle whose mother was working on a theory that she could stop her
from crying by slapping her. I talked to her husband, a chiropodist from
Oregon, who seemed surprised to find any civilization in Canada and
wanted "to see the little graft this here Dr. Locke is running."[1] He was a
mangy looking Irish mongrel I didn't take to much, and I almost felt
inclined to defend Dr. Locke on general principles.

I had three hours in Montreal, went to bed soon after getting on the
train, and found next morning that John Branscombe was on it, married.
He was married Friday night to what looks like a considerably better
half. From Bathurst down to Moncton I talked to the trainman, whose
name is Cormier, a next-door neighbor of ours who is quite a friend of
Dad. He probably has the best library in Moncton, and has been collecting and reading standard works on anthropology, comparative religion
and evolutionary theory for twenty years. He undoubtedly knows far
more about comparative religion than anyone in Emmanuel College.
Very dogmatic and violently anti-clerical, full of Haeckel and Frazer
type of materialism and rationalism. Somewhat narrowed by a profound conviction that all theological writers are either fools or deliberate
liars, and quite surprised that I had read or even heard of any of the
books he had read. The Acadian Frenchman is naturally a liberal free-
thinker on good terms with the English, in contrast to the Quebec
habitant, who is nationalist and obscurantist. The latter are gaining
ascendancy through their superior spawning faculties, and are trying to
foment racial quarrels here. Cormier is part of the vanguard of an agnos-

tic tendency which I think will absorb eventually most of the urban population of French Canada. He made me feel . . . . that he, a mere trainman, should . . . . while I, who had been to University . . . . Fill up the blanks with something pious and patronizing.

Dad has been in Sydney[2] and is not yet home. Mother is an old woman now, quite old, and looks rather ghastly with her large white face, the lines of her mouth arching down to her chin, her close-cropped gray-white hair and a growth on the side of her nose. The partially insane aunt died on July 28.[3] Mother's life up to Howard's death[4] becomes more real to her all the time, and the rest of her life less real. I'm not quite real to her now, except as a kind of after-image of Howard. She read my Delius article[5] and said she didn't know anything about that man Delirious.

The piano is in wonderful shape, considering how little attention it's had, but is frightfully tinny—the felts have all been banged off the hammers. And do you know, I actually left after all without taking Barbara's book[6] with me, which Barbara mustn't know.

My love to the family, and I suppose Harold [Kemp] is a champion bugle-burper by now.[7] I must stop now and take this to the station, where I have to claim my trunk.

Oh, my darling!

Norrie.

1 Dr. Malhon W. Locke, a graduate in medicine from Queen's University and a member of the Ontario Medical Association, practised medicine in Williamsburg, Ont., about forty miles south of Ottawa. Locke developed a theory that numerous ailments were the indirect result of faulty foot posture, and the special foot treatment he provided was reputed to have had uncommon curative effects. Some considered the reports of his successes to be a hoax. See Rex Beach, *The Hands of Dr. Locke* (New York: Farrar & Rinehart, 1935).
2 The major centre on Cape Breton Island, Nova Scotia.
3 NF's mother, Catharine (Cassie) Howard, was two weeks away from her sixty-sixth birthday. The "partially insane aunt" was Elthea (Dolly) Howard, the oldest sister of NF's mother.
4 NF's older brother Howard was killed in World War I.
5 "Frederick Delius," *Canadian Forum*, 16 (August 1936), 19–20.
6 See Letter 92, n. 1.
7 HK's younger brother Harold was a musician, though his principal instrument was the cello. He had apparently been practising the bugle at Gordon Bay.

131. HK to NF   [*Gordon Bay, Lake Joseph, Ontario*]
Aug. 13th 1936.

My dear,—

I was so glad to hear from you so soon, and sorry that you had a bad journey. If it had not been for the pile of New Yorkers you gave me I should have been very doleful indeed. But I applied myself to them very diligently. I had a letter from Barbara quoting two English jokes, beginning as she says, her anti-New Yorker campaign right away! She gave me all sorts of information about train service to Moncton—regular fare, time of arrival in Montreal etc etc, but said there is no excursion until September and the date is not yet known. {Pause: Harold [Kemp] bought a new fish line and got the hooks caught in his pants, but I pulled them out}. I'll not know about that week-end for a little while yet but will certainly come if I possibly can. On the other hand, I don't want you to delay long for me because you could be spending your time to good advantage sight-seeing in London and I feel rather a pig for keeping you here this long.

What did your mother say when she opened your trunks? I hope they arrived safely enough. Perhaps your father would know where to get a heavy wooden box for packing your books, as I am sure you will need another trunk unless you use boxes. Besides, your trunk would suffer less damage that way. You can nail up the box, board it up and put ropes around it and everything should be all right.

Cormier sounds like a welcome diversion! in that long train journey. (Spot would be better for the stoker!)[1] Speaking of opinionated individuals,—I practiced with John Willis last night. He brought his sister Hope—a girl of about nineteen but dressed in pink and her hair in long pigtails, and she looked like an English school girl of thirteen. But she probably went to a school in China run by English mistresses. She is staying home for a year in Halifax and will then go to London to train as a nurse in St Bart's Hospital. J.W. played a little better than last time and I pulled him up short every time he made a mistake. He insists that he has never *counted* since he began. He will when I'm through with him. At any rate, he *does* take correction with good grace and is coming again to-morrow night. He told me he was writing a three thousand five hundred word thesis, with great impressiveness. But I thought that did not seem out of the way for an essay, and asked him what was the subject of the thesis. He said, somewhat less confidently, it was an account of two weeks holidays up here. The events of same—a trip to Midland[2] etc. Mom asked if he'd put in the day he went fishing with her, and he had! So I asked him why he called that a thesis and, not to be put down, he laughed and said he might get an M.A. for it some day, in some university. Quite a lad. Doesn't approve of the S.C.M. in Halifax and says the leader is nothing else but an infidel, who was kicked out of McGill for spreading his philosophical ideas. Bronson, I believe his name is. Chemistry professor, or something in science at any rate.

One day Harold [Kemp] and Mom went fishing and I was just coming back in the row-boat when Daddy came down with Mrs. Meyer. She had come over to call in the afternoon and Daddy was out in the garden, stripped to the waist as usual. However, she started right in and chattered to me while he went back to work. She said she'd tried time and time again to get Mr Meyer to come over but he was so busy always with his garden and when he'd come in he would say he wasn't shaved etc, so she decided to come over herself to show us she had not forgotten us. She seemed to know I had been in Toronto, and said "You didn't bring your friend back with you?" I told her that by that time you were in Moncton, New Brunswick, and she said she had liked your looks, *such* an interesting young man, and such lovely hair! Beautiful colour, like spun honey. I could not help admiring her taste but I did think she might have tried to get over *while* you were here and not—oh well.

Yesterday I started to write a letter for Daddy to Miss Faircloth, one of his lip-reading club people, and I wrote out the notes on a lecture given at their conference. Then I thought my writing is so bad just now,—I'll type it. So I did! I typed it once on the onion skin paper and Daddy wanted it on good paper so I did it over again. It took a long time but I was very proud of myself when it was done. My hand is terribly stiff for some reason, and I can't write properly.

I have just finished Winifred Holtby's "South Riding,"[3] which came a few days ago. It seems quite a good book, and certainly I did not leave it until I had finished. She had quite an ingenious idea and showed all the mixed motives behind county politics in South Riding, class consciousness popping up here and there and she has woven together so many different characters and ticked them off with great precision that what looks like a most formidable list of dramatis personae at the beginning becomes a very readable story. From the wrapper I discover that she is dead and this was finished shortly before her death.

Several more letters have been returned from South Africa[4]—we still don't know who the culprit is, but Marion [Kemp Harrison] complains of our not writing. She sends her very warm congratulations to you on hearing of the Royal Society Award.[5] She seems to be flourishing and I expect you will be an uncle around Christmas time, if my calculations are correct.

I hope by this time you are feeling more accustomed to being at home, and that your mother is more used to seeing you. Three years is quite a long time for her, and she will probably think you have changed quite a bit. Is the growth something serious? Do give her my love, even if she has never seen me. Oh Norrie, *do* you think she would like me to come for a week-end? I want to, so much, and I hope she will like me and I'm scared to death. I'm not really, but I am a little.

Be good, my dear, and go to the dentist and all that. *Couldn't* you get a decent boat from Halifax? After all, Quebec's some distance back. I imagine you'll be a pretty good sailor and you don't need too much luxury.

Send me a line soon. I'm missing you an awful lot, but I just don't think of it, and devote myself to the typewriter.

I love you.

Helen.

P.S. Re Meyer episode. She invited us to send Harold [Kemp] over to get some of their beans. When told of it Daddy said he'd be damned if we would, and gave her a somewhat dirty suggestion with regard to said beans. (She was not here, of course, by that time.) But when Mom returned, tired, and without any fish except one small one, and there was nothing to eat for supper, again characteristically, she sent Harold over without consulting Daddy at all. So they treated him very well and he was most impressed with the garden, and came back with two baskets of the most beautiful beans I've ever seen or tasted.

Harold had dinner at Island View Hotel last Sunday as we discovered some friends of ours staying there and he took them fishing in the morning. Now he is learning to dance, wants me to coach him on table manners and his accent! He still intermittently talks of ants in his pants for practice ———

H.

1 HK first wrote "spot," crossed it out, and replaced it by "diversion."
2 A town on Georgian Bay, about forty kilometres south of Lake Joseph.
3 *South Riding: An English Landscape*, a novel by Winifred Holtby (London: Collins, 1936), published a year after her death.
4 Marion Kemp, HK's younger sister, had gone to live in South Africa, where she married Ernie Harrison.
5 NF had received a $1500 fellowship from the Royal Society of Canada to spend a year at Oxford studying the symbolism of Blake's prophetic works.

132. NF to HK   Moncton, N.B.
Thursday morning [*13 August 1936*]

Postmarked 13 August 1936; addressed to HK at Gordon Bay, Lake Joseph, Ontario.

Dearest:

I have been talking to a very obliging but extremely muddle-headed passenger agent who will probably cause me to change my plans, but as it is now he is telegraphing to reserve a third-class booking on the good ship "Alaunia"[1] which sails from Montreal Sept. 4, at 10:30 a.m. It was while I assumed that he knew something about it that I let him talk me into taking a Montreal instead of a Halifax boat—the Halifax ones are very slow, no cheaper, stop at Newfoundland and land at Glasgow or some such place. The Alaunia will drop me in London. So I think I'll plan to leave here the afternoon of Sept. 2, & arrive in Montreal the morning of Sept. 3.

Dad came home on Monday night. He looks very well, much heavier than when I last saw him, being up to 160 pounds or thereabouts. All kinds of energy: he carries agencies for four Ontario firms and says he's getting all the business for all of them possible to be got in the Maritimes. He wants to get out of here though, and is trying to get agencies for Quebec and the Maritimes so he could live near his old home.

Mother likes to talk to me, so I've abandoned the idea of work—all I'm doing is reading a bunch of sniggering Restoration plays who keep pointing out for page after page how extraordinarily funny a cuckold is. Mother tells me all her dreams, extraordinarily vivid ones, full of Biblical symbolism & quite startlingly like the Pilgrim's Progress. She has always regarded her mind as something passive, worked on by external supernatural forces, and is very unwilling to think that anything might be a creation of her own mind—besides, it flatters her spiritual pride to think of herself as a kind of Armageddon. She told me that once she was working in her kitchen when a voice said to her "Don't touch the stove!" So she jumped back from it, and something caught her and flung her against the table. Half an hour later the voice came again, "Don't touch the stove!" She jumped back again and this time was thrown violently on the floor. When Dad came home for dinner he found her with a black eye and a bruised shin. I have read a story by Thomas Mann in which he tells of seeing a similar thing in a spiritualistic séance:[2] that story was the basis of the priest's remark to the ghost in my *Acta Victoriana* sketch: "If you are very lucky, you may get a chance to beat up a medium or two."[3] Mother has also heard noises like tapping and so on, and was tickled to get hold of a copy of a *Reader's Digest* in which a writer describes having gone through exactly similar experiences.[4] The best way to deal with mother is, I think, to get her books telling of similar things that have happened to other people: she's not crazy, but might be excused for thinking she was if she didn't realize that such things are more common than she imagines. She was delighted with my Acta story, and I'll try to get her that Mann thing and C.E.M. Joad's *Guide to Modern Thought*,[5] which has a chapter on those phenomena.

When you come down to Toronto again you might see if you can find a December Acta—the one with an article on the Ballet Russe in it.[6] I seem to have come away without one, and I should very much like to have my three discussions on opera & ballet with me in England.[7] Also I think I left my Legouis & Cazamian at your place.[8]

Mother thinks the quintuplets are wonderful and has that big yellow Star Weekly picture of them in the living room and several others in the kitchen.[9] Oh, well.

Norrie.

1 A Canadian Cunard White Star ocean liner.
2 NF is apparently referring to the episode involving Ellen Brand toward the end of Mann's *Magic Mountain*—the section entitled "Highly Questionable" in chapter 7.
3 "The Ghost," *Acta Victoriana*, 60 (April 1936), 14–16; rpt. in *Northrop Frye Newsletter*, 4 (Winter 1991–92), 25–7.
4 Louis E. Bisch, "Am I Losing My Mind?" *Reader's Digest*, 27 (November 1935), 10–14.
5 New York: Frederick A. Stokes, 1933.
6 NF reviewed a Ballet Russe performance in *Acta Victoriana*, 60 (December 1935), 4–6; rpt. in Northrop Frye, *Reading the World: Selected Writings, 1935–1976*, ed. Robert D. Denham (New York: Peter Lang, 1990), 4–7.
7 The other two are "Current Opera: A Housecleaning," *Acta Victoriana*, 60 (October

1935), 12–14; and "The Jooss Ballet," *Canadian Forum*, 16 (April 1936), 18–19; rpt. in *Reading the World*, 1–4, 7–10.

8 Emile H. Legouis and Louis Cazamian, *A History of English Literature* (New York: Macmillan, 1929).

9 The reference is to the famous Dionne quintuplets, born on 28 May 1934. A picture of them, *The Dionne Quintuplets*, painted by Hilda G. Taylor, appeared on the front page of a Colour Gravure Section of the *Star Weekly* on 11 January 1936.

133. NF to HK   Moncton, N.B.

Postmarked 18 August 1936; addressed to HK at Gordon Bay, Lake Joseph, Ontario.

Dearest:

Your letter was a long drink of cold water in a desert. I had an idea it would come today, so I didn't do anything at all—just sat around and waited for it to arrive. My ticket has come through from Montreal—I get a whole stateroom in the "C" deck, for $82.00. It's a tourist class, berth in the summer season, they say. I was planning to put my books into a box and have Dad send the box to me by freight after I arrived. Oh, dearest, my pet—do you think you *could* come to Montreal? You see, in my last letter I carefully avoided suggesting it, because I didn't think I had any right to ask you to do that. Well, I still haven't any right, perhaps, but— well, the passenger agent sold me that Montreal boat pretty easily, just because of the chance. Every time I think of seeing you again my stomach feels as if it had electric wires in it. So don't blame me if my spine wobbles a bit—besides, it's only polite to invite you, anyway, isn't it?

{Mother has just called me in to see the two-year old girl in the next house, who is sitting, completely oblivious, between the window blind and the screen, as naked as the day she was born.}

Of course I should love to have you come down here, and Mother would too, but if I said Sept. 4 chances don't look so good. My only hesitation about having you down here was that my parents don't understand a lot of things they would have to understand before I could tell them about the relation which actually exists between us. In other words, I couldn't offer you in my home the hospitality you and your parents offered me in Muskoka, and I am a little ashamed of that. Mother would love you, dear: and I'm sorry I sent that last letter with all those scary stories in it—don't misunderstand them please. I'm getting more used to here by now, and don't feel quite the same way I did when I first came—like a total stranger—the same feeling, exactly, I had on my first day, or week rather, on my field.

Sunday afternoon the ex-girl friend[1] showed up. She's living now in Saint John, but was here for a weekend and finally decided to look me up, after some hesitation. We sat and talked, and gradually her giggles got less nervous and she became quite attractive. She'd been sick all last year, and finally discovered that her teeth were all poisonous. She's wearing false teeth now, and looks very healthy. She's not working, but is going to move up to Hamilton, where her boyfriend has been transferred, and intends to marry him next year. She leaves August 27 for a month's stay in Toronto, where her brother is. So you may be meeting her, after I come back. She showed me his picture, so I had to show her yours, and we agreed we were pretty lucky. He looks all right—first decent man she ever had. She invited me down to her cottage, on the Kennebecasis river, near Saint John, this weekend, and I think I'll go—it means a day or two of fresh air, swimming, and talking socialism with her father. Her coming to see me pleased me very much—I like her better all the time, I think, as I get more remote from her, and feel less paternal about her.

You remember the two boys who used to come for tutoring in modern literature? One of them sent me the stories of Thomas Mann today,[2] with a note saying that it wasn't payment for the huge debt of gratitude he owed me (big words I am grateful for but didn't quite understand) but only a testimonial. Anyway, it was very kind of him and bucked me up a lot. Besides, I was wondering how to get hold of that book. I dropped into the Public Library and found they hadn't bought anything new except *The Golden Bough*, which they kept out of sight behind the desk, so I took two volumes of that and left. I think young Vipond will be writing me about problems other than literary ones—he said he would anyhow.

I ran into Fred Kirby the other day—the only boy of my own age I achieved anything like intimacy with in Moncton. Then he went to Mt. A[3] and I to Toronto, so we didn't see anything of each other, and when he came to Toronto he was always going to look me up and didn't. He was interested in commercial art, spent two years at the Art School, knows Carmichael, is married, lives—or just did—on Browning & Ellerbeck, and is now handling the advertising for whatever Danforth weekly is trying to put the Spotlight, which I've seen in your home, out of business. He'll look me up again before he goes, and I'll tell him to go and see you sometime, as he would be quite a welcome addition to our acquaintance.

Thank you for sending Barbara's [Barbara Sturgis's] letter on—I was planning to ask you for it in my next letter. I congratulate Barbara for having disinterred two authentically English jokes. But one swallow, or even two, won't make a summer, and nothing so obvious as a joke would ever make *The New Yorker*. There's one store in town that sells that magazine, thank God. The Aug. 15 one contains a swell parody of Huxley.[4] Give my love to Barbara when you write. I'm very proud that my typing class is doing so well—why not a few well-chosen lines to dear teacher? Thank Marion [Kemp Harrison] for her good wishes. I *am* sorry about whatever fatuous idiot it is keeps sending your letters back. I'm dreadfully homesick for Gordon Bay. And anyway, I want to see you. The more intimate a relationship is, the more subtle it becomes, and the more skill and delicacy is needed in managing it. Letters are clumsy, blunt tools at best.

Sunday night I went to hear our new minister—new to me, anyhow. The type that shovels into a formless sermon the results of his last week's reading. The choir is worse. Three years ago, chanting the Lord's prayer, it would make a crescendo at the end—it's the same chant as the one used in Vic Chapel. Now they simply jump from soft to loud at the beginning of it. I noticed that, because I noticed three years ago that the crescendo got sloppier every Sunday. I get a bit morbid in church. I spent the entire service trying to figure out what the Prelude was. It was the Andante from the Mendelssohn Violin Concerto.

There's a mountain ash tree beside our house, and I picked a bushel of berries for mother, who is going to make jam or jelly out of them. This town has two magnificent new buildings, a post-office and a high-school. It's a good clean town, with all kinds of flowers and lawns and gardens and trees—quite healthy to look at. Vera won't be coming home, I don't expect—too interested in her boy friend, who takes her to horse races.

I think Mrs. Meyer's explanation, if it was one, pretty lousy—they'd go other places, so why all the absorption in the garden when she proposed getting an eyeful of the spun honey? Just jealous, that's all.

Getting a passport application off is a hell of a nuisance. I got the mug snapped by a photographer who said: "I was talkin to a fella, over this way a bit, who told me that just before that Louis–Schmeling fight,[5] not too far, they made so sure, hold it, the nigger would lose, smile, they gave him a shot of dope {click} before the fight started."

Mother said rather wistfully today that a mother always lost a son when a son married, and gained one when a daughter married, so she supposed Mrs. Kemp would be gaining a son. I do wish Mother would let me talk to her as I would like to, but the barrier of her complete self-absorption is always there, beside an unalterable difference in our ways of looking at things. Mother, like most of her family, needed a training in some difficult technique like one of the fine arts—all that genuine inspiration & terrific emotional power frittering away in backwoods Methodism is a waste of genius.

My love to your family, of course. Oh, darling, I love you so—every inch of my body and every convolution of my brain remembers you. But I daren't think of you too much—not yet.

Norrie.

1 Evelyn Rogers.
2 *Stories of Three Decades*, trans. H.T. Lowe-Porter (New York: Knopf, 1936), an annotated copy of which is among the books in NF's library, now at the VU Library.
3 Mount Allison University. See Letter 3, n. 2, above.
4 Wolcott Gibbs, "Topless in Ilium," *New Yorker*, 12 (15 August 1936), 25–6; the parody is of Huxley's *Eyeless in Gaza*.
5 The 1936 heavyweight boxing match between Joe Louis and the German champion, Max Schmeling, in which Schmeling defeated Louis; in the return bout the same year Louis won with a first round knock-out.

134. NF to HK   Moncton, N.B.

Postmarked 20 August 1936; addressed to HK at Gordon Bay, Lake Joseph, Ontario. NF has just received a letter from HK, which is missing, in which she told him that she was having difficulty renting a flat, that Millicent Rose had run into some kind of problem, and, apparently, that she feared she herself was pregnant. She also mentioned something about one of Sigrid Undset's books.

My pet:

Your letter just came. Thank you for the vegetation—there is not a sign of fall yet in this country. The mountain must be lovely now. I am very sorry about your flat—that was a pretty dirty trick, it seems to me, at this time of the year anyhow. But with Barbara's [Barbara Sturgis's] vigilant eye on the job, apartments being offered everywhere for the next season, and so on, perhaps you won't have to look so hard, and if the owner has any moral sense at all, he may help in the chase. I'm sorry too that you're sick again—perhaps when you get down to Toronto you had better see a doctor about what's holding you up. But don't jump to conclusions quite so quickly this time—I've been away two weeks, remember. And forget about my bleatings for you to come to Montreal—it's far too much bother and expense for you, besides taking you out of the city at the time you ought to be there.

I went over to see Cormier the other night. He takes a magazine called the *Literary Guide*,[1] run by a group of people called Rationalists, a sort of anti-clerical cult. There's a Rationalist club in Toronto which meets every Sunday. I was very much disappointed in it (he lent, or rather gave, me a few copies)—it's a snuffling, canting, self-righteous, priggish little magazine, incredibly sectarian and narrow-minded. The magazine itself is one of those publisher's rackets—its review section designed to advertise their books and knock other publishers'. However, I got a good bibliography from him, as he has some really good things, and some very rare and valuable books.

This morning I saw a little woman struggling with a huge purple suitcase which she had to set down every few feet or so, so I caught up to her and offered to carry it. She was English, and asked me if I were. I said no, and she said she thought I must be because of my voice. Mehton,[2] here I come!

I ran into a chap I used to know called Vernon Stewart. He used to work in a bank which ruled that no employee could marry below a certain salary. He married, and they fired him when they found out. He has another job and a baby now, and lives for the summer at a seaside resort near here, where he has invited me—I may go. His wife was a first-cousin of the ex-girl-friend—still is, of course.

I have been summarizing a couple of volumes of *The Golden Bough*, and the more I read of fertility festivals the more I realize *The Winter's Tale* is one. Apart from that I'm not doing much. This town, being so close to the sea, is deserted in summer, and even if it weren't—well, I'm known chiefly by name and sight rather than personally around here. I'm uneasy walking on the streets, as I never know when I'll pass someone I don't know or can't see plainly. When I do know them, all the conversation is renewal of acquaintance, which is stiff and awkward. So it's really not much wonder if I'm homesick here. Particularly when it's not really home.

Spain worries me—there's no doubt that France and Italy might go to war.[3] Logically, Britain would stay out, as she is neither Communist nor Fascist, her government sympathetic to Italy and the people to France. Besides, it's too barefaced a lineup—Britain has to have more hypocrisy than that before she'll fight. But Britain's capacity for blundering and bungling her way into war is well-known, and, once in, it's jolly old England forever, no matter what she's fighting for. However, I still don't expect war yet, on England's part anyhow.

I guess I'm signed up with the *Alaunia*—I've got my ticket anyhow. If you don't come to Montreal I could go and see my aunt, who is trying to raise a half-grown hellcat named Gloria [Garratt], who is a legacy from the partially insane aunt, who adopted her. She's apparently one of the orneriest youngsters in Montreal—badly brought up, of course—she's eleven now. My aunt writes about nothing else but her troubles with her hellcat. She's alone with her, too. Mother keeps telling stories about early days in her family before she was married.

Not feeling so well—reaction, I guess—not enough exercise here. I wrote to E.K. Brown about the Wyndham Lewis article & asked him what the hell.[4] That ten pounds would be a big help in England. Could you give me the address, sometime, of that place you stayed in London? Or would a hotel or something be better? Living in London is a problem that leaves me at a bit of a loose end.

Well, I seem to have got to the yammering stage, which means I'd better quit. I'm sorry about Millicent [Rose]—it's curious what a mess Communism makes of some people's lives. Sylvia Johnstone, Norm Knight, and others. It can't be the right religion. I agree with you about Sigrid's uterine complex—her father was a doctor.[5] In the last part of the book, called the *Cross*, it's just one fuck after another. Still, it's a way of keeping warm in the North. But if you could get to Montreal—oh, shut up.

Norrie.

1 *The Literary Guide and Rationalist Review*, published by C.A. Watts in London; it began publication in 1894.
2 Merton with a posh English "r."
3 The Spanish Civil War had begun in July 1936, and by mid-August the nationalists and the republicans were engaging in battles of a ruthlessness that shocked the world.

Tension between France and Italy had grown from the time of Italy's invasion of Abyssinia in September 1935, and the subsequent sanctions by the League of Nations against Italy as an aggressor brought Italy into opposition with France and Great Britain.

4 NF's "Wyndham Lewis: Anti-Spenglerian" was published in *Canadian Forum*, 16 (June 1936), 21–2. Apparently NF expects to be paid for it.

5 See Sigrid Undset, *The Cross*, vol. 3 of her trilogy *Kristin Lavransdatter*, an epic story set in fourteenth-century Norway. Although *The Cross* does contain recollections by the heroine of passionate scenes with her husband, NF's account of the conclusion to the novel is somewhat exaggerated.

135. HK to NF   Gordon Bay Lake Joseph Ont.,
                                                            August 21. 1936—

Addressed to NF at 24, Pine Street, Moncton, New Brunswick.

My dear:

I am afraid I can't meet you in Montreal. Things are very complicated for me just now. I can't afford it, I have to find an apartment, and I have to stay home and take care of myself and what ails me. Barbara [Sturgis] has been chasing about and peppering me with letters and post-cards after she found out about the owner of the Bucket[1] moving in, and digging up some awful places to live in. So I am going down on the 24th to get at the business, as dear knows what she would take in a panic. Then Daddy has been urging me to come home—i.e. not so much need of a flat this year, and the family could use the money. Roy resented it last year that I moved out, and if he had not had to work so hard and worry about money so much he would not have failed. All partly my fault perhaps. They—Mommy and Daddy are not urging me etc. but the situation is rather damnable. Roy is not making anything much this summer and things can be no different next year in a financial way than they were last. I ignored the need last year, and if I move out I can't help much and get to England too. I don't think I want to pass up England and a raise is very doubtful. I have written to Dot Drever to sound her out on having Barbara [Sturgis] come in with her and Ev Stewart, but in the meantime I am going down to look for a flat. I don't know what Barbara will say if I decide to throw up the whole scheme, but I will tell her all about the financial difficulty and I think she won't cut my acquaintance. Barbara, in her desire for rigid economy, says she wants to save enough to get back to college before it is too late, so she ought to sympathize with my desire to keep Roy in college. And Harold needs those music lessons. I may have to have some kind of treatment for I seem to have missed a month—it may not be serious, and please don't worry at all, my dear. I feel quite well.

I have been practicing the typewriter and find some difficulty with the right hand margin. Of course the bell doesn't ring very regularly, but I have to keep looking to see when I'm coming near the end of a line. Otherwise I have no great difficulties other than stiff neck from looking at the book so long. Will enclose one page for criticism.[2] I have not worked at it every day, I am afraid, as recent events have put me off work now and again.

Daddy and Mom were both pleased with your message. I think your photograph is lousy and I think that photographer should have his throat cut. But passport photos are all alike that way.

I'm glad you saw the ex-G.F.[3] and hope you enjoyed the weekend at the What's-its-Name River. I was quite amused at you two sitting there reminiscing armed with photographs of your absent loves and congratulating yourselves. It reminds me of my relief at meeting Al Sedgwick and being told he had found the right girl at last. I needed to suffer no further pangs of remorse then!

That *was* nice of your pupil to be so appreciative. Tell me, this young Vipond isn't any relation to the Anglican preacher of St. Andrew's Church in Todmorden is he?[4] The one which is affiliating with St. Luke's. It's an unusual name.

We had a bright idea about the new music room for you and me. There is an old settlers' log cabin at Barwood Sea—the house where all the Hamers were born—John and Fred etc. It's over fifty years old and the logs are as good as new practically because of whitewash inside and clapboarding outside the building. If we could have it moved log by log and put in our back garden it would be ideal. It belongs to Hatherlys at present and is not put to any use except as a storeroom. We are going to see whether we could get an option on it and perhaps buy it in a few years. You'd love it, and it could probably be bought for a song. If you and I ever do consider a house for ourselves here, this is *the* best idea of all, to my mind. There is an upstairs to it, and downstairs there are three rooms at present, one having been used at various times to house the hens and stable the horse. But it could all be cleaned up. The floor is of huge wide boards and there is a stairway going up through the centre of the room. It's a swell idea anyway.

Oh dearest, I would so like to meet you but there are no cheap fares, and the other anxiety does crop up. I feel all at sixes and sevens with Barbara [Sturgis] fussing so much, too.

You don't think that your mother could be induced to look upon *me* as a daughter *gained* rather than the means of losing her son? After all, my family practically lost me last year, so far as my being with them was concerned.

There was something else I've been trying to remember. I think you would be well advised to send a note to Wilson Knight and Kay Coburn right away so that they will know when to expect you. If they are both off on some trip or other you will feel pretty flat. It's only fair to both of them and to yourself to give them a bit of warning that you are coming soon, for life gets pretty complicated in England, especially when people have such a limited time there.

Mom and I called on Charlotte Cronin last night. She has been here all alone for several days, but enjoying it very much. She asked very kindly after you, and said you looked like a genius.

Nothing much is happening here. It rained to-day and there was a heavy windstorm last night. We got up in the middle of the night to pull up the rowboat.

I have my rug well on again. Will soon have to put aside all such things.

My love to you.

H.

1 Apartments located in a house at 340 Huron St. on the western edge of the U of T campus; Ayre notes that "Bucket" was a clipped form of The Bucket of Blood, the name given to these apartments by John Creighton, parodying the name of an English pub (105).
2 HK enclosed a page of typed notes on "The Subject-Matter of Romanesque Art."
3 NF's ex-girlfriend Evelyn Rogers.
4 Les Vipond appears not to have been related to the Anglican minister of St. Andrew's Church referred to by HK; he was the nephew of Rev. Francis Vipond, the United Church minister NF mentions in Letter 136.

136. NF to HK   Moncton, N.B.

Postmarked 25 August 1936; addressed to HK at 205 Fulton Ave., Toronto, Ontario.

My dearest:

I got home at 9 p.m. and found your letter. I thought I would start this tomorrow morning, but here it is one o'clock and there is no sign of sleep yet. Anyway, it is tomorrow morning.

Darling, darling, darling, I'm so sorry about you. I suppose you know how useless it is for you to tell me not to worry. I don't do anything so definite as that: I just ache and hurt, curse myself for ever leaving you, and wish I could do something. I keep telling myself that I can't have caused it both times, that there must be something else the matter, but that doesn't work. Please let me know everything—how much your treatment will cost and so on. And if it really isn't anything much, God knows I'll pay your fare to Montreal if you want to come, but if you think it's better not to, all right. What about bus excursions?

My little girl—I don't quite know how to say this, but I won't sleep till I do, if then—it almost seems as though your parents waited until my back was turned before starting in on you. And sure enough, here you are in the middle of the one problem I had asked you to avoid. We had already discussed the whole question at some length, and it's frightfully inconsiderate of your parents to start raising a fuss now, instead of months ago. "And Harold needs those music lessons"—as though we hadn't already discussed Harold and his music lessons. I thought if you would carry out your plan and live with Barbara [Sturgis] it would save you from being stampeded in every direction by your family. It isn't treating Barbara quite fairly, is it? Don't blame me if she rejects your solicitous proposal to herd her in with Dorothy [Drever] and Evelyn [Stewart], shrugs her shoulders and walks away. Roy [Kemp], of course, has no business whatever to "resent" your doing what you like, and to say that you were responsible for his failure (and, I suppose, for losing the intermediate boxing final too) is monstrous—I had no idea that your father was capable of making such a statement. Apparently he, like your mother and like yourself, is apt to blurt out the cruelest thing in his mind if he feels worried. If I were you, I should hesitate before giving up the plan you spent so much time and thought on last year. To me, at this distance, it seems as though giving up the idea of living independently and returning to the bosom of your family was one of two steps, the second being giving up the idea of going to Europe and passing your examination, on exactly the same plea. What you do in the first instance is your own business; what you do in the second is partly mine: but the two things seem to me to be connected. If you get so bogged down with Harold's cello lessons and Roy's tuition fees and your mother's household and church worries and your father's financial difficulties and Marion's pregnancies that it eventually becomes your duty to stay home next summer, it will be a very bad arrangement for both of us. That is what I am afraid of. I know exactly the sort of appeal your family makes to your sympathies—it comes out in such a preposterous remark as "After all, my family practically lost me last year, so far as my being with them was concerned." Do you feel that Roy "is lost to the family" this summer, or even that Marion is? and they're much more lost than you are.

                                                                4 a.m.

Well, I think I'll leave it. It may be cruel to lecture you like this when you are probably feeling worried anyhow, and, of course, you didn't ask me to butt in, but I think I'll leave it. Because, even if you are quite right, or your family is, about the economics of the arrangement, my warning about the second step still holds. It's a little disheartening to find you stampeding so promptly after I leave away from the one thing I had considered settled. If you're offended by anything I've written, you're still stampeding. But what you decide in cold blood will silence me, as far as the first step is concerned.

Your typing is quite good, as far as I can judge—a memento mother found kicking around here to that effect really belongs to you now.[1] Touch good and even. Two spaces after a period and a colon, use capital O for figures on your typewriter (American ones have a figure 0 where your hyphen is), don't say ST., but St., don't get mixed up with u and y,[2] and don't tackle such hard stuff just yet. Can't tell about rhythm (important) and speed (less important) of course, but it looks very promising. Thanks very much, and send more. Good Lord! I'd better get some sleep.

10:30 a.m.

I had my weekend at Renforth, of course. I went down on the bus, with a vague idea it would be cheaper—it wasn't, and I shall never go by bus again in New Brunswick, for a little while anyway. They're paving the road between Saint (they're particular about that)[3] John and Moncton, but it isn't paved yet, and as it was fine going down I was choked with dust all the way—the bus would get behind a truck or something and the road would be too narrow to pass. Coming back it rained. Of course you haven't much idea what a heavy bus can do to a gravel road which starts out like a washboard and ends up more like a nutmeg grater—but anyhow, I'm resting up today to get over the shock. Mr. Rogers took me out driving in his car around the Saint John valley Saturday night. Sunday it poured rain all day. We (Mr. Rogers and I) went into town to hear Mr. Seeley (the minister who used to be at our church here in Moncton) and in the afternoon we drove around the city—I saw the biggest dry dock in the world among other things. Saint John is built on hills and is a very impressive, dingy, dirty, dilapidated, poverty-stricken city. Climate English—wet and foggy most of the time—and the city looks like an abandoned Lancashire cotton town, I should imagine. It's the oldest incorporated city in Canada, and looks its age—the decrepit, miserable hovels of unpainted houses are covered with meaningless woodwork carving and decoration, which serves now only to catch the soot. There are large wealthy residential sections—the greatest and sharpest contrast between rich and poor ways of living to be found anywhere in Canada, I should think. Yet it was settled by Loyalists, whose descendants spend all their time gloating over their loyalty. To look at the town, you'd think it would be Canada's Glasgow, but apparently the only people in it who have the slightest trace of a social conscience are Mr. Rogers & Mr. Seeley, both fairly well-to-do. Mrs. Rogers is suffering from some nervous disorder or other, and has to stay in bed. Evelyn is going to her boyfriend in Hamilton this Thursday, and was both nervous about going and nervous about my being there (I gather he's inclined to be jealous). She had the curse besides, I think. Sunday night she was acting like a five-year-old—I gather the boyfriend spoiled her pretty badly when she was sick last year—flouncing all over the house, turning to static on the radio and producing horrible noises, while Monday she sulked all day, answering all my efforts of conversation in monosyllables. She was like that before, but not so bad. The last twenty-four hours I sat around and suffered, waiting for the bus to come. No swimming, of course—too cold.

The difficulty about writing to Wilson Knight & Kay [Coburn] is that I haven't any London address. However, I'll write anyhow. I got my passport, but the damn fool who copied out my statement that I was a "Student" got it down as "Steward": I don't know whether that will make any material difference or not.

Vipond's father is a minister, but I had always assumed a United Church minister—however, it may be the one you mention. Dorothy [Drever], bless her heart, also sent me a book to read on the boat— "National Velvet" by Enid Bagnold[4]—I don't know it at all. Your plan for our music house is lovely, and like you to think of it. Two years, darling, and we can do what we like, more or less.

Oh, dearest, I hope by the time this gets to you, you won't feel so sick inside as I do. It's the same feeling I've always had away from you— that's my only reason for getting steamed up about the Montreal trip, which of course is a silly idea from your point of view. It's like those horrible Nazi tortures where they tie down a Communist and then beat his wife in his presence with a rubber hose to extract a confession from him. Something like that always seems to happen to you when I can't do anything about it. God watch over you! My dearest girl.

N.

1 A small pin, apparently one NF had received in a typing contest, that he enclosed with the letter. HK acknowledges its receipt in Letter 138.
2 These are all mistakes HK had made in the typing sample enclosed with her last letter.
3 Before "Saint" NF had written "St" and then marked through it.
4 A children's novel about a fourteen-year-old English girl who wins a horse in a raffle, trains it, and rides it in a steeplechase (London: Heinemann, 1935).

137. HK to NF   205 Fulton Avenue
                                                              Aug. 25. 1936.
                                                              5 P.M.

Postmarked 26 August 1936; addressed to NF at 24, Pine Street, Moncton, N. B.

My dearest,

We came down yesterday, Mom and I. At present I'm undergoing treatment, but I think everything will be all right in another week. There is a little complication in the way of a burn which must be healed first, and the trouble with this kind of operation is one can't talk about it! I mean not to anyone like interested female friends. The thing has gone on for two or three weeks, and the burn must be healed before it spreads infection, and before the other operation can be done. But I'm quite healthy and haven't felt very badly except a few times in the mornings. It will cost $25 I think unless anything more serious happens. I feel like an egg for asking you just now, but could you help me a little?

I have just 'phoned Barbara [Sturgis] who is coming here for dinner to-night. I'll be able to tell you her news later—but she says she's quite cheerful. I wrote to Dot [Drever] and she wrote to Ev Stewart about having Barbara come to live with them—neither of them want a third person very much, and they will be in Yvonne's [Yvonne Williams's] place until November or maybe January. But I expect we'll get a cheap place if we look long enough and there certainly isn't room enough at home. If only the damned gallery would pay me enough I could spare the money for Roy's fees, and I could do it yet if I gave up the idea of Europe next summer. But we need not decide that yet.

Harold and I are trying to say "Mother" as we think it's time we did, so I'll try to work it into my letter-writing to you for practice. Anyhow, Mother is getting a lot of preserving done, and her excuse for coming down early with me is that she had to come on business for Daddy. She is going back to Gordon Bay as soon as she can. She was wonderful, the way she handled the whole affair, phoning various people and explaining to the woman who is handling the case. She backed us to the last ditch, explained the situation to this woman, who by the way, is very competent, experienced and sympathetic, and she told her that this went on with my parents' consent and how brilliant you are (!) I think she can fix me up before I must go back to work, that is, she may do it on Saturday of this week. If not it may be the next week-end. So I can't very well go to Montreal.

I have been in bed all afternoon reading New Yorkers. It's raining again, has been off and on for several days now. Daddy may get fed up and come home if it keeps up too long.

10.30

We've spent a very companionable evening looking over advertisements and with Mother phoning some places. She and I will start hunting to-morrow. Barbara [Sturgis] went over to see the Bucket[1] and she talked to the woman downstairs who is pretty mad about having the owner move in to see how much coal they shovel on the furnace. She says the owner will not be there all the time but has a daughter in fifth form high school who will be there for this year's school term. I'm just wondering whether the girl will want the place for the next four or five years if she decides to go to college! Barbara will probably come over here with me after this weekend and Mother will go back to Gordon Bay, and Harold will come back here. It's all rather complicated and we don't know when Roy will turn up.

There isn't anything very new, and this is a rather pedestrian sort of letter, but you know how it is with house-hunting etc. Barbara went and met the train yesterday, but we came on an earlier one, so she was preparing to meet us again to-night when I 'phoned. We're all very cheerful now. My parents are pretty marvellous, aren't they!

We have to wait until 12.30 to give me a douche and Mom (Oh hell) Mother is bored waiting and it's only 11.20 so she's going to can some more fruit.

With my love

H.

P.S. Mrs. Smith has been telling Mom *how* badly you felt at leaving— Mom says she has a very tender spot for you. Fred [Smith] was asking for you this morning. Also Ev Stewart.

1 See Letter 135, n. 1, above.

138. HK to NF   205 Fulton Ave., Toronto 6
                                          Thursday 11 P.M. [*27 August 1936*]

Postmarked 28 August 1936; addressed to NF at 24, Pine Street, Moncton, N. B.

My dear:

Your letter came to-day, together with the little pin which had me greatly mystified at first! I'm glad you think I'm not doing badly.

Yesterday we spent househunting and find everything very expensive. Janet McLean's on 24 St. Joseph Street is the best yet at $35 a
month—three rooms plus kitchen and bathroom, on the top floor. We
may get two others to go in with us. Don't be dismayed, it really is
awfully difficult to find anything and Barbara's [Barbara Sturgis's] ideas
are very definite on some lines. I have given it a rest to-day as other
things were more urgent. We were dead-tired last night after walking
all afternoon, having dinner with B. [Barbara] at Sherbourne House,[1]
and looking some more.

This morning we moved the big bed out of the middle room and put
some of my stuff in pro tem as it will be some time before we get a place
I think. Then at two o'clock the nurse popped in to say that she'd been
talking to the doctor about the infection around that burn and he said it
would have to be burned away before an operation and unless he did it
I would have to wait three weeks for the operation until it healed under
the nurse's care. I could have the whole thing done this afternoon then,
and get it over with. Have to pay $10 more to him. But it seemed best to
get it over and done properly as she said the sore might spread and if it
had not received prompt attention it would have spread in further—
ulcerated womb, or something of that kind. So she drove me to his office
and it was all over very quickly except that I started to have cramps as
I've never had anything before in my life. I stayed there until four and
she drove me home and I've been lying down ever since. I had cramps
spasmodically until nine o'clock but I'm all right now except that I feel
as if I'd been eating green apples. Mother says cramps are inevitable in
childbirth, so I guess Sigrid Undset wasn't exaggerating much. Mother
'phoned to find out the address of a different woman at first but it seems
she has been in the reformatory and won't be out for a month. She's
been doing this job for twenty years and never lost a patient but someone must have told on her. These two today are very careful about
everything and I expect this nurse knows a good deal more along this
line than many doctors—she had helped Mother once when Dr. Hannah
Reid said she wasn't pregnant, but she had been for four months. I'll be
better to-morrow and Mom goes back up north for two weeks. Barbara
is coming to keep Harold and me company.

Darling, I'm afraid I really can't come to Montreal. I have to rest for a
few days—I'll be having the curse all next week probably, and can't
stand up straight yet. I'm going to be all right as I said, but I can't take
any risks—the nurse said I'd have to go easy but that I could go back to

work on Tuesday. And the job will keep me hopping. There's a Mr. Chisman out from England—he arranged the Exhibition Art Show last year and this[2]—and he's here with his daughter and would like to see me. Baldie [Martin Baldwin] told me to look him up or not just as I like—he's kinda conservative. About fifty and his daughter around seventeen, so I can't take them to a cabaret exactly!

My boarding house was 90 Guilford Street—people named John Walter. WALTER. Why don't you have your letters sent c/o Canada House, Trafalgar Square. You go there as soon as you arrive, sign the register and collect your mail,—no charge and everyone does it. Canadian newspapers there and magazines, but that's no thrill! Why don't you look up Cameron Caesar at 44/46 Frederick St., Gray's Inn Road, Terminus 5819, unless he's moved.

You said I might be meeting the ex-g.f.[3] sometime after you return. She sounds like a silly bad-mannered little fool and I don't wish to meet her, and I don't expect you will be bothered seeing her again. Thank goodness her father had the decency to treat you as an invited guest—he sounds very decent, and I'd like to meet one half of the St. John Socialists. I can appreciate Vera's tea-party tactics in view of recent developments.

Next day—noon.

Everything's over but the shouting—the curse started in last night. I'm still in bed and feel the odd pain here and there. The nurse was in this morning and says the doctor uses a new method that no one else in Toronto knows about. He learned it in Germany two years ago. He uses no instruments and it's absolutely safe, so there's nothing to worry about.

Mom went downtown to get her eyes examined but she'll be back soon and I have been reading more New Yorkers. There was a story about Rose O'Neill who invented kewpie dolls—she does sound an ass. There were two articles about this new conductor of the Philharmonic, Janssen, who seems to have all the virtues dear to Alger fans.[4] Anyhow, I'm going through a year's New Yorkers and it is good fun, although I'd rather like to taste some of the Champagne they keep advertising.

Mother is back now, and while she was in Simpson's she talked to a woman there who has a house on Huron Street. She knows of two places nearby that may have rooms to suit us. Barbara [Sturgis] 'phoned last night saying that she'd asked two girls to live with us, neither of whom I know. Which strikes me as somewhat high-handed, since she didn't ask me about it. I suppose you will say I did the same thing, but the case was not exactly parallel.

I want Mom to post this as she is going out now. Now don't you worry any more my dear. I love you.

H.

1 Sherbourne House Club, located at 439 Sherbourne St. E.
2 See Letter 128, above.
3 See Letter 133, above.
4 The articles HK refers to are Alexander King, "Kewpie Doll," *New Yorker*, 10 (24 November 1934), 22–6; Robert A. Simon, "Local Boy Makes Music," *New Yorker*, 10 (24 November 1934), 38, 40; and Robert A. Simon, "On Seeing Janssen—Rachmaninoff Returns—A Quartet's Finale," *New Yorker*, 10 (17 November 1934), 79–81.

139. NF to HK   Moncton, N.B.

Postmarked 29 August 1936; addressed to HK at 205 Fulton Ave., Toronto, Ontario.

Darling. I'm nearly crazy, what with worrying myself sick over you, getting post-holes dug in my face every morning, and discovering how my money has melted away—I'm afraid my statement that I could pay your expenses to Montreal and back was a bit hysterical. I got my ticket to Montreal some time ago, and am forwarding you $15—the total cost of the operation, you said, would be around $25. That leaves me $13 to pay my dentist with—now if he costs more than that, I'll have to cash some of my English traveller's cheques, in which case I can forward you another $5 or $10, perhaps. If there are any complications to make the operation more expensive—well, we'll just have to cash more cheques. If that fool E.K. Brown would do something about my article before I leave I'd be all right, but he shows no signs of doing so.

My last letter seems to have been a rather unnecessary outburst, except that in your last one you said "I could spare the money for Roy's fees . . . if I gave up the idea of Europe next summer. But we need not decide that yet." You're a rather hard girl to live away from, sweetheart. I thought, having planned and discussed and talked over and agreed on a course of action for a year, that we had clearly decided it. I've only been gone two weeks—do I become non-existent in that time? To say nothing of your own plans. *Please* don't be quite so irresponsible, my darling. You see, you can hardly blame me for answering the letter I've got instead of the one you're just about to write, and now your plans are jumping up and down just the way they did last summer, when I had to take some kind of dope to get to sleep nights.

Well, there I go again. And I think your parents are wonderful and your mother gets my very particular and very deep thanks for the superb way she is handling this business. Also I approve of changing Mom to Mother: the older form suggests a prize fighter explaining to his friends of the radio audience that he did it all for Pop 'n' Mom.

You will have heard of Hull House, the progenitor of all social settlement work, founded by Jane Addams, who died recently.[1] It's one of the big things in Chicago. Vera writes:

'We went first to Hull House. There were about thirty people there from all parts of the country to make a tour of the House. We had a terrible guide. I have never seen such a person there before. I shudder to think what Jane Addams would have done to him. I hope now she is dead the place is not overrun with such parasites. He was oldish, unctuous, lazy, ignorant, and overbearing. He did not want to show us anything we had come to see: he wanted us to listen to him talk. Some man asked him a question and he said, "Well, we do not undertake such work here yet, but, now that Miss Addams is with us no more, doubtless we who have vision will make thorough reforms." Jane Addams, whose "vision" built up a Settlement House that has been copied in thirty-seven countries, who was so honored that at her death flags in all countries flew at half-mast, and for whom foreign countries issued special memorial postage stamps! Well, after half an hour in one bare, hot room, and twenty minutes in one just in the process of redecoration and what looked like the rest of the afternoon in another, while one after another sadly disappointed person slipped away, one mother came up to me and said they had driven all the way from West Virginia to give their children, who were interested in settlement work, a chance to see Hull House, and they had just one day in the city, and what could they do? So, for the honor of our fair city, I went to battle. I told Mr. Collier gently what we were interested in, and reminded him still gently that most of us were pressed for time. He said there were no "Work Rooms" such as I mentioned, and added insultingly that ignorant people made his work as guide very difficult.

So I said that after all we weren't interested in his opinions, but in Jane Addams, and the upshot was that we saw the Work Rooms. Whenever he turned away from an interesting part, I turned toward it, and the group followed me instead of him. Fortunately I know Hull House thoroughly. But Mr. Collier doesn't like me, I am much afraid. We saw the lovely pottery work done by the foreign children, the great rug Gandhi sent to Jane Addams, with its queer card in his handwriting. He grew the flax himself, spun it and wove it all for her. We saw the rooms where nearby children are bathed Saturday night, and the beautiful weaving done by old foreign women, bewildered and lonely in the great city with the strange language, who come to these rooms to teach blind and crippled children basketry, rugmaking, fine sewing and the rest. Altogether, we saw most of it, even if Mr. Collier did say he always knew there'd be trouble when a nosey redhead came along. One tall silent Negro, head of a great Negro Southern School, gave me his card when we left and said, "I'm very glad we had a redhead along."' What a girl!

Now, darling, if you need more money, let me know right away, and I'll get some of these cheques cashed. I can see one point about England next summer—the possibility of this cropping up again without your parents to look after you, and I shall be acquainted only with the most disgustingly pure-minded people. But don't ditch everything just because somebody else has been talking to you. Still, I suppose it would be easier to get help if you were married.

Mother reads all the essays I brought home and seems to enjoy doing so—she says she can understand them as she goes along, but couldn't explain them to anyone else, which makes little difference as there's no one else to explain them to. Something—my aunt's death, I think—has started her brooding—she's covered up a rather fine picture of her family (of which 6 out of 10 are now dead) with my Emmanuel picture. I'm getting Dad a necktie and Mother a book of Schweitzer's for their birthday, August 30.[2]

I think I forgot to mention in my last letter that I saw Cormier again— he took me to see a pig-headed old fool of about 70 who reads his rationalist magazine and much the same books—deaf, and uses his deafness as an excuse for his pig-headedness. Rationalists seem to have only two ideas, that Jesus never lived and that the church has always persecuted. So I got Sun myths and public school history bellowed at me—or rather across me, as I took little part in the conversation—all evening long.

Darling, I love you so much—you are always the same, present or absent, and the sweetest and bravest of all girls.

N.

1 Addams, the well-known social reformer and feminist who had founded Hull House in 1899, died in 1935.
2 NF's mother and father were both born on 30 August 1870.

140. HK to NF   [*Toronto*]
Sunday night 11 P.M. [*30 August 1936*]

My dear:

I am sending the guide to London and the Sacrifice of Isaac[1] to the boat. I have looked for your Legouis et Cazamian and cannot find it. Roy has a copy but I find no other and his name is in his. I don't remember your leaving it here at all. I will dig up a December Acta but it will have to go to England as I probably won't get it in time. Barbara [Sturgis] asked me to-night whether you had taken the book on Oxford with you so I gather it was a loan not a gift but there is no hurry for its return. I have written notes to A.M. Beattie and Norman Langford and the books will go back to them to-morrow. Will give the keys to Roy when I see him. Perhaps you'd better ask your ticket agent about "steward" on your passport. Did you get it for "All Countries"?

You might do well to look up Cameron Caesar as soon as you get there, because he has a good cheap boarding house and would be glad to hear from you. It is a little distance farther than the one on Guilford Street but you'd have someone to talk to. Otherwise, why don't you look up London House and stay there for awhile? I'm sorry that I haven't the address, but it is very near Guilford Street—it seems to me it is in Mecklenberg Square. You'd probably find it in the 'phone book. However, the Walters would very likely be able to fix you up at this time of year but you'd better make sure and drop them a note. For if you arrive on a Sunday they may be out and you'd have to dicker with some manservant who doesn't know what's what. 90 Guilford Street charges 30 to 35 shillings per week for bed & breakfast. Each dinner is 1/6 and you have to let them know in the morning if you'll be in. A hotel would charge more, most of the small Bloomsbury places charge 5/6 a night and Walters' rate is 5S at most. (Unless he's raised the price.) I've marked the spot where the house is—you see it is just around the corner from Russell Square Station on Bernard St.

{Roy and Harold are just arriving now—Roy 'phoned from the Don Station so I'll have to stop soon.}

The eating places are not so hot just around Guilford Street. The one by Russell Square Station is fairly good. The Golden Tortoise in Marchmont Street is a female place and they soak you rather. Go over to Charlotte Street to Bertorelli's or the other Italian place. I have never been in the German restaurant there. You'll find a Lyons or an A.B.C. everywhere and the food is terribly standardized. There is a cafeteria in the Y.W.C.A.—the Y.M.C.A. is right across the road—both near the corner of Tottenham Court Road and Oxford Street. I don't know whether the latter has a male cafeteria but men do go to the Y.W. sometimes and the food is very good.

Next morning. I talked until 2.30 with Roy last night and we seem to have been going ever since. It's now twelve hours later. The nurse has just been in,—she is the most discreet woman and always breezes in on a friendly call. I can go back to work to-morrow and except for a slight back-ache I am completely recovered and I feel just as I usually do under such circumstances. I am to see her before I go to you next summer so that this will not happen again. Oh my dearest, don't take my last few letters too seriously because I was worried when I wrote them, about the money and everything but I had enough in the bank to cover it and I had to pay before I could be treated at all. And please don't send me any more because I know how you need it just now. If you need any more before your Christmas instalment let me know and I'll be able to tide you over by then.

Affairs are much better with Roy than we thought. He cleared sixty-odd dollars above his expenses and although he looks dog-tired just now he will probably be better. What got him down was the drubbing Mrs Cork gave him when she settled the bill—regular vixen when she has the reverse side of her exuberant temperament showing. She charged Roy with the most ridiculous things—she bragged about his photography to all comers but accused him of neglecting his duties and she hadn't wanted him to spend time on photography she said. Also, he'd lied about his singing ability. And nobody wanted to listen to his fiddle playing. And he had no right to take the job if he was subject to stomach trouble—she thought she was getting a hefty he man, etc etc.

The dose she handed him was pretty hard to swallow, the sort of thing only a woman can get away with alive. Her accusations were so hysterical and unreasonable that we have been asking since whether she was sore at Roy because he wasn't a bit more of a cavalier in his manner toward her. She is ten years younger than her husband but it may be she wanted a little more attention than she was getting. I don't know. But Roy is very cheerful, is thinking of doing the Lincoln Hutton essay even yet.[2]

{11.10 P.M.} Barbara [Sturgis] and I have been out looking at another place on Huron Street to-night but it would not do at all. It looks as if we will settle on the St. Joseph attic and get another girl to come in with us. We dropped in to see Peggy and Helen to-night. Helen James has just recovered from an attack of intestinal 'flu and Peggy is in bed getting something that started with the curse and she doesn't know what the next move is. She asked where you were and when you were going. It seems that Mary arrives in New York next Friday.[3] Peggy tried to get in touch with you early in July, but of course you weren't here. Their apartment is pretty stunning—$50 a month plus garden.

I'll send this along now as it is getting late and I must start to work to-morrow. I hope I won't have to do much standing—it gives me a back-ache.

I'll probably think of some more things to-morrow by way of advice.

My dearest, I'll be there next summer, you'll see! Now do take good care of yourself and DON'T FORGET THE FRUIT SALTS FOR SEA-SICKNESS!

I love you so much. H.

P.S. Vera's description was marvellous—*what* a girl!

1 This was probably either E. Martin Browne's play *The Sacrifice of Isaac* (London: Philip Allan, 1932) or the medieval play of the same title that was on the reading list for English 3k, a VC honour course.
2 An essay for the Lincoln G. Hutton Scholarship competition at VC.
3 Peggy and Mary are quite likely Peggy Roseborough and Mary Winspear, two members of the Blake group.

141. NF to HK   Moncton, N.B.
                                                                Sept 1–36

Telegram addressed to HK at 205 Fulton Ave., Toronto. Even though HK had announced four days before receiving this telegram that she could not meet NF in Montreal (Letter 138), they did meet at the Bonaventure Station on Thursday, 3 September, where they had a day together before NF sailed to England. Her change of plans was perhaps recorded in a missing telegram to NF (another letter would not have had time to reach him before he left Moncton on the afternoon of 2 September).

MISS HELEN KEMP,
   CANT POSSIBLY ARRIVE BEFORE EIGHT STANDARD THURSDAY MORNING AT BONAVENTURE STATION MEET ME THERE. NORRIE.

142. HK to NF   205 Fulton Ave., Toronto, Canada
                                          Thursday night. Sept. 10. [1936]

Postmarked 11 September 1936; addressed to NF c/o Canada House, Trafalgar Square, London, England, Empress of Britain: Quebec.

My dearest:

   Barbara [Sturgis] has just told me that the Empress of Britain leaves on Saturday and I am trying to get a note to you for the time being. So many things are going on just now—we have been keeping house ever since I came back from Montreal—Roy went back to Gordon Bay—Barbara moves into the apartment to-morrow and I probably shall soon— Daddy comes home and I'm tired of batching. Have finished that article for "The School"[1]—it is quite good and they'll want another very likely. Barbara made all sorts of pencil marks all over it so it will bear close scrutiny. I am very grateful to her. She seems to enjoy detective work on verbs. Norah [McCullough] came back to work to-day and we're getting pretty busy. I have plunged into work as hard as I can and we'll make things hum this year. I 'phoned Mrs Arnold to-night about German lessons and she would like to teach me herself as she would like to read History of Art. So that will be great fun and keep me working hard. I had Roy Daniells in to dinner last Sunday when Barbara was away—he started at once to count up the number of months, weeks, days and hours it would be before I saw you again—it is a long time! But I said one sleeps about one third of that time.

I wrote to your Aunt[2] and told her about art classes in Montreal for Gloria [Garratt]. She was marvellous to me and I'll always be grateful to her for coming to the boat that day. She brought me to the train after giving me a lunch and climbing the mountain a second time. I meant to write to tell your mother all about your departure but simply have not had time. Everybody is very interested in what you are doing—Norah, Marge Boultbee, Rody Courtice, Peggy [Roseborough], Dorothy [Drever], Roy Daniells, John Jones [Harwood-Jones], etc etc, Mrs Arnold. There is one great advantage I have this time in being surrounded by all your friends. I talk to Barbara [Sturgis] by the hour it seems, often about you, and she doesn't mind a bit. Sallee Creighton said she was always talking about her husband and Roy [Daniells] said I'd do it too—he seems to be right!

I have written to Edith Burnett about you and I hope she bucks up and sends you an invitation to tea or dinner. I will write to Helen Lowenthal soon and perhaps to Madge [Willis]. I do hope you are finding some people to talk to and look up Cameron [Caesar] right away because he is coming home very soon.

Miss Kortright at the gallery is leaving at the end of the month to be married and it occasions some ribald remarks to the effect that there is still some hope for the rest of us. Beatty suggests that we buy her a swell nightgown but I can't see Baldwin subscribing to that!

Had an interesting time this morning when a Persian Jew came in with some Persian book covers, drawings, mirrors, several illuminated copies of the Koran in Arabic etc. He said he was a descendant of Jews from the Babylonian conquest. Mr Baldwin called me down to look at the stuff and it was interesting to see the Persian read the text and count the dates according to the Mohammedan calendar. It was all stuff for Currelly,[3] though, not for us.

It is nearly one o'clock and I'm dead tired. I can't think of anything definite to tell you there are so many things. I took a wedding gift to Ruth Hodgins to-night from the Conservatory crowd, she is being married on Saturday. One thing I could not bear is to go through the process of showers and teas. She looks all tired out what with being entertained until about two every night. Rody Courtice was lunching with her husband the other day when I ran into them and she told him all about your confession of faith—she said why don't I go over next summer and get married—It sounded quite simple. Norah [McCullough] started in to tell me to-day all about Pegi Nicol living with some young man about ten years younger and how some of her friends are cutting her on that account. Oh my dear, you and I have been so fortunate, and so shielded from all that sort of gossip—and we've been very fortunate in other ways. It makes me very humble.

I forgot to tell you to get a bus map from the bus conductor. With that and the underground you should be able to get about. I do hope you are happy and seeing lots of things and have a good boarding house. I'm so glad I went to Montreal, it made all the difference in the world to me. I'll write a much less spluttery letter soon I hope, but you get the idea. I'm trying to keep awake and catch a boat and tell you that I love you and to look after your underwear all in one breath.

Your ridiculous

Helen—

1 "Loan Collections from the Art Gallery of Toronto," *School*, 25 (October 1936), 105–9.
2 NF's aunt Hatty Layhew, who ran a boarding house in Montreal.
3 That is, for the Royal Ontario Museum of Archaeology, of which Charles T. Currelly was founder and first curator.

143. NF to HK   Plymouth, Devon
                                                              [*10 September 1936*]

Postmarked 12 September 1936; addressed to HK at 205 Fulton Ave., Toronto, Ontario, Canada. Written on board the Alaunia, *a Cunard White Star liner, and posted from Plymouth, Devon.*

My dearest:

I do not wish to insult you by remarking that I am writing to you because I am too bored to do anything else, but really, life on shipboard is pretty deadly. You sit around and stand around waiting for your meals, get into a desultory conversation with somebody when you are both painfully aware that you are deliberately putting in time, you look unsuccessfully for someone to play checkers or ping-pong or shuffleboard with, and find either that the apparatus is engaged or that you beat the stuffing out of somebody the day before and he is avoiding your eye. You drift into the bar and out again, and, above all, you read. Friday & Saturday were lovely bright days, Sunday, Monday & Tuesday bitterly cold, with a great deal of rain & fog, Wednesday & today full of marvellous sunshine and everything's happy. (If I seem to be a bit incoherent, put it down to the boat trio which is sawing a Chopin Nocturne in half beside my left ear.) As I have been badly constipated ever since I got on the boat, in spite of my assiduous devotion to the fruit salts, I was a bit groggy one morning and have had intermittent headaches, but so far have had not the slightest tendency to actual sea-sickness. The three stormy days laid out a few men, about half the women and nearly all the children, but the worst is pretty obviously over, if the Channel doesn't raise hell. The piano is a bit of a nuisance: I betrayed my knowledge of it, and now have to refuse politely when asked for a "tune," though I played Haydn and Mozart for half an hour Sunday afternoon. Aunt Hatty's two books were of unequal value: H.G. Wells' "The Dream" was Wells at his best,[1] and ideal shipboard reading, but I didn't reach the second sentence of the other. Then I read three books in the library and finally started on Thomas Mann. The early stories are rather disappointing—they are all written to a Mauve Decade formula of some wretched underdog committing suicide through self-distrust and an unmerciful woman.

The passengers are rather dull—mostly ultra-respectable small-town people going back home to England. One very decent electrician who has been through the War and has some rather interesting reminiscences. There are some nuns and Franciscan monks on board, and he told me a story about a colleague of his who was summoned to fix the wiring in a convent whose occupants had taken a vow never to behold the face of man. He followed some nun who had obtained special permission from the bishop to communicate with him down a corridor, she ringing a hand bell through a continuous flurry of retreating skirts. "Madame," said the electrician, "do you think I'm the parish bull?"

What do you know about a man called Pavitt? He was educated in England, of Lithuanian extraction, to judge by his beard, came to McGill to teach architecture and founded an Art School in the Gallery in connection with the university, which his wife now runs, then switched to floriculture or some kind of experimental farming. He's going to settle in Norfolk, run an electric cable under the soil to warm it up, raise red, white and blue asters a month or two before anybody else, and clean up money at the coronation. He apparently paints quite well and says that two examples of his work are in the Toronto Art Gallery's permanent collection. He knows a few interesting people, including Edgar Wallace. Face, voice, smile, manner of speaking something like [Norman J.] Endicott, but a lot more self-assurance. Curious limitations to his knowledge—knows all about Ruskin and Oscar Wilde, but thought Milton was a contemporary of Charles Lamb and that 1927 was Beethoven's *ter*centenary. Stuck to it, too!

Then there is a young girl from McGill, graduated last year in science, going either for a month's holiday or a year's research in London, depending on how the mood takes her. Profusion of light hair, very attractive if you find a horse face and buck teeth attractive—I do, rather: I always liked Helen Stephens' looks.[2] Central European mongrel— mother Viennese and father a Jew. Handles a pencil adroitly and has picked up money by sketching people on board. Knows my cousin Alma Howard.

Also a woman from the Sun Life, Montreal, who knows the twins[3] quite well. Miss Hersee—by her own spelling—she could be a relative.[4] Squat and low-slung with an arse that looks as though it had been designed for a much larger animal and stuck on her by mistake—I like her well enough, but that's just my reaction to the English female's upholstering. I asked her for her name—there's a certain reluctance to give names on board ship, as though contacts had better be kept anonymous.

A missionary from the headwaters of the Congo. Stupid woman, prudish and thought *Green Pastures*[5] blasphemous, but she remarked that she disliked Schweitzer on the ground that he made such a point of his having "sacrificed" a great musical and academic career for Africa. She could not understand that that was a sacrifice: it was a privilege. There was some pretty genuine courage behind that, all the more so for being unconscious. A good many people, after all, think Schweitzer had so much courage that it must be at least partly quixotic: she saw through the whole pose, for it must be partly a pose; Schweitzer to her was merely a missionary who whimpered and grumbled and apologized and disgraced his profession.

Evenings I spend mostly in my stateroom: I can't stand the air in the lounge. There is always a whist party or something else I don't do well going on, so I push the clock on an hour and go to bed. I can't seem to get enough sleep.

Your letter got here almost immediately: a lovely thoughtful solicitous letter, which will prove very useful. I don't know whether I said adequately enough how much I appreciated all the work you did, like sending off the Last Puritans[6] with appropriate notes, besides your supreme gift of coming to Montreal. We must certainly see Montreal again—Pavitt tells me we must have walked right by a French Impressionism room. I got a very nice letter from Jean Cameron too, mailed at Quebec, or rather delivered at Quebec.

One gets a certain sense of claustrophobia, and I shall be glad to land. I love you unspeakably in both elements.

Norrie.

1 A novel by H.G. Wells (London: Jonathan Cape, 1924).
2 NF is perhaps referring to Helen Stevens, a classmate.
3 Hazel and Evelyn Howard, the second and third of Eratus Howard's four daughters.
4 NF's oldest uncle on his mother's side was Hersey Howard.
5 A Pulitzer Prize–winning play by Marc Connelly (New York: Farrar & Rinehart, 1920); it portrays the story of God in heaven and his people on earth as told to a group of Sunday school children. The play was made into a Warner Brothers movie in 1936.
6 This seems to be a reference to HK's returning F.P. Ladd's *The Last Puritans* (New York: Lupton, 1912) and other books, accompanied by notes, to A.M. Beattie and Norman Langford. See Letter 140. NF may, however, be referring to Santayana's *The Last Puritan* (1935).

144. HK to NF   205 Fulton Ave.,
                                                                     Toronto 6, Ont.,
                                                                     Canada
                                                       Sunday Sept. 12. 1936.

Postmarked 14 September 1936; addressed to NF at Canada House, Trafalgar Square, London, England, Via New York: "Normandie." *Although the letter is dated 12 September, Sunday was actually 13 September.*

My dearest:

Barbara [Sturgis] tells me the Normandie is sailing from New York in a few days, so that I hasten to send you a few more words. There is very little by way of news since the last letter but that doesn't seem to matter.

Daddy came home last night and as we were all away, Harold at the exhibition and Barbara and I at Dot Drever's, he had to climb in the cellar window. Roy is staying up north, writing the Lincoln Hutton essay and mother stayed there with him to cook the meals and go fishing. Barbara moved into St. Joseph Street yesterday but stayed here to-day and will go there to live after to-morrow. Daddy says that he has just had a letter from Uncle Well [Kemp] announcing that while he and Aunt Clara were with us Albert took his young wife to Petrolia Hospital where the baby was born. Now if that is not the height of reticence, I can't think of what is! Uncle Well was a little shamefaced in his letter and said he could not see how two women could be together as much as Mother and Aunt Clara were without it being mentioned. Daddy is thinking up a retort.

Do you know, for a day I thought I was all over my trouble, but on Friday it started again! That means that I have been having the curse for two weeks and it's still going on. You don't think I'm beginning to resemble the ex-g.f.[1] do you? (!) I went to see the doctor again yester-day—he gave me some medicine and said it was probably my regular period coming round once more, and if it wasn't better in a week to drop in and I might have to have a little operation. I'm quite certain I won't though, and I feel much better to-day.

Dot Drever is beginning to feel a little restive about her job, she is tired of being shifted from place to place. I had a long talk with Jean Elder who seemed to think Dot is going off her rocker a bit what with not getting a steady job, and going all high-brow over art, music and Chinese painting and modern poetry! So I defended Dot on every count and Jean ended up by admitting that I was certainly a good friend of Dorothy's and she hoped I'd stand up for her as well if the need arose! It made me a little sick to hear of Marg Torrance *saving one hundred dollars* a month in Sandwich and still others complaining of the difficulty of living on fifteen and seventeen hundred a year! Marg is saving to marry Eric [Gee]. I expect Jean Elder is a little better off this year and she likes the school at Port Credit. There is a niece of Prof. Sissons that she is very friendly with. It made me mad to have her criticize Dot's clothes and talk as if Dot was degenerating and had something wrong with her that she didn't get a job.

Was talking to Barbara [Sturgis] about that story of Norah's [Norah McCullough's] about Pegi Nicol's friends snubbing her for living with a young man, and Barbara said she wouldn't snub any friends of hers for doing it but she would not do it herself and—well I gathered she had made up her mind on the subject. You and I have a very innocent air, evidently. The prospect of next summer must be somewhat carefully considered I suppose. I'll no longer be able to act as I see fit without

someone knowing what is going on. I'm not getting a fit of the Mrs
Grundy blues, but I'm just making allowances for the fact that I'll be
making a good many new friends and acquaintances this year who will
take an interest presumably in yours and my affairs. There are so many
people who know about you and there may be a few soon who'll have
begun to be conscious of my existence—why the devil *do* we have to be
prominent citizens? Ugh!

Mrs Arnold 'phoned to say that she'd teach me German whenever I
liked to begin. Says they hope to see a great deal of me this winter and
whatever am I doing without you? I said I was being just as busy as possible. I've certainly kept so up until now and it will likely continue, if not
I'll find another language to study! God, I've got to keep busy to stave
off the widowed feeling.

Dorothy [Drever] says that George Johnston and the other Vic man,
J.C. Taylor, are in London now, and also that Yvonne [Williams] and
Esther [Johnson] will be there until the middle of October. Address
them all at Canada House. Why don't you look up Yvonne, you'd probably have some fun and might meet Edith Burnett sooner. You'll have
got there by now, it is ten o'clock our time. I have been picturing you
going up the Thames to Tilbury and going by train past all those funny
little pocket-handkerchief gardens and houses on the way to London. I
suppose you landed at Euston or St. Pancras,[2] and then what did you
do? Were there any nice people on the boat? I have thought of you so
much this week, surrounded by ocean and nothing else. I do hope you
weren't sick. Harold sends his love. Will send some New Yorkers soon.

I just remembered. I was going to tell you about John Jones [Har-
wood-Jones] who is definitely going to do graduate work in philosophy.[3] He is at present trying to get a donship or whatever you call it, but
he has to wait until Jerry Riddell looks him over. I wish you were here to
give him a good word, but I can't think of anything I can do about it
without appearing to meddle. John has been working at the Parliament
buildings all summer and has been wangling various things in order to
keep on next year. Of course he has had quite a fight with [Walter T.]
Brown and the Chancellor, they would help him if he goes into theology
but he won't commit himself to that this year. He may later, but he has
definitely decided to take this year out. He talks of getting married
sometime before he's forty, and as he is living at the home of Lorna
Thompson and is away with her for the week-end, things point to L.T.
as a fairly serious aim in view. He says that theology was all right for

you but he is your age now, before he begins, and that he cannot hope to run it the way you did, as he can't study several things at once. All these details he gave me in the course of the lunch I had with him the other day. He thought you'd be interested, and so did I, so here is page five, on John Harwood-Jones.

Roy Daniells asked me if I thought you intended to write to anyone this year besides me—and I said that I thought you might be induced to do so. If I have to be the go-between for all these messages, such as John Jones, you can see that I'll have to begin typing with great zeal. So do please write to Roy!

I'm going to bed now, must be on the job to-morrow. Good-night my dear———

H.

Next night. I could not resist adding a line before I take this down to the post-office. Have put in a busy day with Norah [McCullough] correcting the Educational bulletin. We went to Hart House to-day to see Will Ogilvie's murals in the chapel.[4] They really are lovely, although the contrast between Ogilvie and pseudo Gothic wood carving is rather marked. They are going to transform it with curtains.

Have just been reading Lismer's letters to Norah—he's a marvellous man, there is no getting away from that. He says Vincent Massey is disgusted that they don't get him to look out for pictures now that he is in London for he is Honorary President or something of the kind.[5]

Barbara [Sturgis] is now on St. Joseph St. and I am still here but will move toward the end of the week. Will be very glad to get settled. Norah visited the Fairleys on Sunday. I expect to meet Barker Fairley on Wednesday as we are going to see some pictures of his.

There was big excitement in the papers about the wedding of Fiorenza Johnson to Col. Drew.[6] Baldwin was there. He evidently knows George Drew who is about forty-five, and the bride (daughter of Edward J.) is my age.

Must take this to the post-office. It is a rainy day. I think I will count up the days until June, just out of curiosity. I do hope you are all right. Incidentally, I seem to have completely recovered by now. It is very curious, you seem to have given me some sort of overwhelming energy that knits me to you forever and ever, I love you so.

I had a card from your aunt[7] to-day in answer to my letter. Will send you a copy of the article I wrote[8]—it isn't much but will show you what I'm doing.

Norrie, I do hope that the London climate is not going to make you feel woozy because I don't know what to do about it. Hope you'll be writing soon.

Helen.

1 Evelyn Rogers.
2 HK is referring to two London railway stations: Euston Square Station, the terminus of the London and North Western Railway, near Euston Rd. and Tottenham Court Rd.; and St. Pancras Station, the terminus of the Midland Railway, at Euston Rd. to the west of King's Cross Station.
3 John Harwood-Jones went on to study philosophy at Cornell and Johns Hopkins, and later got a B.D. degree from McGill.
4 In 1934–35 Will Ogilvie had painted murals, designed to represent the communion of saints, over the panelling on the south wall and in the lunette over the altar of the Hart House chapel.
5 Massey was honorary president of the AGT.
6 Fiorenza Johnson, the daughter of the well-known opera singer Edward Johnson, married George A. Drew, who later became premier of Ontario.
7 NF's aunt Harriet (Hatty) Layhew, whom NF and HK had seen in Montreal the previous week and to whom HK had written after the Montreal visit (see Letter 142).
8 This is apparently the article that HK wrote for the *School*. See Letter 142, n. 1, above.

145. NF to HK   London

Postmarked 15 September 1936; addressed to HK at 205 Fulton Ave., Toronto, Ontario, Canada.

My dearest girl:

One day in London. The rest of the voyage was all right: the Channel was as clear as a bell. We got into Havre in the early morning, but I was too exhausted to get up and look at it. My stomach is a bit upset, and I feel correspondingly dyspeptic, but everything else is all right. I saw the chalk cliffs at Dover, and the lower Thames at sunset, both worth seeing. Plymouth was lovely too—everything I could see of England from the boat looked eerie, subtle and mysterious, like something on another planet. The confused mass of subdued colours all running into one another, the hazy misty air, the arrangements of clumps of trees, hedged farms, and sand, all made it look convincing and still vaguely unreal.

Getting off at the dock was a long business. They hardly glanced at my passport, and I rode from Tilbury to London with my missionary friend and Miss Hersee, the last giving me her address and an urgent request to look her up. The missionary goes to Brussels to study tropical diseases.

I got a flop-house of sorts for 6/6, and early this morning started for the path of least resistance—90–92 Guilford Street,[1] in other words. I've moved in bag and trunk, and got a quiet little room on the rear end. How much does one tip the servants, and what servants, at these places? I haven't met anybody in the house yet—I missed dinner as my clock was packed in my trunk and they didn't ring a bell. This morning, when I was cautiously feeling my way around St. Pancras Station (St. Pancreas as the missionary insisted on calling it) who should I run into but Pavitt, whom I mentioned in my last letter. It goes to confirm my belief that in almost any strange city you are bound to meet somebody you know. I had lunch at a hideously overdecorated Italian place and then started for Trafalgar Square, for no particular reason except that it sounded like a place to go. I took a glance at the map before starting, and, though I took a wrong turn on the way home, owing to the fact that the streets change their names and directions like criminals, got along all right. I asked two wonderful policemen to confirm the route, and found that they answered my questions in exactly the what-the-hell-do-you-want-to-know-for tone of American policemen. When I got to Trafalgar Square I saw a dingy looking factory chimney with a man on top who looked like Napoleon from the back side, but I suppose would have looked more like Nelson if I had gone around to the front side. I didn't, however, as I was getting slightly dizzy from dodging this south-paw traffic, and went into the National Gallery. That was a silly idea, as I was in no mood to get anything out of pictures, and I came out with a rather confused impression of the Virgin's blue robe, St. Sebastian's belly stuck full of arrows—rather apt, that, coming just when San Sebastian has fallen[2]—St. Jerome's lion and rock, and the mutilated end of the infant Jesus' penis (which is frequently the focus of the whole picture, have you noticed?), tons and tons of gilt, and my own face regularly recurring in every masterpiece. It might be interesting to trace the influence of glass frames on the appreciation of painting—perhaps an over-subjective criticism may be nothing but the result of the critic's physical inability to see anything in the picture but himself. Do you know, every female, in every Titian picture I have seen, gives me a sexual stimulation, which is as involuntary as it is unwanted. I noticed that at Chicago, and noticed it again today—a little automatic reflex shiver every time. Other pictures sometimes, but Titian always. That might be a good tip to Millicent [Rose] for her thesis.

Tomorrow I shall go to Canada House and get Cameron Caesar's address. I don't quite know what to do with my three weeks—I came over here to get the dope on Blake, and that means work. My sight-seeing is bound to be rather haphazard—there's not the remotest possibility of doing it systematically, even when one cuts out all the very spot where stuff Muirhead is full of.[3] In the meantime, I have discovered that the cats' houses of parliament are just outside my window, and I, instead of sightseeing, am overhearing. Well, I sound as though it were you instead of I who had never seen London, but you know how I am. One thing about London so far which was both totally unexpected and very delightful are the Belisha beacons, the orange globes which decorate the city as though it were carnival time. Sunshine today—no rain or fog. And I love you so much that the Atlantic seems to separate us no more than a wainscoting—it can keep me from seeing you, but it cannot make me love you less.

Norrie.

1 The boarding house in Bloomsbury, just off Russell Square, where HK had stayed the previous year after her return from Italy.
2 In the Spanish Civil War San Sebastián fell to the nationalists in early September of 1936.
3 This awkward expression seems to mean "the very spot where the guidebook (Muirhead) is full of information."

146. HK to NF   Apartment 3. 24 St. Joseph St.,
                                           Toronto. Canada ———
                                           Sept. 21. 1936

My dearest:

This is Monday evening and Barbara [Sturgis] says the Queen Mary leaves New York soon. I moved in here on Saturday and have been tacking down linoleum and that kind of thing before and since dinner. It is Barbara's turn to cook the dinner this week, I do it next week. Leukie has not come in yet but she will appear at the beginning of next month.

You'll love this place. I think that we will try very hard to keep it on. Perhaps you and I could live here when you get home again. It is much nicer than the Bucket, is quite separate from any other people in the house, has three rooms, lots of cupboard space, a good sized hall and kitchen and bathroom. There are hardwood floors in excellent condition and the woodwork is painted cream. A godsend to me! The kitchen and bathroom walls are a sort of paddy green colour, very cheerful. We have a gravel roof at the back where we had breakfast last Sunday morning with great pomp. The trees are so tall hereabouts that they come up to the roof and the vines creep over the brickwork. The house is right near Yonge Street and you can hear the street-cars a little more than I like. But that is bearable, I think. Last night I left the front windows open and a marauding tomcat walked into my bed. I kicked it clear over to the other side of the room and it leaped out the window only to return again several hours later. I woke up to hear some paper rustling and the cat scrammed.

Dr. Arnold was in to get some pictures to-day and I attended to his needs so he asked me out to lunch. One of those intimate, very intense conversations followed, provoked by some beer and his German temperament. Evidently I go down better alone than with a crowd of philosophers. I told him he liked to dominate a crowd and he said it was a harsh word but he did nevertheless. He said he thought it was because he had been ordered about by an older brother when he was young, then he asked me where I came in my family. I had said that I did not mind particularly being dominated in some things—so he suddenly turned and said "—Norrie must dominate too." I said I knew that perfectly well, picturing how amused you'd be at this whole conversation. This led to your thinking apparatus, and I switched the subject to Victoria College, knowing how he feels. I think he is a little intolerant and foolish in his dislike of Methodist hypocrisy and the stupidity of middle aged women with nothing to do. I don't think he has much sense of humour. We talked a little about Roy Daniells. By the way, Ev Stewart has been having a fight with Ted Avison and Roy has been consoling her. Dot Drever tells me that on about last January Roy was busy proposing marriage to Ev at every drop of the hat and Ev ridiculed the idea telling him he'd not know where to get a license. Roy then was terribly hurt and was a faithful dog Tray all over the place.[1] He still says he feels the same about her, but she insists she loves Avison, even though she does kick him out every other time he calls. Arnold said Roy had an incurable habit of falling for some girl, distrusting his own powers, and proposing on the spot before someone else ran off with her. I feel a little worried, with you away across the ocean I've got to work off my mother complex somehow. Guess I'll have to try and marry Roy off to somebody. But I wish he'd stop giving women chances to step on his neck. It doesn't do.

I've got to hurry up to Charles and Yonge and post this now. We continue to be as busy as possible. Did I tell you Miss Kortright is being married?

Do write to me soon my dear, and God bless you.

H.

P.S. Harold Taylor leaves this Wednesday—in two days time that is. You might leave a note for him at Canada House.

1 The allusion is to the faithful dog in Stephen C. Foster's "Old Dog Tray," a graceful melody with a mawkish text, published in 1853; "faithful as old dog Tray" became proverbial.

147. NF to HK   London

Postmarked 21 September 1936; addressed to HK at 205 Fulton Ave., Toronto, Ontario, Canada.

Darling:

I've hardly been anywhere this week, but I've gone around a little, and I think I can find my way around Bloomsbury and Westminster fairly well. The constipation is holding out like the rebels in Toledo,[1] and I may have to dislodge it in the same way they were. My gut seems to have heard of this English reserve or something. Damn this pen. So I stay in more than I like, but should get over it soon.

I went down to get Cameron Caesar's address at Canada House, found it wasn't there, and then remembered (a) that you had given me his address in a previous letter (b) that I was a silly ass. So I went home and verified (a) and called on him that night. We've had lunch together three times—the three following days, that is. He's in the throes of Communism now, and greeted me with the well-known Communist butterslide: When I came over I didn't have very advanced political views, but now (proudly) I've gone pretty near all the way to the left, whereas you, who are already quite well advanced, should go all the way very soon. The first time we lunched he took me through University College laboratories, showed me, quite clearly, how various sets of apparatus worked, showed me the cabinet containing Jeremy Bentham's skeleton which is opened at every council meeting because he provided in his will that he was to preside at all such meetings,[2] and then took me into a photographic exhibition and discoursed learnedly of cameras. He told me (you are probably familiar with the story, but it was new to me) that there's a park nearby originally a cemetery, with a monument in the middle to the memories of those whose graves had been cleared away or made into benches. Then he told me that Jean Cameron, Elizabeth Gillespie and Elizabeth Eedy[3] had dropped in on him and he accompanied the first two down to Victoria Station, where they were supposed to meet the third, who had some shopping to do. He said he had no idea that such bad cyclists could get anywhere: whenever one would look back to see if the other were coming she'd fall off her bicycle. But he got them shepherded down to the station and there they waited three hours for Elizabeth Eedy, getting into a panic for fear she had been killed or kidnapped. "Perhaps," said Cameron, "she went to the wrong station?" "Oh, no; Elizabeth wouldn't make a mistake: if anybody has gone to the wrong station we have." So they pulled out their tickets, and sure enough they were for Waterloo Station. Another story you probably know which was even better: Eleanor Clements worked in a Technical School beside another girl and they didn't speak for six months. Eleanor thought she had struck English coldness and priggishness in the matter of introduction at its very worst. Finally she discovered that the girl was also a Canadian, and had precisely the same opinion of her.

The third time we had lunch he brought along a friend of his, an American doing some social service work with the Congregational Church who had just returned from Russia and was feverishly enthusiastic about it. We had a long talk in Cameron's room afterwards which sounded on all sides very much like the conversation of the young hero in *Beauties and Furies*.[4] Still, that can't altogether be helped, in a country where everybody automatically babbles nervously about Hitler and Mussolini and Russia and Spain and the French War Office chiefly as a partial relief from the haunting fear of an outbreak of war. Cameron and I are typical examples of students flogged by that fear into taking a morbid horrified interest in a repulsive political situation because we have a vague feeling that it's our duty to do something, if it's only to talk, not because we know or care anything about it. Of course, Cameron has read a great deal, subscribes to a left-wing book club[5] and takes Communist magazines, but I don't believe he'd care a damn about it if all were quiet on the western front.

The extraordinary grey horror of this dying world which settled on me after I had left him one day, combined with the fact that I was all alone in a strange country and separated from the one person in that world whom I loved intensely enough to enjoy staying in it, made me feel very depressed and miserable, and on a sudden and rather silly impulse, I called, without warning, on Miss Wedgwood, who lives just around the corner from me—really part of the same building, in fact. I was a bit distraught, I looked as though I had been struck by lightning, in a way that only I can look, I was rather embarrassed as soon as I had got there for having surprised her, and although they (she and her room-mate) were extremely cordial, God only knows what they must have thought of me. However, Miss Wedgwood called me and dated me up for lunch next Wednesday and has written to this friend who has been connected with the Jooss Ballet.

My passport was nothing: they simply scratched out "Steward," wrote down "Student," and put the High Commissioner's seal on it. I got a letter from Mother enclosing a letter from Emmanuel College telling me to let them know if I was going to do any B.D. work this year and card from Mary Winspear written at Salzburg. You might thank her for that if you see her, and please give me your address and Dorothy Drever's address.

Impressions of England: Shopkeepers give you wornout coins in change and then refuse to take them back, so you have to use them for tips. I foam slightly at the mouth whenever I pass a second-hand bookstall, and reflect that they might have given me fifteen thousand dollars just as well as fifteen hundred. They have a "Penguin Library" of paper-covered books for sixpence, some of the best things available in lighter fiction being included.[6] There is a Honeydew, exactly like the ones at home, in the Strand.[7] There may be good-looking women in London, but I haven't seen any, and short skirts in this country are a mistake. When the male limbs were exposed and the female ones covered, England was a great nation and produced Chippendale, but now that conditions have been reversed, everyone fusses because the country is not on sufficiently solid foundations. And a gramophone is a gramophone, while a phonograph is one of those horn and cylindrical record things. Or so I'm told.

I have written to Professor Hooke, Kay Coburn and Wilson Knight. Hooke wrote from Sussex and said he wouldn't be back before Oct. 5. Kay didn't answer: I guess she's gone. Wilson Knight wrote, saying he was just leaving for Southampton—he's sailing back on the *Alaunia*— but that I was to go and see his brother.[8] He talked to Blunden and got him all enthusiastic about me, and told two or three other people at Oxford I was coming, but didn't say anything about de la Mare. I don't know if you remember John Hawkesworth, of 3T3,[9] or Donald Stuart who graduated with me in Theology, or Joyce, John's sister and Don's wife, 3T5 or thereabouts. Anyway, I ran into her on the street—Don is investigating prisons in England and is living at the Warwick House, in (I think) Great Russell Street. She said they'd look me up, of course.

The boarders here don't seem to be bad, though I haven't met many yet. There is a Churchill Eisenhart, who is exactly what that name would imply—a horn-rimmed spectacled American graduate student in statistics at the University of London. Very friendly and quite a good head— Princeton, and knows Izzy Halperin and John Blewett. His father heads the graduate school of mathematics there, I think. Eats with his fork in his right hand and will saw any meat short of vulcanized beef with the edge of it, just as I do, though I am abandoning those tactics now. The only person who has mentioned my accent, though Cameron said he was horrified the first time he heard a Canadian accent and that Jean Cameron nearly split his ears, though he wasn't conscious of anything with me. Eisenhart has an irritating way of dismissing you when he's through talking to you, but that's probably his executive instinct.

Then a chap called Dickinson—born in Vancouver, educated in Yorkshire, leaving Canada as an infant, and an attaché to the British Consulate at Beirut, Syria. Is studying Arabic and Russian, came home with a nervous breakdown as a result of the Russian, and goes back in October. I talked to him all one evening about Syria and we got quite friendly, so we decided to take in a Queen's Hall prom Friday night—Beethoven night—I had missed the Bach one. So we strolled over in the morning, put down a camp-stool and got a seat all right in the prom. section. Dickinson brought along a friend called Maurice Ridgion, long, lean, solemn, but a good sense of humour. I know I should build things to scale, but I did expect Queen's Hall to be larger than Bloor St. United Church,[10] and this business of filling up the downstairs section with a miniature jungle bedecked with icebergs, and water that trickles irritatingly in your ears, strikes me as silly. The concert was probably excellent, but I was listening in a completely uncritical frame of mind, and old Sir Henry [Wood] could have put anything over on me. The Coriolan & the Eroica were the main bits, together with a piano concerto played by a ravishingly beautiful blonde. Frank Bridge was present and conducted two of his own things. Next day the three of us met at Lyons and had lunch, then walked through Hyde Park and Kensington Gardens, stopping at Epstein's Rima, the Peter Pan statue and the Round Pond where they were sailing model boats. Then down past the Albert Memorial (Jesus! I'll never be the same man again) south to the Victoria and Albert Museum. We had tea and then Ridgion and I went to the Savoy to see Lady Precious Stream.[11] It impressed me as a very slickly tailored piece of chinoiserie, and to anyone who had seen a real Chinese play produced under authentically Chinese conditions it was ridiculous. The players shuffled around and simpered made-in-Hollywood wisecracks at each other, the stage conventions were worked to death—some ass with a dinner jacket and carnation came out to remind us facetiously at the beginning of each act that we would just have to use our imaginations, as the Chinese weren't clever enough to think of scenery, and the orchestra consisted of a dismal squeak offstage, as though someone were sticking pins in a guinea pig, which occurred when someone came on the stage. The audience cooed and purred and thought the Chinese were just too cute for words. No declamation, no orchestral accompaniment, no pantomime, not the faintest suggestion that any of these things existed. It wasn't funny enough to be a parody, however, because of all the jokes and epigrams that were so earnestly and conscientiously shovelled in.

Today—Sunday—I went out with Dickinson to Ridgion's place and heard some of his records—a Mendelssohn String Octet and a Brahms Clarinet Quintet. We went for a walk in Hampstead Heath too.

Give my love to Barbara [Sturgis]—I must drop her a line soon. I don't know if she expects me to look her family up—she spoke as though she did, but I haven't any idea where they are.

There are very few moments, if any, when you are out of my mind—I think at least half of you must be inside me. I feel as though I had only to turn around three times to turn into Helen. And you keep coming into my conversation—I can't keep you out, you're such a talkative girl—all about yourself, too. Nobody can talk to me five minutes without hearing about you somehow, and without realizing that I am prouder of my attachment to you than of anything else. I love you all day long and all night long, and if you would mind stepping across the Atlantic a minute I would soon prove it.

Norrie.

1 In one of the most famous sieges of the Spanish Civil War, the nationalists in the Toledo castle held out for seventy days; they were relieved on 27 September 1936, a week after NF's letter was posted.
2 By the terms of his will, the "Auto-Icon"—a fully clothed coloured wax effigy built on his skeleton—was put on display in a cabinet of University College, London, of which he was a principal founder, to be brought out to attend meetings of the college council. Though this bizarre practice was discontinued, the Auto-Icon still presides over a main corridor in the college.
3 Elizabeth Eedy, a classmate of NF and HK, would become NF's second wife fifty-two years later.
4 A novel by Christiana Stead (London: P. Davies, 1936).
5 The Left Book Club, established in London in 1936, issued a number of titles under its own imprint and offered special book club editions of titles published by Victor Gollancz. For its history see John Lewis, *The Left Book Club* (London: Gollancz, 1970).
6 The paperbound, pocket-sized Penguin Library began publication in 1935, issuing titles in editions of 20,000 copies; the series, founded by three brothers, Allen, Richard, and John Lane, initially reprinted novels, detective stories, and memoirs.
7 The Honeydews in Toronto were combination grill and coffee shops; the one near VU was located at 204 Bloor St. W.
8 Jackson Knight, professor of classics at Exeter College.
9 Hawkesworth was actually in the class of 3T4; his sister Joyce, the wife of Don Stuart, was in the class of 3T6.
10 Queen's Hall, built in Langham Place, Regent St. in 1863, was an important centre of musical activity until its destruction by bombing in 1941. Designed by T.E. Knightly, the building actually housed two concert halls, one with a capacity of 2,492 and the other, suitable for recitals and chamber music, with a capacity of over 500. NF is obviously referring to the second one.
11 A Chinese play by Wang Pao-Chuan (New York: Liveright, 1935).

148. NF to HK   London
                                                            Sept. 24 [1936]

Postmarked 25 September 1936; addressed to HK at 205 Fulton Ave., Toronto, Ontario, Canada.

My darling girl:

Tuesday I was strolling down Charing Cross Road feeling a bit lonesome: I had just been in Foyle's inquiring for two books they did not possess, and as Foyle's are supposed to be the last word in books, I was wondering vaguely whether the joke was on me or on them. Then it occurred to me that I hadn't been down to Canada House for three or four days, and there might possibly be a letter for me. I went down, more for something to do than anything else, and found two big, friendly letters smiling up at me, one yours, the other Barbara's [Barbara Sturgis's]. So I read them there, and took a tube home and read them again, gloating over them until the advent of the evening's hash sobered me down.

Impressions of England: hot milk poured into rancid coffee achieves a result a League of Nations Commission ought to look into. English newspapers are a big relief after the Toronto Daily Star. I got my hair cut, and look as though I had been scalped with a remarkably inefficient tomahawk. Nor does it improve a barber shop to call it a Gentleman's 'Airdressing Salon. Englishmen dress the same way I do, which is a relief. There's a girl here called Miss Charlton who remembers you. The house is full of medical students, who talk to each other in cacophonous jargon and seem to think their superior knowledge of the human body gives them the right to leer at each other.

I haven't seen Cameron Caesar since I wrote last—he eats lunch every day in a filthy greasy restaurant I can't stick, so I haven't been there. I shall look him up, if only to borrow his dinner jacket. Yesterday I had lunch with Veronica Wedgwood, and, as she seemed to be drawing me out, I talked my head off to her. She's invited me to her father's for dinner Monday night. Very friendly girl, apparently quite a close friend of Barbara's. She said she's two years older than Barbara, so perhaps she's not as old as I took her to be at first.[1]

I went to a play of James Bridie with Dickinson tonight.[2] It turned out to be an extremely stupid comic melodrama, which rather surprised me, as I know Bridie can write when he wants to.

Thanks very much for writing to your friends. And I'm so glad you're settling down and intend to make a good year of it. The more I think of the possibilities of marrying you next year, the better I like the idea—it leaves both sets of parents out in the cold, but some difficulty of that nature would be just as likely to turn up the year after that. My views on what I intend doing with two years abroad have undergone a very considerable change within the last few months, and my impatience to marry you has increased accordingly. Some day, perhaps, I shall tell you all about that change—perhaps sometime when we're mumbling gruel together at the ages of ninety-five and seven or thereabouts. But at the moment, what I want, a great deal more than anything else in the world I could possibly want, is for us to come together again as simply and naturally as husband and wife should do,—as though nothing could separate us except death, and that only for a time. I am not exaggerating: I have never been able to regard you, for example, as a help or inspiration to my career; you just won't fit into that niche. My career, whatever there is of it, can only be a help and inspiration toward loving you,— because my whole life is dedicated to you. I don't mean that in any grandiose or solemn way—I simply mean that I can't love you as I want to without preserving my own self-respect, and I can't do that without loving you, because that is the highest standard my self-respect can live up to.

I have just had a note from Don Stuart asking me to meet him at Canada House "some morning"—I wonder if he lives in that place. Tonight I shall drop in on Cameron. I wonder what Cameron lacks—he has brains, humor, culture, courtesy, but there's something missing from his makeup—something in the general direction of self-confidence, I should judge. Going around the photographic exhibition with him was rather funny—he'd wince at every nude he came to, but his standard comment was "I think that's rather conventional, don't you?" I told you about his friend who had just come from Russia—apparently he took one of their planned tours backward and talked to the people rather than to other tourists or guides. Or said he did—he said he used German, which sounds to me like a rather dangerous tongue to use. Now Don Stuart writes: "After being in Russia I'll be glad to get home"—unless he means that he has yet to go to Russia. It seems to me that travel, in the sense of going and gaping at a country as opposed to living there, is not so much broadening as flattening—it makes one passive and uncritical. I've found that true here, anyway. At theatres, concerts, or picture galleries I'm all right, as art speaks a universal language, but my ordinary observation of things is much less active than in Canada, because the things I see don't arise from a familiar enough setting—there's too much inexact and unknown data. This may not be very clear, but my point is that, if one is travelling, one is bound to be in what I call a passive and uncritical frame of mind, so if one goes to a country with a certain set of prejudices, looking for certain things, one gets those prejudices triumphantly verified, or else upset by unimportant details.

Sign in Strand: "Moderation Is True Temperance. Closed on Sundays." I woke up this morning to hear someone whistling "O Had I Jubal's Lyre"[3] out of some back window—surely he didn't pick it up from me. London is a great place to overhear conversations. On top of a bus a drunken woman—surely the world's most pathetic and pitiful object—was holding forth on a long lament to her husband, "Oh, why did I, a north-country woman, ever marry you, a Londoner?" The man was obviously wondering why himself. In a restaurant on Coventry Street a man, apparently a theatrical or vaudeville manager, was arguing with an enormously fat woman who looked as though she might be a comedienne of some sort, trying to get her to sign a contract for a tour of South Africa. He named a certain price, and the woman blazed up and asked if she weren't worth more than that. "My dear, of course you are, but we can't always pay people what they're worth these hard times—heh, heh—and what with the expenses of going to a new country where you're not known—" "What the devil do you mean, I'm not known?" "My dear, I'm not suggesting that you're not known, but publicity costs a lot of money, you know, and it's publicity that helps to make you known—heh, heh—." Eventually he got her consent, gave a gasp of relief that fairly sucked in the roof, and said to the waitress: "Bring this lady a nah-ice cup of tea."

I have been to the Tate Gallery. Just a cursory look around—more to see what I would go to the next time and what I would avoid. It's the most grotesque place I've ever been in in my life—the very good and the very bad so close together. Rousseau and Braque still hold me—in painting I'm still in a state of complete acceptance with regard to certain paintings, a thing I never am in literature or music. That makes me vaguely uneasy—is it possible that my admiration for Rousseau and Braque is owing to their clever exploitation of certain formulae I'm not sophisticated enough to grasp? Frenchmen admire Poe's poetry more than Englishmen do, because Poe's tricks are obvious to Englishmen and therefore fascinating to someone less familiar with the language. It may be something like that with me. The Blakes were marvellous, though I was a little disappointed not to see any unfamiliar ones. I made one mistake—I went on students' day, and paid sixpence for the privilege of seeing old ladies copying the pre-Raphaelites, and some bitch befouling one corner with a bastard spawned from Van Gogh's Sunflowers and her own mind, covering up three pictures I wanted to see with her fat backside, and holding forth on the most reactionary political opinions to anyone who would listen to her. Her voice filled the room so completely there wasn't room for me.

I dropped in to a second-hand bookshop which sells books on occultism near the British Museum.[4] Bloomsbury is a great centre of occultism—you see Theosophy, Swedenborg, Rudolf Steiner and all the rest of the Cosmic Consciousness and Third Eye apparatus everytime you turn around. Even over London as a whole it's one of the three largest groups of advertised books of non-fiction—the other two being Marxist political and economic treatises and books relating to sexual intercourse. Though those in the last group are ostensibly intended for married people, to judge from their titles, I suspect them of being mostly sold to uneasy penis-massaging bachelors. Well, anyway, I got to talking with the proprietor of this occultist place, explained my own interest in the subject, and am expected to return Saturday to meet somebody.

Well, darling, I must get this off. I think perhaps I may do less whining in my letters this year than formerly—I hope I shall have less cause in any case. I feel so much better about you—your German lessons with Mrs. Arnold are an excellent idea. But I miss you dreadfully all the same.

Norrie.

1 Veronica Wedgwood was born in 1910.
2 *Storm in a Teacup,* by James Bridie and Bruno Frank, was playing at the Garrick on 25 September 1936.
3 An aria from Handel's oratorio *Joshua,* first produced in Covent Garden on 9 March 1748.
4 New Atlantis on Museum St.

149. HK to NF   [*Toronto*]
                                               Sept. 25. 1936.

My dearest:

This is just a note to tell you further news. Yesterday morning Jessie MacPherson 'phoned to ask me to go into Wymilwood as don—graduate residence.[1] Do some tutoring in art history and generally spread light. Barbara is getting someone to take my place and I'll leave my stuff in the flat. This is rather too good a chance to miss, I think, and I'm going to make a good job of whatever it is I have to do. Poise, push, that's the thing. I think I can be more sociable than Dr [Florence A.] Smith, at any rate. I don't know whether I'm replacing her or not. They have not made up their minds yet about how much tutoring I'll have to do but Jessie Mac said she wouldn't work me to death. I'll have to get special arrangements made about any evening work here but that can be done. Norah [McCullough] thought it was a grand idea for one's reputation and a connection for us with the University and Daddy could just see Robson being a little impressed. The money saving too I need hardly mention. Just for eight months, my boy, and I'll be able to see you.

Have just finished a little blurb on the Soviet show[2] which pleased Baldwin and Norah. We may be getting places!

Inquire if Birken Howard the architect is still at 90 Guilford St. If so, make yourself known as he was quite friendly with both Norah and me. Last news of Edith Manning [Burnett] was that she was in Albania on holidays.[3] K. Coburn is back here—too bad for you, but she did give Miss Thorneycroft orders to look you up. Bursar of St. Hugh's, a grand woman with red hair and a weakness for Canadians.

Must go to work———don't die of shock!

Love

Helen

1 Dons were young people with university degrees who looked after a house or unit in a student residence, performing some in loco parentis functions and also being available for tutoring and academic counselling. Often graduate students or instructors, or workers in museums, art galleries, or libraries, they were accorded the status of junior faculty.
2 "Exhibition of the Art of Soviet Russia," *Bulletin of the Art Gallery of Toronto*, October 1936, [2].
3 HK later reports (Letter 159) that Edith Burnett was in Dalmatia.

150. NF to HK   London

Postmarked 29 September 1936; addressed to HK at 205 Fulton Ave., Toronto, Ontario, Canada.

My sweet pet:

I forget exactly when I wrote last, but I feel like talking to you again anyhow. I have looked up Cameron Caesar again, borrowed his dinner jacket according to schedule, and went to the ballet at Sadler's Wells with him on Friday afternoon. It's a new English company, which has the appearance of having improved very much over a period of about a year. It has acquired a good deal of competence, but is obviously completely in the grip of the Ballet Russe tradition, and is developing very rapidly in the wrong direction. The first ballet, "Baraban,"[1] was quite good: an Algerian landowner has Italian troops billeted on him, pretends death, the soldiers realize there is nothing more to be got out of him and leave, and he revives. The execution was a bit sloppy, but the music was good. Then two Tschaikowskys, both designed to exhibit individual dancing virtuosity—the last thing a ballet should do—one from the Nutcracker Suite called the "Kingdom of Sweets," which summed up practically the whole programme. Then an excessively feeble attempt at an 18th century Watteau landscape, complete with garden, twilight, lords and ladies admiring a shepherd, negro boys as servants, and statues of Roman gods. Music Handel, arranged by Beecham and grotesquely unsuitable—Handel's strength and virility smashing to pieces all their attempts to be cute. Cameron loves that sort of thing, but has seen all this ballet five times over. You don't seem to have made much impression on that gentleman—he talked about the open-air Shakespeare theatre at Regent's Park, and I mentioned that you had gone with him to see the Midsummer Night's Dream. He said he knew you had been there, and knew that he had seen that play there, but whether you were together or not he didn't remember. The pursuit of pure science seems to include amnesia among its occupational diseases. Then he took me into University College again and showed me some of his experiments with dyes—all about how dyes changed their color in a test tube when acids or alkalis were added. It was very fascinating and incomprehensible. Perhaps it's just common interests we lack—for instance, when I asked about Queen's Hall proms he said dutifully that you said they were very good, but he hadn't been there himself. I offered to read his thesis over sometime for spelling, punctuation and grammar, and he seems very grateful. We have a sort of date to go to the Tower together this week.

I have definitely abandoned the attempt to get a decently cooked meal in the middle of the day, and think I shall try to subsist on a light lunch and a light tea—one saves money that way anyhow. Last night I was with, as I shall presently explain, two very fat women who talked to me about food and were very solicitous about giving me names of restaurants, so perhaps things will look up. I have also abandoned the English climate to its own devices. Beyond the fact that a brilliantly sunny morning seems to be usually the sign of a cloudburst to follow an hour or so later, I can make nothing of it. The last few days have been overcast and the weather has been sultry and sticky, with the thermometer at around 70. This is described by the papers as a "heat wave"; I don't know if anyone died of prostration or not.

Yesterday (Sunday) Dickinson looked me up and we went out to see Ridgion, with plans for a walk on Hampstead Heath. It rained, however, so we went to Ridgion's room (I dislike the word "digs" for some reason) and heard the rest of his records—a Mozart clarinet quintet which made me desperately homesick, as I had last heard it at Douglas MacAgy's on Bloor St., and a Schubert Octet. Then, acting on a suggestion of my own, we went to the Wallace Collection and spent a frightfully exotic afternoon gazing at rococo.[2] I didn't get a long enough look at the big red room where the better pictures are, however, and will have to go back. The snuff-boxes I particularly admired, and anyway they seemed the most direct symbol of all that stuff—elegant, expensive, useless and narcotic. Then we had tea and I went along with them to a friend of Ridgion's—a girl named Nan Kelly, extraordinarily lively and friendly and a professional revolutionary—she works in the Worker's Bookshop in Clerkenwell Green and is something like Mary Winspear, either much less attractive or infinitely more so, depending on whether one takes to rampant Communists or not. She was entertaining four females, all hideous, two fatter than the other two, as aforesaid. None of them were Communists, but Nan seemed to be pulling them all along at various stages of squawking protest. One of them went home and the rest of us went out to someone's home who was putting on a concert in aid of the Spanish workers. Two very fine things—a meso dialogue of Ernst Toller recounting the betrayal and murder of Karl Liebknecht and Rosa Luxemburg by the Nazis which, except for the names, read exactly like an account of the Passion—betrayal, mockery, martyrdom and renewed life for all as a result of the martyrdom, all fitting in.[3] It ended up with prayers for the souls of the saints, starting with Lenin—Trotsky and Stalin being delicately omitted, no doubt as being still alive. Then a play of a strike in Barcelona—two Communists being tortured to confess where arms are concealed. One starts going mad, so the other agrees to talk if they'll shoot the other man, on the plea that when released he'll denounce him as a traitor. They do so, and the strike starts by cutting off all the lights, including of course the prison lights, which was the signal agreed upon. "Now you can shoot me," says the Communist. "Only he and I knew where the arms were: he's dead and you're too late." Then two poems equally gruesome, recited by a female, one called "A Pile of Bloody Rags"—meaning the mutilated corpse of somebody killed in the war. Bloody in every sense of the word. It was a fairly strenuous evening, as you can imagine—a little of that goes a long way with me, and the general catacomb atmosphere was a bit overwhelming. Charge, sixpence each, but as the host said the expenses of the evening were pretty heavy. I don't know how much the Spanish workers will get out of it. I can't imagine why Ridgion & Dickinson went—the former seems to have no definite political views, and the latter is if anything Conservative.

I'll try to get letters off to Roy [Daniells] and the rest, but whenever I think of writing a letter I think of writing one to you, and when that's written it's time to do something else. I'd rather like to keep in touch with Dorothy [Drever] a bit this year. I rather expected that her divergence from the mediocrity magnet would set up an English and History howl.[4] She must be having a rather colorless life in some ways. I do hope she doesn't turn Communist—religions like that are only for people predestined to them, I think, and it would make her very lonesome and unhappy. The trouble with her is that her intelligence and energy don't seem to fertilize her. It sounds silly to say that she needs a sympathetic man, but, damn it, she does, and although I played that role two years ago, I shall never know whether I made a mess of it or not, and at present can do nothing but feel vaguely responsible and definitely helpless.

I arranged to meet Don Stuart at Canada House this morning and found him all right—we walked around and had some coffee at that Strand Honeydew. He's just been making a tour of English prisons and sightseeing, and came back from Russia at the end of August. He had a hell of a time in Russia—they wouldn't let him near any of their prisons: they went through all his private letters and diaries at the customs, they wouldn't let him take photographs of anything, everything was frightfully expensive, the trial of the Trotskyite conspirators a farce, militarism, parades and propaganda everywhere, his wife was completely fed up and the food made him sick. Apparently Russia is taking no chances with possible Fascist spies. His point of view in regard to English prisons seemed to be pretty official—he was greatly impressed by the Wakefield experimental prison,[5] had accumulated a vast pile of notes, all of which have to be carefully examined and censored by the Home Office, together with all articles written for the *New Outlook*.[6] The English were horrified when they found he was going to write articles, even for a church periodical: "Oh, we wouldn't have given you all this information if we had known you were going to write for the press: you said you were just a minister."

Tuesday

I had dinner with Veronica Wedgwood and her father[7] last night. It was quite thrilling to have a chauffeur call for you in the family car, a maid to announce you by name, a butler to say that dinner was served and then serve it—I had read all about that, but never saw the process in operation before. Wedgwood has a fine library, is very interested in Shakespeare, and has some etchings, including two Rembrandts and two Whistlers. Veronica is going to Edinburgh, but we've more or less arranged to meet again at Christmas, unless she happens to come to Oxford during term. She does work on seventeenth-century history, I understand—I've promised to lend her my copy of Spengler when it arrives.

Dickinson tells me he has to take some more time off and raise ninety guineas to persuade a psychiatrist to get rid of his nervous breakdown for him. His appearance is that of the most stolid and phlegmatic of Englishmen. A doctor's bill like that would be enough it itself to start up a pretty big neurosis in me, I told him. It's not easy to win these fights against nervous breakdowns, but it's some stimulus to reflect that it's expensive to lose.

I quite understand your fear of gossip, but, although I don't know much about Pegi Nicol's case, it looks from your description to be in an altogether different category from ours, and I do not know three people in town who would treat them as being exactly parallel. Sometimes I find your views on the relation of morality to convention a little difficult to disentangle. Besides, England is three thousand miles from Canada, and everybody knows already that you are coming across next summer and approves. John Jones [Harwood-Jones] has his nerve with him, but he also has my best wishes. My love to everybody you see—the fact that they see you endears them to me. If my letters sound a bit choppy and scrambled, it's because they get seasick crossing the ocean. They want so much to tell you that I love you, and they hate the Atlantic.

Norrie.

Impressions of England: English shoes fit.

1 Alexander Aliavev's comic ballet *Volshebniy baraban.*
2 A London art museum in Hertford House on Manchester Square, distinguished by the variety of its holdings: paintings, arms and armour, furniture, porcelain, miniatures, and enamels.
3 In 1926 Toller had begun writing an experimental play based on the events leading to the murder of Liebknecht and Luxemburg. He later named the play *Berlin 1919,* but he never completed it, and only fragments survive.
4 That is, a howl from students in the English and history honour course at VC.
5 The Wakefield prison experiment, which developed from the Prevention of Crime Act (1905), involved constructive training and self-discipline for selected prisoners, below the age of twenty-six, who engaged in group work and educational activities.
6 See Letter 35, n. 4, above.
7 Sir Ralph Wedgwood.

151. NF to HK

London
Oct. 1. [1936]

Postmarked 1 October 1936; addressed to HK at 24 St. Joseph St., Toronto, Ontario, Canada. Apt. 3.

Darling, I'm very sorry you're not getting my letters: the last one I picked up at Canada House was dated Sept. 21, and you hadn't even got my Plymouth letter then, which was mailed from the *Alaunia.* I hope nothing has happened, but I couldn't very well have sent you a letter before we landed at Plymouth, now could I? and I wrote you again before I'd been in London twenty-four hours. I wish to hell we'd connect: this business of writing into a void is no good.

I've caught the world's worst cold at last—I'd more or less been waiting for it. To help things along, this boarding house is full of coal gas and quite uninhabitable. And with my snuffle I don't feel much like going anywhere. I think one gets cold easily in tubes—they're so draughty and stifling and overheated. Today I wanted to go to the Tower with Cameron [Caesar], but he's up to his neck in work and can't make it, so I'm at a bit of a loose end. I went to Paddington[1] around ten this morning to get my ticket for Cheltenham—I'm going there to see Wilson Knight's brother tomorrow—then I strolled over to Cameron's and finding myself at a loose end, wandered down to the Temple—a wonderful place to wander—drifted across Blackfriars Bridge, had lunch at the Elephant and Castle, got on a bus and went through Lambeth, across Westminster Bridge, past the Houses of Parliament and the Abbey, up Whitehall, past Trafalgar Square, up Charing Cross Road and home. I'm beginning to feel as though I belonged in London. I like doing that—London itself seems small, and its museums seem so depressingly large. I haven't got past the Greek & Roman sculpture in the British Museum yet, nor have I yet much idea of what's in the Victoria and Albert. Late afternoon, all alone, in a largely empty museum when it's too dark to see anything properly makes me feel how far away you are. Yesterday, for instance, in the Victoria and Albert, I wanted so much to tell you how I disliked Rodin's great steaming lectures on creative evolution, forms emerging, like Dr. Slop, in all the majesty of mud,[2] how I liked poring over illuminated manuscripts in the Book Production Room, how very pleased I should be to have tea with you downstairs. Of course I did tell you, but you didn't hear me, so I had to have tea by myself.

I had more or less gathered from Barbara's [Barbara Sturgis's] letter that you were living at 24 St. Joseph St., but this is the first letter I've been able to send directly there—the others have all gone to Fulton Avenue. I've written you regularly twice a week—no, I'm afraid I skipped one half-week. They should be trickling in by now, of course—it's only that when I get letters from you begging me to write to you I naturally get worried. I wrote to Barbara at Macmillan's.

I didn't know Roy [Daniells] had actually proposed to Ev Stewart—if she actually ridiculed a man as sensitive as he he's to be congratulated on a merciful deliverance. What a brass-headed door knob that woman must be! And it's quite refreshing to hear you gravely agreeing with Arnold that I'm a very dominating sort of person, but you don't mind being dominated, really, as you're the meekest and most submissive of women. You must have touched his misogynist heart. I got a letter from Dorothy [Drever] along with yours—I didn't know she'd be going back to Wellesley Street. Be good to her, Helen—in spite of all her strength and persistence, she's a little lonely, a little lost and a little scared, and I think we're about the only people left she can believe in. And don't try to marry Roy [Daniells] to anybody. He's a man to be discouraged from marriage.

I met Donald Stuart again at Canada House, along with Joyce and her cousin, a chap called Jim Brown, from Trinity. He's been in Paris a month and London a month. Rather a weak, flabby face, but he may improve on acquaintance—we've arranged tentatively to see Eliot's *Murder in the Cathedral* some time.[3] We all had lunch at Lyons, cursing the coffee and the vegetables. Another one of Donald's many woes in Russia was an irritation in a very unwise place to have an irritation. So he contemplated it, wondering if he had or had not got a case of gonorrhea on his hands, terrified to go to a Russian clinic—he'd been through one and it was filthy—scared to tell his wife, and eventually saw it disappear. We went down to Buckingham Palace just too late to see the foot guard change, went back to Whitehall and got elbowed by policemen into a place where we saw the horse guard change. So what? Then we went down to the Abbey and looked around vaguely, walking all over people like Fox and Pitt and Canning.[4]

Tuesday and Wednesday nights I went by myself to Queen's Hall. Tuesday was a Haydn-Mozart concert, and I got a camp-stool and a seat for that. The Surprise, the Mozart G minor and Myra Hess playing Mozart's D Minor Concerto. Fair to middling—she's a good general practitioner but I never did like her Mozart. The ability to play Mozart properly seems to be a faculty separate from the ability to play anything else. The audiences at Queen's Hall applauded everything vigorously, good or bad—they give Sir Henry [Wood] an ovation when he's being an exquisite artist and they give him another when he's being a sentimental old jackass. The next night was a Bach concert, with that concerto for two violins. This time I had to stand—that is, stand half an hour in line outside the theatre, stand around half an hour waiting for the concert to start, stand all through the concert. And the London County Council says you can't sit on the floor or put your coat and hat on the floor, and the management says you have to give up any stools you may own before going in, so you get nicely framed on all sides. I suppose it's all done to cultivate that playing fields of Eton spirit. On both nights I saw somebody carried out in a dead faint, so it must be hard on some people. Oh, well, the concerto was superb, and it's such a relief not to have to worry over what the devil the woodwinds are going to do next. They played a Mozart serenade for wind instruments, just to show what they could do.

I love you so much, my sweet pet. I do hope you have got all my letters.

Norrie.

1 Paddington Station, the terminus of the Great Western Railway for the west and south-
   west of England.
2 The reference is to the squat man-midwife in *Tristram Shandy*; Dr. Slop, having been
   summoned to the Shandy household to deliver Tristram, is described by Sterne as
   "waddling through the dirt" on the back of his small pony; when he finally arrives, covered with clay, he does so in "an explosion of mud" (Laurence Sterne, *The Life and Opinions of Tristram Shandy, Gentleman*, vol. 2, chap. 8).
3 T.S. Eliot's play about Thomas à Becket, first produced at the Chapter House of the
   Canterbury cathedral in 1935. It played at the West End Theatre in London from
   November 1935 to March 1937.
4 That is, walking on the memorial tombstones of the English statesmen buried under the
   Abbey.

152. HK to NF   October 3rd 1936
                                                        10.30 P.M.

*This letter, written on the stationery of the Fenway Hall Hotel, was posted from
Cleveland, Ohio, where HK, Martin Baldwin, Norah McCullough, and Gordon
Webber were attending an exhibition mounted in connection with the twentieth
anniversary of the Cleveland Museum of Art. Almost four hundred pieces were
shown at the exhibition, including a Titian and a Raphael from the Louvre and
works loaned from England, the Netherlands, Germany, the United States, and
Italy.*

My dear:

Norah [McCullough] and I are having *my* first experience with col-
lapsible beds in a very bourgeois looking room here. Mr Baldwin drove
down with Gordie [Webber] and Norah and me, and we have just had a
very good meal at a Swedish place nearby. It is run by Swedes and
patronised by a great many art students some of whom made the crock-
ery and decorated the walls and painted screens with grotesque
humans. It is Saturday night and we have been driving all day through
towns full of colonial clap-board houses. Mr Baldwin was quite full of
information about periods and told us that there were carpenters' books
circulated all over the country in the 1870's and earlier, full of designs
for cornices, mouldings, pilasters and so on, and that the Greek revival
was responsible for the miles of Ionic pillars one sees on front porches.
We passed through Buffalo and saw the most magnificent grain eleva-
tors I've ever seen. Then there were huge piles of coal gleaming in the
sun, dark blue and darker shadows; there was a heap of yellow sulphur

against dark red machinery; there were great towering black funnels and girders and tremendous bridges and boats and tugs going up and down the river. All the way here I was holding you by the hand to myself just to be sure you were with me and seeing everything too. It has been a lovely day, my dear. We have not yet got in touch with the people at the museum but will do so to-morrow. The show has been prolonged another week. I am overjoyed that I was included in this party, and Mr. Baldwin is being awfully nice. He makes lewd remarks every so often but that is his way. Said to-night he asked Miss Kortright if she wanted him to tell her the facts of life and for a moment I almost thought he had. We gave her a present and she departed full of love for us all, even though she had been fighting the day before with Miss [Jean] Cowan like any alley cat. Poor woman, she will probably improve no end with a husband, and getting away from her parents who are very old, I gather. There's nothing like admiration to make a woman blossom, and I hope her husband does that for her. She can't be naturally such a vixen.

I am very comfortably settled in Wymilwood by now. Started a letter to you a few days ago,[1] just before your letter arrived, but I was too exhausted to finish it and will probably toss it in the waste basket when I get home. Roy Daniells has asked me to help him chaperone a Middle House[2] hike on Tuesday night. As it is Harold's [Harold Kemp's] birthday I have asked him to shift our party to Wednesday night which he will likely do. I think I am getting on fairly well as a don. Mr. Baldwin teases me a good deal about deans and gaiters, and this morning when he called for me at Wymilwood he said it made him feel like the monk from Siberia who finally eloped with the Mother Superiah—you know the limerick.[3]

Eleanor Caesar is in Wymilwood so I asked her to have dinner at my table last night.[4] She brought along a music student and I asked Norma Thompson, the head of the house to come too. We had a very merry little party and I begin to feel that I'm not such a dud socially at all. Jessie MacPherson wants the don to mingle a lot with the students in that way, and not always eat with Miss Manning.[5] She wants me to help get some pictures in the residences, and later on to give some talks on picture appreciation. I am to be on hand at Sunday teas and one night a week for coaching in art history, but so far my duties have not been arduous. I have given out house-keys and presided at the house meeting. The arrangement is ideal for me this year as it relieves me of all housekeeping problems and gives me more free time than I could possibly achieve in the flat. Frances Russell is taking my place and that end is quite well arranged.

I'm very sorry that you have been having trouble. Possibly you are better by this time. I hope so, because there is nothing more miserable than the general congestion caused by changes of climate and diet. Mother gave me some pills for you, but unfortunately I left them at home. They were given her by the nurse who looked after me, and they helped Roy very much.

Your stories about Cameron [Caesar] were very good. Dot Drever said he was a Communist now. I had heard about the wrong station episode from Jean Elder, but you give the other side of it much more graphically as usual. I am so glad you are finding some people to do things with. You have gotten over the worst now, darling, once you know a few people to talk to, even if they are colonials and keep on giving you the colonial's impression of the English. Not that these do particularly. I told Barbara [Sturgis] you had gone to see Veronica Wedgwood and she was very glad you had, and did not seem to think it at all out of the ordinary for you to have been unceremonious. I'm glad you went to see her. Barbara was surprised that I had not given you the address of her family, as she thought I would do so if I thought you would not be bored seeing them. She is always a little reticent about them, especially about her father, for she seems more interested in her mother. She doesn't exactly say that he's a dud, but I sometimes wonder. Her mother is a more vital personality, and it may be that the father has spent his life and his talents worshipping at the silver shrine until he has become merely a pale shadow beside her. I found him very kindly and pleasant, and I was really quite fond of them both. There was a grandmother too, a beautiful old lady, but she died last winter. They live at 12 Inkerman Terrace which is near Earlscourt Station. Name is under Roland Sturgis in the telephone book and you had better drop a note to Mrs Sturgis first.

Dorothy Drever is still at 81A Wellesley Street and will be there until January. After that I don't know. Barbara is at 24 St. Joseph Street. I am at 84 Queen's Park—until May, if I'm not fired.

Another glorious thing about the Wymilwood affair is that I can help Roy. He has to pay the full amount of fees as that absence from lectures idea was no good. He is working away on the Lincoln Hutton essay now, and I'm getting a gallery check for the first instalment of some seventy odd dollars.

I think I mentioned that Kay Coburn had received your letter asking to meet her in Oxford. I *am* sorry you didn't meet there but I think she came home a week earlier. Miss [Alta Lind] Cook is full of Salzburg and is studying singing now. I talked to her at the Sunday vesper service for the frosh. She asked about you. So does everyone.

You are a little hard on Lady Precious Stream. I don't think it pretends to be a reproduction of a Chinese play exactly to the letter. Of course I didn't have to listen to a fatuous idiot giving cute remarks.

Last night I dreamt I slept with an elephant. That one goes down with the chased-by-a-gorilla-down-main-street-of-Ottawa dream. Only he was a very kindly sort of elephant and his trunk was soft and really didn't get in the way much. I hope I dream of you to-night. I'd much rather.

I'll tell you more when I've got out to see some of the buildings to-morrow.

Monday evening

We have been very busy, as you will imagine, what with seeing the exhibition and Mrs Dunn and hearing the lectures by Thomas Munro and Mr Milliken, the director. It is nearly time for dinner and Norah is having a nap. I must get this letter aboard the Queen Mary, so that I'll finish it off in a hurry.

If I didn't realize that you were seeing fine things in London I'd be inconsolable at your missing this show. Of course there were a number of pictures which were in Chicago, so they're not unknown to you. Early Italians, two beautiful Duccio's belonging to John D. Rockerfeller Jr., Memling, Van der Weyden, Holbein, Titian, Tintoretto, three *grand* El Greco's, and the best show of modern French that I've ever seen, all the way from Corot to Picasso and Matisse. They had the Duchamp "Nude Descending Staircase"[6] which was great fun. Redon's "Orpheus" was there and a lovely mysterious Rousseau called "Night of the Carnival." The Derain girl in pink which we had in Toronto was in the show, but they had improved it greatly, with a new frame.

Munro lectured on French painting this morning. He gave a very competent résumé of developments, just a little prosaic in his manner. Milliken was almost Latin in his enthusiasm and in the richness of his vocabulary. He spoke extremely well, on Siena and Florence and their artistic development, and painted the background of the movements—I

was spellbound by his language. Had to whisper somewhat imperti-
nently to Norah at the end about St. Milliken in ecstasy, but I really was
impressed. He did what Lismer likes to do, but I felt he had his work
better in hand; his sentences were not so involved and he spoke simply
enough but in the language of an Italian scholar rather than too much
looking down to the audience. Perhaps he can do this more readily in
Cleveland where they've got a longer tradition than we have in Toronto,
I don't know. Perhaps he has more people who know about art history.
But as I say, I was impressed, and encouraged to think that a gallery lecture can be kept informal and yet be as full of meat as his was. Norah
and Gordie stayed late after the gallery was closed and saw some children's drawings. I would have gone too, but we had an altercation with
an officious guard. Norah sailed through imperiously, Baldwin was all
for obeying orders, got sore at Norah, marched out and took me with
him. I thought I'd best indulge in my favorite occupation, and got out
the old oil tank once more, and soon all was happy again. We've had a
very busy time and it is no wonder that a little temper is lost now and
again. Mrs Dunn is the woman who began the children's art classes. She
talked away like a dynamo when I was there and she kept on going for
an hour nearly when she was talking of the children's work. She has
been there for eighteen years and is in her sixties but she is so full of
energy it makes you a little anxious.

We're all tired out and may not do much to-night. Last night we
dropped in to see the streets of the world at the exposition[7]—good fun
but full of junk. We hope to get an early start to-morrow and get home
around six in the evening,—the trip down took a little over eight hours.

I'm sending you a couple of post cards. There weren't many in colour,
and their photographs were fairly costly, so I'll limit it to these and
show you the catalogue when you get home. (!) Which won't seem long,
my dear, at this rate. Here in these United States there seems to be a tax
on everything just as in Montreal, so that when you think you've bought
a post card for ten cents it is eleven, or a meal for forty-five and it's
forty-seven.

I'll soon begin sending things to Merton, in fact I might just as well
send this letter there, judging by the date. I hope you meet the people
you've been hoping to see, right away, and are not lonely at all. Now
you know, don't you, how I felt when I was away from you, and how it
is not so hard for me this year, knowing a little of what you are seeing
and where you will be. If I could have prevented that horrible lost soul

feeling in London I'd have done whatever it was—I hope you'll never feel quite as down as I did sometimes. But of course you won't, because you're going to a real university, and you've made friends already. Once you are feeling better then I will not feel so concerned. Gordie sends his best and hopes you will see some exhibitions and tell us about them.

Baldwin has just called up to see when we eat, so I must stop. Write to me as much as you can, and I'm sorry that I left those pills at home. But you'll be better now, I hope. And I love you very much.

Helen.

1 See Letter 155.
2 One of the four houses of the main residence at VC.
3 "There was a young monk from Siberia / Whose morals were very inferior. / He did to a nun / What he shouldn't have done, / And now she's a Mother Superior."
4 The custom was for each of the dons to sit at a different table in the dining room in Wymilwood, the Women's Student Union.
5 Jessie Macpherson played an important role in helping to liberalize the policies governing women's conduct in the residence halls at VC. On her retirement in 1963, Frye, who was principal of VC at the time, observed that "through the earlier part of her administration she had the difficult and delicate task of adjusting the rules of women's residences to the changing patterns of social behaviour, aiming at a sane and relaxed discipline which would keep both the respect of the students and the confidence of parents" (*Victoria Reports*, 13 [May 1963], 21).
6 See Letter 57, n. 1, above.
7 The Great Lakes Exposition, which was taking place at the same time as the exhibition at the Cleveland Museum of Art. The museum show, in fact, was the official art exhibit for the exposition.

153. NF to HK

London
Oct. 5 [*1936*]

Postmarked 6 October 1936; addressed to HK c/o Art Gallery of Toronto, Ontario, Canada, S.S. *Normandie.*

My sweet pet:

I got a letter at Canada House from you this morning dated Sept. 25, and you still don't seem to have got my first letters to you. Last Saturday a letter came from mother to Guilford Street—she'd got my Plymouth and first London letters the same morning—Sept. 23. It's not going to be much fun living in England if I can't trust the English postal system. After all, a freighter should have got those letters to you by the 25th.

Congratulations on the Wymilwood appointment, darling: it's a wonderful idea, you'll do splendidly at it, and it turns your coming over next summer from a financial gamble into a pleasure trip. Whoever thought that idea up deserves a Nobel Prize—and yet, it is a perfectly logical move to make, and you're the logical person to make it with. Don't let bigger and flashier girls overawe you—that would be your main difficulty as a don. My very best wishes to you, darling—it'll help keep Victoria College in the family. I am very pleased, and if Victoria is really going to do something intelligent with you instead of getting you to draw them signs everything may turn out even better than I had ever expected.

Friday I went to Cheltenham to see Wilson Knight's brother.[1] The train trip was fascinating—it was like being dragged through one Constable painting after another, and I like these funny little trains that sidle off so apologetically—everything is built so close to the ground in England. Knight is different from his brother—much less reserved and introspective. It's hard to carry on small talk, generalizations or personalities with Wilson: we talk exclusively about literary subjects. His brother is equally friendly and equally intense and enthusiastic about symbolism, but is much more interested in me as a person and is more flexible in his general outlook. The Knights are the only people I have met who really speak my language, and I sat there drinking gallons of cider (I have been pissing pure apple-juice ever since) and talking and listening as I had never talked nor listened before. Knight's politics I don't like—more sympathetic to Fascism than Communism, full of a mystical devotion to the army, which he regards as the embodiment of ideal character training, and inclined to regard the Oxford Group[2] very seriously—but somehow that doesn't seem to matter when we talk the same language. Cheltenham itself is a perfect background to such a set-up—a health resort, beautiful, sleepy and cultured, full of private hotels of a most devastating respectability, inhabited by retired army and government people. Knight lives in one of those sepulchral hotels: I can't imagine how he stands it. He's a professor of classics in Exeter University and is bringing out a book on the labyrinth in religion and art.[3] In the middle of our political discussion, he said: "The essential point about you is that you're not an escapist," which is the highest compliment it is possible to pay me, I think—or anybody else for that matter, but particularly me.

In the evening he brought in a repulsive youth named Berry, who is a poet the Knights are patronizing.[4] This person took us over to his house to hear Beethoven's 9th on the radio. He worships Beethoven, largely because he accepts a sort of Nietzschean strong-man philosophy—admires Hitler, of course. Along with this goes a nature mysticism like Lawrence—if you ever get around to reading Lawrence's *Plumed Serpent*, you will see how closely an exaggerated respect for nature and her works is bound up with Fascism and its belief in war as a purgation of the spirit. The poem this ape read us was full of Lawrence's kind of *pot au feu* philosophy—he admired volcanoes for one thing, and was ecstatic about being part of a huge stewing cooking hellbroth. Knight prefers him, as a poet, to Day Lewis, whom he also knows, I think with some justification—as there's no doubt the son of a sod can write, and write superbly. Only, he represents everything in this world I detest and fear. When a man goes to the edge of a precipice, part of him wants to jump over, and when civilization approaches a precipice, there is always a group seized with an insane desire for suicide. That's what the Fascists represent, and what he represents. Now I object to being told that, because the law of gravitation is so much greater than I, I ought to smash my brains out as a sacrifice to it. Knight said: "He's a very nice boy, but I'm afraid you rather hate him." I said fervently that I did. However, we're not the worse friends for that, if you understand what I mean. Knight explained that he was really on his worst behavior, as he hadn't too much self-confidence and what he had he lost after five minutes with me. Knight gave me one or two names at Oxford—Veronica [Wedgwood] has also given me a letter.[5]

Yvonne [Williams] and Esther [Johnson] called up Thursday night. I went to their home—Esther's aunt, as I understand—and had dinner. I would have had a nice time except for a huge Scandinavian sow, who was some sort of scientist in Toronto and is going back there from Denmark. She barged in, quite unexpectedly, and held forth in a strident monologue about her worries in connection with getting a dog into Canada. As this Great Dane had come in a taxi, I had to escort her home through the tubes—fortunately she lives in Russell Square—but hardly got talking with the two girls at all. Last night I went to see Cameron [Caesar] again—he'd been down with a crowd of about half a million people, who turned out and stopped the Fascists from parading through the Jewish quarter, and was feeling very cheerful. We may have to cancel our trip to the Tower, as he's up to his neck in work, trying to finish his thesis and get home to his job by the end of November. Today I ran into Ernie MacQuarrie on the street riding a bicycle. Two years ahead of me at Emmanuel, just missed the travelling fellowship but got a much better one which gives him three years at Cambridge.

I am afraid I am going to be pretty short of money by around the beginning of December, so it's possible I may have to call on you for a short-term loan before my $750 instalment comes through. I seem to need such a disheartening number of clothes. Sunday I went to Ridgion's again, and today I went down with Dickinson to buy clothes. Dickinson bullied half a dozen stores into various stages of dignified protest, and eventually produced a rich brown sports jacket, a close approximation to Harris Tweed, for 27/6, gray flannels for 10', and a lemon yellow pullover sweater for 9'. I'm all woolly. I've been moved out of my room into a smaller, cheaper and noisier one, and have lost two stamps and thirty cents in Canadian money in the process.

I still get a nervous twinge and a feeling of nausea when I think of how far away you are, but it won't last forever. My love for you will.

Norrie.

1 Jackson Knight.
2 See Letter 46, n. 6, above.
3 Jackson Knight, *Cumaean Gates: A Reference of the Sixth Aeneid to the Initiation Pattern* (Oxford: Basil Blackwell, 1936).
4 The young poet was Francis Berry, who had published two books of poems: *Gospel of Fire*, with an introduction by G. Wilson Knight (London: Mathews & Marrot, 1933), and *Snake in the Moon* (London: Williams & Norgate, 1936).
5 This is perhaps the undated letter of introduction to Trelawny that Veronica Wedgwood gave NF. HFF, 1991, box 3, file 1.

154. NF to HK   Paddington
                                                          Oct. 8 [*1936*]

Postmarked 9 October 1936; addressed to HK at 84 Queen's Park, Toronto, Ontario, Canada.

My little girl:

Two days ago it was your birthday, and I wanted very badly to write to you, but I took a warm bath in a cold room, and it's been headache, wretchedly sore eyes and a vacant mind, so no letter got itself written. I think of sending you greetings on your birthday rather than a week or so before it, because naturally celebrating your birthday comes more appropriately from one who gives thanks every day that you got born than from you yourself. Besides, it's as much my birthday as yours. Exactly a year ago—again a delay of two days!—you came back to Toronto, and by doing so made yourself my wife, and by becoming my wife ended my adolescence. I mean by adolescence the period in which I collected materials for building the sort of life I was cut out to build. I had the materials; I knew in a general way I was a pretty froggy sort of tadpole and would never turn into anything different, and I knew I would do the sort of things I had to do no matter what happened. But the point is that a life to be any good has to mean something to the person who lives it as well as to other people, and I couldn't find anything that would give my capacities any value or meaning to *me* until I was sure of you. Now I'm all right—I can go ahead building and planning. You have the power to destroy that building at any time, if it pleases you, but until then at any rate I am secured by knowing that everything I can achieve in contributions to "culture" or "the intellectual life" or whatever abstraction you please, as long as I can keep pouring them out, has another name, and that name its real name, Helen.

So, while I am desperately lonesome for you, I am not lonely. I don't mean only that I have enough people to talk to and enough to occupy me, though that enters, but also that what I am doing here grows naturally out of my love for you, as well as out of my own urge to advance, the desire of Victoria College to have English-trained professors, or the will of God or the pattern of twentieth-century thought. All these other things are admirable enough, but I shouldn't care to be left alone with them. It's bad enough to have to sleep by myself, without taking a Purpose to bed with me, personal or impersonal. But you're part of the scheme now, and everything that happens, if it fits in with the fact that I love you, is all right.

Why do I protest so much? Partly because I am a little nervous at seeing you holding my happiness in your volatile and temperamental little hands. Partly because I am one of those people who have to give some form of expression to their feeling or burst. And of course I may be simply dramatizing myself, overwhelming you with flatulent words and egotistic emotions over a comparatively simple matter. That is your own opinion—or at least it has been your opinion—so I have gone into it more carefully and from more points of view than you ever did. And what emerged was: it is quite true that I sound like an intolerable prig and am making an abject fool of myself continually. And I don't care; and I shall never care. I don't mind if you laugh at me and say to yourself: "That's Norrie hypnotizing himself again." Because a love which is dignified can never be more than liking or respect: love itself is ridiculous and grotesque, like the sex act itself. I could hardly be a lover without being a clown first. That is because I am blissfully and completely in love with a very real woman. Why do they say "head over heels in love" if they don't mean that a lover will do absurd things, like writing absurd letters to bore his sweetheart with?

I go up to Oxford tomorrow, travelling light because I love you.

Norrie.

155. HK to NF   84 Queens Park. Toronto.
                                                    Sept 30. 1936.

The first two paragraphs of this letter were written on 30 September: as HK says in her letter of 3 October (Letter 152), she had begun a letter "a few days ago." On 10 October, she added the current letter to her earlier note.

I'm firmly installed here, have had the house meeting to-night and have given out scores of keys. Dot Drever came in as soon as she knew about this and gave me her advice. I think I'll be a pretty fair don, feel a little depressed to-night because of too much social activity. We had a tea at the Art Centre[1] yesterday and a big members' tea at the Gallery today; I've been moving AGAIN, and working like a nigger at correcting bulletins, etc. Had to take round a group from the Angel Factory this morning.[2] It was rather fun, for they were nice girls and some were quite interested in pictures. I figure rather largely in this month's bulletin, what with five hundred words of blah on the Soviet show.[3] Marge Boultbee wanted to know where I got my material and I said from the catalogue introduction, same as she had. I dressed mine up a bit, though, and it wasn't bad. The middle paragraph seemed a little jerky as to rhythm, I thought, but I'll improve next time.

I just pulled out one of your letters written in July 1932. It rather gave me a start, the working in and out of your very logical brain in response to my affectionate advances. Poor Norrie! I wish you were here to let me bewilder you again. Oh hell, I can't write to you to-night. I'm so tired I can hardly hold a pen. I had better leave off. I'm going to Cleveland this weekend.

October 10, 1936.

Just pulled out this pad and found the above note started before the Cleveland trip. I got back from Cleveland on Tuesday at six in time for six-thirty dinner, then went with Roy Daniells to a Middle House hike at Lambton Mills[4] with the new don of North House, named Miller, and a girl named Cunningham. Very badly organized, it rained, nothing began until after ten, and I was annoyed because I passed up a birthday celebration at home to go to it. Besides, one isn't too full of energy after driving over three hundred miles. Work continues at the gallery,—complicated by the curse and constant interruptions and bad management of one kind or another. A crowd of thirty odd teachers arrived an hour before I expected anyone the other day, and nobody was back from lunch except Baldwin and myself. However, he talked to them. Heaven knows what he said and I'm sure they didn't know, but it was a gallery talk. You see the Soviet show was open that night; it had just gone on the walls; we were still writing labels for the print room and arranging a showcase full of books and dolls and small pamphlets on modern Russia. The catalogues had not arrived from New York and Aileen Galster was frantically lettering signs to tide over our difficulties. And in came a hundred more teachers, the ones I was expecting. However, all hands went at the pump, Norah [McCullough] and Baldwin talked on the show and I took groups down to the centre where Gwen Kidd and Dorothy Medhurst looked after them. All this happened yesterday, and while there was a formal opening at the gallery there was also this big brass hat reception at Victoria.[5] They gave me a red badge to wear and dubbed me hostess-at-large, so I felt I had to go. Mother came over and sewed me into Norah's dress, and I finally got there. What a life! The dress was very effective, if you can get the idea from my fashion drawings.

The Governor General[6] was on hand and all the stuffed shirts in town. God, what a bourgeois affair *that* was! Hundreds of people, the crush was pretty stifling. There were covered carpets stretched from Vic to Burwash and to Emmanuel, and there were exhibits in the library of Emmanuel. I felt damnably single, I can tell you, what with everyone

turning up with husband or wife or fiancé. These Vic family affairs are
all very well if your family doesn't happen to be in Merton. However,
Miss [Margaret] Ray snapped me out of that by saying "Oh you married
women!" and introduced me to Moff Woodside as Norrie's fiancé and I
thought the family'd better be well represented. I spent the evening
alternately receiving congratulations about the donship and answering
questions about you. Roy [Daniells] suggests that I type out an expur-
gated edition of your letters for general circulation and Jerry [Riddell]
even offered to edit the collected letters of H.N.F. I do wish you would
send a note to Roy and to Art Cragg who seems a bit gloomy in Emmanuel without you there. I ran into George Morrison who stuck to me for
the rest of the evening and solved the man problem. I didn't feel it was
adequately solved, but still he was someone to talk to. I'd forgotten how
he danced though, and felt some regret later when he gripped me con-
vulsively and crushed all the roses. Graham Millar was there with his
sister and Dot Drever told me in an aside that Mildred's infant is about
to arrive at any time.[7]

I'm taking on the Women's Lit Art Group, that is in an advisory capacity. I start on Tuesday with Mrs Arnold, who is one grand woman. I'm
rather appalled when I think of what I've got to get through this year, but
I'll do it just the same. "The School" printed my article and gave me 8
bucks for it.[8] I'm just about broke again. Will be for some time.

I didn't realize that I sounded impatient about letters. It is always a long time before the first one can get here, that's all—ten days for you to cross and sometimes another ten before the letter arrives here. Your first one came three weeks after you left, and I've had about five I think altogether. You're really doing nobly, and you know how much I devour them when they do come. I had hoped you'd be feeling better, but then you catch a cold—*are* you dressing properly and wearing your underwear etc—you know all my stock questions.

Thank you my dearest, I'd like to have tea with you anytime you say, but I'd much rather have it somewhere else than in the V & A lunchroom. The Morris tiles used to give me the blues. Have you seen the library at the V & A? It's supposed to be the best art library in the world. So Webb said, at any rate. There is a rather pleasant room up near South Kensington Tube Station which is more cheerful than the V & A liverpot-pie-suet-pudding atmosphere.

I think Ev Stewart is all right—anyone might have teased a man in the situation as I heard of it—she stopped as soon as she realized what she had done. The other night at the so-called hike—another excuse for a dance—Roy [Daniells] left me flat to make a date with Leith Ferguson, and he kept up a certain adolescent vivacity whenever she was anywhere near. I recognized the symptoms for I've done it myself lots of times. Dorothy [Drever] says that on Sunday night after Roy had left their place the Finnish girl 'phoned there and asked very crossly for him. They finally said she had the wrong number. At that moment he was very likely feeding me a chicken sandwich, so you can see that poor old Roy is being fairly hounded to death at this rate. The Finnish girl is in charge of the art group and is very attractive. There's really nothing like a fascinating foreign accent, especially in a foreign girl.

By the way, Norah [McCullough] has been entertaining the grandson of Jacob Burckhardt,—Civilization of Renaissance in Italy. She met him in London, and he is here on his way to New York where he is to work in chemistry somewhere. Beautiful youth, I quite lost my heart to him. Young Dick Mulock is in town but I have not met him yet.

Don't stand for anymore Prom Concerts, I'm sure it isn't good for you. Was so glad that you were visiting Wilson Knight's brother. Cheltenham will be very beautiful just now—I was there with Marian Higgs.

I must stop and get to bed. The don and the other appendages of Wymilwood are served breakfast in bed on Sundays so I have eight hours more to wait. I think I'll start gathering some interested souls together to listen to records, Arthur [Cragg] offered to lend me some. I'm rapidly losing any fear of people—there just isn't time. And I seem to be manufacturing conversation at quite a rate. Perhaps I'll be able to pour tea sooner than I expected. I keep on being amused at being adopted into Vic family party with you away, I'm still rather dumbfounded, but I'm here and it seems to be all right. If the Smith [Florence A. Smith] held this job last year I certainly can. But I feel like a widow with a lot of children. One month gone. By now you'll be at Merton, but Kay tells me that Nichol Smith is giving Alexander lectures here[9] and going to California for the winter. Dreadfully sorry, I hope it doesn't make too much difference to you.

One thing I beg of you—on all the bended knees you like, preferably yours—*do* get your hair cut by someone who knows how. And make them leave it long. One look at your passport photograph nearly gave me hydrophobia. Find out who is good and sit on him until he gets the idea. I can't bear it.

Thanksgiving Day

 The post office tells me I may catch the Normandie if I hurry with this. I have been in Wymilwood all morning, playing the piano and getting my clothes in order. Roy [Daniells] has a bad cold and I asked him to go for a walk this afternoon. Yesterday I went on a hike with Jean Cameron, Jean Elder, Dot Drever, Elizabeth Gillespie and Olive Brownlee. Cooked supper on the wet ground. Nothing much happened. I am enjoying a quiet weekend after a very hectic two or three weeks. I must get to work on German nouns and verbs later on to-day, and there is no news. I hope your cold is better.

My love to you.

Helen.

1 An experimental children's art program initiated by Arthur Lismer and funded through a grant from the Carnegie Corporation, the centre opened in October 1933 at 4 Grange Rd. in Toronto; students selected from the Saturday morning classes at the AGT attended classes at the centre three afternoons and one evening per week.
2 The United Church Training School at the southeast corner of Yonge and St. Clair was known as the Angel Factory.
3 See Letter 149, n. 2, above.
4 An area on the Humber River in Toronto's west end that derives its name from an old

flour mill at one time located on the river bank just below the Dundas St. bridge, and from the village that grew up around it. Home Smith converted the mill into a restaurant, tea room, and dance hall, similar to the Old Mill, but the premises were destroyed by fire in 1915.

5 Lord Tweedsmuir presided over a reception held at VC on Friday, 9 October 1936, on the occasion of the centenary celebration of the granting of the Royal Charter of VU. Fifty years later NF presided over the sesquicentennial celebration and in connection with the observance delivered a sermon on 5 October 1986 at Metropolitan United Church in Toronto.

6 John Buchan, Lord Tweedsmuir.

7 Mildred Oldfield Millar, Graham Millar's wife, was expecting a baby.

8 See Letter 142, n. 1, above.

9 The Alexander Lectures at the U of T, named for W.J. Alexander, professor of English at UC, 1888–1926, were instituted as an annual series of public lectures (usually four) in 1929. The lectures were ordinarily published. D. Nichol Smith's appeared as *Some Observations on Eighteenth-Century Poetry* (London: Oxford University Press, 1937).

156. NF to HK Oxford
Oct. 11 [*1936*]

Postmarked 11 October 1936; addressed to HK at 84 Queen's Park, Toronto, Ontario, Canada.

Darling:

Sunday in Oxford. I am completely surrounded by shell: I have no curiosity: don't want to go see anybody, or go for a walk: just want to sit in my room, devour books nervously and feverishly—one a day of these sixpenny paper-covered Penguin things, quite good—and write to you. I'll get over that, of course. Becoming a freshman again has its temperamental difficulties. Repetition always calls up associations; if one cries for the first time in fifteen or twenty years, a host of childhood memories come back with a rush. So I feel the same awkward, coltish seventeen-year-old coming back again. Several reasons—the obvious one that it's all new and I'm lonesome and ill at ease. And I feel a sense of being shut in on the campus. So at Toronto—the first year it was all campus, and I felt haunted by it—then the city grew and the campus faded out, till last year I was a citizen of Toronto, married to you, and only kept the college as a centre of gravity. But there is no Oxford—not for me at least—except the University, and the feeling of moving like a separate disembodied spirit among lights and crowds, which makes me love a city so, will have to remain in abeyance. Where at seventeen I definitely needed the pressure of a social group, here I want to choose my own friends. I shall eventually, of course: but just now I want to be by myself, and open out to others gradually.

Well, I'm beginning at the wrong end as usual. I got up here Friday and was assigned to my room before lunch. It's in the Mob Quad[1]—origin of name unknown, long series of stories invented to explain it—fourteenth century. My room is about the size of the Senior Common Room at Burwash. A chesterfield, two armchairs, seven wooden chairs, a bookcase, two desks, two huge windows with window-seats. Then a bedroom—bed, chair and commode. Also a large central table I eat my meals on. Also a fireplace with an electric grate which stares at me silently and warms up very gradually, a perfect symbol of Oxford. My slender belongings look very meek and deprecating. The scout[2] seems to be all right.

Friday afternoon LePan dropped in, and [Joseph] Reid, the only other man on this staircase, from Manitoba. We went for a walk—Oxford has done the secluded academic retreat stuff very well. Curious word, retreat: it seems to imply that the acquisition of knowledge means stepping backward, with one's diffidence and caution increasing at every step. It's a pedant's word: the pedant loves to think that great knowledge is simply the revelation of greater ignorance. Knowledge is power, however. Reid has asked me to breakfast tomorrow morning, and LePan to tea tomorrow afternoon. Reid tells me the ghost of Duns Scotus is supposed to haunt his room: they raised the floor, but the ghost walks at the same level, so maybe I can see his feet and ankles dangling from my ceiling. I hope so, anyway.

A large pile of letters and circulars waiting for me here. One from Edith Burnett, sent too late to catch me to Canada House. One from Barbara [Sturgis], all breathless disjointed questions. One from Kay Coburn, one from Roy [Daniells]. And a circular from every firm in the city and society in the University. My fingers are numb from tearing open envelopes and my brain dulls at the incessant requests to buy lounge suits for seven guineas.

Although I have a huge purple pisspot, estimated capacity five quarts, I have to walk over to the New Buildings, several hundred yards away. One wonders how they managed it in the fourteenth century. Out the window, to mortify the flesh of the passers-by? Out in the landing, for the scout to collect? Into the fireplace, to save money? Wood and coal cost money, and the Hindus burn cow-dung.

Blunden seems a very good head and quite prepared to be friendly. Gentle soul on the whole, I should think, but with an unfortunate propensity to assume I know more about the subject than he does. Bryson, the Anglo-Saxon tutor from Balliol, seems to be all right too, if he does wear dinner jackets at five o'clock. Wonder if he's any relation to the Christopher Bryson who married my cousin Jane Howard, the judge's daughter, and took her to India. I wouldn't have thought of it only a clipping from a Montreal paper fell out of one of my notebooks about them. And if I say again I shall work this term, it's because this time I have better reasons than an uneasily moaning conscience can provide. I know where I am, working; then I have a certain amount of self-confidence, and there, until I am a little more at home in this grey, misty world of snuffling Englishmen, I shall remain.

I shall not be unhappy here, but neither shall I ever be positively happy; happiness, for me, is only to be found where you are, and I realize as I never have before the fact that there is a certain radiance about you I can never find in anything else I am in contact with—I read over what I wrote on Blake this summer, and can hardly face it—I wince at every paragraph because it calls up some luxuriantly happy scene at Gordon Bay, something in which you figured.

Could I have transferred this feeling to another woman instead of you, if I had met someone else? It's unthinkable: I can't imagine loving anyone else, nor have I met anyone who showed any possibility of meaning what you mean to me. So around my love there is always a mystery: why, in a world that seems to make so little sense otherwise, did something so inevitably right happen apparently by accident? Because it's all right, even the wrongs. I know that now. My religion was, I think, the last thing to centre itself around you.

Oh, my darling! Words and words again. And you so far away.

Norrie.

1 The quadrangle at the southwest corner of Merton College; the origin of the word "Mob," as NF says, remains unknown.
2 The term for a servant to the resident Oxford University students. NF's scout was a man named Day, who was about forty-five years old at the time. According to Rodney Baine he had been gassed in World War I, and as he had not completely recovered, he occasionally had to be relieved of his duties. Rodney Baine to RDD, 12 December 1995.

157. HK to NF   [*Toronto*]
                                                                Oct. 14. 1936.

My dearest:

Can you hear the hellish row that is going on downstairs? It is the
Music Club getting under weigh. Crawford is trying all the usual tricks,
Charlie Jolliffe has done his turn and the chorus is now very nearly in a
state of hysteria with exaltation. It is the greatest example of mass hyp-
notism I know. In two shakes I'll be down there standing on my head
too. Crawford uses his musical gifts in a way that I consider just a bit
immoral. However, I suppose a musical binge of this sort really does the
kids a lot of good, a sort of purgative that works off energy, and most
people need to work off energy.

The Lit tea was this afternoon and I gave a little spiel on the art group,
then hurried away to hear Nichol Smith lecture on Pope. I really went
because he was connected some way with you, but I did enjoy myself.
Even though I remember nothing of Pope, I was intensely interested in
his lecture, and would have dragged down my copy of Bronson[1] if I
hadn't had some German to do. To-morrow he lectures on Johnson and
I must not miss that. We had Barker Fairley to lunch down at the centre
to-day and he said Nichol Smith was rather dry—I didn't think so, however. Mrs Hubert Kemp was there too—I mean at the Art Centre. She
has just returned from Russia and she is doing a Friday gallery talk for
us.

Roy got his essay on the New Deal off to John Jones [Harwood-Jones]
who is typing it for him, last night.[2] I was at Arnolds' having my first
lesson. They seem to be running a sort of pension this year—John helps
in the house and runs the furnace. There is a girl there too, but I don't
know anything about her. The house work is done by a woman, and
Mrs Arnold is very busy with her course in Psychology.

Last night I had dinner at Annesley[3] and invited the dean to tea here
on Sunday. And to-night Roy Daniells asked me to chaperone a Middle
House tea with him on Sunday. When I suddenly remembered the dean,
he said "Bring her along too," and was quite stubborn about it. The
egg—he said he'd 'phone her and ask her too—which would be silly
from several points of view, as he is reversing the order of precedence
and you can't treat the dean as second fiddle. It's his affair, however and
in the meantime until further notice I'll be here on Sunday! Jessie

MacPherson is a great gal and I like her very much. I've made one boner, giving a 2.30 leave to one girl in the absence of her don, but J.M. partly took the blame. Only the dean ever gives out a late leave.

Mrs Arnold wished to be remembered to you in my next letter. Both were asking for you. Harold [Kemp] started to-day to take lessons from Marcus Adeney who is very enthusiastic about him. Harold is going to give up the Scouts as he has very little interest there anymore, so I expect he will work hard on the çello, and he likes Marcus very much already.

Eleanor Caesar tells me Cameron mentions you in his last letter. Incidentally, I didn't go to see Midsummer Night's Dream with him in Regents Park. I went with one of the old maid school teachers I met in Cambridge. Give him my regards. I suggested to Eleanor that we should hold a sort of binge when he comes back, thinking of Angelo's,[4] and she said, let's have a banquet in Wymilwood! So tell him to beware!! I'm getting to know my people better now, and I have managed very well so far to talk to the kids and I think they will like me well enough. Last night I found an exchange student from Manitoba named Lois Phillips. I said "Are you any relation to W.J.?" and she said "yes, he's my father." So I said: "do you know Sherman Wright?" Answer: "Yes, he's engaged to my sister." She told me further that he is working in Ottawa for the government on architecture of some kind.

Fairley told me that L.C. Knights has a permanent appointment at Manchester now, and he thinks he is married. I'm glad—he needed a job badly, and I hope he has a nice wife. I liked him very much and I'm sure you will too if you ever see him. He came down one night I remember, with an article he'd written on pedantic Shakespearian criticism,—called "How Many Children Had Lady Macbeth?"[5]

Did I tell you I'm doing a lecture on The Rococo Spirit in Painting for Ruth Home's museum lectures? Later on I'm doing Late Eighteenth Century Painting in the same course—the two lectures slated for the Art Gallery of Toronto. Am trying to read some German on the Rococo spirit. Don't know any vocabulary yet, however, and it is very slow going.

It is a blessing that I am so busy and have other people to think about than myself or how much I miss you. I kept looking over the crowd in Hart House to-day for a fair head—I always do in that theatre. It is a relic of the days when I first fell in love with you—and the music club is doing a finale that nearly gets me down at this moment. Do you remember the lump in the throat that the final chorus sometimes can give you? And you probably wouldn't remember how I watched you from the other side of the wings the night I was prompting and you were stewing about the pitch of the soloists?[6] I think you went home with me that night. It was about the first time.

Well my darling, I am picturing you in Oxford now and I am so very proud of you. It helps some to have the Arnolds like you so much and speak so highly of you. Roy Daniells said the other day that [Pelham] Edgar is due to retire the year after next, just when you are due to come back, "if," he said "you do come back." He seems to confidently expect that you'll get a wonderful job in England. They're not exactly floating around are they? I practiced some r's to-day just in case.

W.G. Constable is lecturing on this side of the water—in Buffalo soon, I understand. Dry stick, but he has a name, and America is a fertile field.

At last the party has broken up. Crawford did the "Theologians" in the minor with the chorus singing it very well.[7] They're all clearing out now. Guess it's time for bed. I wish I could be with you to-night.

Your

Helen.

1 Walter C. Bronson, ed., *English Poems*, vol. 3, *The Restoration and the Eighteenth Century* (Chicago: University of Chicago Press, 1908). This volume was on the reading list for English 2e, an honour course at VC.
2 Roy Kemp had written an essay for the Lincoln G. Hutton Scholarship, a prize competition open to all students at VC. He was successful, as HK reports in Letter 170, below.
3 One of the women's residences at VC.
4 A popular dining lounge located in a hotel at 144 Chestnut St. in downtown Toronto.
5 HK is apparently referring to a portion of Knights's book, if not to the book itself: *How Many Children Had Lady Macbeth? An Essay in the Theory and Practice of Shakespeare Criticism* (Cambridge, Eng.: G. Fraser, The Minority Press, 1933).
6 During their second year at VC, the Victoria College Music Club, for which HK was the pianist, staged Gilbert and Sullivan's *The Gondoliers*. NF was operating the arc light for the production, and HK was on the other side of the stage with a prompt book. Though not love at first sight, this assocation was the beginning of their romance.
7 Perhaps Arthur Foote's composition "Ships That Pass in the Night" (1921), the lyrics for which come from Longfellow's "Theologian's Tale."

158. NF to HK   Oxford
                                                              Oct 20 [*1936*]

*Postmarked 20 October 1936; addressed to HK at 84 Queen's Park, Toronto,
Ontario, Canada.*

Darling, I'm sorry to have been so long getting a letter off: it's just the
usual feeling of being suspended in the air, like Mahomet's coffin.[1] I've
worked very hard most of the week, on my first paper for Blunden. It
was on Chaucer's early poems,[2] which are all in the usual symbolic,
visionary form of medieval poetry, and as that happens to be the kind of
poetry I know how to read, the paper grew and grew as I worked on it—
I spent every waking hour of Saturday, Sunday and Monday on it, practically. Blunden said very flattering things about it, but he obviously
isn't very fresh on Chaucer. That's the weakness of the tutorial system, I
think: the tutor has to pretend to know everything when he doesn't, like
a public school teacher. Not that Blunden bothers to pretend much. I
think he likes me, and spoke of taking me out to see Blenheim palace.[3]
However, he absolutely declines to take the initiative in deciding what
papers I am to write. Next week I tackle *Troilus and Criseyde*, & may do
something with Shakespeare's *Troilus and Cressida* too. I should be
rather good on the Shakespeare—I just gave that play a careful reading
almost exactly a year ago, and it did something to me—seemed to numb
something in me, or paralyze a nerve centre somewhere. I've never been
the same man since.

The rest of life is a bit dull as yet. It's very difficult actually to meet
people—when you have breakfast and lunch in your room, you keep by
yourself. Not that I want to meet people much—the freshmen here are
such utter children, less mature, I think, than even the average Victoria
freshman in some ways. They're nice kids but it's difficult to say anything to them when there's so much to explain, so to speak. I had one in
here one afternoon who talked religion and politics at me for three
hours. He was trying his ideas out on the dog, so to speak. I questioned
so many of his assumptions that he was pretty shaken up, but it will do
him good, and I think he liked it. The Canadians, [Joseph] Reid and
LePan, I see occasionally—Reid is on my staircase, as I told you, and
we're the only ones on it. The other night a kid came in and asked Reid
if he'd ever seen the ghost that is supposed to haunt this particular staircase, as he had, a week ago. I thought he was drunk, but he wasn't,

though he admitted he might have been dreaming. There was another man in Reid's room, a Scotchman, and we discussed ghosts, I bringing out my story[4] to show that they existed at a certain level of perception. The Scotchman, who also reads English (Reid is in Mathematics, a Rhodes) was quite overwhelmed by my systematic mind, praised me for about ten minutes on end, and left us at about half-past two, after firing questions at me like "What is your ethic?"

There are three Rhodes men here in first year, two reading English. All Southerners—there seems to be a tradition of Southerners coming to Merton. One from Mississippi—Baine, large, good-humored drawling type, has fed me marvellous coffee in his room twice (Maxwell House) and is interested in music. He says he plays some of Roy's things: Mendelssohn Concerto & the Handel Sonata. I *must* get a piano, although, if I have to pay for it in advance, it will leave me with about one pound for the rest of the term. I'll have to get Blunden to dispatch an S.O.S. to Ottawa around the first of December. It's tying up all my money in this silly deposit (£30) that's left me short. The other Rhodes man is Texas—[Alba] Warren, sawed-off shrimp, all right, but a bit on the bumptious side, I think. We three have a tutorial with Bryson at Balliol for Anglo-Saxon.

If I don't join the Badminton Club I'll have two pounds for the term, but I'd rather like to learn to play Badminton. As a freshman pointed out to me, having to walk, fully dressed, several hundred yards to the New Buildings rather discourages the gut, and it needs stimulation.

Esther [Johnson] and Yvonne [Williams] were in Oxford this week. They sent me a note, and we had tea at a place called Kemp Hall. Lovely name. They brought along a vaguely clerical person who lives out near Keble College and is apparently an expert on church architecture in general and stained glass in particular.[5] Also a girl named Elizabeth Fraser[6] I met at the Art Gallery with Norah [McCullough] one day. She's settled in Oxford as it's a good market for her formal design and illustration work. We parted with expressions of esteem and promises to come together later. I may give a tea for her and LePan soon. She looks interesting. As Baine said: "Ah caint go these hyah English women 'cause they're all sao (sah-yow is closer to it) ugly."[7] Esther dropped in to say goodbye two days later, and I showed her the college in the three minutes or so she had to spare—Chapel, Library, Hall and Quads. That night we had tea we went to the Blackfriar's Priory for complines.

Saturday night I went with Baine and the other Rhodes man from

Exeter to a string quartet in the Town Hall—the Mozart thing Hart House played the night I wrote them up for *Saturday Night*,[8] a rather dull Dohnanyi, and Brahms. They got better as they went along. There are times when I find the reasonings of Rhodes committees a little difficult to follow, but it was a good evening on the whole. ·

I have just received a note from Miss Thorneycroft asking me (a) to go to a concert with her Thursday afternoon (b) to go for a drive Saturday afternoon. I'm afraid it will be (b), as a rather too pious young curate, who is taking his first year in theology here (apparently one can do that) and is married, told me if I was feeling the lack of a home atmosphere, would I come and have tea on Thursday? I think he is a bit anxious to cultivate someone a bit older than the other Freshmen.

The man who canvassed me for the Oxford Union,[9] which I'm joining for the sake of its library, asked me what sports I was going in for. I said none. He said "Don't you play any games at all?" I said no. "What, not any at all?" I looked him straight in the face and said no. He stared at me a moment and then said "Neither do I."

The worst feature of Merton College is its bloody electric chime, which clangs with a terrific row every fifteen minutes. It stops after ten o'clock at night, thank God, or I'd never sleep: Corpus Christi complained about it some time ago.[10]

Thanks for the postcards—nothing in England will ever console me for missing Cleveland. I'm so glad you're having a good time—you should have a marvellous year, and I think of you as filling the breach for the Frye family. Also I meekly cringe under your annihilating snub about tea in the V and A—I didn't even see the floor; the only really essential idea I had in mind was that I wanted to see you.

And I still do.

Norrie.

I was so glad to get your Cleveland letter—it was the first definite information I had that you were getting any letters from me—I almost cabled.

---

1 NF perhaps picked up the simile from a note in *History of the Decline and Fall of the Roman Empire*, where Edward Gibbon says, "The Greeks and Latins have invented the vulgar and ridiculous story that Mahomet's iron tomb is suspended in the air at Mecca"; chap. 15 of *The Decline and Fall*, later published separately as *The Life of Mahomet* (New York: Sheldon, 1961), 175.

2 Probably the untitled holograph essay on Chaucer in the NFF, 1991, box 37, file 12.

3 A castle designed by Sir John Vanbrugh for Blenheim Park, an estate near Woodstock in Oxfordshire.

4 The fable entitled "The Ghost," which NF wrote for *Acta Victoriana*, 60 (April 1936), 14–16.

5 A man identified as Long by NF in Letter 167. Long is also often referred to in Elizabeth Fraser's letters to NF in 1936 and 1937. See HFF, 1991, box 3, file 1.

6 Fraser, who was a Canadian artist and book designer living in Oxford, was twelve years older than NF. Ayre describes their relationship as a "lonely hearts" one that "centred on discussions of art and the damnation of poverty" (133). The Fraser side of this relationship is revealed in her letters to NF during his stint at Oxford. See the HFF, 1991, box 3, file 1.

7 Baine and Charles Bell often affected an exaggerated southern accent, especially when they were around British students. Between themselves they never used it. Rodney Baine to RDD, 12 December 1995.

8 NF had reviewed the Hart House String Quartet's performance of Mozart's String Quartet in D Minor, K. 421, in *Saturday Night*, 7 December 1935, 23.

9 The Union Society at Oxford began as a debate society in the early nineteenth century and developed into a student centre similar to Hart House at the U of T.

10 Corpus Christi College was next door to Merton, directly to the west.

---

159. HK to NF   [*Toronto*]
                                                              October 22. 1936.

My dearest, your letters are coming right along now, and I am so glad you are writing to me often, it does help the separation a little. I am waiting to hear how the first week at Oxford strikes you and then the next and the next after that. I am so glad that LePan came to see you right away, by now you will be feeling a little more at home. You won't be in for any of the sort of hazing Freshmen are given here, surely, and I cannot imagine what a fresher at Oxford has to do. The size of your room sounds appalling—would you like an orange crate or a cheese box?

While I think of it: I am dreadfully sorry. I can't send you any money I'm afraid, because I borrowed $65 for Roy's fees and won't get it paid back until too late to be of any use to you. I'd ask Roy Daniells for some but think it would be better if you did that yourself. Let me know if you haven't arranged anything and I'll see what can be done. At present I'm living until the end of the month on a dollar that Beatty lent me. The 65 has to be paid back before the end of the year because of the auditors and I'll need a little to come and go on. Perhaps I'd better talk to Roy [Daniells] about it anyhow, because if I wait until you have time to send word back to him you may be penniless before the check arrives. You don't say how much you need, and I have no idea of how low the funds are.

We are terribly busy. I'm always saying that but it is still true. 185 teachers came this morning from ten to twelve for a talk on picture appreciation. Norah [McCullough] and Baldwin had to take them for my members group was at eleven. There aren't many registered, but the group was intensely interesting. Mrs Coryell is back and Miss MacBeth and Miss Robinson. Some new ones too. I got them talking about what they like in pictures and what they expect to see; showed them Assyrian sculpture and Japanese painting, Frith's Derby Day and a fifteenth century Persian miniature. Several other things too, and we didn't have time to talk about Russian ikons which I expected to end up with. One realist began to back down and look for something more than accurate representation—she said I'd given her a new idea, and I wound up by asking them for some quality which might be common to primitive art and West European art—shot them Clive Bell's significant form,[1] acknowledging that that was *one* aesthetic hypothesis. I told them the standpoint of some modern critics exalting the primitive above Renaissance art. They certainly talked and I do think it went across pretty well. I feel ever so much more sure of myself this year for some reason. Monday night we had the monthly review of exhibitions. Lismer usually does it but Norah and Baldwin and I took charge. 120 people out, quite enthusiastic. Boris Berlin gave us a good deal of information about the Soviet [show], and Dot Medhurst said each one of us took it from a different angle. I think I can give a better talk this year, I seem to speak more easily at any rate, and my voice doesn't go back on me. Next Saturday the children's classes begin and Norah is organizing everything, Tillie Cowan has been 'phoning people all week. Marge Boultbee has a stenographer sending out Van Gogh publicity. Norah has a swell girl in Mrs Smith's place who is very interested in the work—name is Peggy Kidder. Freda's [Freda Pepper's] place is being run by Gwen Kidd who has a librarian's training and will step into that job if and when Freda comes back. She is very efficient and has lots of ideas. The bulletin goes to press to-morrow and I've got to turn out 100 more words on Van Gogh, but I seem rather stuck at present.

Mrs [Herbert J.] Davis was in to-day with Barker Fairley and was asking for you. Kay Coburn and I are trying to have a tea this Sunday for the Briegers,[2] asking the Davises and the Arnolds.

The Vic Art group is coming to the Art Centre once a week if they get a sufficiently high enrolment, and there are about 25 people coming to me every two weeks for art appreciation at the gallery. And I'm to do a little tutoring if anyone needs it. It is all very good fun and slightly wearing, especially as I've got to work like sixty at German. I seem to be pretty highly organized at present but nothing much has gone wrong so far. We're having a house party on the 21st which I'll have to chaperone. The best thing to do is invite a man and dance too, so I'll have to ask Roy [Daniells] again, in return for that little job I did for him at the hike. But he gets the best of the bargain because this is going to be a good party. Just think of two years from now, you and I functioning in that way. Two months are nearly gone.

This week's Saturday Night ran a photograph of the Governor General shaking hands with Bickersteth, with the Chanc and Mrs Wallace in the background and the other dignitaries scattered around about. "Photo by Roy Kemp"[3]

11 P.M. Barbara [Sturgis] has been in for the evening and has just left. I had not seen much of her since I moved in here owing to extreme busyness. I read her some of your remarks about Merton—first Sunday in Oxford. Unfortunately, I have to come to a dead stop now and again, if you *will* talk about purple piss-pots and myself. I do think you ought not to use a purple one, I shouldn't like it myself, but I dare say I couldn't abide their sanitary arrangements anyhow. Couldn't you suggest that they partition off one end of the Senior Common Room[4] and install a bathroom? It would make you popular at once I am sure, and you could begin farming out bathroom privileges. I woke up with a start lately with a nightmare in which I thought I had given one of your last letters to an utter stranger to read, and how I snatched it back when I remembered what you had said in it.

I am awfully tired and must turn in soon. There is no use, this year I can not afford to get too exhausted because each day is as strenuous as the one before it. I wish I could hold your hand and go to sleep peacefully. I don't stop to think much of how far away you are, I don't dare. I just go around with you on street cars and go for walks with you along University Crescent in the evening and think of how much you would like it. And I'm always very happy thinking about you and how nice you are. BUT BY THE WAY—how DOES the lemon yellow sweater look??? It sounds just a bit weird to me, but perhaps Oxonians dress that way. Also—PLEASE be careful of your haircuts—I really do mean that. Barbara [Sturgis] had a letter from Veronica [Wedgwood] who likes you very much and her father was evidently charmed to have you to talk to. I had a letter from Edith Burnett who was away in Dalmatia when you were in London, and still wants to see you.

My writing seems to be getting smaller all the time, do you think I'm parsimonious?

ANYHOW, I'M SENDING YOU A LOT OF LOVE

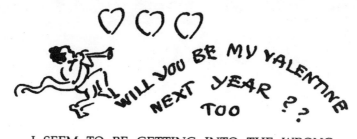

I SEEM TO BE GETTING INTO THE WRONG SEASON, BUT THEY'RE ALL THE SAME SO FAR AS YOU'RE CONCERNED. BESIDES, YOU'RE NOT A CLOWN. WHAT IF I SHOULD CABLE THIS,— I'M JUST A LITTLE NUTS. HELEN.

1 One of the central ideas set forth by Clive Bell in his book *Art* (1914). Bell invented the term "significant form" to denote "the quality that distinguishes works of art from all other classes of objects"—a quality not found in nature but common to all art and existing independently of representational or symbolic content. Bell's theory was important in advancing the view that more attention should be paid to the formal qualities of art.
2 Dr. Peter Brieger was newly appointed to the Department of Fine Art at the U of T in 1936. Prior to this he had been assistant at the German Institute of Fine Art in Rome, lecturer on the history of art at Breslau University, and member of the staff of the Courtauld Institute of Art, 1933–36, during which time he gave additional lectures at the University of London and at Oxford. His lectures at the U of T were on seventeenth- and eighteenth-century painting and sculpture, and on the art of the Middle Ages.
3 See *Saturday Night*, 24 October 1936, 20.
4 HK is referring to NF's room at Merton; in Letter 156 NF had compared the size of his room to that of the Senior Common Room in Burwash Hall.

22. Frye and Kemp at Gordon Bay, ca. 1936 (courtesy of Susan Sydenham)

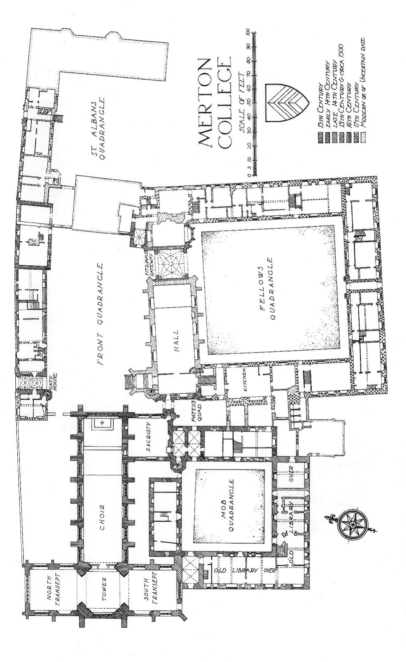

MERTON COLLEGE

SCALE OF FEET

13TH CENTURY
EARLY 14TH CENTURY
LATE 14TH CENTURY
15TH CENTURY & CIRCA 1500
16TH CENTURY
17TH CENTURY
MODERN OR OF UNCERTAIN DATE

ST. ALBANS QUADRANGLE

FRONT QUADRANGLE

HALL

FELLOWS QUADRANGLE

FITZJAMES GATEWAY

PATEYS QUAD

KITCHEN

SACRISTY

CHOIR

NORTH TRANSEPT

TOWER

SOUTH TRANSEPT

MOB QUADRANGLE

OLD LIBRARY

OVER

OLD LIBRARY OVER

GATE HOUSE

23. Plan of Merton College (reproduced from *An Inventory of the Historical Monuments in the City of Oxford*, Royal Commission on Historical Monuments, 1939)

24. Illustration by Elizabeth Fraser for *Plato's Academy*, 1936 (courtesy of Oxford University Press)

25. The Fryes, 1937 (courtesy of Susan Sydenham)

26. The Fryes, 1937 (courtesy of Susan Sydenham)

160. NF to HK   Oxford
                                                Oct 27 [1936]

Addressed to HK at 84 Queen's Park, Toronto, Ontario, Canada; the post-marked date is illegible.

My darling girl:

I should be very happy here if it were not for your absence; but every once in a while a sudden twinge comes, or else some Toronto scene—invariably with you in it—arises in front of me and I realize that I am an exile after all. I love you so. Don't mind if my letters suddenly turn introspective on you—naturally it's thinking of you that makes me that way. You should be seeing Esther [Johnson] and Yvonne [Williams] before you get this, so we can see each other at second hand at any rate. Incidentally, I got a very friendly letter from Elizabeth Fraser issuing a general invitation to any sort of meal at any time. I think I shall take her at her word—it's that kind of note—and besides, being able to connect with your circle of friends, even at this distance, means a good deal.

I'm glad you liked Nichol Smith's lectures. He must be doing rather better than he does here—LePan said he wrote to his sister and asked if he preserved his Oxford habit of repeating everything twice to make sure that his audience understood there was nothing in it. His absence makes no difference to me—he'll be back. He isn't anyone I'd ever meet, except to hear give a lecture occasionally, but he might be induced to take an interest in me.

The work is going strong—I keep putting a hell of a lot of work into my papers. I have just finished the *Troilus and Criseyde* thing. I didn't get into the Shakespeare, as there were 8000 lines of the Chaucer, and I think I worked as hard over it as I ever did over those theological essays that used to bring in such an impressive list of firsts. I think Blunden approves all right, but his main interest is in things like natural imagery of the 19th c type. I can't write about that intelligently, as I don't think in those terms, and neither did Chaucer. So what Blunden says is that the paper is a very fine piece of work, that Chaucer was quite a poet, that that picture on the wall he bought for ten pounds at an auction, and the catalogue described it as School of Poussin and dated it around 1710: would I give him an opinion on the date? also the next time I pass St. Aldate's Church,[1] would I take a look at the font cover there, which has been varnished out of existence, and which looks medieval, but is, he thinks, sixteenth-century Flemish work done in a medieval tradition, and let him know what I think about it? So I get up and stare solemnly at his bloody picture, and then announce that my opinion on the date of a bastard Poussin is not worth a damn, and that my qualifications for pronouncing on Flemish font covers are exactly nil. Well, no, I let him down easier than that, so that he thinks I know far more about it than I actually do—you know my methods, Watson.[2] I can see where I shall have to marry you and make you live with me at Oxford next year in sheer self-defence.

Impressions of England: the women at Oxford have a terrific inferiority complex. There is a man called Herapath,[3] who eats at the Senior Common Room in Burwash, who told me that when I got to Oxford he would write to his maiden aunt, who, he said, was a "dear old soul." The dear old soul turns out to be the Principal of St. Hilda's. She and Miss Thorneycroft both sent me invitations to tea on the same day; and each said that if I couldn't stand the idea of entering a woman's college I was to say so and they'd make other arrangements. I went out carriding with Miss Thorneycroft into the Chiltern Hills Saturday afternoon—this *is* a magnificent country. The richness and variety of autumn coloring, particularly the beeches, is I think subtler and more satisfying in many ways than the Canadian fall, if less brilliant. I had a glorious time and fairly got drunk on color. We went back to St. Hugh's for tea. She showed me over the college—dining hall, library and one of the rooms—and it was all so light and airy and cheerful I told her that she had most of the compensations for 13th century glass. The dear old soul doesn't feed me till tomorrow. Miss Thorneycroft is a grand woman: I probably impressed her as a rather dim bulb. I know very little about canoeing in Canada.

So far I've gone to two lectures, one by Blunden and one by Abercrombie. They're rather bad, but I may go to some more, as it's a good way of meeting some of the other people in the course. The method of lecturing is very similar to the sort of thing you described at the Courtauld—an endless niggling over minutiae and in hopeless disproportion to the very general scope of the course. By the way, the new volume (the last) of the *Cambridge Medieval History* came out this year—I hadn't noticed it particularly in Toronto. It has an article on Gothic art by Constable which is fairly good,[4] although it's probably all in your notes, but the bibliography in the back might be useful to you. I notice also that

McInnes has an article on Canadian water-colors in the *Studio*.[5] He makes it fairly plain that he knows very little about it, I think.

Apparently the tradition I think I mentioned, that the ghost of Duns Scotus haunts this room and the one above it as well as the library (which is really an extension of my staircase) is quite well-known and of some standing. He has a long and cold way to come, as he's buried at Cologne, but I can see where the legend of his haunting the library would originate: Merton had the best library in England during the Middle Ages and all of Scotus would be here, being the greatest English scholastic and a Merton man. Then the Reformation came, this library was plundered, the manuscripts torn to pieces and thrown into the quad, and of all authors the one singled out for especial destruction was Scotus. I asked my scout if he had ever sensed a ghost on this staircase, and he said no, but various people have put on surplices and awakened people by putting cold hands on them. He said a nigger had this room once, and that someone came around the middle of the night and blew a big trumpet in his ear, shouting "Fire" and put the end of a fire-rope in his hand, which is just inside the bedroom window. The nigger grabbed the rope and shinned down into a tank of ice-cold water a colleague had prepared for him, and spent the next few days prowling around with a huge knife in search of his tormentors. I told the scout I'd keep my piss-pot full and near at hand for people like that, but he said I didn't need to worry. I expected the Freshman's brawl to be held here, but for some reason they held it across the quad. I didn't go: I intended to drop in at the end, but [Joseph] Reid and Arnott invited me to supper in Arnott's rooms, and I didn't get back till one, after the party was over. It doesn't seem to take much to make an English schoolboy drunk.

You may notice that the envelope has a twopenny stamp on it. There's a sad story behind that: the day I came to Oxford I got a cheque-book from the bank and was charged two shillings for it. I emerged cursing the Oxonian rapacity that soaked you two bob for a cheque-book, and went to get some twopenny stamps to put on them (cheques). Then I discovered that they were all stamped, there being twelve of them, which had accounted for the price.[6]

One of my old tooth fillings has fallen out of my head as a result of trying to cope with one of Baine's caramels, so I'll have that to worry about until I can get it fixed. I don't know if I mentioned the Reverend Brimley Howells, a freshman here who is ordained but wants an Oxford degree, and cottoned to me as being older than some of his colleagues, also as a theological student who had already read his course and could suggest books. He is married, has a church down by the waterworks,[7] also a house, to which he invited me for tea. He exudes righteousness in a rather uncomfortable way: he assumes that his moral standards and yours are much higher than most people's, and so we can talk over the heads of the unregenerate. It's curious that a snobbery which I take for granted when it's intellectual or artistic I resent when it's moral. His wife is a typical English housewife: large, buxom, pleasant, hospitable, virtuous blonde, very interested in Canadian ideas about English food. The food at Merton, apart from the vegetables, is very good, but I expect nothing but decadence from a nation with its belly full of decayed Brussels sprouts.

If the music around Oxford doesn't improve I shall grow tone-deaf. Friday night I went to hear Iturbi, who I thought was good. He made a frightful mess of the Mozart (the first in your edition, which I had heard Schnabel play much better, though God knows he was bad enough) and the rest was the tub-thumping virtuoso—Liszt and the galumping Spaniards—i.e., Albeniz and Granados. *When* will pianists learn that the only way to play Mozart is to play him in the completely transparent unaffected way his chamber music is played, and all the querulous barbs and thumps and rushings of time which they think represents expression is all bad taste? Sunday night the "Griller" string quartet came to Merton College and gave a concert in the hall—I don't know who they are, but they're bad. The first violin sounded as if he were playing with four steel strings, and the rest weren't much improvement—the 'cello was the best. They played a Haydn, a Beethoven and a Mozart. If they had spent their time on two quartets instead of trying to tackle three they'd have done better.

J.C. Taylor came over from Cambridge to see LePan and called on me Sunday afternoon. He's doing Philosophy Tripos there, and seems thoroughly satisfied with it: the department of philosophy there is probably the best in the world, now that Germany has gone to pieces, and they've organized it much more systematically than at Toronto or Oxford, where it's practically all history of philosophy. Jim seemed to think it was awfully funny to see me in Oxford, but gave me a warm invitation to call on him at Cambridge—if I had any money I'd go, as I'd like to see the Blakes in the Fitzwilliam, but can postpone it till next term. Besides, he may be in London at Christmas—[George] Johnston is there, just around the corner from Walters'[8] in Lamb's Conduit Street, refusing jobs in order to devote himself to writing. He asked me if I didn't feel a sense of relief in escaping from Toronto. I said no, thinking of you, and he shrugged his shoulders and gave me up as a hopeless sentimentalist.

I intended to write this letter last night, but [Joseph] Reid came in and said one of the two university dailies, the *Isis*, had asked him to go to a cinema and write a criticism of it, and would I go with him and write the criticism? Or maybe its a weekly—I don't know; I've never seen a copy. So I went to the cinema—the first I had been to since whatever it was we saw last together (ouch!) in Toronto—and wrote it up.[9] The editor, or whoever the official was we took it to, seemed very pleased and said it was much brighter than usual. It was called "Wife vs. Secretary," which I think was in Toronto months ago—one very obvious reason for not going to cinemas in London is that you've seen them all—and was a triangle with all three parties innocent as well as very rich—one of these how-to-be-sophisticated-though-virtuous pictures. Or at least the picture said that the husband and secretary were virtuous, despite circumstantial evidence, but I couldn't see that the issue would have been affected if they were not, as there was no hint that the wife believed her husband's protestations when she went back to him. It was an interesting example of the way censorship induces hypocrisy.

Well, we're getting close to the end of another month of separation. It really won't be so terribly long—not to look back on it at any rate. But this year is nothing to me compared to two years ago—we're bound together for good now, and I shall love you as long as I live.

Norrie.

1 A fourteenth-century church, restored in 1863, located just within the old South Gate of the town of Oxford.
2 The oft-repeated rejoinder of Sherlock Holmes to his assistant and foil, Dr. Watson, in Conan Doyle's short stories.
3 This is apparently John N. Herapath, who served as a don at VC for one year and published a short story, "Good Work," in the *Canadian Forum*, 16 (December 1936), 19–21.
4 W.G. Constable, "Painting, Sculpture, and the Arts," *Cambridge Medieval History*, vol. 8, ed. C.W. Previté-Orton and Z.N. Brooke (Cambridge: Cambridge University Press, 1936), 718–72.
5 "Canadian Water-Colours," *Studio*, 12 (October 1936), 208–9.
6 The postal rate for a letter to Canada was one and one-half pence.
7 St. John's Church, almost one mile south of Merton College on Church St., west of Abingdon Rd., and just to the east of the Oxford Corporation's water works.
8 The boarding house at 90 Guilford St., owned by John Walter and his wife, where HK had stayed after her return from Italy in 1935. See Letter 138.
9 For the review, entitled "Three-Cornered Revival at Headington," see *Isis*, 28 October

1936, 14. NF implies that he wrote the review by himself (in Letter 165 he refers to the review "I wrote up for Isis"), but as the published version is signed "J.R.," the Canadian Rhodes scholar Joseph Reid takes credit for having written it.

161. HK to NF

Toronto, Ont.
Wymilwood———
Nov. 2. 1936. 7.30 P.M.

Postmarked 3 November 1936; addressed to NF at Merton College, Oxford, England, Via New York: "Queen Mary."

My dearest: I have just telephoned the Post Office and find that I may make the Queen Mary if I hurry. I was going to write you a longish account of the doings of the last week or so, but the unforeseen happened: yesterday I got an attack of nervous indigestion, fainted, whooped and was put to bed. Fortunately I was at home and everybody was quite solicitous. Roy carried the corpse upstairs, Harold came in from time to time and smoothed the blanket, Daddy came up to see how the patient got on, and Mother sat with me and did her knitting and I enjoyed it immensely. I stayed home from work to-day and slept all afternoon. {Georgie Green just dropped in for a minute before a meeting of the Alumni executive. They're having a big party next week. She is terribly big-eyed about the don's room in Wymilwood.} The Van Allens are back from Edmonton. They went out about two weeks ago because their brother was dying with pneumonia. He is on the mend however, and we all feel terribly relieved. Miss [M.M.] Van Allen is the dietician here and her sister [Blanche] works in Simcoe Hall and lives with her in Wymilwood.

I haven't a great deal to tell except work, work, work. It makes me feel rather worn out by the end of the week, and wishing desperately that you could make some sort of weekend arrangement to come and see me. Perhaps in another decade or so that might come about for people like us. Modern marriage across the oceans with weekends spent together. It would cost a good deal in balloon fares, I suppose, but if you are apt, as Roy Daniells firmly believes, to land a big job in England, I certainly won't be able to do the same. My job seems to be growing here on this side of the water, and I'll have to learn to handle a 'plane and come to see you weekends or be like Vera Britton[1] who married an American and lives with him for six months of the year.

Barbara has just 'phoned to say that she has just had a lovely letter from you and that it quite makes her feel that she is back again. She is coming over to see me in a minute or so to tell me all about it. Your last one to me came on Saturday morning. You were about to go driving with Miss Thorneycroft, you had just written an essay on Chaucer, had had tea with Esther and Yvonne and Elizabeth Fraser and had £2 in the exchequor. I am awfully glad that you are making friends. I think it will be much easier in Oxford: it is a civilized place, not the bleak jungle that Bloomsbury is at first. Jungle is much too warm a word. Arctic desert is how the Courtauld struck me, too. If you get what I mean. I feel rather sorry for the two American Rhodes men coming up against you in a group, and as for the little man who told you all about religion! I always wondered what you'd do to Millicent [Rose] if you had met her. At any rate, I can picture you feeling fairly much in your element {blast this ink!}[2] writing an essay each week. Roy Daniells was saying on Saturday that he wondered whatever the university would do if there ever came a really creative person to the faculty, someone who would pour out publication after publication and not be bothered with all the social duties of dons. I expect you will start something when you get back to this comfortable sociable smug little college.*

Barbara has come and gone, delighted with your letter. What a nice man you are! She says that the weakness of the tutorial system may partly be in Blunden's management of it, since her tutor always sent {God *damn*} her to specialists in particular subjects, but that arrangement may cause complications financially and some people were stuck with the same tutor all year.

Barbara said she had dinner on Sunday with the McInnes family & Prof. Alford was there. They talked about the policy of having children in the gallery. You recall, it was McInnes who wrote that nasty letter last year which upset things a bit. Alford, the big Grampus, said he didn't think it did any good to have children given talks about pictures, they learned so little, and the classes might as well be stopped. Mrs McInnes complained that the children smelled. Barbara tells me all this, so I told her just how much damage McInnes had done with his letter. After the Ed Dept had sent out letters inviting all sorts of groups, including schools, to come to the Van Gogh show in the afternoon for talks etc—

---

* Last week there was a luncheon for the newly wedded wives of professors—Kay McMullen and Kay Riddell—and for Grace Elliott who is taking Bea Abbott's place this year (BA has T.B.) full of warm welcomes etc.

the council takes upon itself an experiment. No lectures are to be given to children in the galleries during the Van Gogh show. All such work is to be done in the print room upstairs: the youngsters can go through the Van Gogh show later but without formal talks. You can picture the difficulty we will have playing traffic cop what with Miss [Margaret] Wilson's classes and other groups having to dodge each other on the stairways—and if there are people in a room looking at pictures we are not to disturb them but poke our noses into some other place where the children will not bother anyone. All this for the sake of a few non-stinking members!! They wouldn't tolerate the children at all except for the fact tht without the children we'd have next to no attendance whatever. And Alford! The presumption of that man! I'm getting a knife ready for his hide. He was quite rude about lending a book to me the other day after Dr. Brieger had lent it but suddenly asked Alford if it was O.K. and Alford point blank refused to and treated me like a small worm he'd never seen before. *So*, next time he wants some lantern slides in a hurry, hum, well—worms have a way of being small and insidious and nasty. However, I haven't time to waste over a big pasty faced ox who won't take any exercise. We asked him to do a review of the exhibition and he intends to do a lecture with lantern slides. Now the review is *always* something using the pictures on the wall, and fairly informal. *He* stubbornly declines to do that and will give us a formal lecture, in spite of the fact that we've already got [Robert Tyler] Davis from Buffalo doing a formal lecture on Van Gogh. It will probably be a damned sight better than Alford on Van Gogh. I'm sorry, I feel a little mad at Alford.

Art Cragg just 'phoned, I had asked for the address of the man who would grease the gramophone for me. The Clare père and mère are moving to Toronto and will live in the same house with Ida and Florence [Clare]. Earl is coming too and will go to Oakwood Collegiate. Arthur gave a talk on Sunday to the girls at the Ontario Ladies College about his mission field. Says he'd like a letter from you, that he quite forgives your writing to me, but he thinks he ought to come before Barbara Sturgis, and when I said you'd written to J.R.D. [Roy Daniells] he was quite put out. He really was pretty mournful about you being out of Fifth House when I was talking to him at the Centenary reception, he says he misses you more than the rest of the house put together. Do write to him my dear.

Well, to-morrow I get back to the fight. On Wednesday I have this lecture to give to a group who have enrolled for a course of lectures at the museum,—The Rococo in Painting. It's fairly well in hand I think. I get

$10. I'm not having a German lesson this week and on Wednesday night a fourth year student is coming for some help with an essay on Chartres and Donatello. The Vic students come to the gallery every two weeks so I won't have them again until next week—I think they enjoyed it last time and I certainly have the bright ones coming.

I read part of your letter on Saturday to Roy Daniells who took me out to tea and gave me some help with Baroque & Rococo. He said: "Isn't it just like Norrie to run into someone, e.g. tutor, first off who doesn't know as much as he does about the given subject!" We talk quite a bit about Coburn & [Florence] Smith. I think Dr. Smith is pretty pathetic as a woman—she may be splendid as a footnote artist, but she giggles and squirms, she has fishy white hands and complains about not keeping them ladylike. I'd hate to see the rest of her anatomy. I'm being catty, but I find her rather a bore, and I do try to like her. Roy wonders what they'll do with you when you come back, whether they'll put you above those two women, which will break some hearts, or whether they'll put you beneath them, which he says will be ridiculous.[3] I don't care what they do. I want you back here in a hurry. I'll chaperon any number of parties, I'll pour tea like an Amazon, I'll give Sunday teas for Freshmen and listen to their ideas about football, I'll wear a velvet hat with an ostrich plume and grow a front and behind to go with it to show the official prof's wife—I'll do *anything* that's necessary if only you'll come back and marry me and make me the happiest girl in two continents. {The ink has a tendency to clot just where I'm extra emphatic so it must have some sympathy with my views}

P.S. I sent you 2 bundles of New Yorkers last week.

Well, anyway, look what *you're* going to live with!

I must run away and post this now before it's too late. I'm very sorry about my remark regarding the Morris tiles. I had a couple of very bad night-mares in that lunch room and some very agonizing moments at the V & A in the early days and that's why I twinge now and then as if I had a tooth-ache. You mustn't mind, I'll meet you anywhere, I'll go with you anywhere, I'll sit and have tea with you in a coal bin or a dung-heap, I'll do anything you say, but I don't want to stay away from you for two years ever again.

I got side-tracked letting off steam about Alford. I'm glad you met Elizabeth Fraser—she is from all accounts a pretty remarkable woman. I met her here in the spring but saw her only for a few minutes. Also, about the money—*could* you get any borrowed from your deposit, or could you get Blunden to wire? I mentioned the fact to Roy [Daniells] on Saturday but he did not offer to help out and I wasn't sure of his mood and did not ask him outright for help. He may be rather hard hit himself as he has been going to an osteopath all fall who charges plenty for his treatments.

Another thing I forgot—not that it is all that important—on Sunday George Clarke phoned up—he's pulling teeth at Uxbridge now, where Pete Colgrove is. I told him he'd better get the town interested in pic-tures. He said he would return a book of Daddy's that he's had for about three or four years,—but he didn't. He *is* a total loss, now, wouldn't you think that using the book as excuse, he would at least *return it*?

John Creighton still has no job. One down South somewhere did not materialize even though he went so far as to hunt for a flat, and finally the job wasn't given to anyone. Sallee [Creighton] is pretty mad at Vic but Roy says she never was given any hope of anything permanent. Still—

Say ——— *am* I going to talk to you all night?!!

I wish I were. My love to you, my dear,

Helen

---

1 Unsure of the spelling, HK has written "ain?" above the last syllable of "Britton." Vera Brittain married George Catlin, a professor of politics at Cornell University.

2 HK's pen was flowing too freely, a situation that also occasions her outburst—"God *damn*"—in the next paragraph.

3 At VC the academic titles below the rank of professor were, in ascending order of importance, fellow, reader, instructor, and lecturer. In 1935–36 NF held the position of reader; Coburn, who began her career at VC in 1929 with a sessional appointment as

fellow in English, and Florence Smith had both become instructors by 1935–36. When NF returned in 1937, he was appointed instructor, and Kay Coburn was promoted to lecturer.

162. NF to HK   Oxford
Nov. 3. [*1936*]

Postmarked 3 November 1936; addressed to HK at 84 Queen's Park, Toronto, Ontario, Canada.

Sweetheart:

The notorious month of November is here at last, and by all appearances I shall not see the sun again until next Easter. A fitting symbol of the dark underworld to which your absence has consigned me. I am imprisoned by rain: my electric light ("all rooms are furnished with the electric light"—Quotation from college bulletin, and the subtlest use of the definite article I have ever encountered) burns all day as nature and England are mourning for you outside. I sit indoors like a convict, and look like one. It's easy to say, get yourself a decent haircut. Just you try and get yourself a decent haircut in a strange land. I ask people to recommend me barbers, and they gleefully consign me to some maniac who can't make up his mind whether he wants to produce a Mohammedan saint or a monk out of the object in front of him. The recommendation is based on the fact that the same maniac has cut *their* hair properly, as though that were a valid argument. Darling, there's no use telling the fool what to do: he just doesn't understand what to do. You people with straight turd-coloured hair don't appreciate my difficulties. I'll try to find the best barber in Oxford, and that's the best I can do.

Listen, pet, I told you I was short of money because I tell you everything, not because I was hinting for you to send me some. I can live in Oxford all right without cash—everything goes on a bill to be paid next January—all I'm worried about is whether those Ottawa people will come through by the end of this term or not. Don't worry about me: I'll manage somehow. I think I can stay here during the vacation if the worst comes to the worst. I have been rather handicapped by the lack of money, but that doesn't matter so much this first term. But if you really want to do something for me, my own self-sacrificing little girl—WHEN

THE HELL ARE YOU GOING TO COME THROUGH WITH SOME
NEW YORKERS?

I've got a piano moved in. I ordered a typewriter, but it didn't come,
so I think I'll let it go—Blunden never asks to see my papers, and I can
borrow [Joseph] Reid's for any Blake work I may get done. What money
I save by scrawling my letters and essays can go on the piano. I went
over to Scott's and picked out the best piano they had—which wasn't
any too good, as they've been pretty well looked over, so they brought it
along, measured the staircase, measured the piano, decided not to argue
with the fourteenth century, and took it and me back to the store. Very
unwillingly I chose, if you can call it a choice, a wretched little abortion
with strings about a foot high and an action like a steam calliope, which
eventually filtered through to my room, after getting covered with several pecks of plaster from the ceiling of the staircase. However, all the
keys are present, so I started on it. That was Saturday. Sunday Baine
came over with a violin and some music—he had told me that he played
a violin. He had the Handel Sonata in A, the Beethoven Romance in F,
the Mendelssohn Concerto and a book full of a lot of other things,
including some Tartini variations and Corelli's La Folie. Considering
that he's out of practice he's a remarkably good player—very accurate
and thorough if not brilliant. I had a swell time, needless to say. He lives
in the Fellow's Quad, where they don't allow musical instruments
played, but the general impression the authorities have given him is that
if he wants to practise they won't say anything. In the evening a red-
headed Freshman named Corder came in with the rest of Roy's repertoire—a book of Beethoven sonatas and the César Franck. He was a
complete contrast to Baine—he thought he was a lot better, but was a
rather sloppy though very glib and plausible sight reader. That may be a
defect in English musical training due to their greater insistence on
Beethoven than on Mozart. Anyhow, there's another young freshman
here named Mellor who also lives in the Fellow's Quad and has to borrow pianos to practise on who is the most extraordinary combination of
remarkable technical agility and carelessness—I never realized before
how much technique could dispense with the problem of getting the
notes right. He makes horrible noises actually, but his gestures are so
impressive he seems to be unconscious that there's anything else to
playing. Incidentally, Baine, who comes from the South, is going to
leave for Italy directly he leaves Oxford, and wants me to go with him if
my money comes through. I don't think I shall, but it's an idea. The

other Rhodes man, Warren, makes the night hideous[1] at dinner by his sneers at English climate, English tutorial systems, English fussiness and red tape, English vegetables, and so on, all of which the English receive very meekly, but assume that if I don't burst forth in similar maledictions, it's only because I'm too polite. It puts me in a rather compromising position: I don't like saying: "Not Rhodes—Royal Society of Canada" too often, and it's even more difficult to say that I simply adore their sanitary arrangements and so forth. However, I don't think I give too bad an impression. I'm giving up political discussions, as practically everyone in England is either a Fascist or a right-wing sympathizer, and I obviously can't assume that everyone I talk to shares in the main my own views, as I could in Canada.

More teas. The Principal of the Postmasters yesterday. He and his wife both very nervous and self-conscious. At 5:15 he vanished suddenly without explanation, and at 5:30 his wife announced that she was going down town, and would we please get the hell out? There were four of us. Last Tuesday the Chaplain, three of us this time. The Chaplain's best topic of conversation is obviously cricket, and having settled the fact that we don't play cricket in Canada, the conversation (I had to take what conversation there was) shifted uneasily from Aberhart to the Gospel of Saint John—I don't quite know how we made the transition— until we left, whereupon there was a big gasp of relief on each side of the door. These English officials are not exactly volcanic in their heartiness. Then there was the Principal of St. Hilda's tea, which I think I mentioned before. The old girl was really a frightful-looking battle-axe— great protruding jaw propped up by three chins. A girl there from Vancouver, in training at whatever the English call a Normal School here,[2] and apparently a graduate of St. Hilda's. Quite attractive in a hatchet-faced sort of way—plays golf and looks it, not too intelligent.

Wednesday, I think it was, I dropped in on Elizabeth Fraser and she gave me tea. She's illustrating a book by some maniac of a Greek professor who wanted to excavate Plato's Academy—why, I don't know,— and build an international school for the preservation of world peace on the site. The householders living on Plato's Academy told him to clear out, so he sorrowfully returned, shaking his head, and wrote a book in Greek, with an English translation made by someone else, about the swell idea he had. It's full of immense turgid sentences like: "Life did not now present itself in the guise of alternation between pleasure and pain, but as one great mission and trust, as one great task which it is each man's duty to help carry forward; and as far as the narrow limits of my knowledge allowed I conceived that from the advance of the science of the human mind will emerge an unimaginably great and noble Something of which the least of the immediate results will be the idealization of humanity and the supreme beautification of the life of Man."[3] Now this ungodly tripe appears simply to have swept Elizabeth off her feet: she has been working like mad for a year on illustrations to it—God knows the book could stand a definite image somewhere—her ideas have been gradually developing the way mine have on Blake, into a more and more objective unity all the time, and she regards herself, the publisher, and the translator as initiates into a sort of cult, or at any rate talks that way. I'm afraid that even to please Elizabeth, I can't pretend to like such horse shit; but I think I shall avoid discussing it when I return the book to her.

Mother writes that Aunt Evelyn [Howard]—the judge's wife whom Aunt Hatty [Layhew] feels snubbed by—is very interested in my being at Oxford and will write to some of the people Jane [Howard] knew, who I think was at St. Hugh's. It's very kind of her and quite in character, I think.

I feel at the moment like shutting myself into the Bodleian and staying there until you come over with the sun. But even in hibernation I should dream of you.

Love,

Norrie.

Blunden improves. He threw flowers at my feet yesterday, I think because my paper was clever, vague and short—Canterbury Tales.[4] Told me I'd made a real contribution to criticism, etc. etc., and then talked about Blake for the rest of the hour.

N .

1 The allusion is to *Hamlet*, 1.4.54.
2 In Canada the older teacher-training schools were called "normal schools." In England the older ones, which were residential and religiously affiliated, were called "voluntary colleges"; after 1902, nonresidential teacher-training institutions, called "council training colleges," were established.
3 The book that Elizabeth Fraser illustrated, *Plato's Academy: The Birth of the Idea of Its Rediscovery* by Pan. Aristophron, was published in London by Oxford University Press in 1938. The edition, handsomely printed on handmade paper, contains thirteen full-page, two-colour illustrations by Elizabeth Fraser, plus an illustration for the endpa-

pers. Only the first illustration is autographed with the initials "E.F." The passage NF
quotes is from p. 31. See illus. 24, this volume, for one of Fraser's illustrations for the
book.
4 NF's paper on the *Canterbury Tales* has not survived. But the paper he presented to the
graduate English club at the U of T in 1938, "A Reconsideration of Chaucer," includes a
section on the *Canterbury Tales*. As NF incorporated his Oxford paper on Chaucer's
early poems into his Toronto talk, it is likely that that talk borrowed from his *Canterbury
Tales* paper as well. "A Reconsideration of Chaucer" is in the NFF, 1991, box 37, file 4.

163. HK to NF   84 Queens Park Toronto.
                                                November 8. 1936—

Postmarked 10 November 1936; addressed to NF at Merton College, Oxford,
England, Via New York: "Normandie."

My dearest: Another Sunday gone, this time a fairly eventful one,—
dinner with Cameron Caesar's mother who is visiting Eleanor, the
Mozart Requiem at Bloor St. United Church in the afternoon, with Barbara [Sturgis], our tea for the Briegers, then a Wymilwood musicale
with Wilma Stevenson. The Requiem is pretty magnificent music, but I
don't know how wise it is to put on a performance of it in that stuffy
church.

Kay Coburn really managed the tea. I just asked the Briegers and they
are charming. You will like them very much. The Davises, the Arnolds,
Kay, Roy (Kemp) were originally invited. [Herbert J.] Davis had to
phone at the last minute that he could not come because Mrs [Gladys
Wookey] Davis and Elizabeth Anne were sick. Will tell you something
else about them later. Kay [Coburn] then asked Jerry Riddell and Kay to
come and Jessie MacPherson and John Creighton. They all came but J.C.
The Briegers got here right on time and apologized for coming so soon,
and suggested that they walk around the park for a few minutes but I
kept them here and showed them the house and they were very much
impressed with all the grandeur I'm living in. Kay Coburn told him
Canadian students were *soft* and it surprised him a good deal as he
thought they were all hardy and strong and rugged. It was a grand
party, with everyone talking intelligently to their neighbours and there
were no bad moments, both Dr Brieger and his wife are exceedingly
accomplished in the matter of conversation. The Arnolds, I think, had a
good time, and I certainly did, for I got a chance to talk to Jerry about
you, and that's always a help. Brieger told me his version of trying to

meet Gordon Snelgrove—he said he never showed up and always looked the other way whenever they met on the stairs at the Institute.[1] He also told an amusing incident—coming home from Paris he and his wife were in the same compartment as Gordon Snelgrove and Miss Davies, the girl who got first class standing this year in her B.A. exams. They talked about the Courtauld Institute and Brieger could not help but overhear the conversation and there was no opportunity of letting them know he was on the staff. He said it was very amusing. I know about what that conversation would be like and I dare say it was!

Mrs Davis was going to give one of our reviews this month on Van Gogh, and she borrowed some books, getting ready for it. But just before our posters were printed H.J.D. [Herbert J. Davis] 'phoned Norah [McCullough] and said that she could not do it, that, um, er—she was ill and had been ordered to bed for a month by the doctor, and, well, that she was about to produce another child! By that time Norah had gathered the general trend anyhow, but she said he was very sweet and naive about telling her. So when they did not come to-night I was not surprised. I met Mr Davis the other day in the Diet Kitchen[2] and he asked for you—twice—and would like to hear from you. So please be good and write to him—you really should anyway. Roy Daniells says that Edgar is retiring in a couple of years, that he and Pratt will look the ground over and write to you around April outlining what courses you will likely be taking eighteen months from then. That is to give you time to load your gun. I can hardly wait until you come back, but I suppose I have to be patient. By that time people will be accustomed to seeing me about anyhow and I'll fit in with the rest of the fixtures.

I have to postpone activities in German for most of this month because of the Van Gogh show. But after it is over I'm going to make tracks. Brieger asked me how long I was in England to-night, and several things about the Institute, and I had another moment of panic about that *bloody* diploma—I didn't show it of course. I've *got* to write that off in June or I'll worry about it still, and it isn't worth any more trouble of that sort.

Barbara [Sturgis] came to read your letter to me—did I tell you?—and then the next day there came another from you and I was very pleased. I have a sort of resurrection at the sight of your writing on an envelope and go about happy for the rest of the day.

Last night Roy K. took me to see Wilson Knight's production of 'The Winter's Tale' and it was glorious![3] I don't know when I have enjoyed anything so much. And I liked to think that Knight is a friend of yours and that he does such good things and I was so glad Shakespeare had written that play. I had never read it and all I knew of it came through Charles and Mary Lamb. Murray Bonnycastle was in it—rather too beauteous always, I feel. A string quartette—Margaret McKay who used to play çello with Lucy Cox and me was in it. They played the incidental music, and Madame Lasserre had directed the dancing. Tom and Joan Fairley also had small parts.

Our house party here is on the 21st—Roy Daniells is going to chaperon with me—he 'phoned on Saturday and asked me to reciprocate at Middle House party on the 27th, so I'll have some use for the purple evening gown beside gallery openings.

Don't mind if I talk about your coming home to marry me—I really mean just coming home to live with me again. I feel always as if you are here now, especially at times like The Winter's Tale and Mozart, and I am so proud and pleased about you.

I forgot to tell you about the Rococo lecture on Wednesday—another group of a dozen old ladies ticked off—I don't know how orthodox on Rococo I was but I think it was interesting and I did not lack words at any rate. I analyzed Baroque picture design compared with Renaissance (Wölfflin)[4] and led from Rubens into Watteau and then the rest was easy. Showed lots of pictures and I think they liked it. My Thursday class is now eleven people and I'll be doing Van Gogh for two weeks[5] I expect. Hope I don't lose interest in Van Gogh—it will be fatal!

Various people have seen my article in The School[6] and one teacher has come in on the strength of it, to borrow pictures.

Have been somewhat under the weather again all week. The nurse said it was the beginning of intestinal 'flu, which has been going about. However, I have not been in bed with it, just felt like hell. Saturday the usual arrived and I gave up and talked to Dot Drever all afternoon. Did I tell you, by the way, that DOT HAS A PERMANENT APPOINTMENT? I don't think I did. It is at Earl Beatty School, teaching commercial work, but she likes it, and it is a regular job. She is very well, working hard, has to go to night school twice a week. Has had a recurrence of man trouble—the ex-fiancé's father told her last week that ex-f. is still willin' and that it's her move. She feels he might do a little moving himself, but the revival of that affair, even the mention of it, has her a little worried.

I go to bed thinking of you, and I wake up thinking of you just the same. I'm often rather surprised you're not with me when I wake up. I like to dream and I think I'll not waste any more time staying awake!

My love to you, my dear.

H.

Monday Nov. 9.

This evening was spent with the dean in council. All evening we talked about smoking, providing smoking rooms and private entertaining rooms for the students and so Jessie Mac [Macpherson] is going to bring up the question before the Women's Council and see what can be done. She's a good scout, but very conscious of the position she is in, moving slowly to keep from antagonizing people whose attitude she knows from long acquaintance with Methodism. Dorothy Forward it was who kept on bringing forth more suggestions. They're going to fix up the Annesley tea room for entertaining and the women will all be allowed to smoke in their rooms and to entertain men at definite times, in their rooms. None of this is *law* as yet, but may come about in the near future. Dorothy Forward is in the Botany department and used to be a demonstrator when I studied Botany—I like her much better now that my connection with her no longer entails the breeding of flies in bottles and such-like.[7] Helen Brown is in the Psychology department. The new woman from Australia Miss Nickle is in the Geography department. [Florence] Smith, Coburn, and Kemp, you know. Florence Smith had the curse to-night and looked like the devil, and Coburn knitted a yellow garment all evening. Times are certainly changing around here but not any too soon I'd say. We went out for coffee afterwards to the Park Plaza[8] and had *coffee* in the beer parlour and did not smoke because the dean was there. And after the smoking question was gone over the discussion turned to sex relations and F.S. [Florence Smith] said there was a lot of sexual intercourse going on in Toronto, Jessie Mac told of one case in London, England, which proved that conduct was a good deal less rigid than here, Dorothy Forward talked of couples travelling together in England on their holidays, for the most part platonic arrangements. F.S. said yes, it might be platonic on the woman's side but how long did it remain so with the man? There is no doubt about it, you men are all a little unsafe to be with (bless your hearts, says the widow pro tem). Anyhow, you get the idea. Altogether

I'd say the dean and the dons are not so bad at all. Oh yes, there was one other thing that came up. For the sake of stimulating Conversation we are to think of Interesting People to invite for dinner to come and talk to students afterwards and they can be from the university staff or elsewhere. Then, if university staff, do we invite the wives? Wives are a blight, said Kay [Coburn] and F.S. almost simultaneously. But they'll have to be invited. Various discussions regarding what to do with the dim bulbs, so I said if I were a dumbegg professor's wife I'd a damned sight sooner stay home than be dragged in because it was the done thing, thinking vaguely of Coleridge discussions and Arnold's philosophy party. And then I had to turn the sentence somewhat adroitly to a general sympathy with wives in general realizing that very soon I'd be exactly in that position and mentally noting that refusals are in order to joint invitations to Conversational Orgies in Women's Residences. If it gets too painful I'll get myself invited to lecture in South Africa and leave you to it. Norah [McCullough] says Lismer sent a message to me to the effect that there is no end of pioneering to be done there in the line of lecturing.[9] I said yes, that's all very well, but I'm somewhat attached to Toronto, but Norah said you might go too. Let's do it sometime.

Van Gogh opens to-morrow—Barbara [Sturgis] is coming with me and possibly Freda Pepper's Fred Brown. I feel very much mellowed toward Fred since he had a studio party that Sunday and played records and had a good baritone sing and Jack Kash dropped in etc etc. Fred and this baritone Eric Tredwell are going to come to Wymilwood next Sunday for the musicale.

Jerry and Kay [Riddell] were entertaining eight freshmen after our tea party on Sunday—Roy [Daniells] says Jerry is much more sociable than he used to be, talks more easily to students. And Kay is, of course, a past-master at the art of tea-partying.

I must get this off to the post box. The streets are wet and it is nearly mid-night, and I must post this at Charles and Yonge to be sure it goes off on the 7.30 morning mail to get to New York in time. It is really quite thrilling to think of the journey this bit of paper is about to make, I hope you like all the little marks on it. I wish I could roll myself up in a carpet like Cleopatra and arrive in Merton and wait in the shadows with Duns Scotus.[10] I wish I could fold myself up in this letter and creep into your waistcoat pocket and stay with you for a long time. I will be your Tinker Bell but I'll not be angry ever and I'll be very quiet and let you read

Chaucer and Shakespeare and Blake and Johnson and I'll only tickle your ear occasionally. And I will NOT be a BLIGHT.

Good night my dearest man. I love you so very much.

Helen.

1 The Courtauld Institute of Art, where Peter Brieger had taught before coming to Toronto.
2 A restaurant located on the north side of Bloor St., near Bay St.
3 Wilson Knight's production of *The Winter's Tale* was staged in the Hart House Theatre 5–7 November 1936.
4 The reference is to the German art historian Heinrich Wölfflin (1864–1945), whose *Principles of Art History, The Art of the Italian Renaissance,* and *Classic Art* were available in English translations in the 1930s.
5 HK lectured on Van Gogh to the Thursday morning study group on 12 and 19 November. In the first lecture she used reproductions of the paintings; the second was a review of the exhibition at the AGT.
6 See Letter 142, n. 1, above.
7 Dons with experience in non-college subjects were hired on an annual basis; Forward was a "science don."
8 A hotel near the U of T campus at the corner of Bloor St. and Avenue Rd.
9 Lismer had gone to South Africa for a year at the request of the government to lecture to teachers and to establish children's art classes.
10 Duns Scotus, the renowned scholastic philosopher, studied and taught at Oxford, and, as NF has remarked in Letters 156 and 160, the ghost of Duns Scotus is said to haunt certain rooms at Merton, including his own.

164. NF to HK								Oxford
Nov. 10 [*1936*]

Postmarked 10 November 1936; addressed to HK at 84 Queen's Park, Toronto, Ontario, Canada.

Sweetheart:

There are times when I feel acutely conscious of the minor discomforts of life in England. It is no doubt frightfully vulgar of me to refer to the trivia of daily existence in this venerable and other-worldly seat of learning, but really. Here I am sitting with a whisker half an inch long, waiting for my scout to take away the water I washed my face in out of my wash-basin and give me a chance to shave. There's no place I can put the water except into my pisspot, and *that's* full of piss. Meanwhile the hot water he brought me has got cold, and I shall have to heat it up again in an exceedingly temperamental tea-kettle. The capacity of said pisspot is considerably less than at first reported, now that I have calmed down a bit—hardly more than three pints, actually. So no doubt you can infer another minor discomfort: waking up with a distended bladder in the middle of the night, staring speculatively at the half-inch or so left at the top, and wondering whether it will take what you've got or whether the danger of overflowing it is great enough to make you dress and go your shivering way to the New Buildings. Minor discomfort No. 3: shaving in front of the mirror when the room is so damned cold you cover the mirror with a thick film every time you exhale, and can't see what you're doing.

To switch the subject to civilization for the moment. Thank you very very much for the New Yorkers. You *are* a sweet little girl. It was just pure nerves that made me bark for them in my last letter. The idea that you might have forgotten to buy them owing to pressure of work or something nearly made me collapse. I spent a marvellous weekend with them. It was just as well they came when they did, as the boots took my shoes Saturday morning to repair them and didn't return them till Sunday morning—I had to go to Hall in my tennis shoes.[1] After Hall I got some coffee and settled down for a long evening with them—I'm quite reconciled to everything now. *How* that magazine sustains that incredible prose style the way it does I simply don't know. And I don't want to know. All I can do is gape in admiration and shiver in delight. Thanks for the Mail and Empire clipping. How Pearl McCarthy sustains her prose style I don't know either.[2] But for the last three days I've been purring and cooing like a cement mixer, and in the intervals have thought what a swell girl you are.

I had a tutorial again with Blunden last night. Blunden was vague again—obviously doesn't quite know what to do with me but would like to be helpful. I shall have to be careful with that man. I mentioned Skelton, and referred to a very bad editor of Skelton as a congenital idiot. Blunden was tickled—he had written a very unfavorable review of that very edition, and had received a rather abusive letter from the said editor in consequence. It was the right remark, but I could just as easily have made it about one of his friends. Speaking of wrong remarks, this man Baine made one, I think. Recently Blunden gave a very good lecture on a minor 18th century poet called Young, and had a swell time quoting bad passages from him, quoting jokes on him, and setting his inflated ideas beside his achievements. As we were coming out of the lecture, I said to Baine: "There's no doubt that a bad poet provides better material for a good lecture than a good one." This went away down into Baine's subconsciousness somewhere, and next day he had a tutorial with Blunden, who asked him something about the lectures he was attending. Baine started a long harangue which went definitely to show that most of the lecturing around here was extremely bad, and after complaining lustily for ten minutes, suddenly realized that it was high time to start exempting present company. So, realizing like many a good scholar before him, that the best way of saying exactly the right thing would be to quote me, he said: "I enjoyed your lecture on Young very much, but then I suppose it's easier to lecture on a bad poet than a good one."

Sunday I went to tea with one of those martyrs who invite colonial students and tell them to make their place home while they're in Oxford. Three of us. Hostess a gentle Anglo-Indian, Host very genial and intelligent. An Irish woman there who looked quite bright, so I got talking to her. She asked me where Toronto was and I explained as well as I could. Then she asked another man where Vancouver was (his home, of course) and he explained as well as he could. Then she asked me if Toronto was anywhere near Vancouver. Which reminds me. There's a solemn individual in horn-rimmed spectacles named [Arthur] Jackson who spends dinner time prying information about America out of Baine. In the course of this he has been forced to realize that America is very, very much larger than England, and he has got a bit fed up with that. Last night he asked Baine if the place where he lived (state of Mississippi) was subject to floods. "No," said Baine loftily. "I live in the eastern part of the state, and of course you must understand that the state is nearly as wide as the whole of England." "Quite so," says Jackson, "but then I always thought the Mississippi River itself was as wide as the whole of England." To return to the Irishwoman. It developed that she is a painter—studied in Chelsea but has never heard of the Courtauld Institute. I asked her if she'd exhibited, and she said vaguely, "Yes, in Dublin—not in London." She said something about [John] Constable. I said I was sorry to have missed the Burlington Exhibition of Braque, Matisse and Picasso. Those names were new to her, and she asked me to tell her who they were. I started on Braque, and mentioned Cezanne. She said: "Oh, yes, the man who does all the ballet dancers." So I gave up, and when she said she thought Constable had done what all these Impressionists had tried to do but had got beyond it, I just let her say it. I didn't have the energy to mention Blake. The third man present was an offensive domestic animal from South Africa, who treated me to a stentorian biography of Cecil Rhodes on the bus going home and said that Rhodes was very like Hitler in some ways, as both were unmarried. He'd been to Germany. Said he thought the Jews would respect the thoroughness with which the Nazis got rid of them, whether they agreed with the policy or not. There are times when I find the reasonings of Rhodes Scholarship Committees *very* difficult to follow.

I got a very welcome letter from Barbara [Sturgis], conveying the devastating news that Veronica's father is Sir Ralph (Rafe, I suppose) Wedgwood.[3] I am absolutely sure I sat there and shouted "Mr. Wedgwood" at him all night. Somebody should warn me about these English.

I got a desperate note from Elizabeth [Fraser] the other day, so I went around to see her. That fool who wrote the book she's illustrating has been turning down her designs, which get better as the book gets worse. They are very remarkable drawings, I think—she has a fine sense of design and a very unusual imagination. The printer has been breaking her heart too—she had drawn a crushed, huddled-up nude figure which he said would suggest "to anyone who had been in Egypt"—why there I don't know—someone defecating on the banks of the Nile.[4] The drawings are to my mind just as sincere as the book is faked, and as concrete as the book is vague, which is saying a lot. She's a very remarkable girl, and it's a pity she hasn't something decent to illustrate. I can't say I blame the fool, as her drawings have very little to do with his text—she thinks they have, but they haven't—but as he hasn't anything to say it doesn't matter. He could hardly be expected to realize, however, that the sole merit of his book is in its illustrations.

Apparently the story of Duns Scotus haunting this staircase is flourishing—I don't know whether I told you or not that a silly ass came up here one night swearing he'd seen it. Well, some dim-witted imbecile with a brain like a London fog identified that same silly ass with me, so I've tried to bore a hole through his skull to let the idea evaporate. I hope I succeed before he decides it's a good story.

Last Tuesday I went to a lunch held by the League of Nations club—speaker a Jew talking about Palestine. Very good speech addressed to a not too intelligent audience who asked questions about all the points he'd already dealt with, so that he gave his speech over again, complete with perorations.

I've talked to a lot of people but I haven't said anything important. Charlie Chaplin is here now, but I didn't go—I had the New Yorkers. However, I told as many people as have brought up the subject to go and see it. 1066 and All That is on the stage here now,[5] but I haven't bothered with that. [Joseph] Reid goes to Paris for Christmas—I'd like to go, assuming I get some money.

There is no doubt that if I were to try to sacrifice you to my career I should get a very poor exchange. Here I am, in the greatest university in the world, studying the only subject I care a damn for, and still all I can think of is how much I want you, and how much more I want you. Seven months to keep telling you I love you without proving it.

Norrie.

Did you know that the word "Kemp" means giant, or athlete or warrior of enormous physical prowess, from the same root as "champion"? Silly name—you really ought to change it, you know.

1 The "boots" was the person in charge of cleaning the students' shoes. The scout would tag the shoes and give them to the boots to clean or to have repaired.
2 The reference is to an article by Pearl McCarthy, "Canadian Academy Has Strong Exhibit," which appeared in the Toronto *Mail and Empire*, 6 November 1936, 5. The article praises an exhibition of Canadian artists at the AGT.
3 NF had not previously known about the peerage of Veronica's father.
4 The drawing is opposite p. 36 in *Plato's Academy* (see Letter 162, n. 3, above). The printer was John Johnson.
5 A play by Walter Carruthers Sellar (London: Methuen, 1931).

165. NF to HK   Oxford
                                                  Nov. 17 [1936]

Postmarked 17 November 1936; addressed to HK at 84 Queen's Park, Toronto, Ontario, Canada.

My sweetest pet:

I woke up this morning when my scout came in at 7:30 with my subconsciousness registering the fact that I was going to get a letter from you today. Then I went to sleep and dreamed about you for an hour, and woke up and went into my living room and picked up your letter, not even realizing that I ought to be faintly surprised at its presence until later—somehow or other I saw your letter around the corner. I love your letters—you wouldn't believe what a physically bracing effect they have on me. I know you love me, but I'm a sort of Shylock in a way—I prefer seeing your name signed to the statement.[1] *What* my lawyer would do if you decided to run away with some other man! I warn you, I'm saving them all carefully. And, look here, I'll do my best to get letters off to all those people, but it's not as easy as it sounds. At first I thought I could write letters in the evenings, but that idea is not so good—the climate is getting into my bones now and after dinner I feel disgustingly like bed—my eyes play out sooner here, too. I was amused by your descriptions of life as lived by the presiding spinsters in Wymilwood, particularly at the Smith's [Florence Smith's] remark that a lot of sexual intercourse went on in Toronto (poor old girl: they should breed a special kind of stud for that sort of female. I've been wrestling with one exactly like her all week—the woman who edited the definitive {I'm afraid} edition of Wyatt,[2] my favorite poet as I think I said. She reduced me to a sort of incoherent splutter when I came to write my paper. Wyatt was a lover of Anne Boleyn's, and was arrested when she was: the spinster's Appendix F is designed to prove that Wyatt never, never actually went to bed with Anne, but that "on the contrary, the relation between them was an agreeable one.")[3] Darling, if you think I'm going into Wymilwood to carry on Cultured Conversation, with a lot of Goggle-eyed Gorgons without you there to protect me, you've got a second guess. Bless the Wookey's heart; I hope it's not another girl.[4] Now, I must really stop purring and cooing over your letter and pass to the less attractive topic of myself.

Blunden last night. Paper on Wyatt: by no means a bad paper, though not very well organized: I didn't start writing it until ten that morning, and the splutter over addle-headed critics as aforesaid also interfered. Blunden said he had noticed that all his students who really understood what poetry was about liked Wyatt, which was no doubt a compliment. That man must listen to my papers more carefully than I thought. I was listening to a lecture of his on Chesterton last Wednesday in which I suddenly heard a paraphrase of a passage in the last paper I read him, followed by an application of the general principle it embodied to Chesterton. After the lecture he nodded cheerfully at me and said: "I stole from you, but unwillingly: and it was only petty larceny anyhow." I'm just going to take what Blake there is over to him: I want the "favorable half-yearly report" to get to Ottawa before the end of term. I don't want to stay here during the Christmas Vac. if I can help.

Tuesday I had Elizabeth [Fraser] in to tea, and she told me all her troubles with her pseudo-Platonist.[5] She's beginning dimly to realize now, I think, that her drawings have nothing to do with his burbling, and is rather depressed about it. She wants to write herself, and illustrate what she writes. Saturday we went for what started out to be a walk around the country, but which ended up in a pub-crawl. We had morning coffee in Kemp Hall (nice name that place has) at eleven, and started up a tow-path north-west of here.[6] It was a marvellous day, bright sun and dark rain-clouds on the opposite horizon, everything full of the subtlest lighting and colour-effects. This landscape almost paints itself, but then it does it so quickly—the sun goes behind a cloud for a minute and then you have an absolutely different picture. It would break a painter's heart, I should think—that is, a real painter: but I should think the temptation to sit down and dash off a bad water-color on the spot would be almost irresistible to a bad painter. I like this particular stage of the fall (autumn, these silly people call it), when the trees are almost emerging in black outlines, but still keep a few rows of russet tufts on them. We had lunch in a little village called Wytham (these villages and their inhabitants are exactly what one sees pictures of and reads about at home, which gives one rather a shock) and then discovered we were in a blind alley, as all the land around there is privately owned and they keep people out when they want to shoot pheasants. We started up a road and asked a long individual with two pointers snuffling along behind him how to get around his property—he was obviously connected with it—to somewhere else. He wore a green hat. He told us if we went through a farm "we wouldn't do any harm"— rather a subtle remark, meaning essentially that we wouldn't get shot in the pants by a pheasant-hunter, and the naïvete of the Englishman's worship of private property it embodied kept me laughing for the rest of the day. So we started toward the Thames, but instead of getting to the towpath ploughed along through a swamp, me getting my beautiful gray flannels soaked with muck and my shoes—I don't know what the Boots said the next morning, and probably couldn't set it down if I did know. Elizabeth almost wept and said she ruined every day she planned, but I was really having a very good time. We had tea in an even more post-cardish village called Eynsham, and started up a highway, of all places, but it was getting dark and Elizabeth wanted to flag a bus and go home. We stopped one—a very swanky one for this country—and the conductor got out, glanced at our shoes, and said that this bus was much more expensive than another which would be along in ten minutes—one-and-six. We got in. Then we went home and had high tea in Kemp Hall (swell name that place has) and then I went home with Elizabeth & stayed there until half-past ten, Elizabeth's landlady,[7] who is a very sweet old soul, sending up some coffee for us. Elizabeth, as I say, wants to write—she's got all kinds of ability, generalized; how successful she'll be in focussing that ability I don't know. She feels the lack of a systematic training, wanted me to give her something to read, got frightened after I made a few suggestions and said she'd write instead. God knows what one can make of the girl. Her relief at finding someone who wouldn't blush and look the other way when she powdered her nose and who wouldn't think she was a fallen woman if she wanted to go find a bush in the course of the walk suggested that she had been making rather a fool of herself in front of Englishmen recently—I suspect she has a genius for that.

Friday I had tea with another Oxford Martyr, which is what I call the people who make a profession of inviting overseas students. Mrs. Haldane—J.S. Haldane's wife and J.B.S. Haldane's mother—super old lady, I should imagine. Miss Thorneycroft was there—I talked to her a bit, and then my former martyr, Mrs. Boyd, got into a corner with me and opened up on India. She was swell. Her husband is somebody very big and important in India, and she had gone with him when he went to administer a Mohammedan Native State. The ruler or Nawab had married three times, having an heir by his first wife and an eight-year-old boy by his third. The said third wife was precious but cunning, and was determined that her boy would be made heir. So she pretended friendship to the real heir, encouraged him to drink and go with women a bit, and then went to the Nawab with the most horrible stories about the vices he'd been engaging in. The Nawab, who was a senile old fool, listened to her, disinherited the heir and sent him to a small village, where he took to drink and strange women in great earnest. The British government heard of it and sent an officer into the village to straighten the boy out. The boy impressed the officer as an extraordinarily decent kid, so he persuaded the Nawab to reinstate him. So he came back and inside of a week was dead, undoubtedly poisoned by the old girl. Then the Nawab died too, which left the eight-year-old the ruler, and at this point Boyd[8] took charge. He had the most frightful time with the old girl, who simply raised hell all the time, filled the youngster up with horrible stories about Europeans till he got so scared he didn't open his mouth for six weeks or thereabouts, and insisted on two servants' guarding him all the time. The point was, of course, that they wanted to give the youngster some education. At that he nearly died on their hands, as he developed enteric fever—he was very delicate, being carried everywhere, so that at the age of eight he could hardly walk across a room. The night nurse saw one of the attendant servants putting something into the boy's mouth, and she dashed over to extract it, and found it to be a wad of paper with a passage from the Koran written on it—a priest had given it to the mother to smuggle in. And so on. It was fascinating, this Oriental melodrama suddenly appearing in the middle of a respectable Oxford drawing-room. There was a young girl by the name of Purcell who talked to me for a while—I said something about her name and she told me she was descended from him, and that she expected I just hated his music. That led to a conversation on music more or less paralleling the one on art I had had at Mrs. Boyd's. Oxford seems to breed a curiously weedy sort of virgin. Mrs. Haldane said she'd give my name to yet another martyr, a sister of Mr. Brett, who specialized in Toronto people.

Last night Baine dragged me to the first cinema I'd been to in England, except for the one I wrote up for the Isis.[9] "Ceiling Zero,"[10] all about flying aeroplanes—quite interesting except that it was full of officers rushing around bawling orders at the top of their voices so fast they were quite unintelligible. The behavior of Oxford cinema audiences is most remarkably unpleasant—a constant succession of derisively imitative noises when anything except comedy is being shown. The English public schoolboy seems to take a long time over being an English public schoolboy. Also another film based on the usual hermaphroditic theory of love—that the most decent man in the world will make you miserable if he isn't the one you reely luluv.

The S.C.M. here held a discussion meeting Sunday night and [Joseph] Reid dragged me over. A Presbyterian minister droned for half an hour on the theory of the atonement—the English S.C.M. is not the Canadian S.C.M.—and then someone got up and said: "I brought a friend of mine here, and there he is. He's a Unitarian. He doesn't believe in the divinity of Christ." Or words to that effect. Whereupon everybody pitched in on him and had a grand old heresy hunt. Actually they were very much ashamed of themselves afterwards and apologised to him, but it was amusing enough while it lasted. I think I shall cultivate the S.C.M. a bit, as I should rather enjoy setting some of these Anglo-Catholics by the ears.

Jackson Knight has two ex-pupils at Oxford, a Hewlett who is here, and a Jenkins at Corpus Christi: Hewlett gave Jenkins and me tea yesterday. Jenkins and I will not get along—he's another one of these Cheltenham Fascists—but they are both very nice boys, and talked to me about music. Jenkins thinks music began and ended with Beethoven.

Sunday night a man called Elson dropped in to see me. He does work in medicine here—I had met him at Walters' in London, where he was boarding.[11] He came to the college knowing nothing about my name except that it had a y in it. The porter somewhat illogically sent him to Warren, so, with some misgivings, he went to see Warren, stared at him solemnly for nearly a minute, said "You aren't the one" and vanished. So Warren said. I've asked him to lunch.

In the course of writing this letter I went to a League of Nations lunch and listened to Gilbert Murray. Magnificent old man, but couldn't say anything except that there's nothing wrong with the League: it's not the fault of the League ideal if the world is being slowly brutalized into a gangland.

I wish you wouldn't get things like intestinal flu, poor child. I do hope you're all right now. Bless you, darling, and keep up the good work. I'm sorry Alford is such a toad, but it will give you something to fight for—just give him an unmistakable impression that you despise him—nothing less subtle would touch his ego. I wish I could have seen Wilson Knight's *Winter's Tale*. My love to everyone you see—I'm giving you enough to supply Toronto with.

Norrie.

This letter contains some of the worst prose ever written in Oxford. If it doesn't make sense, just ignore it.

At the Gilbert Murray lunch today a Maltese Rhodes Scholar from Hertford was sitting beside me. He looked at the various female examples of sartorial perversion drifting past us, and said: "There are some wonderfully beautiful women here, aren't there?" I spent the next fifteen minutes staring eagerly around the room, and the following fifteen deciding not to go to Malta.

N.

1 In Shakespeare's *The Merchant of Venice* (2.3), Shylock agrees to lend money to Antonio on condition that he sign a bond stipulating that he forfeit one pound of flesh from any part of the body that he, Shylock, may designate.

2 NF is referring to Agnes Kate Foxwell's edition of *The Poems of Sir Thomas Wiat*, 2 vols. (London: University of London Press, 1913).

3 What Foxwell actually says in Appendix F is that "no fact has been discovered concerning any relationship between Wiat and Anne Boleyn, while *certain interesting facts tend to prove that the intimacy between them was an agreeable one, of short duration, and ceased altogether after 1527*" (*The Poems of Sir Thomas Wiat*, 2:254).

4 Gladys Wookey Davis, the wife of Herbert J. Davis; the birth of her child was imminent, as HK announces in Letter 163.

5 Pan. Aristophron. See Letter 162, n. 3, above.

6 Kemp Hall was a two-storey stone and timber-framed building just to the northwest of Merton College, off High St., between St. Aldate's and Alfred Streets. The outing that NF goes on to describe took him and Elizabeth Fraser northwest along the towing- path of the Oxford Canal to Wolvercot, and thence west along the Thames towing-path to Wytham, the northernmost village in Berkshire; from there they headed west again to Eynsham, which took them back into Oxfordshire. The distance between Oxford and Eynsham is about ten miles.

7 A Mrs. Bachelor, whose boarding house was at 55A High St. in Oxford.

8 Sir Donald James Boyd, a British civil servant in India, had served as the commissioner of the Rawalpindi division in northwest India from 1927 until 1934; at the time NF met him he was a finance member of the Punjab government, a position he held until 1937. The Mrs. Boyd NF mentions—one of his Oxford "martyrs"—was Sir Donald's second wife, Winifred.

9 See Letter 160, n. 9, above.

10 A 1936 film, directed by Howard Hawkes and starring James Cagney as a womanizing, devil-may-care pilot whose fate catches up with him.

11 Walters' boarding house. See Letter 160, n. 8, and Letter 138.

166. HK to NF
[*Toronto*]
November 19. 1936.

My dearest: I've run out of proper writing paper and I should be in bed, and I've nothing much to say, so I'll just fill ten pages more than likely. Your letter of Nov. 10 came yesterday, and makes me wonder when I wrote to you last. I have been so very busy lately, you can imagine, with the Van Gogh show in full swing. We are dated up for every afternoon and evening this month and Marg [Wilson] is starting on December now. The show is over on the 13th. Fortunately we take turns at coming down in the evenings,—I was just out two evenings last week and two this week, so it really is not too bad. We have huge mobs of women and children in the afternoons—high schools, technical schools, study clubs etc etc. Peggy [Roseborough] brought Branksombe Hall and Mary [Winspear] brought St. Clement's School[1]—70 of them at once. Tonight I had to be hostess so to speak, for 200 odd women from the university who came down under Miss Ferguson's wing to listen to a lecture by John Alford. Shades of Lismer! Their idea of integrity is so different—Alford is so painfully insistent on neatly putting Van Gogh in the right category—Lismer's object would be to make people *see* something vital in his work. Alford *ummed* and paused and pawed the air for words and pretty well killed poor Van Gogh so far as that audience went. There isn't too much use in giving people a critical evaluation of a man's work in cold blood: what they want is a warm and glowing appreciation of his work and a clue to what he's getting at. Alford started with a comparison between classicism and romanticism or intellectual and emotional art, showing examples of a Greek statue, the Parthenon, Raphael's School of Philosophy, and a German crucifixion and a painting of Turner. Then he pointed out that Van Gogh was an emotional artist and overworked his comparison between Vincent and Brueghel and went on to the biographical details, and I must admit he did show some general sympathy with the man's super-sensitiveness and his colour harmonies and his feeling of the pulsation of life in everything around him. And just as I was forgiving Alford for his beginning—in which he also showed S. Sophia and Byzantine mosaics for no reason that I could see—he talked of formal relationships etc etc— Alford wound up by telling people that Van Gogh was never a first rate artist because his emotion predominated over his reason and that his later work is marred by too great a subjectivity of approach. Regular wet blanket. A fine way to end a lecture, when you've got two hundred students who are all agog to see a show and you send them away saying it's a second rate artist anyway but still worth looking at!!! Holy suffering horse-shit! Barbara [Sturgis] was with me and we have been pulling apart J.A. all the way home. I had to say some polite words to him about his lecture, which I did quite sincerely. I told him I liked his attempt at the beginning to explain what to look for {but I didn't say how long-winded he was and how he could have done much better with *two* slides instead of the number he used} I said I was interested in his treatment of the insanity question {he had quarreled with Robert Tyler Davis of Buffalo who lectured here on Monday and who called it epilepsy}, and I said it was refreshing to hear his summing up at the end, which was a thing we would never do in talking to groups who come for a talk and some tea. I don't think he got my point. I really think that Brieger will outdistance Alford in popularity in no time.

I must go to bed after all that tirade.

Furthermore, Mr Frye, I haven't got straight hair. There are several distinct waves in it, and as for the word you used to describe it may I remind you that there is another form of excretion lighter in colour than the one you mentioned, which might more fittingly describe the hair of some other people we know. So there!

My study group turned out with twelve people to-day and they want a consecutive course—they still continue to talk and I feel much encouraged. I lectured to the Dames Club the other day, expecting to talk to 27 people, there turned out to be forty-five of them with Principal Brown's wife in the front row! So I held forth and a few days later the secretary sent me a note saying that their visit had been the best yet (and they come every year.) So that goes into the appreciation file along with the other applesauce.

I'd consider changing my name perhaps—no, I wouldn't consider it at all. I wouldn't need to spend that much time on the question. I'm afraid you're a goner, my boy, or I'm a comer—whatever way it works out, so that we can be together.

Sunday Nov. 22.

Another peaceful Sunday morning—breakfast in bed—bath—shampoo etc, and a letter written to Esther Higgs. She is Marian Higgs' sister and is staying with relations in Paris, Ontario, and is coming to see me for a week-end soon. Marian Higgs, you will remember, went with me to Paris the first time to see the Italian Exhibition, and I spent a weekend at her home near Cheltenham. I didn't write to her about you because I thought you'd be bored probably, as you would have no interests whatever in common with either Marian or her family and you've already had several vague geographical conversations with English people.

We should have had our house party last night but only five people wanted one and it was cancelled. Oak Lawn, the other graduate house, didn't have one either, so Helen Brown and I sat in front of my fire all evening and told each other how much work we were getting done—both of us lying flat on the floor with our feet in the air and both of us nearly asleep. I had asked J.R.D. [Roy Daniells] to help me chaperon, and when I had to cancel it he did not do the right thing, from my point of view i.e.—take me to a show, which I think you would have done in that case. Now wouldn't you? I had a very nice time last weekend, however. Douglas MacAgy and I went to see Libeled Lady—William Powell, Myrna Loy, Jean Harlow etc, and it was grand fun.[2] Douglas has gone to

Cleveland this weekend—keeping in touch with Thomas Munro about a job there. Then Roy [Daniells] 'phoned up in a hurry to get me to come to Middle House tea on Sunday as his men had pulled a fast one and put on a tea before he knew it. I was at home in the morning—Roy [Kemp] was playing with Albert Fuchs who stayed for dinner, then Roy and Harold and I played trios and then I hurried back here to find that J.R.D. had been trying to get in touch with me as his tea started at four-thirty, not at five. We *met* the party leaving as we approached Charles Street, and so the two chaperons had tea unchaperoned. Then later the rest of Middle House plus females descended en masse and we all indulged in animated conversation for some time and suddenly they all rose and scrammed as quickly as they had come, leaving us with another don plus *his* woman. Englishman, new to Baldwin House this year. I've forgotten his name. Jerry Riddell ambled in and expressed his doubts about the whole system of letting people have teas unchaperoned in their rooms—it seems there are some people they wouldn't trust. The whole thing leaves me a little puzzled: here are the women trying to get as much freedom as the men, and the dean thinking of allowing teas in women's rooms without chaperonage—and now the senior tutor gets squeamish and wonders what people outside will think if they pass by and see flocks of women at tea-time playing musical chairs in the men's common rooms! I said I couldn't see how the rapture and roses of vice[3] could flourish much in that dull olive green atmosphere. The protective attitude of Victoria College seems a matter of great curiosity to me—I don't see how we can make the world *safe* for anybody. It is an impossible idea. From some points of view I've done all the wrong things, myself—but most of them are the right things—except that of course I couldn't have lived with you in residence very well, and we can't provide a co-educational residence yet. Miss Addison told Jessie Macpherson last week at a conference of deans of women from all over Ontario that the dean should be writing and doing research and lecturing on women's rights, women's education and goodness knows what. Which somewhat bothered J.M. Helen Brown said some time ago she spoke to her about the privileges of a don in widening the student's horizon etc etc, and Helen thought she sounded critical of the present régime in the women's residences. It certainly is different now with a young dean and dons like Dorothy Forward—science, Miss Nickle the geography woman from Melbourne—very good scout, Helen Brown—child psychology, Coburn, Kemp, [Florence] Smith. None of us at all strong on the religious viewpoint of Miss Addison's day. Anyhow, I'm staying all day to-day and trying to spread some light. Owing to Van Gogh I still don't know all the students by name even, let alone personally. But that will come in time, I hope. I must get dressed now for dinner.

Blue Monday.

I must send this off to you now. There is no more news: for the rest of yesterday I went for a walk with Barbara [Sturgis] and came to the residence for tea and called on Jerry [Riddell] and took back Ukridge.[4] The sight of two such happy people as Kay and Jerry was enough to give me the hump yesterday—I wanted the whole world to be just as miserable as I was. It is just reaction from Van Gogh excitement I suppose—have had my nose in that gallery so long that I don't know what to do away from it. And I'm tired and disgruntled at being all by myself without you, and it doesn't help one bit to remember all the millions of women who are lonely too.

But cheer up, my girl! This *will not do*. I heard a funny story yesterday about something that happened here on Hallow E'en. Someone from Burwash called Annesley and asked if there were three short girls who would go dancing with three small men. The girl who answered was a freshie, but not short. She thought this was too good to pass up, so she said she wasn't short but she didn't mind dancing with short men, so it was agreed. She got another six-footer and a medium sized girl, and they all dressed up ready to go. Presently the Annesley doorbell rang and they went to meet their swains. On the doorstep were three Burwash milk-cans with "HOMO" written on them! Well!! They got the don and they wondered what was the next move. Helen Carscallen, that blessed little imp, took matters into her own hands. She phoned Burwash, each house in turn, trying to get the don. But finally she got Roy Daniells out of bed and she told him, or whoever answered, that three Burwash men were over on Annesley front steps IN A TERRIBLE STATE, trying to get in. She said in most agonizing tones, it was hard enough for them to keep their own girls straight without taking care of Burwash men too, and would someone come over and take these men home as they certainly weren't capable of taking themselves back to bed. *So*, the story goes, Roy got dressed and went across the street and got Jerry out of bed, and they rounded up three of the huskiest men they could find in Burwash to take these drunks home. Kay Coburn said it was the grandest sight of her life to see them on the doorstep, all armed to handle the three stewed inmates of Burwash! The story ends there, but I understand Helen Carscallen is in for a lot of razzing from Burwash lately.

It is late, I must go to work now. I'll send you some more New Yorkers to-day. I've seen Capek's Insect Play[5] and Ruth Draper, this weekend. Ruth Draper visited our staff meeting at the gallery and I'm a very warm admirer now. You must see her when she comes to England soon.

Hope there's another letter from you soon—

Love H.

1 Both private schools for girls of all ages, still in existence; Branksome Hall was opened at 10 Elm Ave. in 1912, and St. Clement's at 21 St. Clement's Ave. in 1922.
2 A 1936 MGM film, directed by Jack Conway and starring, in addition to those mentioned by HK, Spencer Tracy.
3 See Letter 23, n. 1, above.
4 HK had returned P.G. Wodehouse's Ukridge (1924), which NF had apparently borrowed from Jerry Riddell.
5 A 1921 stage drama by Karel Čapek, translated into English in 1922 as The World We Live In (The Insect Comedy).

167. NF to HK

Oxford
Nov. 30 [1936]

Postmarked 30 November 1936; addressed to HK at 84 Queen's Park, Toronto, Ontario, Canada.

Darling:

I have put off writing you day after day, but no letter has come for two weeks, so I shall have to start this letter to you without one of yours to go on. I got two immense letters last week, one from Barbara [Sturgis] and one from Dorothy [Drever], which were a joy to read, though they took me all morning. Dorothy is worried about the challenge of Communism—I've seen it coming her way much longer than she realized—I think I mentioned it to you before. She's probably in for a bad time, but I don't think permanently. Try to look after her a bit if you can—she's worth it, busy as you are. Barbara is at her best in her letters, I think—she can sustain an amazingly friendly gurgle for page after page. I like her letters very much.

I have seen a good bit of Elizabeth [Fraser], off and on—last Saturday we went to the Downs in Berkshire, where she lived last year. We left on the train for Didcot, had breakfast in a pub. in a town called Blewbury, walked over to the little village of Aston where she had lived and called on a friend of hers, then walked across the Downs[1] for ten or fifteen miles. The last part of the trip—a cinder road—was rather dull, but the first part—over the Downs in one of those amazing mists that turn everything into a blue-green grey haze—was lovely. Elizabeth knows the Downs very well, and makes an excellent companion, for that part of the country in particular. The only thing that spoiled it was the presence of a regiment of ruffians murdering pheasants on all sides of us— the result was that we had to keep to the roads, and climbing a clayey hill with a mist in our faces and a wire fence on each side, with all the silly popping around us, made us feel as though we were going over the top. One of the old Roman roads provided a trail for us. We had no lunch, and we were nearly starved when we got back to Blewbury for tea. We got back to Oxford about eight, and I forsook Elizabeth and went to my room, finding one of my tame violinists ensconced there. Naturally, after fifteen miles on the Downs, I didn't play very well. Warren heard us, and came in to offer criticisms, which annoyed me. I lost my fountain pen in the course of the trip, hence this oblique memorial in pencil.

Elizabeth had had me over to tea the preceding evening to entertain a very apologetic Jew[2] who lives next [to] her in the boarding-house. It wasn't too successful a meeting, as he seemed rather afraid of me, Elizabeth was no help at all, and things ended up a bit indecisively. This week I had Elizabeth over to tea here to meet Douglas LePan, whom she liked, though she was rather prejudiced because she doesn't like his father. They got along quite well, and, though I was rather nervous and spasmodic as a host, I think I got things organized all right. Saturday we went for a walk again, with Elizabeth's landlady,[3] who is all right, but the day was a bit disastrous—we lost our way in an incredibly muddy track and came home with our feet full of cow-turds.

Other events equally trivial. One cinema, with Baine—"My Man Godfrey"[4]—really very amusing. The main plot was hopeless, but it looked as though someone who was a bit of a genius at dialogue and characterization had been handed the world's worst plot and told to make something of it, and had succeeded. As well-sustained a comedy as I've seen since the Chaplin picture. Then there was a dismal Englishman studying medicine here whom I met at the Walters' and who looked me up here—I mentioned him, I think.[5] I had him here to lunch, and, although I fed him fairly well, he was difficult to talk to—politics was about the only thing we clicked on. He asked me to dinner with him at Exeter last night. Exactly the same food as Merton serves, in the same kind of a Hall—a big lumber-pile in the roof and portraits of very distinguished and very dead alumni covering up the walls. Exeter is a rather down-at-heel sort of place, having less money than Merton.

There is an organization here called the Bodley Club, named after the founder of the Bodleian, who was a Merton man—apparently it's the only non-athletic group in the college except another beer-swilling outfit. It keeps itself limited to twenty members and is therefore considered awfully exclusive. LePan belongs to it: he brought me along to a meeting last week—an American Rhodes Scholar of German ancestry reading a paper on the dragging of America into the war. The conversational discussion afterwards was fairly bright—a bit forced, but the Club is said to be quite good as College Clubs go. I was elected a member after I left—I'm rather glad, as it's as good a way as any of getting to know the Best People. The mature students have obviously monopolized it.

[Joseph] Reid upstairs gave a lunch yesterday to two Canadian Rhodes men and invited me along. He had to read a paper somewhere on Canadian politics and invited our criticisms. It's curious how one has to go away [to] discover one's own country. At home I should never have said that Canadians had any nationality, and that they consisted of Americans of whom a few imitated the English unsuccessfully and a few Frenchmen tried a rampant jingoism which came off no better. But there definitely is such a thing as a Canadian. The other men were all Westerners, but somehow everything all fell into place immediately—there was a kind of mutual understanding I could not possibly have got with Americans or Englishmen. The political discussion helped (we shared the same prejudices) but it wasn't essential. I noticed the same thing with Douglas [LePan] & Elizabeth, to a lesser extent—Elizabeth is more contemptuous about her Canadian background than she needs to be—actually she feels a little out of place in England, and resents the adjustments she has to make—but she is a Canadian, just the same, and it makes all the difference. I don't know if I mentioned a large, pasty individual named Long I met at Yvonne's [Yvonne Williams's] tea here. He promised to look me up, but never did, and is, I gather, a rather inconvenient friend of Elizabeth's. She wants me to help entertain him tomorrow night and persuade him to take a trip to Canada. So you see, blood will tell.

Baine, Warren, and a New Zealander named Joseph, whom I'm thrown in with a good deal, improve on acquaintance. Baine is about the best chess player in Oxford & Warren about the best golf player, which makes me feel very humble. Baine is winning, if he has not already won, a university tournament, the winner of which is usually one of the seven selected to meet Cambridge: but the club, terrified at the prospect of having an American Freshman as a candidate, have already selected their full team, so Baine has challenged one of the members of the team and is apparently beating him badly. Warren & Joseph are Catholics, the former the usual muddle-headed reactionary of the Cronin type,[6] Joseph a surprisingly radical one. Joseph is the most intelligent of the three, I think. It's interesting to know a Southerner like Baine, hating northern industrialism frantically, full of a mixture of non-Conformist prudery and local patriotism, regarding Warren as a kind of traitor because of the Northern ideas he acquired at Princeton. Warren said yesterday in Bryson's tutorial that the Southerners acquired their accent from negro nurses, whereupon Baine exploded like a geyser and fizzed away for about fifteen minutes. Bryson tried frantically to compromise peacefully on Anglo-Saxon, and I grinned and remarked that we seemed to have struck a neurosis. Baine is very tall and bulky, and can't go out without a huge overcoat and muffler—he's spent the entire term trying to keep warm. He looks funny with me breezing along beside him with my yellow hair & pullover. The other day I went into Warren's room around twelve & found him suffering from a terrific hangover—he'd been out to a Thanksgiving dinner the night before and was wondering about the people he dimly remembered having asked to tea—whom he asked, what day and what time of day they were coming, and why he'd ever asked them anyhow. I suggested that he go out and get himself a glass of tomato juice. He said he needed a whole can of tomato juice. I told him to get a whole can of tomato juice. He stared at me stupidly and said: "I haven't got a can-opener."

I have decided not to write a paper for Blunden tonight. I'm going to go in and twist his neck with my bare hands. I've scared the shit out of him, in the Burwash phrase, and I'm just beginning to realize it, and to comprehend why he gives me that dying-duck reproachful stare every time I finish reading a paper to him. He returned the Blake with the remark that it was pretty stiff going for him, as he wasn't much accustomed to thinking in philosophical terms. I could have told him that there was a little girl in Toronto who could follow it all right, without making any more claims as a philosopher and far less as a student of English literature. So I think I'll start cooing to him.

I was in the English Reading-Room of the Bodleian some time ago, looking for Tillyard's book on Wyatt—much the best thing on the subject.[7] I couldn't find it and told the old griffin at the desk. He complained that I was probably just too lazy to get down early enough to get hold of the book in the morning, and I said that was possible, but that it had more likely been lost. So, with much sighing and groaning, he looked it up in the list of lost books, and sure enough it had been stolen for about a year. "Yes," he said, "some dishonest person has taken it," glaring at me as though I were the thief. I suggested it might be replaced. Well, he didn't feel like replacing books: somebody else might take them again (giving me another glare), and he thought it was better for the gaps to remain as warnings to other students not to steal the remainder. I said maybe, but it was the business of the Bodleian to see that all books published in England were in it. "Well—how important is Wyatt, anyway? You're the first person who has ever asked for the book, you know. And who is this man Tillyard?" I said important enough for a paper, that I was not surprised if Oxford students knew very little about Wyatt if there were no books on him, and that Tillyard was a Cambridge don who had written a very important book on Milton. "Oh, well, if he's a Cambridge don we wouldn't have heard of him: we haven't got the book on Milton." I said "I know you haven't, and it's a wonder you've ever heard of Milton." (Milton, and incidentally Wyatt, being Cambridge). By that time our exchange of insults was getting fairly good-humored, and after I had told him that the book was published by O.U.P. in spite of its Cambridge lineage and would only cost about seven and six anyhow, he said he'd do something about it, and after several months I might see the book on the shelves. However, he brought the book around to my desk the next day, so he must have been impressed. I had a very brilliant American Rhodes man named Espey in to tea the other day and he said he also complained to the griffin about something in his first term and the griffin said "You're one of those Americans, aren't you?" Some weeks later Espey was copying a map, with a sign in front of him saying you can't trace maps, and the griffin said "Can't you see you're not allowed to trace maps?" "Yes," says Espey, "but I'm not tracing the map: I'm copying it." "Hm. Well, you're not supposed to have one of our books between the inkpot and your notebook." "Quite so, but the book is nowhere near the inkpot, and I'm using a fountain pen." "Hm. Well, I just thought I'd tell you."

I've written an SOS to Ottawa and have asked Blunden to endorse it, and he says he has done so. I shall go back to Guilford Street as soon as I get my money, but expect to be stuck here for a little while anyhow. I hope not: I've got a bit of wanderlust in me: I've had enough for a little while of this other-worldly paternalism, and would like a big city again and myself all alone in it. From a social point of view I have, in Dr. Spooner's words, tasted the whole worm,[8] but there have been reasons for that, what with the paralyzing effect of entering a new country, particularly this country, the work I've been doing, and an invincible shyness which is only gradually wearing off. Also, I've been handicapped by a lack of money. Next term I'll probably expand a bit, take in a few more concerts, and illuminate myself generally.

The term has gone very quickly. Two more terms of the same length,[9] and I'll see you. Oh, darling!

Norrie.

1 The Illsley Downs. Didcot is about nine miles south of Oxford, Blewbury another three miles to the south, and Ashton just over a mile to the east of Blewbury.
2 A Mr. Finegold, who is mentioned in Elizabeth Fraser's letters to NF. See HFF, 1991, box 3, file 1.
3 See Letter 165, n. 7, above.
4 A 1936 Universal Pictures film starring William Powell and Carole Lombard.
5 A man named Elson, mentioned by NF in Letter 165.
6 HK's Cronin relatives were Roman Catholics.
7 E.M.W. Tillyard, *The Poetry of Sir Thomas Wyatt: A Selection and a Study* (London: Scholartis Press, 1929).
8 The Rev. William A. Spooner rebuked an Oxford undergraduate with one of his best-known spoonerisms: "You have hissed all my mystery lectures and tasted the whole worm. You must leave by the town drain!"
9 The Oxford terms for 1936–37 ran from 11 October to 5 December, 17 January to 13 March, and 25 April to 19 June.

168. HK to NF

[*Toronto*]
Dec. 3. 1936.

My dear: I am grabbing a few minutes to send you a line or so as I am told the Christmas mail closes at 5.30 to-night. Van Gogh still going strong: gallery open every evening until Dec 10 with groups coming and being talked to in one way or another. And now the annual Christmas concert is to be arranged. Victoria continues as before. Last Friday I helped chaperone {sp?} the Middle House At Home. It was a beautiful party and I had a very nice time. Saturday I took Roy [Daniells] to see Barbara [Sturgis] and Frances Russell—he said that Frances' poem[1] in the latest Poetry Magazine was to his way of thinking, the best in it. That man is forever having Sunday teas and getting me to come, and of course I enjoy it very well as Wymilwood doesn't tax my powers to any extent. He 'phoned last night to arrange for this Sunday, and I have seldom heard him in such a hilarious mood—this man Hanford from Cleveland who was lecturing here last week wired him lately offering him a six weeks summer school lecture course in Milton at *ninety* dollars a week! Roy says it is a big joke but he lost no time in answering in the affirmative. He tells me Pratt says that on towards the spring they will send you an outline of courses and will more or less give you your choice so that you'll have another eighteen months to think it over.

Roy (big brother this time) has to have an operation on his nose, as Dr. Nelson Tait said he'd be deaf in a few years if he didn't. So it is to be on the 19th of December. Last Monday morning we had a cable from Ernie [Harrison] saying that Marion had done the trick—on Sunday afternoon. A big boy—and we're all now aunts and uncles![2] He says she is very well too. We didn't expect that to happen until Christmas but you never can tell exactly and Norah [McCullough] says the first one often arrives a little early.

Peggy Kidder is just typing a letter to Zwemmer's[3] about a book I am sending you, 'Masters of the 20th c. Album II'—modern French painters. I haven't the vaguest idea whether it is good or not but it should have some fairly good reproductions and I hope you'll like it. I can hardly think about Christmas—we may get a Botticelli from New York—I mean we certainly will, only it may be a Ghirlandaio instead.

You should see the whoop and holler Toronto's new morning newspaper is making about the King—Headline this morning is that he will probably abdicate in a day or so and go into exile with Mrs Simpson.[4] Percy Bilkey was quite worked up this morning. Told me the King must be nuts, and that woman wasn't any good anyway. She's forty-two, says he, and she's gone through two men already. And Percy went on to give me his idea of the English divorce laws and how it was all cooked up anyway, and to illustrate his point he stopped in the centre of the long gallery, talking in no delicate whisper, and said "just take an example—

Supposin' you were my wife, s'posin' we were married, and you went away with the King for six months, could you blame me for gettin' sore?" I choked him off there as I couldn't listen any longer to the idea of my being his wife. Cornishmen are a queer lot.

I wonder what you are doing for Christmas. I shall be thinking of you, you know how much I think of you. I wish I could have written you a proper letter but there just hasn't been time.

I went swimming last Monday night and it was grand fun. I go on the night when faculty members and professors' wives go in. I shall be so glad when I really get to be one of the wives.

There has been a great deal going on lately but I can't remember just now with my mind tied up in the Renaissance, Madonnas for the Print Room and Van Gogh etc etc.

I love you so much, and I hope you will do something very nice at Christmas. Jerry [Riddell] keeps asking for you whenever I see him. So does everyone.

I nearly forgot to tell you. I met Phyllis Foreman {God damn the telephone!} in the Danish Restaurant at noon, with Ellsworth Toll, no less. And, *my dear*, she came over to me, all blushing, and said: "Do you want to know a little secret? We're just going downtown to buy a ring!" So I heartily blessed her and it would have been all right if I hadn't had to talk to the future spouse who bellowed as if talking to five hundred people, asked me if I were drawing any more maps etc. I knew Phyllis was engaged, as I heard she was blushing all over St Christopher House about it.[5] Ah me.

I must stop. The office is in full swing again and I must post this. Bless you, my dear. I shall be home for the holidays.

Helen.

1 Frances Russell, "And Laughter Unquenchable . . . ," *Canadian Poetry Magazine*, 1 (July 1936), 40.
2 Irwin Hubert Harrison, born 30 November 1936 in Rhodesia. Marion Kemp had arrived in Bulawayo, Southern Rhodesia, on 25 March 1936; she married Ernie Harrison on 9 April.
3 A bookshop on Charing Cross Rd., London, specializing in titles, both new and used, on art, architecture, film, and design; Anton Zwemmer, a Dutchman, opened the shop in 1924.
4 The new morning newspaper was the *Globe and Mail*; it began publication in 1936, uniting two dailies, the *Globe* and the *Mail and Empire*. Edward VIII abdicated the throne on 11 December 1936 in order to marry the divorced U.S. socialite, Wallis Warfield Simpson.

5 A settlement house originally founded by Presbyterians in downtown Toronto near
   Bathurst and Dundas Streets in 1912 to engage in educational work among the poor
   and train social workers for Presbyterian institutions; after the union of the Presbyterian, Methodist, and Congregationalist churches of Canada in 1925 it was associated
   with St. Christopher's Settlement United Church.

169. NF to HK   Oxford
                                                        [8 December 1936]

*Postmarked 11 December 1936; addressed to HK at 205 Fulton Ave., Tor-
onto, Ontario, Canada.*

Dear Helen:

Vacation time. Nobody around but a bunch of dispirited youngsters
writing Pass Moderations exams.[1] No money, and the Royal Society
doesn't care. I'm sending them a cable tomorrow—it may help and it
probably won't. I can stay here until the 19th and then I leave for London, money or no money. I'm simply going mad in this place. Dismally
cold, wet, clammy, muggy, damp and moist, like a morgue. The room is
always as cold as a barn—I can't play the piano because the keys are too
cold. The mice are all over everything—they've eaten all my food, and
shit all over my dishes. I've got a cold, and I feel like hell. It rains all the
time. The sun sets around three o'clock in the afternoon, I think—it's
hard to tell. I can't work, I can't think straight, and I've just had a cold
dismal lunch in that great bung hole of a dining hall. Ow-oo-oo!
     Everybody's cleared out, of course—Baine and Warren have gone to
Italy, cursing me for staying around and doing a lot of work. The day
we come back—I shall probably be a water-baby in the Cherwell by
then[2]—we write two exams, one for Bryson on the sixteen hundred lines
of *Beowulf* we're expected to read during the Vacation, and one for
Blunden on the work we've taken.

                                                             Friday.

     I feel better now, having put in a fairly concentrated dose of Elizabeth
[Fraser] since Tuesday, when I wrote the above. Elizabeth *is* a sweet
girl—besides, I owe her a pound. I went out and had tea with her Tuesday, after walking around Oxford for two hours trying to keep myself
awake, and as it was so foggy I could hardly see where I was going I

managed to succeed. Wednesday we went out to a little 14th century church in a place called Northmoor.[3] I was to bring this pad along, but left it in Elizabeth's digs in the morning. The point is that they had dug several pounds of plaster out of the north transept, revealing a tangled mass of red lines and flakes of gilt Elizabeth said were paintings.[4] So Elizabeth started tracing them and I held her tracing paper for about half an hour. Then we decided it was too cold to work, and went to the local pub. to get warm. We spent the rest of the afternoon there and I started a letter to Barbara [Sturgis], but didn't get very far with it. Yesterday I did absolutely nothing at all—God, I've never been at such a loose end—it's because I feel so helpless without money—except send a cable. I *do* hope the Secretary of the Royal Society isn't too bloody a fool. Elizabeth came in for tea and I started playing for her—I've got a little more spring in my wrists now. She doesn't know anything about music, and came around again this morning to get her ears opened. The freshmen I see at meals are all right, but naturally pretty busy, and they'll all be gone by Monday. Your letter of the 3rd came this morning. My congratulations to Marion and commiserations to Roy. Actually, the baby is much the best thing that could have happened—the fuss made about it in July was quite inexcusable. It's true we won't see her for a long time, but that's less important to her than to us.

Yes, we've had Mrs. Simpson too, only our news was later—you being closer to U.S.A. knew all about the abdication weeks before we did. I'm sorry he abdicated, as he seemed to know his job, and definitely had a social conscience compared to this imbecile Parliament—I suppose that was really why they wanted to get rid of him. No doubt he found the pattern of bourgeois rectitude set by his father a bit strenuous. It's probably the death-blow to the prestige of royalty in the country, which is a frightful calamity, I'm afraid, as royalty seems to me to be, or at least to hold together, the most effective opposition to a military despotism. In any other country this would be a paradox: not so here.

The events of the last week of term didn't amount to much. The Bodley Club met again and some depressing individual who didn't know anything about Samuel Butler read a paper on Samuel Butler, and was criticised by someone who knew even less. One of the dons was present, and he and I took the subject in hand. Next night a couple of New Zealanders—Joseph I think I mentioned, and a friend of his over in Balliol—dropped in and suggested a pub-crawl. Between us we drank most of the beer in Oxford, and as I had had a pint of cider at dinner, the effect wasn't happy. I hadn't been in bed long before I felt a bit queasy, and was soon thankful I had a wide washbowl. After that I was all right. My scout said nothing—it's routine to him. Someone else had occasion to ask him once about a graduate who was under his care some years ago. "Oh, a very gay young gentleman, sir; very gay indeed. Wet his bed every night he did, sir." Next morning I had a splitting headache— never again will I ever mix fruit and grain alcohol—and staggered over to the local Lyons for some tomato juice. I stared dismally at the menu and found it not, so I flagged a waitress and said: "Haven't you got any tomayto juice?" "Tomahto juice? No, sir; we don't keep it." "Didn't any- one ever tell you that tomayto juice was good for a hangover?" "Oh, yes, sir; we've heard that in England too." Now I ask you if that was a chari- table way to treat a man in my condition. The Balliol New Zealander was a good head—one of those unfortunates who are interested in noth- ing but modern literature, and take classics because they think it will be good for them. He had only one idea at that time—to rush down to Lon- don and find a woman to sleep with. He's probably happy now. Both men are Catholics—Catholics seem to suffer acutely from celibacy. The New Zealander said if he didn't find any women in Oxford he'd bring his fiancée over. I didn't ask him what his fiancée's point of view would be. I had an amusing conversation the next night with a California Rhodes man named Espey. I retailed the New Zealander's grievance to him, and he said it reminded him of an appalling vacation he spent in Paris with two insufferable youngsters from Harvard who had heard, like Florence Smith, that a lot of sexual intercourse went on in France, and proceeded to get themselves drunk and look for it. Both were vir- gins, and although they found women easily enough, Espey learned from them both next day that they still were. One had gone sound asleep, and had been wakened and ignominiously shown the door.

I've been invited to Blackpool for Christmas, but there'd be no point in my going—I should get to London. Several people have offered to lend me money, including Blunden, but I haven't taken it—I may regret that later, of course.

Oh, well, things might be worse—I don't have to look at pictures of squalling babies on the front page of the Toronto Star, for example. And thanks very very much for the New Yorkers—they helped a lot at a crit- ical time. At any other time I'd say they were worth their weight in gold. Miss Thorneycroft took me out last week to a Beethoven violin sonata recital—I think I told you. And I think you're a swell girl and I'm head over heels in love with you and I wish to God you were here or I was there or both of us were together, anywhere.

Norrie.

1 The first public examinations at Oxford for the B.A., often taking the form of a diploma in a special subject.
2 The allusion is to Charles Kingsley's *Water-Babies* (1862–63), a story about Tom, a chimney-sweep, who falls into a river and is transformed into a water-baby. Oxford sits at the confluence of the Cherwell and Thames Rivers.
3 A village in Oxfordshire, about six miles southwest of Oxford.
4 It is not clear which of the medieval wall paintings Elizabeth Fraser is tracing, but among those in the church at Northmoor are a crowned Madonna and "Our Lord in Glory."

170. HK to NF   205 Fulton Avenue [*Toronto*]
                                                    Dec. 14. 1936 —

My dearest:

I am sending some letters off tonight on the Queen Mary and I had expected a little more time but the mail closes at 7.30 to-morrow morning and no word as yet to you. I am at home but expect to get out on the long trail again presently—Wymilwood is my centre of gravity these days. I shall move home for Christmas and then go back again later. Your last letter came on Thursday and it was just in time to cheer me up again, for you evidently let two weeks go by also. I am very sorry. I just did not realize how the time was going. The Van Gogh show went down off the walls this morning so life will be a good deal easier from now on, I hope.

Such events as Christmas dinners, tea parties, the usual festivities, Burwash carol service last night, formal dinner party at Annesley next Friday, informal one at Wymilwood last Friday, lunch to-day with Miss Ray at Bienvenu.[1] Discussion: the King, bless his heart—i.e. Edward VIII. Everyone has been in a perfect turmoil here, and the papers have been pretty disgraceful. You have been out of it all and probably can't imagine how bad the American papers can be at times. I mean with this much time at Oxford you may have forgotten some of the vulgarity of the American tabloid. "Wallie meets Eddie," "Wallie in doctor's care"— etc. It has been pretty sickening. Now, of course, the Star is beginning to turn its machinery to build up a myth around George VI and we see him with his happy family and hear about how different he is from the late King, going to church on Sunday etc and sitting quietly at home with his wife who has influenza, poor dear. Preachers from all across Canada are quoted re the sanctity of home and family and the great trouble that has been averted. However, I gather that Canterbury is making a howling ass of himself, telling what evil ways Edward has fallen into.[2] The King's speech of farewell was one of the most impressive and heart-rending messages I have ever read. Not only that, beyond its evident sincerity, and simplicity, it was a piece of work of the most consummate cleverness, perhaps all unwittingly done.[3] I did not hear it, unfortu-nately, but Mother says it made Daddy weep, and he was not alone in that. We have heard so much talk, there has been such uncertainty and so many wild reports that one feels completely exhausted by it all. It has been a great victory for the Church, I suppose, and perhaps has done a great deal of good in rousing people to some sense of the solidarity of the empire—that is what Newton Rowell said, something about the empire machinery running smoothly. Hell, I think we let the King down, and that he was railroaded into the whole mess by the slandering yellow sheet American press. People stand around on streetcorners and the old girls yell about home and mother—they all scurry for shelter when a question like divorce comes up. Too many cling to their meal-tickets. Dorothy Forward says she almost interrupted a conversation in Britnell's[4] the other day between two self-righteous old prudes who had everything settled to their satisfaction.

Well, my dear, I did not mean to start on that subject. Here is a bit of news that is rather exciting: Roy won the Lincoln Hutton with his essay on the New Deal,[5] and we all feel pretty happy about it. Kay Coburn was all excited and Barbara [Sturgis] phoned to congratulate him and I nearly burst with pride and joy. I think I told you in my last about Marion's boy arriving. We have had no word since the cable.

It is past mid-night and I must post this now and go back to Wymil-wood. I do hope you arrange something more pleasant for Christmas than Guilford Street. Write a note to Edith [Burnett] or to Barbara's mother, or get Elizabeth [Fraser] to do something for Christmas day if nothing else materializes. But I am sure someone will invite you to spend it with them—I hope so. We are all missing you—Harold wished me to send his greetings, Mother wondered what you'd be doing, Daddy and Roy add their bit to the general message. By the way, Eleanor Caesar tells me that Cameron wired, he's got his Ph.D. and sails for home on the 16th, so I am going to be reception committee if he comes through Toronto. Barbara's home address is 12 Inkerman Terrace and it's in the phone book under Roland Sturgis—her father. I really must go now, will try to collect my wits in a few days to write you a decent letter.

To-morrow night Barbara is having a dinner-party at the flat. She asked me to come and help her out, the point being that the party is for Wilson Knight. Bob Orchard will be there too and I'll do my best but I do wish you were along. I'm so glad you've got Blunden properly impressed. What about chances of publishing the Blake? Is there any mention of that?

Harold keeps asking me whether I am going up north this summer. How does a summer in Muskoka appeal to you—or shall I come over there as we planned? Where the money is to come from I still don't know, and the rates have gone up, but I can't worry about that.

My love to you

Helen.

1 A restaurant located at 29 Bloor St. E.
2 On 4 December the archbishop of Canterbury, Cosmo Gordon Lang, had issued a statement calling on the British people "to refrain from speaking directly on matters which have arisen affecting the King himself and his subjects." On 13 December, however, he broadcast a message to the nation in which he spoke of the dark tragedy surrounding the abdication of Edward VIII, a message that many found offensive.
3 In a radio address delivered on 11 December 1936, Edward VIII commended to the British people his successor, George VI, who, the king said, "had one matchless blessing, enjoyed by so many of you and not bestowed on me—a happy home with his wife and children." He added, "I would have found it impossible . . . to discharge my duties as King as I would wish to do without the help and support of the woman I love." George VI was crowned on 12 May 1937.
4 A bookshop on Yonge St. in Toronto.
5 See Letter 157, n. 2, above.

171. NF to HK Oxford

Postmarked 17 December 1936; addressed to HK at 205 Fulton Ave., Toronto, Ontario, Canada.

Darling:

The Royal Society came through all right, with fifty pounds. Apparently I have to make a half-yearly report to Pelham [Edgar], he being my Canadian Supervisor.[1] They didn't tell me I *had* a Canadian supervisor, which is one reason for the hold-up.

I go down to London Dec. 19. I've been working quietly in my room. My only extravagance when the money came, apart from taking Elizabeth to dinner, was two volumes of Scarlatti—I've been doing a good deal of playing during this vac., as there's no one in the Mob Quad and I can play at any time of the day or night without anyone's hearing me. There are only a few left for meals now—two Australians, two Scotchmen and two Englishmen besides myself.

This letter will probably be late for Christmas—so of course will whatever I send you when I get to London. Thank you for the Zwemmer's book you mentioned you were sending. You rather took the wind out of my sails, as I had more or less assumed that anything I would send you would also come from Zwemmer's. However, London is a large and various place. I am getting a bit impatient with having the Atlantic Ocean sitting on all our Christmases—however, it won't be long until being separated from you for months on end will be only a sleeping nightmare instead of a waking one. At present Christmas is nothing but the fag-end of the year for me. Maybe in a few years there'll be so many descendants borrowing your stockings to hang up, the way I used to borrow Mother's, you'll have to spend your Christmases bare-legged.

Saturday Elizabeth [Fraser] and I went for a walk to a little village near here called Cumnor.[2] It was a lovely rainy day, with a carpet of golden-brown, maroon and madder leaves, pale green grass and black soil. Both of us felt fairly poor, as we had only a pound between us, but we went home and had supper, and then I came back to Merton to get something to read to Elizabeth and found the Royal Society's letter. The evening got perceptibly brighter after that. Tuesday we went to Aston again, the place Elizabeth lived last year. We dropped in on a lovely old lady—not so old at that—and her young nephew, who is studying at the Royal Academy of Music. He went out with us when we started walking, but as he's got T.B. and has to be careful he soon came home. We went into a little village called Compton[3] and had lunch, in a hideous parlor, waited on by an old man with two ideas (a) it seemed more like spring than winter (it did, too: it was a moist, hot, sappy sort of day) and (b) if Mrs. Simpson had only been a widow aaaah! He almost smacked his lips. Then we went into another village called Aldworth, which has a very interesting 14th c. Church with a lot of stone statues inside of some

Flemish family[4] who came over in Edward I's time. Some of the statues (they were recumbent, of course) were amazingly good—the women were quite unsuccessful, as they obviously were trying to avoid suggesting a body and couldn't let them sprawl properly—but some of the men were fine. There was a small lion too with a most lecherous expression on its face, some old carved pew-ends, and a yew in the churchyard a brochure said was a thousand years old. We had to walk back to Aston[5] for our tea, as all the pubs. were closed for some reason or other.

You speak of "Toronto's new morning newspaper"—I wonder if that would be the Toronto Globe and Mail I saw quoted in an Oxford paper and put down to provincial ignorance.[6] When A.E. Killam of Montreal bought the Mail & Empire in order to fight the St. Lawrence waterway he tried to buy the Globe too, and seems to have succeeded. Sometime you might look up this man Pavitt I met on the boat and see if you really have any paintings of his—I was quite interested in him and wonder how his coronation asters are getting on. Damn this bloody pen—cost me five and six and won't function at all.

I was examined last day of term by all the dons and the warden, the process being known as a donrag. Said donrag lasted ninety seconds, & consisted of a speech by Blunden and a purr from the warden. I mentioned it in my letter to Barbara, which I filled with the sort of Oxford gossip that doesn't get into my letters to you, on the principle that she'd come around and read it to you.

I don't think Blunden liked my thesis much—he said something vague about all the sentences being the same length—what I think he really resents is the irrefutable proof that Blake had a brain. I am afraid I shall have to ignore him and just go ahead.

This is a filthy letter—please excuse it. I'm at a bit of a loose end—perhaps London will improve matters. I don't think of you any more at Christmas than I do at any other time of year, or I should be quite unable to think of anything else. Don't mind me—it's just that everybody else has gone home to their mammas and left me cursing the Atlantic Ocean.

Norrie.

1 NF made his report to Edgar in a letter, dated 28 December, which he wrote while in London, mostly devoted to reviewing his plans for the Blake thesis. The letter is in the Pelham Edgar Collection, VU Library.
2 A Berkshire village, about four miles directly west of Oxford.

3 A small Berkshire town, about sixteen miles south of Oxford.
4 The church at Aldworth, a village two miles east of Compton, contains the tombs of the
   De la Beches, the Flemish family who came to England with William the Conqueror
   (not in the time of Edward I, as NF says). The small lion NF describes is on the tomb of
   John, the brother of Lady Joan De la Beche. The male stone figures were so tall that the
   villagers referred to them as the Giants.
5 A walk of some five miles.
6 See Letter 168, n. 4, above.

172. HK to NF   [*Toronto*]
                                                       Dec. 24. 1936.

My dearest, I have just re-read your letter postmarked Dec. 11 and
feel considerably relieved that the end of it is more cheerful than the
beginning. I am dreadfully sorry that your money did not come
through, and I feel seven different kinds of skinflint for not being able to
send you some. I was just paid yesterday or the day before, and I have at
last finished paying back what I borrowed for Roy's fees. I'd have
cabled you some then i.e. about 2£ (!) but considered that by now you
must have borrowed from someone in order to get to London. I do hope
you have looked up everyone you know. Roy [Daniells] has just had a
card from Harold Taylor at 44 Russell Square, and he sounds a little
lonely—living with Saul Rae, Roy says, wondering how that combination is working out. Cameron Caesar just 'phoned me to-day on his way
home. I'm going to visit Dot [Drever] in Guelph this week end and hope
to see him then. He asked me whether I wasn't sorry to be back, and I
thought that was an unfortunate beginning for him. He will feel very
strange at first, after two years away, just as you will when you come
back, but the strangeness wears off after a time. There is nothing like
having absorbing work to do to make one fit in, and he has a job waiting
for him here. Except for the political business I'd say he is in quite a
good position just now.
    Did I tell you that Roy won the prize for the Lincoln Hutton essay? I
believe I did. He's had the operation on his nose too, and is lying around
recuperating and reading. We are manufacturing the usual Christmas
excitement around home, especially Harold who is taking Marion's place
as Christmas enthusiast. We have a little tree and I have been out shopping for small things. We are to be alone this year and we will miss you
like anything. I sent a card to your mother and said so. I had a sort of fellow feeling, remembering how many Christmases you had been away

from home. I sat and thought and thought and worried how I was going to write the greeting on that card—after all it was the first one I ever sent to your family. And Roy was sitting opposite me and writing a letter to Jessie Johnston whom he took to the Hart House Masquerade this year— he tore up page after page until there was a pile of four pages rejected. The fifth won out and was sent. So when he said anything about my pen-biting all I had to do was look with scorn at his letter. Harold did not help matters at all: he kept practicing the most bull froggy sounding exercises on his çello in the next room and asking how our letters were progressing. Then he'd offer suggestions and keep an eye on the clock because he boasted that he was practicing for two hours this time. He really is doing very well, and plays in two school orchestras now. When we try playing trios he reads quite well. You'll be surprised when you hear him. Also, his voice has cracked and he recently got a job as Father Bear in Bessie Ayres' marionette show at the Heliconian Club.

I've got a raise—$900 a year instead of $750, beginning last October, but I don't get the benefit of it until January. Let me know whether I can help you then.

I have some bad news for you. Lou Epstein has cancer of the throat and is in Mt. Sinai Hospital and not expected to get better. I did not hear of it until last week when Norah [McCullough] mentioned him: Edmund MacDonald had spoken of one of the most brilliant students he ever had, dying of cancer. Norah 'phoned the doctor who said he'd had all kinds of treatments and a nerve operation recently to relieve the pain. Roy said he'd been to New York last year to see a specialist and had got a very raw deal. Roy met Epstein through Isabel Ricker several times. There is also the story that Epstein was nearly bled white in his college days paying alimony or some such thing to a girl that he'd married when he was eighteen and that he is still supporting a child. Roy said the New York doctor had not treated him because he was a Jew and had no money, but Norah can't see why he would go to New York for treatment when there are good cancer specialists in Toronto. Anyhow I've asked Mrs Arnold whether anyone is looking after him and she is going to find out more about him—she had no idea that his throat condition was so serious.

Charlie Holmes has a job as a civil servant in Ottawa, Grace Elliot told me at the Annesley dinner the other night, and he is pretty lonely and disgusted with the town. However, since he has just been there two weeks I told her he should be more optimistic. I've written to the Carmans to look him up. I nearly said "Oh Betty Burt is there" and then stopped in time, considering that Grace would hardly appreciate my introducing him to an ex-flame. The Christmas dinner was all very well: everyone in best plumage and in the cloak room afterwards some of the dowagers compared notes on Moff Woodside's wife's clothes at the president's reception the night before. Times like that I feel like throwing a bomb at the bourgeois dames. Miss Nickle, the don from Australia, has some amusing stories about her tea with the archangel Michael[1] who offered her cigarettes, and how she talked Socialism with Mrs F. Louis Barber who she discovered was one of the Best People so tried deliberately to give her a jolt or two.

Barbara's [Barbara Sturgis's] dinner the other night was very successful from some points of view—Bob Orchard and Wilson Knight talked to each other most of the evening and thus enjoyed themselves. Knight expressed surprise at my knowing you and I affected a casual acquaintance with you which led him to maintain vigorously that you were about to publish the best book on Blake written up to the present. He said it was unfortunate that Blunden is your tutor in some ways because his interest is not in Blake—more in little histories like the life of Keats' publisher.

As a mildly academic question: is there any objection to our getting married this summer? Does it matter if an Oxford undergraduate is married? After all, you are not a minor, and I am beginning to pull out white hairs, so your spouse is a pretty hoary female.

I must go to Danforth[2] now and post this. It is a sad mixture of news items, I'm afraid, but I will try to write something more amusing in a few days. I must get to work on German next week as I have not done anything about it for two months now. The bands and choirs from different churches are singing everywhere to-night, I wonder what you are doing this Christmas Eve. I am so glad that Elizabeth [Fraser] is on hand to cheer you up a bit when necessary, and I've no doubt she is glad to see you too. What about Veronica Wedgwood?

I love you very very much, my dear, and I hope you get my little book before long. I will send you some more New Yorkers on Monday.

Helen

1 John Hugh Michael, an expert on the book of Revelation, who taught New Testament at Emmanuel College.
2 Danforth Ave., two blocks south of the Kemps' home on Fulton Ave.

173. NF to HK   Paddington
                                                                        Dec. 30. [*1936*]

Postmarked 31 December 1936; addressed to HK at 84, Queen's Park, Toronto, Ontario, Canada.

Sweetheart:

I'm staying with Edith and Stephen [Burnett], and I've been here for a week. I like being here, although it isn't the easiest place in the world to work, and Edith and Stephen are very good to me and have made everything very pleasant. They went down to Kent (Stephen's father's home) for Wednesday and came back yesterday, leaving me in charge. The day I came down (Dec. 19) I went to tea at Lady Francis Ryder's—the lady herself has retired, and a number of "hostesses" are there to be maternal. The first time I went it was horrible—the place was full of fat New Zealanders in the butter business and corn-fed females who discussed the weather and Mrs. Simpson. I went back on Wednesday and found (my brains are completely addled: I haven't the energy to fight anybody)[1] a solid mass of Canadians, including Saul Rae, a Rhodes man—no, he can't be Rhodes—he's at the School of Economics—Kylie, I guess—who recognized me and gave me the addresses of all the Canadian colony in Bloomsbury, including Henry Noyes and Harold Taylor. I shall start looking them up soon. The tea was much better, the hostess, a Mrs. Fry (she affects the curtailment) being a very intelligent woman and drawing us out for all she was worth. I got an invitation to lunch on Christmas Day which I took rather unwillingly, as I wanted to remain hermetically sealed on Christmas, but saw no good reason for declining. The place was in one of the most complicated parts of Kensington and took a long time to find. Rae was there again and two exotic females—a Latvian who did most of the talking (I never met anyone from the Baltic States who didn't) and a Viennese. Neither very interesting, though the latter was funny: the hostess asked her if she spoke French and she said: "Fluently, madame, and Italian too." The house itself was a bit depressing: a parlor a solid mess of unpleasant furniture, a fireplace with Ionic columns on each side with relief carvings of females holding up sheets over their navels with one hand and balancing grapes and things with the other—all in the sort of marble that never looks clean—a wedding-cake ceiling, and so on. The host was Gladstone's grandson and looked it. However, they were very pleasant and I had a good time. On Boxing Day Elizabeth [Fraser] came down—she was getting a bit fed up in Oxford—and we went out to dinner and went to see *Murder in the Cathedral* but Elizabeth got sick, almost fainted and had to be brought home in a taxi and sent to bed with a hot-water-bottle. Sunday she was all right, but we didn't do much except go to Soho for dinner, which I didn't like much. Monday morning Amy, the maid, came in and announced that she had spent Christmas neither drunk nor sober, but "just happy." I don't know if you met her, but she's sweet—wide and good-natured and sentimental. We went out to Hampton Court that day, saw some rather dim pictures, and then completely exhausted ourselves staring at that *glorious* Mantegna[2] for over an hour. Mantegna must be the very greatest painter who ever lived, no matter what anyone else has done. Incidentally, the day I came down I went to Zwemmer's and got that book for you. My mind rather misgave me—it's a rather pompously pedantic sort of Christmas present, and the paper is the sort you cut your fingers on and I would have liked a few colours, but I was told with some hauteur by the clerk that reproducing processes would only caricature the artist's intentions, and it was the only thing they had on Mantegna and I had come in with a sort of *idée fixe* that I'd get something on Mantegna, and I didn't have the nerve to look a Zwemmer's clerk in the eye and say "And what other painters have you?" So there it is.

Well, anyway, Tuesday we went to see *Murder in the Cathedral* again. It's a wonderful play all right—read it sometime. It will probably come to Toronto anyway. The chorus of women was full of the loveliest poetry, and as a play it came off very well. I had reserved tickets for this performance, but through a very fortunate error (at least I assume it was an error) we got seats in the front row of the dress circle, where we were practically breathing down the actor's necks. The female functionary who had fluttered around Elizabeth Saturday evening and offered her peppermint lozenges came up in the intermission and said "Are you feeling better now, dear?" Elizabeth left early to get the last train back to Oxford, which leaves at eleven and is called the "Fornicator" by the Oxford students.

I had a card from Baine, in Italy and still cold. Also an SOS call from [Joseph] Reid, who is in Paris and doesn't know any French. Which reminds me that Edith [Burnett] and Elizabeth and I went to see a French film called *Le Kermesse Héroique*[3] which had some rather good

Breughelesque scenes, though the plot was the same dreary triangle with the fat cuckold.

Oh, dear, life with Edith is strenuous. I had got this far yesterday. Just before lunch. Then a hideous Jewess with a voice like the breaking up of an ice floe (I wonder if I ever make that unpleasant series of nasalized honks?) came in, and her fat stern had hardly disappeared through the door when in came the incarnation of Toronto—a girl named Ruth Gunther who knows Jean Wishart. Bishop Strachan School,[4] undergraduate drawl, an art student, but otherwise exactly like all the other females I have endeavored to introduce to Pope and Marlowe. I had scarcely viewed her stern with satisfaction when in came two relatives to dinner. They were quite nice, but they didn't leave until I was too exhausted with being pleasant and too stupefied with drinking sherry and a poisonous red Spanish concoction to do anything but sleep.

I have never missed you more since I went away than I do now—the same physically sick feeling I had two summers ago and never thought I'd have again. Oh, Helen!

Edith sends her love.

Norrie.

Surely I've mentioned your Zwemmer book, which I liked very much. I haven't decided whether to leave them there or take them out and frame them—probably the former. Thank you, darling.

N.

1 For "found" NF had first written "fought" and then cancelled it.
2 *The Triumph of Julius Caesar*, a famous series of tempera paintings executed by Mantegna in 1485–94 for the Duke of Mantua and bought by Charles I in 1629.
3 A 1935 French film, directed by Jacques Feyder, satirizing the daring and resourcefulness of wartime citizens threatened by invaders.
4 An Anglican-affiliated private school for girls founded in 1867, the year of Confederation. Originally located on Jarvis St. in downtown Toronto, it moved to its current location at 298 Lonsdale Rd. in 1915.

174. HK to NF   [*Toronto*]
                                                                Jan 6. 1937.

My dearest: I'm beginning to feel like a pig for not writing to you— work is the only excuse. I worked all through the holidays—the days I had off I spent on mild celebrations like eating turkey and a trip to Guelph for two days. The rest of the time was gallery and Greek sculpture. My study group begins again to-morrow and I'm apt to have a dozen women, and I'm going to give them a dose of Greek sculpture. And I have the curse, which always takes away any brain power I may ordinarily have.

Thanks so much for the Mantegna, my dear. It is very nice of you, now at last I have a German book of my own to read, and the gallery does not possess the Klassiker der Kunst Mantegna, so I'm one up on them.[1] I haven't had more than four German lessons and they were back in October. What I'm to do about it I don't know, everything is so complicated, with our gallery programme as full as usual. We've got Dr Held lecturing on Flemish art two nights a week, and he is so good that I feel that I should attend his lectures. German Jew from Berlin, lecturing for Carnegie people.

The residence goes on as usual. I'm at Addison House this week (ex New House)[2] because the don went to San Francisco for holidays and is not back yet.

My raise went through all right. Baldie [Martin Baldwin] told me to-day that the committee would not make it retro-active from October, as they say they lose $4000 a year on the gallery etc etc, but this year I get $900. I just lose a matter of $45 which is nothing to a millionaire but considerable to me, as I told Baldie. He said he was ashamed of them but did not feel he could disagree lest they give me nothing. I told him that was a bit thick when I saw high school teachers with their $1700 a year (Marg Torrance: Sandwich) and he said he felt the same way when he saw American directors getting twice as much as he does. He gets $4500 per year and Mr Milliken at Cleveland gets $15,000 I think. However, it is all a matter of scale, and I would say that the $150 is a lot more use to me, proportionately, than it would be to Milliken. He tells me that Band brought up the point about losing people like Freda [Pepper] if they don't loosen up with their money. Norah [McCullough] fully expects Dorothy Medhurst to be asked to go to Detroit next year to help Freda. I'm not really crabbing, you know, just—.

Roy and Harold and I went to hear Stravinsky conduct Petroushka and the Firebird last night.[3] Harold brought a young lady named Georgina Gibson, who plays the çello and is in the two orchestras Harold plays in. He is getting quite fond of her and spent his Christmas money taking her to the concert, and as we thought he was a little young we went, too. Especially as I had asked him to go with me, in the first place, only to find that I was too late. So it turned out very well. Stravinsky certainly made the orchestra do things that MacMillan never managed.

My dear, my dear! Your mother sent me a Christmas card and I was so happy! That was awfully sweet of her—at least it was signed Mr and Mrs H.E. Frye but I thought it was more likely to be her writing. I was so glad that your money came through at last. The Mail and Globe is the new morning paper bought by George McCullagh who claims to be taking the best out of the two old papers. Hell of a rag.

I am so sick of having no time to send you a decent letter. I haven't told you anything about the Tudor Singers'[4] concert at the Gallery or the children's entertainment or Dorothy [Drever] or Cameron [Caesar] whom I saw in Guelph just after his arrival, or anything else. And I've *got* to do something about this class to-morrow now, and I said I'd drop in with Dorothy Forward to see Florence Smith at ten. (Getting chummy, you notice. I intend to.) I don't know anything about Roy Daniells—he's still telling Ev Stewart she's the only woman he'll ever marry. I tried to get him in the holidays but he was never in, or else nobody answered the 'phone. So I don't know what sort of time he had.

I feel so strange having all this busy life away from you. The year is going terribly fast, too fast for the amount of work I hoped to get done, but wonderfully fast when I think of you. I'm so glad Elizabeth [Fraser] is there to go walking and exploring those marvellous churches. Barbara [Sturgis] went to Washington for New Year's. I haven't seen her since. She has a relative there. I love you *very* much, and I hope my accent won't strike you like a meat-axe when next you hear it. Oh I remember, we did go over *that*. Here's some gossip. Kay Riddell is said to have gone home to her mother twice this fall because of arguments with Jerry—(1) she is an Oxford Grouper and (2) doesn't want him to smoke in the house. Did I tell you Fred Housser died just before Christmas? What about Spain?

Helen.

Your nephew: doing well, Irwin Hubert Harrison.

1 HK's Christmas present was Fritz Knapp's *Andrea Mantegna*, first published in Stuttgart in 1910; she quite likely received the 2nd ed. (Stuttgart: Deutsche Verlags-Anstalt, 1926). Knapp's book was vol. 16 in the Klassiker der Kunst in Gesamtausgaben series.
2 HK has written "137" above "New House," meaning 137 Bloor St. W.

3 Stravinsky was guest conductor for the TSO concert at Massey Hall on 5 January. On the same program, Sir Ernest MacMillan conducted Brahms's Symphony No. 4.
4 A choral group directed by Healey Willan.

175. HK to NF   84 Queens Park, Toronto.
                                                        January 8? 1937.

Postmarked 14 January 1937; addressed to NF at Merton College, Oxford, England, Via New York: "Bremen." *The question mark HK puts after "January 8" implies uncertainty about the date, and indeed her opening remarks indicate that the letter was begun on Sunday, which was 10 January.*

My dear: Back in Wymilwood once more, Sunday morning, under Laura Muntz Lyall's 'Mother and Child' with hymns coming up through the floor from a church service over the caretaker's radio. Miss Manning has just gone to the chapel service with Blanche Van Allen, both unwillingly, but the Chancellor sent Miss Manning an invitation to come with a friend and she feels that it can not be ignored. The preacher is a man named Vipond who was in Blanche Van Allen's year at college, and therefore the prophet lacks interest for her.

I believe I got a letter off last Wednesday by a miracle of sorts—Sunday morning here sometimes is about the one saving of my sanity, and this is definitely such a time. I was in New House: now Addison House, all last week but moved back thankfully last night. Breakfast at Annesley Hall with Kay Coburn reading the newspaper, Jessie Mac [Macpherson] reading the newspaper, Florence Smith uncommunicative though mildly affable, Miss MacDougall the young dietitian from Mac Hall sweet amiable, timid and without many ideas beyond her food problem, Dorothy Forward as usual willing to talk about something and not particularly grumpy. About once a month over there I come in for a concerted attack about something. The first time it was about music as an accompaniment to eating or conversation—Jessie Mac tackled me on that because I had not remonstrated with my girls when she was in to tea one Sunday and the radio was left on quietly. I suppose you agree with her on that point, but when you've got a crowd of people that need to be melted a little, a gentle noise in the background seems to help. So there I was defending that position, I being very little accomplished at debating. The last encounter was Kay's [Kay Coburn's] attack on my well-meaning remark that Pride and Prejudice I had heard was well worth going to see for the costumes alone.[1] (Florence Smith had expressed disappointment in the dramatization of it but admitted it was pretty nearly impossible to telescope the dialogue and please her with conversation which she knew thoroughly.) Kay pounced of course and supposed that I would go to any poor play for the costumes, and would I go to Pride and Prejudice for the stage setting, and what rank heresy anyhow. One trouble with being in the first stage of the curse is that I blush so easily, and can not get any action when stuck against the wall and prodded. I thought of Gordon Webber and how he'd enjoyed the play in New York and described it when he returned, knowing nothing whatever of Jane Austen and regarding the language as something quite foreign. (God what a sentence!) Maybe I'll spend my life like Goldsmith in Johnson's circle, stuttering and stammering when a remark is addressed to me.[2] However, I did not come off so badly, as I held out for the dignity of setting and costumes in ballet for instance and the appeal to the eye through form and colour and movement and Dorothy Forward and the Smith [Florence Smith] helped me out a little. Naturally, I think all that is outside the real reason for enjoying Jane Austen, but then I don't see why Jane Austen need be dramatized. I said someone had complained about the Tudor Singers not being in costume, and I thought that was rather silly because Willan's idea is to put across the informality of Elizabethan family singing. So there I was on the other side and Kay gave up her attack.

Yesterday I went with Norah [McCullough] to the Picture Loan Society—did I tell you that it started about three months ago?[3] Gordon Webber, Gordon MacNamara, Norah [McCullough], Douglas Duncan, Rik Kettle, Pegi Nicol are the committee. They are giving the first one man show this week—Carl Schaefer. I rented one of Webber's called "Pink Rock," a lovely thing with green sumacs and blue sky sketched in above great folds of MacGregor Bay stone. It is opaque colour over brown paper and very swiftly done. Mounted on grey—looks marvelous against my white wall. Douglas Duncan has just acquired a very delicate African Sketch from Will Ogilvie—a study in rhythmic lines, touched up with brown and reds very delicately—just a small thing. Douglas is a nice soul—yesterday was the first time I had talked to him much.

Did I tell you that Pegi Nicol married the man a week or so ago—I mean the young man she was living with, not Duncan![4] I forget these things.

I'm going to see Alford on Tuesday, about the exam. We're getting a heavy programme lined up for the February architects' show and I *don't* see how I can do any extra work. German is still a lost cause, except that I do a little from time to time at translating titles. We have asked Lescaze to come and give a lecture, if he can't we may try for Lewis Mumford. Dr. Held is still giving the Flemish painting series. He was feeling very depressed before his lecture the other day and if I had not invited Ramona Laplante to dinner I would have taken him out somewhere and cheered him up. Norah [McCullough] did however, gathering up Gordon Webber and MacNamara and they went to Little Denmark. I chatted away with him before dinner and found out he was worried about Baldwin who had been rude to him, and he'd just received news of the death of an old professor of his, and that he was sick of the monastic life of Hart House where he was staying, and tired of jumping from Toronto to Detroit and London and Toronto then a week touring the Maritimes then back to Toronto etc. After dinner he got up and prepared to leave saying in his German way, he'd have to go back to his Hart House and its Mr—Mr—Mr. Stickelbitch,[5] fumbling for the name. Peggy Kidder wondered whether he knew what he was meaning in English!

Wednesday night.

Darling, I've been to Alford, I went yesterday. Yesterday opened gloriously with a letter from you, all about your stay with Edith and Stephen [Burnett], and I was so glad you were all right. Then I went to see the old mugwump and he advised me not to attempt it this spring— thinks I should enrol as a graduate student and come to his lectures. Well, maybe I should, but *after all*, I have a job in the daytime, and while I could get off for some lectures—well it is impossible. He says, of course if it is a matter of doing it for my job he wouldn't bother, but if it is a case of getting a job somewhere else it would be a good thing to have academic qualification from a recognized institution. He is so discouraging and so pompous and dull and afraid to commit himself. There are times when all I can do is to hate him, helplessly. However, Douglas MacAgy turned up last night and we went for a long walk and had some beer, and Douglas told me some of his adventures lately with Alford, who is on very shaky ground in aesthetics and laid himself wide open to attack the other day. He has been attending a few of MacCallum's lectures Douglas said. Anyhow we had a very cheerful time and I felt better.

Here it is, the middle of January. I've done some work on Greek Sculpture. Just how long it would take to organize what I know on the rest of the field (!) I don't know. And there isn't an earthly chance of getting time off before May to work at the stuff consistently. It is all so silly—here I have a wonderful job, full of interest which keeps me hopping all the time, and I'm worrying because I haven't got academic qualifications. Just the same, I feel on devilish thin ice sometimes. Then I go back to work and feel that we are making history in these parts, and devil take the diploma. Look at all the diploma students who have no jobs! Baldwin is quite discouraging about the diploma business—thinks I'm crazy to think about it at all. But then I don't take his advice very much to heart. If only you weren't in England things might be a little simpler—I might spend the summer in New York for instance, and start a course there. I very definitely need some further training soon, and of course it might be possible next year to do some work under Brieger or Alford, but this high pressure stuff is not easy, and you know how I like Alford.

I wish I knew what you intend doing next summer. I suppose you will travel on the continent, unless war breaks out all over the place. You should go to Italy in the spring, if you are going, the weather is best then, it will be glorious. Summer is too hot. You should go for Easter and get in touch with International Student Tours and go with a gang, it doesn't matter, you leave them as soon as you arrive, and it saves a good deal. Several pounds. Ask Miss Thorneycroft for the address. Peggy Kidder talks of going to Europe on a freighter and I may go with her. It's very cheap, but slow. I could meet you in London and I suppose we could go somewhere—I feel so vague at this point, not knowing what your ideas are on the matter, when your term ends, what the financial situation will be next year, what you feel about my last proposition. If only you were here to talk to, but all these bewildering problems have to wait and wait and crawl back and forth across the ocean. I am very tired of the Atlantic. You are not thinking of coming home next summer I suppose, or are you? What about getting a job in the summer school for six weeks here? {Just an idea that occurs to me at the moment.} You said you wanted a year to roam around by yourself— what if I stay on this side this summer and come over the *next* year? {Oh Lord!} I've got to get something settled soon because I'll have to see about boats, and coronation time is VERY BAD.[6] I could not leave here before May 24th anyway, I suppose, with this don business to think about too. It really is not too bad—in spite of my grumbling about Kay Coburn etc, I'm enjoying it immensely.

The Annesley At-Home is this Friday. I don't think I will go, in spite of the invitation. I don't want to have to dress again, I don't want to take Roy Daniells, and I'd sooner do other things with Douglas MacAgy, and Roy (Kemp) is going with Helen Carscallen. So it's all rather difficult, and as I have a lecture to give to Ruth Home's museum women, I'd better get ready for that. Classicism in France, end of 18th c. I'm going to summarize the first lecture on Rococo for contrast, define classicism—show Greek sculpture etc, then compare it with Greek ideal as understood by Raphael—in School of Athens for instance. Then dive into Ingres and David and the rest. I think it should be all right. I have learned something this year at any rate, I enjoy painting and sculpture myself a lot more, and that goes a long way. Had a fan letter to-day from some teacher in B.C. who had read my article in "The School"[7]—much too bowed at the knee but made me feel good just the same.

We've been making out reports to Carnegie, and Baldwin makes wild statements, Norah [McCullough] objects and she and I do the blue pencilling.[*]

I took the Vic people to see Yvonne's [Williams] studio to-day and Yvonne talked about stained glass. She really is remarkable when she is on her own ground, and I was quite thrilled myself. We went to see Jackson one other day[8]—I may have told you. I don't know what we'll do next time, perhaps review the gallery show, or go to see Joan Fairley or something—I'd have to think it over. If I don't take on the diploma thing I might try doing some magazine articles on something or other, I've got one on the Grange I'd like to do, for one thing. I might go see Byrne Sanders and see if I could sell her an article for tired mothers in her magazine.

I weakened on Sunday and 'phoned Roy [Daniells] and we went for a walk, dropping in to see Harold and Bessie Ayres toward the end. Roy irritates me beyond measure, at times, and I could shake him for his lack of thoughtfulness—he is just letting his connection with Peggy [Roseborough] and Mary [Winspear] slip into the past out of sheer indolence.

---

[*] Wild statement: Mr Lismer's enthusiasm etc etc has been sorely missed this year, but on the other hand the staff has ably stepped into the breach and the *work has in no way suffered from his absence* (!) {We yanked *that* out!} Continuing my foot-note I might add that Norah firmly believes in her dismal moments that Baldwin is trying to oust Lismer. I'm not sure of that but I do say he is *the* most tactless man I know of.

Says he has no means of paying back their hospitality, the wretch, and I say—why not take them out to dinner occasionally? But he said he didn't want to and he hadn't time etc etc—and he has loads of time for all his little undergraduate students. And of course I have to do all the organizing when I want to see him, which I do quite firmly whether he likes it or not. But the only time he asks me to do anything with him is when he has to have a gorgon attend his teas, and I'm *not* feeling awfully flattered. However, when I feel the need of masculine company I 'phone him up and feel very fond of him. I suppose it is his courageous bachelor whistling in the dark that annoys me—he keeps on telling me how wonderful it is to live in Burwash as he does, blissfully without care—and then he tells me how wonderful Evelyn [Stewart] is, and then Dorothy [Drever] tells me how devoted he is and Roy (K) tells me how the men have diagnosed Daniells as needing a woman badly and how they speculate about his feminine friends. Then Roy talks to me in his amused way about how funny Barbara and Frances look, and asks me what's wrong with Dorothy Drever—patronisingly, I thought. I was pretty mad about that last, and he said he thought she was a little too ingratiating. So I said yes it was a tendency in her that I disliked but that I felt her association with Ev Stewart was perhaps developing that trait a little too much, that Ev had a tendency to ride over people—that struck home, I saw, so I let it go. Other people can prod with pins, too.

Dot has joined the Communist Party—last fall—this she told me the other night, in confidence, so don't mention it unless she has already told you. Dot is fairly happy, I think, concerned about her mother who is not well, and also about her place in society when she can not openly state her position because of fear for her job. Ricker proposed at Christmas and she settled that score—she thought she had done so before. Then he sent her a copy of "Live Alone and Like It"[9] for Christmas and she didn't know what to do! Dot is patronised by Ev quite a bit, in their relationship, and she allows Ev to boss her, and consults her in household matters which she is quite capable of looking after herself. And she adopts certain cooing baby ways of talking that quite give me the hump. I like Ev Stewart very much, but I wish to God I could find a wonderful man for Dot, who would make her feel a swell gal herself, instead of a pale haired white-faced school teacher who lives with Ev Stewart who is engaged to Ted Avison and sought after by Roy Daniells, and two or three upper Canada men all at one and the same time. Dot has her school made permanent now and she is going to night school. She has debts to pay this year so is not investing in clothes—and she ought to buy something very dashing and get out of the grey coat, black hat, navy dress stuff.

Goodness, I *am* grumbling to-night. With Spain in ruins and Hitler about to pounce, and heaven knows what going on in Europe, I go on at this length about my own little world. Still, it is my own little world and I'm trying to tell you about it. I'll go and post this! Roy said last time I saw him that one thing he was sure of was that so long as you and I had a crust of bread he would have a crust of bread—I, thinking of his feeding me tea so much and agreed that he was laying up stores in heaven. But my hope of heaven was a little nearer than he thought. All I can do is hope, hope, my dearest, lest the world crumble about our heads and everything we care for perish. I had a lovely note from your Aunt yesterday, from B.C.[10]

Helen

1 The Road Company had staged a production of *Pride and Prejudice* which toured theatres in Canada and the United States during 1936 and 1937.
2 Numerous such anecdotes about Oliver Goldsmith are recounted by James Boswell. Goldsmith had, says Boswell, "a more than common share of that hurry of ideas which we often find in his countrymen, and which sometimes produces a laughable confusion in expressing them." Boswell, *The Life of Samuel Johnson*, ed. Arnold Glover, 3 vols. (London: J.M. Dent, 1901), 1:276.
3 The Picture Loan Society, Canada's first art rental, was founded in 1936 at 3 Charles St. W. in Toronto. In addition to the members of the "committee" mentioned by HK, Erma Lennox Sutcliffe was also a founding member. The PLS made arrangements for the public to rent paintings for a modest fee (2 per cent of a painting's value per month) and to buy them either outright or on instalment. Rik Kettle first suggested the idea of the PLS, having come across a similar rental organization in England in 1934. Douglas Duncan became the moving force behind the PLS. See Kettle's account of the PLS in *Douglas Duncan: A Memorial Portrait* (Toronto: U of T Press, 1974), 50–5.
4 Nicol married Norman MacLeod in December 1936.
5 Dr. Held was trying to recall the name of J.B. Bickersteth, warden of Hart House.
6 HK is worrying about the crowds that would come to England for the coronation of George VI on 12 May 1937.
7 See Letter 142, n. 1, above.
8 According to HK's records of the program for her Thursday morning study group the visit to Yvonne Williams's studio was originally scheduled for 7 December, and the visit to A.Y. Jackson's studio for 2 November. See HFF, 1993, box 4, file 6.
9 *Live Alone and Like It: A Guide for the Extra Woman*, a book about unmarried women by Marjorie Hillis Roulston (Indianapolis: Bobbs-Merrill, 1936).
10 According to HK's letter of 20 January (Letter 179), it was NF's Aunt Hatty who was on vacation in British Columbia.

176. NF to HK   London
Jan. 11. [*1937*]

Postmarked 11 January 1937; addressed to HK at 84, Queen's Park, Toronto,
Ontario, Canada.

Sweetheart:

I have been staying with Edith and Stephen [Burnett] ever since my last
letter, and will remain here until the end of this week, when I go back to
Oxford. For some reason or other Merton College hasn't forwarded my
mail—I wrote them to change the forwarding address to here and they
got all confused and didn't send anything but a bill for fifty pounds. I am
going to cut my expenses next term, I can see that. Less of Merton's very
excellent cider. I have just put in the dimmest week I've yet had since
coming to England—six days of reading 1600 lines of *Beowulf* and being
so exhausted when evening came that I could do nothing but go to bed.
Christ, what a language. And such a stupid dreary story.

I got cards from Veronica Wedgwood[1] and Doris McGroggins[2]—I
don't know who she is, but suspect her of having been originally Doris
Livingston. I've been calling Veronica at intervals without success, and
shall go to see her this week, I hope. I have a rather good time being the
oil between the Edith and Stephen cogs—I described the situation here
to Elizabeth [Fraser] as a *Doll's House* deadlock,[3] and I think that's about
what it is—Stephen babies Edith, and Edith is just mature enough to
resent it and make him look a fool, and just naive enough to justify him
to some extent and make her resentment little more than occasional
explosions of ill-temper. She has the uneasy conscience of a woman who
isn't quite satisfied with either housekeeping or a career, though both
attract her, and is at present taking an L.C.C. course in life drawing,
weaving and textile designing, intending to sell her designs later on.[4]
Both are nice, and I like them. Stephen is an industrious stamp collector,
and I have done just enough of that to be able to talk intelligently about
it, and besides I have a Newfoundland set somewhere in my drawer at
Oxford I can give him—Louise Whiteway gave it to me. I do a good deal
of reading to Edith, who likes being read to.

A letter of Edith's you had shown me had led me to believe I would
be walking into one of those frenetic Communist brotherhoods. Actually, they had a Jew staying with them during the summer who bawled
Edith out so often for her lack of a social conscience that she got rather

tired of it. She has no politics at all, and Stephen's amount only to a choice of newspapers. Saturday we had a Canadian banker in to dinner with a noisy and poisonous wife who could have been very charming if she wanted to be, and yesterday we went to tea with them and, to my great disgust, stayed for supper. J.S. Woodsworth's son was there—he's studying at the London School of Economics.

I have wasted more time this vacation even than usual—enough to last me the rest of my life, I should think. The more time I spend with you, the more I seem able to get done. Congratulations on your rise—I never imagined they'd get it into their fat heads you were doing more than $750 worth of work there, especially with Lismer away. Of course I'll marry you next summer, on one very reasonable condition: *Habeas Corpus*. You must produce the body. I can't marry you by correspondence: if I could we'd have had grandchildren already. Perhaps with your rise you will feel more like coming over this summer. I'm not going to rewrite the letters I've already written on this subject, partly because nothing I can say seems to have any effect, partly because I don't want to keep bullying you. I suspect your family of digging at you again. It isn't quite fair to ask me to come back to Canada this summer, but if you ditch your whole scheme of coming over yourself I suppose I shall have to, as I can't very well face the prospect of not seeing you for still another year. My heartiest congratulations to Roy: I'd like to see his essay sometime. The impetus of that should carry him through the year all right.

God, it takes me a long time to write even a short letter, particularly when there's no news. Doris [Moggridge] tells me that Helen Stevens is at Oxford. I must look up Henry Noyes before I go back too.[5]

Lovingly,

Norrie.

1 Wedgwood wrote NF a card on 28 December from Stoke-on-Trent, saying, "I hope to see you when you get back to London in a few days." See HFF, 1991, box 3, file 1.
2 NF means Doris Moggridge; he corrects himself in his letter of 17 January 1937 (Letter 177).
3 The allusion is to the relationship between Nora Helmer and her husband, Torvald, in Ibsen's *A Doll's House*.
4 Edith Burnett was taking a course at the Central School of Arts and Crafts, which was run by the London County Council (LCC).
5 Noyes, who had received his M.A. in English from the U of T, and NF had been in some of the same graduate classes; in 1937 he was studying for his Ph.D. at the University of London. Letter 177 indicates that NF did visit Noyes before returning to Oxford.

177. NF to HK Oxford

Postmarked 17 January 1937; addressed to HK at 84, Queen's Park, Toronto, Ontario, Canada. NF says he hasn't heard from HK since her letter of the 26th, apparently the postmarked date of her letter of 24 December 1936.

Sweetheart:

No letter from you since the one dated the 26th. I'm back in Oxford now, having spent the whole vacation with Edith and Stephen [Burnett]. The last week I tried looking up a few friends. Monday I went to see Henry Noyes—he was in bed with the 'flu. A man named, I think, McKay was there.[1] Henry says he hasn't been doing much on Moore lately, that a book which just came out on him covered a lot of obscure gossip and saved him a lot of work without crabbing his job,[2] and that he's tickled to get the I.O.D.E.[3] The other man, who I think was 36 Victoria, but am not sure, is, like Henry, the son of a Chinese missionary,[4] and he's writing a book—free-lance—on the collapse of the Ming dynasty in China. I had a good time with them. Tuesday I went to see Doris Moggridge—I don't know where I got the idea her name was McGroggins. She was Doris Livingston all right, but with a difference: round, plump, and a bit soggy, with a start on a double chin. Her mind has got a bit soggy too—mostly details of housekeeping. Her husband wasn't much help either. Altogether a somewhat depressing visit. He works in a Ford factory somewhere away out east of London. Thursday, lunch with Veronica Wedgwood. And *she's* writing a book—on the Thirty Years' War.[5] A very charming girl, is Veronica—she's thawed out a little more progressively each time I've seen her. This time she was very much more at her ease than before, and everything went off beautifully. I got *Beowulf* read again, by some miracle, and Friday morning came up here. Yesterday I wrote Blunden's term exam—collections they call them here. It was pretty bad—he seemed to have simply opened his Chaucer at random to pick out spotting passages. I wasn't in very good condition for it either—for the last few days I've been vaguely wondering if the 'flu epidemic is going to catch me—I've been pretty dizzy and even stupider than usual lately. Also I saw Dickinson again, packing up to leave for Russia. He tells me not to send him any counter-revolutionary letters, as he's afraid they'll all be steamed open before they reach him at Leningrad.

Sorry if I barked a bit at you in connection with your coming over this summer. Suppose I go to Italy this vacation: then I'll have just enough money, when the final instalment of my scholarship comes in, to buy a ticket home. Oxford is really too expensive to let me do anything with my vacs.—I was pretty lucky this last time. But of course I could ask the College to advance me enough to keep me here this summer, and certainly marriage in England would be a lot less fuss than in Canada—besides, there'd be visiting my parents to consider. This altogether apart from whether or not you want your diploma. The one thing I do know is that I'm going to see you this summer. I see nothing but a possible I.O.D.E. in the way of marriage, and that's hardly enough to set against the advantages of marrying you, as far as your general peace of mind is concerned.

I went to see Blunden yesterday and he handed me a book on Canada by André Siegfried, which he said he had to read for some reading club or other.[6] I was interested, because Siegfried's translator is this man [Henry] Hemming I told you about—the banker who has bought a hideous Edwardian house and is busy turning it into something very modern and Canadian. Fortunately, he had just finished the book when I was talking to him—Blunden's copy is a proof—and so I have an idea of what's in it.

The Mrs. Simpson you gave me was comparatively mild—one paper had "Teddie gets his tart." Another had pictures of her three men with "The Wallace Collection" underneath. McKay said somebody from Canada had written him saying: "How I envy you, being in England at this moment when history is being made!" I told that to LePan, chuckling hugely, but he wasn't much impressed—said all *his* correspondents had said the same thing.

Elizabeth [Fraser] seems to be all right—she doesn't hurt herself working: just enough to keep her alive. Edith [Burnett] sends her love. When I said to Stephen that you might not, after all, be coming over, he said that *his* house was available if you did come, but I'm afraid that wouldn't do, as they have only one bed, and that a narrow one—one spare bed, that is.

The time should pass quickly now until I see you again. I hope so, anyway.

Norrie.

1 This is almost certainly, not McKay, but Robert Forbes McRae, a 1936 graduate of VC
   who had come from China.
2 This was probably Joseph M. Hone's *The Life of George Moore* (London: Gollancz, 1936),
   the only full-length treatment of Moore published in 1935–36.
3 A scholarship from the Imperial Order Daughters of the Empire; see Letter 86, n. 4.
4 For the story of Noyes's early life in China until the 1970s, see Henry Noyes, *China Born:
   Memoirs of a Westerner* (London: Peter Owen, 1989).
5 *The Thirty Years' War* was published the following year in London by Jonathan Cape.
6 André Siegfried's *La Canada, puissance internationale* (Paris: Armand Colin, 1937) was
   translated by Henry H. Hemming and published as *Canada* (London: Jonathan Cape,
   1937).

178. NF to HK   [*Oxford*]

[*19 January 1937*]

Postmarked 19 January 1937; addressed to HK at 84, Queen's Park, Toronto,
Ontario, Canada.

I don't know why I'm writing you again so soon, sweet, except that
your letter came this morning and the New Yorkers. I expect sending
those magazines is a bit of a nuisance, but please keep on: silly as it
sounds, they mean quite a bit to me. You *do* do them up so well. Thanks
for the snapshots: Harold is good, you diminish, but recognizable
enough to make me feel funny inside. I was very pleased to get Harold's
letter, which was a very good letter, and will try to get it answered
shortly.

Oh, dear, some of your news is a bit depressing: first that horrible
business of Epstein, and now Kay and Jerry. I *did* think they'd hit it off
better—I thought they were so well adapted to each other. Kay cooed,
and Jerry gloated with possessing pride—that sort of thing. It's too bad
mamma is so near—a desert island with lots of bamboo on it seems to be
indicated. The Oxford Group[1] is a pretty insidious menace—I don't
know if I ever told you that you nearly lost your husband to it. One particularly callow infant—in Norm Knight's phrase, just out of the shell
and not quite dry yet—at Merton was talking to me at the beginning of
the term, at first about music. He wanted to know who were the greatest
musical composers, and I said Bach and Mozart. Then about God, man
and the world, about which he had ideas. Well, during the first two
weeks of the vacation I ran into him again. He'd just joined the Group,
and was all starry-eyed. It poured rain, and he talked to me for nearly

three hours while the Mayor of Oxford was trying to explain to anyone who would listen that, in spite of what we had been told, the really truly king's name was George VI. Apparently kings have to be proclaimed by suitable officials in all the towns of England. Where was I? Oh, yes: the Oxford Group was going to nip in between Communism and Fascism and save the world—it was just as revolutionary as they were, but better because it believed in God and they were based on a materialistic philosophy. I raised an eyebrow and said that most of the Communists I had known were hopeless idealists, and that Germany had been living off idealism for the last five months, not having food enough to be materialists. Or so they say. Evidently the German newspapers say the same thing about England: the Hemmings' German servant came back from Germany loaded down with food supplied by her friends for the starving English. Or so Hemming said, but as he's pretty Fascist I suspect some embroidery—his wife was skeptical, I remember. Where was I? Oh, yes. This kid walked back home with me and backed me into every corner of Merton College in turn, haranguing me. I ought to join the Group, because the Group needed all the brains it could get. God, it does. After an hour and three-quarters he glanced dubiously at my frozen pan and said: "Of course, I'm just a newcomer to the Group: you can see I haven't had much experience, or you'd have been in flames by now." Word for word. He said he had a Group friend who was one of the world's greatest authorities on Händel, which is probably Groupese for the fact that he had read some Händel at one time or another. I'd enjoy meeting him, because he's musical. Then a fragment of our earlier conversation filtered into his poor addled brain, and he said "But, then, of course, you're not a Händel man, are you?—you're Bach and Mozart." Surely I haven't told you all this before?

Your efficient tying-up of New Yorkers reminds me of a remark of Stephen's [Stephen Burnett's] in a particularly sniffish mood—"Why are all Canadians so utterly hopeless at doing up parcels?" Edith [Burnett]: "Because we're not a nation of shopkeepers."[2]

Blunden was very pleased with my exam and said nice things. I was disgusted with it myself. If I can make that impression when half asleep, more than half sick and execrably prepared, I ought to be all right on Schools.[3] I've been fighting off 'flu and think I'll eventually succeed. This is a dead secret, by which I mean everybody in general and Norah [McCullough] in particular. Elizabeth [Fraser] has been working on a series of imaginative designs, on the borderline of formal design and literary illustration, with a sort of running lyric in free verse as commentary. Not at all publishable: she simply did it and handed it to me. I don't know what to make of it: first time in my life I've ever been absolutely at a loss. It's easy to say it's remarkable, and it's easy to say it's drivel, but neither statement is in the least true. The poem is unquestionably bad in diction, it's hopelessly vague and cloudy, but its rhythms are remarkable, and the drawings, though equally cloudy and over-abstract, are extraordinarily suggestive. The whole is so bafflingly elusive, and yet so disturbing, that I'm absolutely at a loss—knowing Elizabeth doesn't help either. Blunden has asked me to supper this week, and—this being an even deader secret, as Elizabeth would be furious if she knew—I'm going to take them to him. I've *got* to have an intelligent opinion on them. On reading over the above, I find that I seem to be repeating myself, which reflects the confusion of my mind.

Don't let's talk about plans for the summer until the Easter vac. any way. If I haven't any money left, I'll come home. I won't have enough, certainly, to keep me in Europe *all* summer. Trading Europe in for you would be a pretty fair exchange, anyhow.

Norrie.

1 See Letter 46, n. 6, above.
2 Edith Burnett's allusion is to the statement of Adam Smith: "To found a great empire for the sole purpose of raising up a people of customers, may at first sight appear a project fit only for a nation of shopkeepers" (*Wealth of Nations* [1776], vol. 2, bk. 4, chap. 7, pt. 3). Napoleon, probably without reference to Smith, said, "L'Angleterre est une nation de boutiquiers."
3 That is, honours examinations which were held by all faculties in June of each year. To receive a first on any "school" or subject was a notable distinction, and the colleges at Oxford prided themselves on the number of firsts their students received. The issue that later develops is whether NF will take his B.A. degree by writing his Blake thesis or whether he will stand for school examinations, as Edmund Blunden would prefer. Although NF was nominally enrolled in a B.A. program, in accordance with the Oxford system, his degree would be converted into an M.A. upon completion. As HK explains in Letter 82: "Two years study for the B.A. and enough residence fees and the examination fee and you get the M.A. (Oxon.) without further preamble."

179. HK to NF   [*Toronto*]
Jan 20. 1937.

My dearest: There is a boat going off soon and I'll send you a few disjointed scrawls just to tell you how very pleased I am with you and life in general. Norah [McCullough] had a letter from Edith and Stephen [Bur-nett] all about Christmas and a party at Rose Lamb's and Stephen says you're a swell guy. Norah says they must like you a lot or they certainly wouldn't say so. So I was very glad and—well, I like you a lot, too.

To-day I polished off the second lecture to the group from the museum—did I tell you Ruth Home was running a course of lectures two of which were given by the Art Gallery of T.? The first one was Rococo in French Painting, which I did before Christmas, this one was classicism—David, Ingres etc. I gave them a spot of Raphael and Poussin for good measure and read extracts from Reynolds' Discourses for the English approach to classicism. There weren't many there—six to be exact. There were about ten the time before but I don't think the course had a very high enrolment in the first place and the weather kept some away. Norah says she is going to charge next year for my Thurs-day morning group, if Ruth Home gets a group together like this one we surely can. Then to-night after dinner I had to talk to some students about pictures at Jessie Mac's [Macpherson's] suggestion. I expected about a dozen to stay and there were more like forty, so I had to sit on the arm of a chair and hold forth. Am still feeling surprised at being able to do it. Have just spent the evening getting acquainted with one of the McMaster students that I thought was a Philistine—big brawny, at O.C.E.—but she's all right and we love each other. The don business is going on, I really feel at home in the job by now. Oh dear, I *am* feeling a bit elated.

Your Aunt's letter has just turned up on the desk—she says, writing from B.C. that her big valise was lost somewhere in Ohio and she landed in B.C. without a change of stockings nearly a month ago. Gloria is in a boarding school as she was getting too obstreperous altogether, and she says "she knew no friend she would like to burden with such a proposition." I like your aunt very much.

Oh dear, this is a silly little note but I want to get it off to you and I've a class to-morrow, and I'm going to the Mikado Friday night and there is not much time for a decent letter until the weekend again.

Peggy [Kidder] is looking up the rates for freight boats. Roy won $8 worth of prizes and a lot of glory at the photograph show last Monday.[1] Douglas MacAgy looks green with envy at my Mantegna.

I love you very much,

Helen.

P.S. I am going out to have coffee with Florence Smith. We are getting very friendly as she is interested in pictures and is actually enthusiastic. I melt, I melt!

1 This is not the first time that Roy Kemp had earned recognition for his photographs. Two years earlier he received prizes for six photographs in three categories in a Hart House exhibition (*Varsity*, 16 January 1935).

180. HK to NF
84 Queen's Park
Toronto
January 31. 1937.

Postmarked 1 February 1937; addressed to NF at Merton College, Oxford, England, Via New York: Bremen.

My dearest, on Saturday there were *two* letters from you, and my whole outlook brightened immediately. I do get a bit fretful sometimes in between letters, and I had not heard from you since January 11th. Of course, Beatty says, what do I expect, a letter every few days? There are drawbacks to this don racket, and that is that one gets involved with internal politics and the small feminine rivalries of the place. I am thoroughly bored with them and it will only bring the details into too much prominence if I go over the ground again—so I'll not trouble you with all the stupid details of existence here. I'm afraid you'd have to hear all about it if you were closer, my poor man, but on the contrary if you were closer I wouldn't be here.

There are several sad things to tell you about. For one thing, Dr. George Locke died on Thursday after a month's illness.[1] I think I told you about Housser at Christmas time. It is what makes me so uneasy and so sad—Housser gone, Locke gone, Lismer so far away you so far away. I am dreadfully afraid of war coming soon, and of something happening to you, of Roy having to go and have his head blown off, and Harold soon being old enough to be eligible for slaughter. There is a feeling here of greater activity, the mines are booming and there is more gaiety in Toronto than for some little time. Everyone said New Year's Eve was the gayest since 1929 and oceans of money was spent. There is a new night club in Toronto out near Sunnyside and people are going there to see the fig leaf dancing.[2] Beatty says it's a magnificent place.

Mrs Arnold 'phoned to see how Epstein is and was given more hopeful news but I have a notion the person she asked may not have known. Norah [McCullough] asked me about Dr Arnold the other day—he asked her to go to a dance with him at the German club and Joan Fairley told her afterwards she had gone out with him once, but never again—too much affection. It seems he has been fairly gay at various parties always with someone *not* his wife. Yesterday when I was having my usual German lesson we had tea and I exploded a little about the smugness of Victoria etc. Then Mrs Arnold asked me how I liked Dr [Florence] Smith and I told her I had been liking her much better lately. Mrs A. was pretty scathing about her, but I said she'd probably had a hard life getting adjusted socially and besides she needs a beau. Mrs A: "So have I had a hard life, and who doesn't need a beau? We are all better off when we have someone to admire us—but what would you do if you were married already, and your husband has no more interest in you any more? What can you do then?—" she laughed—"take a university course, like I do!" She changed the subject then. Last week when I was there he 'phoned home and said he would not be in for dinner, in spite of her having invited Sid Gould to dinner—I met her with Sid later in the evening at Eaton's at a French movie. Arnold just clears out for weekends, and her telephone conversation that day sounded pretty strained. I don't know what can be done about it, I expect she is not as fluffy as he would like, but I also think he is being rather a pig. Still, I don't intend to judge the situation too definitely. I suppose when people tire of each other they tire of each other, but the man certainly has the advantage, when she is left to look after three young children and he can flirt with his students and other interesting women he meets about town. But wives here can't do anything of the sort, and when she is cast aside in the little village of Victoria College, it is a little awkward for someone like Sid to find himself in the position of escort because Arnold is off dancing somewhere. I could *spank* him! At any rate, it *is* too bad.

Later—a good deal later. I went to another tea for J.R.D. [Roy Daniells] and I still think Roy's manners leave a great deal to be desired. Charlie Miller, don of North House, lectures or demonstrates in Psychology, was there with Jean Cunningham who works at fashion drawing with Brigden's, and a queer little man from the west named Wright, who farms all summer and does graduate work on Duncan Campbell Scott all winter. He talked to me, and I talked to him—he seemed a timid soul—while Charlie and Jean clowned as people do sometimes when they know each other very well and feel that way, and Roy fussed over supper. I'd hate to marry Roy—I should think he'd be off like Arnold, very soon. I still think Ev Stewart would be the best one to handle him. I'm afraid I feel a little jaundiced because Roy's house teas are a little wearing—he is fussy as I've said, and I have the feeling that I'm there as a good handy across the road sort of filler in whom he takes quite for granted and isn't half as interested in as he is in any of his freshies. This all sounds dreadfully silly to you probably. I like him very much, but I feel just a little bit insulted and fed up. Fortunately I got out and went up to Fairley's where Joan was entertaining all the gallery crowd—the Briegers and Alford were also there. We had an awfully good time. I shall be so glad when you can be with me at parties like that. I asked Roy casually to come, but he had to go back and kick out the people because we met Jerry [Riddell] coming across the street to inspect everything. Roy should have made them leave fifteen minutes before that. We dropped in to see Art Brant who is don of South House—he was having tea at the same time—nice group of people too.

My pen is running dry and I've tried to get away with water for the rest—

I'm sorry about troubling you with the summer. I know that you are running things pretty close financially, and forget that you don't feel quite the same about seeing Europe as I do—and if there's an I.O.D.E. in the offing I suppose it will be wiser to wait. I wish sometimes *your* peace of mind were slightly troubled, though, so you wouldn't blame me for the idea altogether.

Kay and Jerry [Riddell] are really all right I expect—the gossip I retailed to you was sifted through Roy Daniells > Ev Stewart > Dot Drever. Incidentally Dot is getting the jitters about Communist activities—I expect her to start wearing a veil to hide herself any time now, she's so afraid of being found out. She's going through some more hero worshipping and I'm a little tired of hearing how wonderful Ev Stewart is and all her acquaintances.

I'm so glad my dear that you did well on the exam. Mary Winspear sends her regards, Peggy [Roseborough] is working on her Ph.D. this spring. Barbara [Sturgis] showed me Veronica's [Veronica Wedgwood's] very impressive book on Strafford.[3] Your news of Edith and Stephen [Burnett] is refreshing, especially the parcel bit!

What I want to know now is, do you want me to come over for June and July or July and August? Cheaper rates the end of May. I must get reservations in soon and you haven't told me when your term ends. The sailings are pretty crowded and things will be crowded all this summer.

Isobel Sim has left residence again—she weighs 63 pounds this time, so she's home for good. I've been seeing her a little this week,—she's fed up with her course and doesn't care about quitting.

It's midnight now and I've got to write a radio talk on Rubens to-morrow.[4] I'm afraid this letter sounds as if I hate everybody—please don't mind if your wife turns shrewish now and again.

I love you *very* much, and four months to go—

H.

Next day: noon. Gwen Kidd's father attempted to slash his throat last night—now in hospital again. She was called from Fairley's to meet the police wagon on the street and her father all messed up—alcoholic case. They had him in the Psychiatric Hospital but then he said that he'd reformed, and the family were fooled for the ——th time. Miss Latter, University Extension, died. Dr Rose Henderson died at a meeting last Saturday. Daddy earned $8 last week. There's no use my saying I'll put so much aside—There *are* a few demands that I cannot disregard. If you were home you would feel the same way about *your* family, so please don't accuse the family of digging at me again or whatever it was you said. They're not. But if I'm the only one with any money, I can't very well hoard it—you wouldn't if you were in the same position.

However, aside from all this doleful stuff, everything is going fairly well. I just meant to tell you how things are with us—family intends to pay back all my loans, but I don't see how they can very well, so why worry.

I'll go off to lunch now. Rubens coming on slowly.

H.

1 George Herbert Locke (1870–1937) was chief librarian of the Toronto Public Libraries, 1908–37, and a member of the VC board of regents and its library board for twenty years. It had been his suggestion to apply to the Carnegie Corporation for funding for a library, and the successful application resulted in the construction of the Birge-Carnegie Library in 1911. The George Locke Room in 29 Birge-Carnegie, currently the home of the Northrop Frye Centre, was opened 27 November 1937 in his memory with an endowment collected from members of his year by Perkins Bull. Immediately prior to that the room had been the Browsing Room, Dr. Locke's creation, although the original Browsing Room, still in use in NF and HK's time, had been located on the ground floor of the library.

2 Probably The Silver Slipper on Riverside Dr., beside the Humber River. For Sunnyside, see Letter 128, n. 5, above.
3 Veronica Wedgwood, *Strafford, 1593–1641* (London: Jonathan Cape, 1935).
4 The title "Analysis of Rubens' 'Elevation of the Cross' and two Bassanos and Veronese Madonnas—argument re Modern Art" appears beside the date 2 April on HK's list of topics for her Thursday morning members' study group (HFF, 1993, box 4, file 6); however, it seems she eventually passed the topic along to Martin Baldwin, who gave a talk on "Rubens' Elevation of the Cross" on 9 March 1937 in the first of an ongoing series of broadcasts presented on Tuesday evenings on radio station CRCT (a Toronto station acquired by the CBC in 1933). See Letter 186, n. 1, for further details.

181. NF to HK   Oxford

Postmarked 3 February 1937; addressed to HK at 84, Queen's Park, Toronto, Ontario, Canada.

Sweetheart:

I spent several days staggering around holding on to things, not daring to bend over too quickly for fear I'd stay down, and going through a lot of other antics trying not to get flu, wherein I eventually succeeded. It hasn't been too prevalent among students, although half the scouts are down—mine just got back today, to my great relief—I had been collecting half the teapots in the college while a substitute was looking after me. (Damn, I'll have to stop now: one of my tame violinists wants to play with me.)

I have finally persuaded him to try the big fugue in the Mozart sonata in A, so we're happy once more. He's bad in somewhat the same way I am: neither of us can keep time, and we can't learn anything thoroughly. I'm sleepy today, having gone to the O.U.D.S. performance of Shaw's *Caesar and Cleopatra*, a stupid (or at least a tiresome) play badly performed. Their last performance was the *Beggar's Opera*, and in spite of my violent antipathy to that play I enjoyed it—they imported several people from London to carry it, and they did well. Macheath was a little too restrained, and Polly, a beautiful but not much else Oxford girl, was weak, but they made a good evening—these O.U.D.S. things are only 7½ d. on Monday evenings, and worth that, certainly. Sunday night Merton College had their musicale of the term—a Hungarian named Louis Kentner, a simple soul who played Liszt brilliantly (he has an incredible technique) Mozart, of course, badly—far too much expression—and made a very creditable assault on the Beethoven Hammerclavier—if you see Norm Langford you might tell him I've heard that performed.

Elizabeth [Fraser] keeps well but poor—she owes me £1.10.0 now. She's working on several jobs—one, trying to draw those obliterated paintings in Northmoor I mentioned, and another series of anatomical drawings for a doctor. But of course her book, which she gave to me, took up a lot of time. I showed it to Blunden, who said he liked it, and I think actually he did. He seemed impressed anyway. I couldn't trust my own reaction—at times I thought it was drivel, and yet something in it made me keep coming back to it. The girl has brains, and her poetry shows a genuine feeling for rhythm. If only she weren't so inchoate—I think there's a genuinely mystical quality to her mind, which makes her work over-abstract. Well, last Tuesday she and a wall-painting restorer named Long and I went to a town near here called Abingdon, where there's a church with a series of figures on each side of the chancel ceiling.[1] They are kings and prophets alternately, leading up to Christ and the Virgin in the last panel (some of them are out of place), with a tree of Jesse running horizontally underneath them. The Christ is a beautiful Lily Crucifix—his body is in an attitude of crucifixion, but there's no cross—just a lily plant covering him. Late 14th century. Varnished out of sight, and some disappeared when they took the roof off in 1872 and put it back on again. Well, Blunden hasn't seen these, although they're in the next town and he (or his wife) has written a book on church architecture in England. So he's coming to see them this week, and he's coming to tea afterwards, and Elizabeth is coming too. "He probably hates churches," says Elizabeth. Poor Blunden—but if I didn't bully him somebody else would—he's always being bullied by somebody. There's a minor Elizabethan poet named Fulke Greville—a great favorite of Roy's [Roy Daniells's] as well as mine, a very intellectual poet and frightfully obscure at times—quite the thing for a Blake student to be interested in. After my first tutorial this term I said: "I shall be reading Sidney and Lyly this week, and will probably bring you a paper on Fulke Greville: is that all right?" He said: "Er—oh, yes—certainly— except that I haven't read much Greville—Aldous Huxley is very interested in Greville: he started talking about him once, and all I could muster in the way of quotation was"—he quoted two lines—"it wasn't much, but I think I had even that counted to me for righteousness." Blunden and I are definitely going to get along well this term—he's used to me now, and probably my manners are better than they were at first. I went to supper with him one night, with Mike Joseph, the Catholic New Zealander, and had a good time. Sherry, white burgundy, and Madeira. Mrs. Blunden is small, dark, Armenian, and intentionally vivacious, with large brilliant eyes and a kind of electric intelligence that turns on and off.

Fulke Greville has been keeping me busy—like Blake, his religious, philosophical & political views are all in one piece, and it would take at least a month's solid work to read all of him and tie him all up in a neat little sack. I had only a week—there's no good modern edition (Roy wants to do one, but I'm afraid various people are beating him to it) and there was a baldheaded johnny who had reserved all the books in the Bodleian, so I had to beg all the books from him. I had one of my seizures, and worked every day until my eyes gave out for a week on that paper. Blunden liked it very much, I think. These essays I'm doing are mostly publishable, I should imagine: certainly I've collected a lot of material for future books.[2]

Plans for the summer are still vague—a summer at Gordon Bay is an idea that is beginning to take shape more and more. I don't want to meet people in Canada any more than I can help—just half a dozen—but I do want to live with you and grow for a while. I'm maturing here, and have a feeling that this novel, which has been hanging fire so long, will come off if I can have you beside me. Or something like that. Judging from your account, it would have been physically impossible for you to have done any work towards your exams here—there aren't fifty or sixty hours in a day, and that's that.

Did I tell you that Bryson, the lazy devil, called off our *Beowulf* exam? I got another nice letter from Barbara [Sturgis]—I like her. I must do some *Beowulf* for tomorrow now. Baine is away for the day playing chess with the House of Commons. He didn't want to go, but he said it would please his mother. Bless you, darling.

Norrie.

This is a grind's letter—I've been grinding hard.

1 The church in Abingdon, a Berkshire town about five miles south of Oxford, was St. Helen's, the oldest parts of which date from the thirteenth century. The pictures that NF goes on to describe were not frescoes but the remains of thirty-eight medieval paintings on the wood panels of the roof.
2 NF produced a large body of writing for Blunden—"five and six thousand words a week," he wrote to Roy Daniells (RDF, undated letter written in June 1937, box 3, file 2). Except for the essay on Chaucer, NF's Oxford papers have apparently not survived.

My dear: I sent some New Yorkers off a few days ago and the mutt in the Post Office gave me the wrong amount of postage so they were returned for more. However, you'll get them, but a little later by a few days. I also sent some gallery bulletins to let you know what is going on here. Last night was the big opening of the Architectural Show with The Tweedsmuirs present.[1] He gave a speech, quite a good one, which I could not hear because of the amplifiers distorting everything so in the Sculpture Court. René Cera has been here the last few days installing Eaton's exhibit in the Sculpture Court—a mid-Victorian drawing room contrasted with a modern one.[2]

I can't give you much news as this is Saturday morning at the Gallery and you know what that is like. I am trying to catch a boat again with *something* at any rate. I have a miscellaneous lot of news.

Eleanor Caesar at breakfast this morning said that *she* had something to tell me: Cameron [Caesar] is engaged (the cagey old fox!) to Bunny Pidgeon. So I was very properly pleased, and not awfully surprised for some strange reason, even though I did not expect Cameron to be harboring any matrimonial plans.

After two attempts at suicide Gwen Kidd's father passed out in the hospital two days ago, and she is back to-day, I understand. Alcoholic case. Norah [McCullough] told Douglas MacAgy about it and he said he understood that situation pretty thoroughly—only his mother left his father when Douglas was twelve, and I guess they haven't seen him since.

Mother's birthday was last Wednesday,[3] and we went to see the Rembrandt film at the Uptown.[4] It is one of the best things I have ever seen on the screen, the design of each scene is beautifully thought out, and balanced, and the producer managed to keep everything pretty simple—even when he has a few sacks of grain and nothing else, he remembers to keep the whole thing nicely balanced.

Harold played last Saturday in Massey Hall in the secondary schools' orchestra. Emily Tedd's choir and this orchestra put on a very fine programme, I really was surprised.

Wednesday afternoon I took the Vic Lit group to Douglas Duncan's studio and to see Harold Stacey (pewter work) They are both at 3 Charles Street where the Picture Loan Society is this year. I was over there last night with Norah [McCullough]—Robert Finch's one-man show has just come off the walls and Marina Goodier's is going up. Marina, incidentally, is going to have an infant soon. It was two months before she noticed there was anything different in her make-up—she insists it was an accident but they are both going to be terribly pleased. Rik Kettle's wife is also helping the population. I'm going to see the [Herbert J.] Davises this afternoon with Barbara [Sturgis], and I'll have to tell them all about you. You really ought to write to him, if to no one else,—well, Pratt would be all ears to know how you are, I imagine. And Barbara will have to supply details to the Davises about the Don-rag.[5] I wish there had been a letter from you this morning,—but then I wish that every morning.

I hope you are well, and have not caught 'flu. It is hitting some people pretty hard here, and the Infirmary is full.

No news. I gravitate between Wymilwood and A G of T, and do my best with Wymilwood students—The upstairs maid doesn't dust properly now that Nellie got married, and what's to do about smoking? etc etc.

I will send you a note later on.

My love to you

Helen.

1 The Sixth Biennial Exhibition of Architecture and Architects, sponsored by the Ontario Association of Architects, Toronto Chapter, and the Royal Architectural Institute of Canada, was opened by Lord and Lady Tweedsmuir on 5 February 1937.
2 The Walker Sculpture Court of the AGT was named for Sir Edmund Walker, the first president of the gallery; after his death in 1924 funds were raised by private subscription and from the Toronto City Council to build the court and two sets of flanking galleries.
3 HK's mother, Gertrude Maidement Kemp, was born on 3 February 1884.
4 *Rembrandt*, a 1936 film starring Charles Laughton, Elsa Lancaster, and Gertrude Lawrence; it was based on a radio play by Carl Zuckmayer.
5 NF's examination on the last day of the term. See Letter 171, above.

183. NF to HK Oxford

Postmarked 9 February 1937; addressed to HK at 84, Queen's Park, Toronto, Ontario, Canada.

Helen, dear, just settle down and be a good girl and wait till I come over—the year ends around June 20. I'm sorry if I've been unjust to your family, but it's hard to see across the Atlantic, and I could hardly avoid thinking in terms of your letters to me in Moncton. But if you aren't ready to try your exams,—you certainly won't, and it's no fault of yours—there's no reason for you to come over except that I want to see you, and so it's up to me to make the move now. I won't make your situation, to say nothing of your family's, any more complicated or strained than it is. It was just an idea we couldn't work out. And I have to think of things like the I.O.D.E.: I can't ignore them any more than you can ignore your family. So to say that I'm blaming you altogether for the idea of getting married seems rather untrue—I've had that idea a lot longer than you have. But don't worry any more about the summer, or about anything else.

Poor little girl: such a cranky woebegone letter. I do wish I could take you into my arms and quiet your nerves and put you to sleep. Things must be depressing in Toronto with all your friends dying or miserable—I don't know when I've heard of such an aggregate of horrors all at once. Wymilwood, too: there's nothing pettier than female jealousy. Arnold is a swine—he always was: the complete thoughtlessness of a spoiled child combined with a priggish impulse to justify everything he does. He always had a tendency to think that anyone who refused his explanations of his conduct—i.e. flirting with some giggling servant-girl in the German Club because he was being starved for intellectual companionship—was just one of the herd trampling on his individuality. And Roy [Daniells] isn't insulting you, sweetheart. He's being scrupulously honourable about you, and he doesn't do it well, that's all. Besides, anyone capable of falling in love with that Stewart sounding brass [Evelyn Stewart] shouldn't be judged as other men are judged.

Nothing is happening to me. I told you, I think, that I was having Blunden and Elizabeth [Fraser] in for tea. Elizabeth did just what I thought she'd do: shut up like a clam, and Blunden and I talked shop. It was simply another tutorial. The silly girl—she's in love with one of the biggest men in Oxford—the printer at the O.U.P.[1]—and hints darkly of terrible things that have happened, which obviously include the fact that she's managed to make a fool of herself and that he won't look at her. She only sees him very rarely, and it plays the very devil with her nerves, which is why she has these spells of shyness. If she could get away from him and from Oxford she'd be all right. Obviously she's made a big impression on him, which complicates it. I think Blunden liked her, though, and I do think he admired her book. Norah [McCullough], of course, mustn't get hold of this. Actually, it's a more respectable story than I can make it sound—it's practically been her whole life for two or three years. Her flying trip back to Canada, when we met her in the art gallery, was a reaction from it.

I read my anatomy paper to Blunden last night.[2] He said I had two hundred very saleable pages there, but that Jane Austen's admirers would just read my one sentence on her and conclude that there was rape afoot. He lives, somewhat like Ned Pratt, in mortal terror of the scholars, including at times me. It's probably the effect of living with Nichol Smith. Anyway, he asked me what he should lecture on next term, so I drew up all the harmless names I could think of in the 17th c: he said he was tired of the 18th and 19th and was afraid of the scholars of the 16th. Bryson asked us up to his flat for an extra tutorial Friday night. Baine couldn't go, but Warren and I went, and had a good time—he produced beer, a Schnabel recording of the Waldstein sonata, a Picasso sketch, and a lot of conversation about New York—he's very fond of America. Warren doesn't know what to make of him—says he still feels he's typical Oxford, but seems to be a nice chap in spite of it.

I've bought myself a lot of typing paper and am going to get a lot of Blake done. I've got to finish my general book on him before the year's out. Give my love to Peggy [Roseborough] & Mary [Winspear] when—or rather whenever—you see them. Does a radio talk on Rubens mean that you are going to talk over the radio? Oh, sweetheart, I love you so: I feel sometimes as though you simply must appear, right here in this room, in front of me, I want you so.

Norrie.

1 John Johnson, whose position was "printer to the university" at Oxford University Press. Fraser's letters to Johnson, 1935–45, are in the archives of the Oxford University Press.
2 For NF's anatomy paper, or perhaps a later version of it, see "An Enquiry into the Art-Forms of Prose Fiction" in the NFF, 1991, box 37, file 4.

184. HK to NF   [*Toronto*]
                                              Friday, Feb. 19. 1936 [*1937*].

My dearest dearest man! I'm starting a new pad and I'm only going to write joyful letters to you from now on. No more cranky sniffling: I've cheered up. The weather has changed and several things have happened in the last week. I've laid a ghost. I've had two letters from you. I have a new dress—and I still think you like me. And no more people died this week except in Spain.

Norah [McCullough], to begin near the beginning, had lunch one day with the Briegers and they were talking about me, the upshot being that I was to see Brieger about the Courtauld business[1] all over again since Alford couldn't make out what I was talking about. He *wouldn't*. So I 'phoned Brieger, who immediately asked me up for supper and a French film afterwards at Eaton's with the Haurwitz pair—they're in the Physics department. I had a talk with him before his guests arrived, and I may say that I can hardly wait for you to meet Brieger, he and his wife are pretty well taking Toronto by storm. He got the whole story out of me, i.e. my feeling of obligation to McCurry and my bad conscience in general, and my desire for academic standing in Art History—Then said "But what do you *want* to do? If you could go anywhere, do anything you want—would you go back to the Courtauld for the diploma?" I said that I certainly did not regard that of any importance except as a sort of stamp and one that might mean something toward a degree here or somewhere else. He couldn't see it at all—both he and Alford think I should register here as a graduate student next year and take lectures when I can fit them in (which I could do next year fairly well, I think) Brieger talked again exactly as Daddy did—that there was no use becoming a physical wreck trying to work in an examination over and above the gallery job this year. But his final argument was that the disagreement between Constable and his directors was partly over the diploma course which Constable wanted to abolish. Brieger and I pretty well agreed about the waste of time at the Institute and it seems the director had had the same idea for some time. Brieger thinks that the course might be done away with in a few years and ———! Brieger sounds here as if he made up his mind that I should not go back. He did not do that of course, he put it up to me and it was the same this time as it was with Miss Whinney. I am taking his advice because it is what I want to do anyway. He and Alford were the people I was worrying about here—I don't think McCurry gives a rap. So I am just going to forget the diploma and start again. It isn't that I'm turning green at the sight of an examination but there just isn't time for it. Norah [McCullough] says I could very likely get off next year to take certain courses and she thinks it's all to the good. At present the German is going slowly and I haven't been able to work at it this week at all.

To-night we had the Lescaze lecture, last night I was down for the university settlement evening, next Monday there is a lecture by Eric Newton and on Friday the Leo Smith musicale.[2] And so it goes! Lescaze is simply *grand*—you get the idea from the article in The New Yorker {Dec 12}[3] but to hear him talk and to see all the buildings he has designed—! *Now* don't you wish you were in Toronto? Mother came down to hear the lecture—she is looking awfully well—new dress—new hat—and we're much more cheerful this week. We had dinner at Little Denmark and then went to the lecture. We had an awfully nice time and talked about all sorts of things. I hadn't seen her for a week but it seemed a lot longer—so many things happen. For instance, we had a bang-up formal dinner party Thursday night at Annesley Hall when Emmy Heim came to sing. I sat next to Malcolm Wallace afterwards and we exchanged yarns about Goldwin Smith—he is a nice duck. Mrs Shore asked me about Lake Joseph, she remembered Harold learning to swim. Mrs Davis was there too and she told me H.J. [Herbert J. Davis] has been in bed with something. Did I tell you about going up there to tea with Barbara [Sturgis] the week before? I had to answer an awful lot of questions about you. And if I have not said so before I now most *solemnly urge* you to write to H.J.—he is very keenly interested to know how you are liking everything and how the work is going and I could tell him so little of what he is most interested in hearing. After all, he wrote to Merton for you and surely he isn't difficult to approach. You really ought to write to him out of politeness, let alone your friendship's sake.

Oh dear, it's getting terribly late and I must be ready to talk to the combination of the Dean's Council and the Women's Council to-morrow. Should women be allowed any part in the university and if so what and should they compete with men and what is the place of women in community life? And all because of their damned luncheon I have had to pass up a luncheon at the University Club to-morrow to meet Lescaze—*isn't* it the devil?

I'll not talk about summer or Arnold or anything else until I've had some more sleep. It is nearly one. If I were to imagine *very* hard to-night that I kissed you good-night do you think it would make any impression on you? Not to-night, I suppose because I don't know just what you're doing when it is one P.M. here, and you wouldn't get this until a week from now and all this will be history by then. Still a sort of thwarted historical kiss is better than nothing at all perhaps, and I'm sending you one all wrapped up in a warm glowing sort of atmosphere, and I wonder where it will land. Now that is a nice idea to play with—I just wonder where it will land—I'll think about that for a long time—or do you think I could send two or three and have a choice?

Sunday afternoon in Wymilwood—*raining again!* It is no wonder that I send you such stupid letters, this has been such a rainy winter. Much more like English weather than it has been since I can remember, dull rain and everything muddy and too warm days alternating with sudden cold. Fortunately I did not get 'flu but a lot of people were laid low—Beatty and Marge Boultbee, for instance, both had it.

I met Lescaze on Saturday morning so I felt that I was not cheated out of seeing him altogether by the Women's Council and their Round Table conference. *That* started at eleven but I could not get there until after twelve and I had quite enough by two thirty. We had lunch and it was quite interesting to me to meet these people—some were *pretty* stupid—talking about one's philosophy of life and how the dons should impart a philosophy of life to the students. It wasn't that that I object to so much as that sentimental family hold-their-hand stuff. There was really only one woman who was the worst offender and Kay Coburn told me afterwards that she had not over-worked her brain when she was here. The question boils down to the fact that they need more people on the staff and they would like more women so they could have more of Victoria staff as dons in residence. Dons are, of course, supposed to do tutoring and that is why they let the high school teachers go, or else they

resigned or something. But only one person has come to me for any help
and she is a teacher from Sudbury who knows Isabel Ricker and doesn't
need help anyway. None of the dons are doing much coaching, and I
think it is a bit ridiculous having me here on that ground, for instance,
because all I could ever do would be to refer any youngsters who came
to me to certain books, try to get them interested in a subject and tell
them to go see Brieger for more definite information. I told Kay Coburn
a while ago that I wasn't keen on having a sinecure and what *am* I
expected to do? I also have talked to Jessie Mac [Macpherson] asking her
if I should round up all the art students and pump art history into them
but she said no—just go ahead as I am doing. However, I am starting
some cocoa parties this week and expect to entertain people at least once
before Easter.

I put up an exhibition of posters and wrote little notes all over the
place and the students have absorbed something. I suppose an introduction to things by the way is all that one should hope for. At any rate
there is no use worrying.

I went to see 'Ghosts' last night—Nazimova again. Ibsen seems pretty
hysterical and out-of-date. Good no doubt in his time, but he does seem
to pile on the agony.

I've just had lunch with Dot Drever and the sounding brass[4] and
Eleanor Clements, cousin of Brad Clements, one of the people who went
cycling with Cameron [Caesar]. I did not tell them about his engage-
ment, I'd rather like to but wasn't sure whether they wished it
announced yet. Ted Avison has a job, a good one, in Montreal now, and
just left a week ago, so Ev is going out with a different man every night
in the week, according to Dot. Ev is a constant source of wonderment to
her, I expect.

Later 12 P.M. I had got to about the third line above this when Dot
appeared to take me for a walk around the park in the rain. She and I
have not seen much of each other for the last three or four weeks—I
have lost patience a little I am afraid—communism, hero-worship, general awe-struck attitude to culture—oh I don't know what it is. I'm just a
grumpy old hen, that's all.

It is midnight, and I have just come through a driving rain and snow
storm with the wind nearly blowing my umbrella inside out at the corner of Bloor Street. And if I am to get this posted in time to catch the
Queen Mary I must walk over to Charles Street to-night. The added difficulties always make it more of an event sending a letter to you, after a

walk along Charles Street at midnight in a storm. Miss Manning tells me Charles Street is one place she wouldn't go alone—so I feel *very* brave!

Mother said the other night that January is the family's worst month and that they don't want me to worry any more about money because work will pick up soon and they will try to pay back what I lent them, and by all means to come across if I can manage it, although they would like to have you up north if you come home. Harold is all ready with a rousing welcome when you do come—he'd like to see you—he wants some more piano duets. Roy will be at Lake Jo [Joseph] I think. I am trying to figure out some sort of itinerary if I do come over to you. It seems a great shame in a way, for you to come here when you might be seeing Europe. But I have difficulty picturing just what you want to see and how you want to go if I come with you. If you were with a man you might go cycling or walking—you might see a lot more if you didn't have me there. Germany appeals to me, and Austria. But where would we stay—Youth Hostels, Hotels, or Pensions? It gets so complicated when I think of it— and I haven't made any inquiries about railway fares. [Herbert J.] Davis suggested that you might get a job as tutor to someone in Danzig—he might have a few ideas for the summer that would work out quite well. Of course they would hardly include me. After a little more experience around Victoria College I begin to see the wisdom, or at least the necessity of bowing to the conventions to a certain extent and the I.O.D.E. argument is pretty strong. I don't want you to be too much indebted to the college—more and more I am anxious about that. I don't want you to have to spend too many years in this college.

Here's some news for you—Ruth Hebb is now the mother of ——— Dingman Hebb, a boy. Everybody is very proud and pleased. Jean Elder 'phoned to-night and told me about some of our friends—she was at a party at Berna Langford's and she has never heard so much talk of obstetrics before. Which hospital is best for the job, and how Millie Oldfield was Dr. Hilliard's star patient and she suspects Berna of having a second coming and Ivan [Cleaver] is still working in the garage, etc etc. Mrs Dingman told me the other day that Doris Moggridge had mentioned you in a letter to Ruth and that I might be coming over this summer. You seem to be making it fairly clear that I'm coming over—Esther [Johnson] told me so the first thing I saw her! Bless your heart my dear. It will of course be a very bad summer for England, with the Coronation[5] and all.

Oh well, I'll let it go at that and not worry you any more for a while.

I'm beginning to weaken about the trek to Yonge Street—I'm awfully sleepy, and if I don't go you won't get this for some days later. Marian Higgs has just written and asks me to stay with her in Cheltenham.

Dorothy sends her love,

and I mine,

Helen.

1 The issue is whether or not HK should return to the Courtauld Institute in London to retake the exams she had failed the previous year.
2 According to the AGT *Bulletin* William Lescaze's lecture on 19 February was entitled "Why Modern Architecture?"; Eric Newton gave a lecture on 22 February entitled "The Meaning of Modern Art"; and the Conservatory String Quartet's musical evening on 26 February was billed as "A Consort of Viols."
3 Robert M. Coates, "Profiles: Modern," *New Yorker*, 12 (12 December 1936), 28–38—an article on William Lescaze, a leading modernist architect.
4 The "sounding brass" refers to Evelyn Stewart.
5 Edward VIII abdicated on 11 December 1936; George VI was crowned on 12 May 1937.

185. NF to HK
Oxford

Postmarked 22 February 1937; addressed to HK at 84, Queen's Park, Toronto, Ontario, Canada.

Darling: I had just settled down to write to you when Henry Noyes dropped in from London. He looks cheerful. I showed him the library: I'm acquiring a perfect guide-patter about the library—and sent him off again. The Canadians are meeting in Rhodes House this afternoon to discuss agriculture—I don't want to go but I suppose I should. Well, I went; and a very dull affair it was. I feel more cheerful now that I've got a note from a bank saying they want to pay me some money—evidently Papa Edgar finally got his letter off to Ottawa. I was afraid the Bursar here would start asking questions.

I'm stiff. I'd spent most of the week trying to write a paper on T.S. Eliot, and for some reason, although I eventually wrote quite a good paper, I took an enormous time writing it—began to worry about the sentence rhythms and echoing vowels and things to the most morbid extent, so I don't think I shall try to write a paper for Blunden this week. Well, I got all soft and feeling as though I needed exercise, so I proposed a walk to Elizabeth [Fraser] on Friday and we started.[1] The first village we struck was named Elsfield, where there was a church stuck on the crest of a hill with two lovely tall windows in the west end evidently designed for clear glass, but had been filled with hideous fussy stained glass—if they'd been clear we could have had a lovely view of Oxford in the valley below the hill.[2] Well, we soon discovered that the landscape was being befouled with a fox hunt. People were riding all around us and all the yokels were staring and the hounds were baying. As you can imagine, my opinion of fox-hunters is not high, and Elizabeth feels even more strongly about them than I do—there's something so nauseating in the way they dress up for it, making a sort of ritual murder of the wretched little beast. The next village was named Beckley, and its pub was of course all set for the fox-hunters, so Elizabeth and I were parked in a small top-room with the yokels. That would have been all right, only their cider tasted like Orange Crush, and Orange Crush is the most unnerving drink possible for lunch on a cold day, their cheese had apparently just been rejected by their mice, we got practically no butter and the alleged pickles were raw onions which exploded inside us like bomb shells. I dare say you might have enjoyed it, with your primitive impulse to devour raw onions, but Elizabeth and I were feeling distinctly sick when we left the place. The church is a future job of Elizabeth's, when she gets through with Northmoor—not much left of the wall-painting, except a delightful early 14th c. drawing of the Child getting fed in the most realistic way by the Madonna. The next village was Wood Eaton, where there's a St. Christopher[3]—a tiny little church with a huge enclosed pew occupied by the lords of the neighboring manor. Also a large stone building with a sign saying County Library. And a battalion of cows moving along the road with a villager at each end. And no pub. No pub. There was nothing for it but to walk to the next village—Marston, about three miles from Oxford. We did so, trying to figure out a mental picture of a village that had a manor, a church, a library, cows, yokels and no pub. It didn't fit together, and I decided that the yokels just looked at the County Library sign, looked at each other, leered, and went in and had a drink. Well, Marston's pubs don't open till six—there are two of them next door to each other—and it was then five. No. 1 referred us to No. 2, and No. 2, incarnate in a young man in slippers & a newspaper, was out. Elizabeth said that villages so near to larger towns sometimes won't bother to give you tea. So we took a bus and had some tea at home. I eventually missed Hall[4] and got to my room about five minutes before the Bodley Club started filing into it. I was footsore and stiff and tired—it had rained at intervals all day—and hungry. The Bodley refreshments—coffee and beer—didn't help at all. However, I got through the paper and a very good discussion followed, although it was mostly a catechism of me.[5] About six of them knew their Eliot well—one who knew him personally stayed and talked to me till midnight afterwards. Then I drank all the beer that was left—two bottles, apart from four left for the scout—and went to bed, still hungry. The Bodley Club means a lot of extra work for the scout, cleaning up and so on, and the next morning [Joseph] Reid, upstairs, had the boat club in for breakfast—and they have a terrific breakfast when they're training. About ten o'clock my scout, having fortified himself with four bottles of beer, came stepping into my room. "Finished the breakfast?" I asked. "Yes, er, all but the sweet," gasps Day faintly. "Quite a bit of funk for you, isn't it?" I said. "YES SIR," says Day—the only time I've seen him drop the perfect-servitor mask. Then Baine came in and dragged my shrieking skeleton out to Headington[6] for a walk, and in the afternoon I went down to see Toggers.[7] This is the inter-college rowing match—not the big one, which comes off in May, but still pretty big and colourful. The boats are all lined up one ahead of the other, depending on their last year's performance, and then try to bump into the one ahead. As soon as a boat is tagged it's out of the race. Merton started in 7th place, which was much too high for it, is now down to 11th, having been bumped every day—they run six days, three so far. I, being optimistic, had gone down to the first starting-place, thinking Merton would get at least that far, but it didn't—it got bumped by Exeter in about three strokes. Today, after the Rhodes House affair, Reid, who has dropped in every afternoon for tea and consolation, went for a long walk with me, just to keep in training, today being Sunday. So, as I said at the beginning of this paragraph, I'm stiff.

Miscellaneous news: Mrs. Boyd, my favorite Oxford martyr, gave me tea last Sunday—she's going back to India. I think I told you about all the intrigues and murders in the state her husband was regent of—well, the little prince they were acting for has grown up to be a weakling and has just written her husband to get him to run the country for her again.[8] Did I tell you that I ran into Helen Stevens on the street, the day I gave tea to Elizabeth [Fraser] and Blunden? She's married to a Toronto man called Chitty and is working in the Museum—some research job in science. Said she'd feed me but hasn't yet—I saw her again at Toggers. And *she's* fat and double-chinned. LePan has had an offer from Mount Allison and was asking me about the place. Says he has better things in the fire but they're vague—besides, he hopes he may get a fellowship here. It's not really an offer—just a chance of a job. And a man from Corpus Christi came in one afternoon and announced that my first cousin had married his brother. The judge in Montreal's eldest daughter[9] who went through St. Hugh's, married Christopher Bryson of Corpus and went to India with him. This kid is the very nice Englishman who reads Greats[10] well, plays rugger well, talks well, and does them all separately. We didn't make much of each other. I'm not sure I told you that when I got back from Edith & Stephen's I decided that, as Stephen was an enthusiastic stamp collector, the fact that I had a chance set of Newfoundland stamps given me by Louise Whiteway was providential, and I sent them along. I reckoned without the instinct of the true collector, however, and Stephen said he wouldn't thank me for them or put them in his album "until I'd had another think."

A few days ago I was just going out of Mob Quad when I saw a scout propping up a square block of stone that I had always taken for a sort of marble cover—in fact, that's what it is,—and wondered vaguely about, as there's no plumbing in the Mob Quad. It's in the walk just inside the archway. The scout said "Here's a bit of old stuff, sir," and I bent down to look. It's a hole dug in the ground by an anchorite or hermit, over a thousand years old—older than Merton College. Soft, oozy, clammy rock, and no room for him to lie down: he'd have to sleep crouching, or standing like a horse. Ugh! I knew it was around there, but I didn't know just where. They turned it up a few years ago, and it's the oldest building in Oxford, says the librarian, though to what extent a hole in the ground can be called a building I don't know.

The other night in the lodge our only sprig of nobility, the Honourable David St. Clair Erskine (one of our tame homosexuals as well) came in from the Dramatic Society's performance of Macbeth and met Baine, who had just come in from seeing the Marx Brothers in Duck Soup.[11] The Honourable David St. Clair Erskine was tanked up just enough to be affable to anybody—when he woke up next morning and realized that he had spoken to an American Freshman Rhodes Scholar to whom he hadn't been introduced he probably went on the water wagon for life. He said: "I enjoyed the show (meaning Macbeth) very much, didn't you?" Baine: "Very much" (meaning Duck Soup). "I remembered that I had seen it before, but I enjoyed it very well the second time anyway." The Honourable D. St. C.E. (somewhat staggered): "I—I understand they didn't get it all rehearsed in time, and are adding a few scenes at each performance." Baine: "Yes, I noticed it had been cut a good deal, but thought it had been censored." The Honourable Et Cetera: "I liked the leading lady—she's new to Oxford, but she did very well." By this time, there being no leading lady in the Marx Brothers picture, the first faint roseate blush of dawn began to appear in Baine's mind, but he wisely decided the situation would be too much for the H.D. St. C.E.'s poor bewildered brain to cope with at that point.

Thanks very, very much for the New Yorkers and your bulletins, both of which were funny in places.

I'm damned if I'm going to start a new sheet to tell you I love you.[12]

Norrie.

1 The excursion NF describes takes him and Elizabeth Fraser northeast of Oxford, Elsfield being about four miles away. The other villages—Beckley, Wood Eaton, and Marston—were all within a mile and a half of Elsfield.
2 Elsfield was the home of John Buchan—Lord Tweedsmuir—whose ashes, brought home from Canada, lie in the yard of the thirteenth-century church there.
3 A large fourteenth-century wall painting of St. Christopher fording a stream and carrying the Christ child.
4 That is, he missed dinner, which was served in the Hall. See illus. 23, this volume.
5 For NF's paper on Eliot, "T.S. Eliot and Other Observations," see the NFF, 1991, box 37, file 4.
6 A village about two miles northeast of Oxford, along the London Rd.
7 Oxford undergraduate slang for "Torpids," the boat races that took place during the Lenten term.
8 The pronoun references here are confusing. NF may mean that the letter was a request for Boyd to return to India in order to administer the northern state for the prince's mother, who is described in Letter 165. If he does not mean this, then he has mistakenly written "her" for "him" (the prince himself).
9 Harriet Jane was the eldest daughter of Eratus ("Rate") Howard, one of the older brothers of NF's mother.
10 The course of study at Oxford for the B.A. in classics and mathematics (*Literae Humaniores*).
11 A 1933 Paramount film; screenplay by B. Kalman and H. Ruby.
12 NF has crammed this sentence into three short lines at the bottom right corner of the sheet.

186. HK to NF 84 Queen's Park
March 3. 1937.

Postmarked 4 March 1937; addressed to NF at Merton College, Oxford, England, Via Halifax: Montcalm.

I forget when I wrote to you last, whether it was last week or the week before. I can't seem to remember anything these days, except that there is a great deal to do and time is going very quickly. I spent this evening figuring out how I can afford a summer in Europe. I think I can manage it if there are no accidents. I haven't phoned the steamship people yet and I haven't made any definite plans, except that I'll be taking holidays in July and August if your term ends in June. There is always Gordon Bay of course—Roy intends to go up, and Harold—which makes a perfectly good trio and I *might* even let you play with them sometimes if you're good. But no more of that.

This last week has been a little hectic. Ivor Lewis at last made definite arrangements for the Gallery to go on the air for fifteen minutes each week—Tuesday at seven-fifteen. And I'm in charge—gathering material and choosing subjects and all the rest. We start next week. Baldwin will give the first, Bert Brooker the next, Ivor Lewis and Charlie Band will do one each, and so on. I suppose I'll have to do one from time to time but not at the start. We went to Buffalo this week-end, a whole bus-load of us, and saw the Exhibition of Bronzes. And I had a talk with Mrs Davis who does their radio work, and I finally got the news slant on the thing. Local and international art news, our programs etc, children's work.[1] It will be great fun as soon as I learn how to do it, but at present I feel a little anxious, especially when Baldwin is so dependent on others for encouragement. I talk to my group to-morrow, lightly, on Cézanne. These chats are on a pretty low level of erudition, but we have a good time, and perhaps clarify a few ideas. To-night I took the Women's Lit people to see Charlie Comfort in his studio working on the murals for the new Stock Exchange Building at Bay and Melinda Street.[2] He has done eight huge murals as well as stone reliefs for the outside. The picture committee is looking for something to buy and I'm getting a little worried—the O.S.A. show is *lousy* and I really don't know what we'll get.

I've become Jessie Mac's official accompanist, to the joy of all concerned. Alta Lind Cook has been chasing her for weeks and making a great fuss about accompanying her, and it put her in a difficult position, for you know how Alta Lind plays the piano. However, I am to play for her on Monday at the University Women's Club, and Alta Lind is going to be told that I've done a good deal of work on German lieder (!), which I evidently played at sight better than Moff Woodside and Alta Lind.

The dean just came from a meeting of the Victoria College Council at which they proposed to have a faculty club room which would be limited to men. Jessie Mac evidently blew up and told them she quite understood their wanting a men's club room but need they call it faculty?[3] I see more and more what a ticklish position women are in around this place. I'll be so glad when you come back and can blow some of those pompous pseudo-scholars to hell. I do so want you to get the Blake published, and a lot more, and hit this college so hard they won't know what's happened. I didn't mention that the day I had tea with [Herbert J.] Davis, Barker Fairley was there, and when Davis asked so much about you Fairley asked if you were the man who wrote so intelligently about the Jooss ballet.[4] Norah [McCullough] says that on the trip to Buffalo Mrs Gordon Davies was telling her about how very helpful you were with her Blake paper. So there are a few people who are pretty keen about you besides myself, in this town. Esther Johnson was asking for you yesterday and urging me to get to England.

My dearest, my dearest, I sound so terribly prosaic. I don't mean to be but I'm hurrying more than I've done since I left high school—here and there, talking to so many people and having to get to bed at a decent time to keep from being cranky, and all this institutional life. I love it of course, I don't know what I should have done without it, and you away, but I can hardly wait until the summer when I can stop for a little while and look at something with you. Do you remember when we visited the Art Association in Montreal, and all the lovely things we've seen when we've been walking together? This noon I stood on a corner for a few minutes and watched the sunshine on the tops of the trees on University Avenue, and a Jew with a fur cap pushing a cart, and another whipping the horse that was harnessed to his rickety wagon. It was so strange and new, I stood there and forgot time and everything else except that I love you, always.

Your

Helen.

1 According to AGT records: "After consultation with Miss McCullough, Miss Boultbee and Miss Kemp who had discussed radio work with Mrs. Davis of the Albright Art Gallery, Buffalo, Mr. Baldwin made Miss Kemp responsible for the programme. The series was to be planned to interest a wider audience than could be reached through ordinary channels of publicity, and to provide talks which would have a very definite educational value and attract people to the Gallery." Martin Baldwin gave the first talk, "Rubens' Elevation of the Cross," on 9 March; Bertram Brooker's talk, entitled "Annual Exhibition of the OSA," was given on 16 March; HK prepared a talk called "Children in the Art Gallery," which was delivered by Judge Denton on 30 March, and presented her own talk, "The Permanent Collection," on 25 May; Norah McCullough's talk

"Children in the Art Gallery," was given on 18 May; and the remainder of the talks in
the series were given by Martin Baldwin. Edward P. Taylor Research Library of the
AGO, A.3.6.8., File: Radio Talks, Spring 1937.

2 Comfort's murals for the Toronto Stock Exchange, completed in 1937, were the first
murals in Canada to reveal modernist influences.

3 According to the minutes of a meeting of the VC Council held on 3 February 1937, "Professor Fisher brought in a suggestion that the members of the Faculty form a society—
such as a Faculty Club or Senior Common Room—at which members of the Faculty
may meet periodically in an informal manner. He suggested the Men's Faculty Club of
the University of Alberta as an example to follow, at which a member gave a twenty
minute paper on a current subject. This was followed by a discussion lasting not more
than one hour and thirty minutes." The motion was tabled for a month and brought
up again at the next meeting of the Council on 3 March 1937, at which a committee con-
sisting of "Professor Fisher, Miss Macpherson, Professor Sissons, Bennett and Hare"
was nominated to explore the possibility. Nothing further seems to have come of the
matter, however, apparently because of controversy over the question as to whether
or not to include female faculty members. Women were not allowed into the Senior
Common Room at VC until 1968.

4 NF reviewed four performances of the Jooss Ballet in the *Canadian Forum*, 16 (April
1936), 18–19.

187. HK to NF   84 Queen's Park, Toronto
                                                              March. 8. 1937.

Postmarked 9 March 1937; addressed to NF at Merton College, Oxford,
England, Via New York: Queen Mary.

If I hurry I can get a note off on the Queen Mary to-morrow. I met
someone last night who is sailing on the boat on Wednesday, and it
makes me wish that I could just pack myself in a letter and come across
to you on a penny stamp. It seems that I am a god-mother to Elaine Cud-
bird, and I didn't know it. Last night was her confirmation and that was
the first I had heard of my part in her spiritual destiny, so I turned up
with Mother to listen to Bishop Owen dispense platitudes from the pul-
pit of St. Paul's Church.

It is nine o'clock and I have just come from a meeting of the Picture
Committee. They are taking a run at choosing pictures to present at
Senior Day, and Miss Macpherson wants to buy reproductions, so Blair
Laing sent over about fifteen and I have been helping them go through
the Impressionists—they couldn't stick Renoir, liked Van Gogh of
course after all the Van Gogh education that has gone on this year, and
fortunately did not eliminate the Cézanne. Miss Manning sits and

fumes, I can see, for running the picture committee has always been her job and she isn't keen on Jessie Mac taking it over. Kathleen Irwin and the Richardson woman were in to dinner to-night and Kay Irwin kept on loudly shouting "Jessie" all through her tin-horn conversation, which was wildly inappropriate in view of the fact that there were four students at the table along with the rest of us. *Now* I know the Irwin strain though—her father is the collector of all those Daniel Fowlers we saw. Yesterday Kay Coburn and Jessie Mac and I went out to Scarborough, we took the 'bus at ten o'clock and got back here in time for tea. It was a heavenly day with bright sunshine on the snow, and the trees all dripping and shining with ice-crystals, and the earth steaming in the sun all down the side of the Bluffs.[1]

Baldie [Martin Baldwin] does the first radio talk to-morrow.[2] I think it is fairly decent. You would have been amused to see me to-day,—I went with him to the University Club to have lunch with Brooker who is doing the talk next week. Business Men's lunch stuff. I enjoyed it immensely as you may imagine, and felt no end important. Brooker is awfully sweet, I like him very well. He seems oddly unpretentious in his approach to people, simple and very direct and rather disarming. It is not what I had expected at all, for some odd reason. Baldie and I are very friendly these days, which is a good thing. He goes to Ottawa next week to judge pictures for the Coronation exhibition—Canadian painting is being represented.[3] And there is a collection of children's paintings going to Ottawa to be judged for some competition, the ridiculous part of that being that the judges are the same as for the other—Eric Brown, Baldwin, Grier, Alford, Jackson and Southam. Not anyone in the lot who has had anything to do with children's work. Norah [McCullough] gazed rather ruefully at the pictures she was sending down to-night as she told me this.

The [Herbert J.] Davis infant is not to be. Mrs Davis was in Buffalo with us, and that made me wonder, in the first place, and when we were home Norah said she had told her that this child was lost too. Roy Daniells told me that there were two others before this, and the same thing happened. I am very sorry, it is awfully hard on her, and I had counted on that child, for some reason!

I forgot to thank you for the interpretation of Roy Daniells' attitude, which doesn't really help me very much—in order to be scrupulously honourable a man surely need not ignore my whole existence. But I don't mind—he has been rude to a good many other people around here before he was rude to me. Roy [Kemp] tells me that he feels a great tension in the air whenever he goes to see Daniells and that other students have confessed to the same sensation. Poor old J.R.D. I do wish he could get over whatever it is that troubles him. He keeps on talking of his religious experiences and his scars so much that I always feel that he should have a more definitely creative outlet than anything he seems to do here. He still fusses about how much work he has to do, and in that way his reactions seem more like the instability of a woman—too nervous and highly strung. You, for instance, go quietly to work, at a speed that I have never seen equalled, but he fumes away. Why I should talk about Daniells I don't know for I haven't seen him in weeks.

How is the Blake anyway? Have you found a great deal of new material that must be incorporated into it, or are you winding up the first book now? I thought that it had all taken a very definite and nearly finished shape in your mind last summer, so I suppose that you will be working at white heat again now, once you are in the midst of it again. I wish I were with you. I love so much to be with you when you are working.

By the way, all this work on wall-paintings that Elizabeth [Fraser] is doing,—what is it for? Is she doing illustrations for Constable, or Professor Tristram, or Tancred Borenius, or any of those people? It must be great fun though rather neck-breaking and tedious now and then. I must begin to send you addresses if you are going to Italy for Easter. Where in Hades my address book has got to I can't tell, but there is a good place in Florence near the Palazzo Vecchio. Pensione Balestri, Piazza Mentana. There is also Pensione Internazionale, just near there. Both are quite good, and of course, very central. If you are buying guide books you might investigate Muirhead again. I think they are much better than the Baedeker ones,[4] and if you go to Charing Cross Road you will probably get some clean second hand ones if you go in time. I think I told you about getting in touch with student tour people. And go third-class—you save a lot of money and if we could stand it I'm sure you might. Although, as you say, I have quite a passion for garlic and onions which you unfortunately do not share. Hotels in the small places I can not tell you about because I did not take down the addresses and they were just the regular places. We stayed at a pension in Rome which was farther out than I'd go again unless I were staying longer. Hotels in Paris are cheaper across the river—along the Rue de l'Université, Rue Jacob etc there are quite good ones. The one where Higgs and I stayed

was Hôtel St. Yves, 4 Rue de l'Université. Bob Hunter had one even
cheaper a little farther down but I'm afraid I can't give you the address.
That one is near the Louvre, and the Station du Bac—tube station I
mean, and bus-stops are right at the turning of Jacob and Rue des Pères,
and all along the River of course. There are good restaurants right near.
If you want me to send you guide books, I have the Belgium one, and
Paris, and Louvre catalogues etc. If you let me know where you are
going I can send the necessary ones in a hurry, but I fear that I'm a bit
late at that, for Easter is only a few weeks away. Be sure to let me know
if any of these are any use to you.

My goodness, how my writing does meander. Harold continues to
improve. He listens every week to the symphony, and keeps a record of
all the programmes he has heard. He tells me with some perplexity that
Marcus [Adeney] told him he was the most promising pupil he has ever
had, and Harold doesn't know whether to believe he means it or not.
Roy has had first class standing all year in his essays and is the only man
in the course. There are just four women besides himself. He is doing
photographs once a month for us at the Gallery and is just finishing up
his work on Torontonensis. He was offered the editorship for next year
but is turning it down. The Branscombe boy—brother of the man you
know has had a terrific amount of work on it this year and Roy doesn't
think it is worth the 200 odd bucks they pay for it. Marion [Kemp Harri-
son]—did I tell you?—writes hoping I will not be old maidish and give
her advice about the infant. She is beginning to moralize in her letters
about the joys of motherhood and how awful it is to pass them by and
live a thwarted life—she urges me not to wait too long in having a family, and talks about the baby's constipation at some length. Ernie [Harri-
son] writes quite cheerfully and they both ask how you are.

I thought I'd stop at that point but I guess I won't after all. That was a
strange story of yours about the oldest building in Oxford. I can't imagine what a hole covered like a manhole, yet used a thousand years ago
as a hermit cell—will look like now. You seem to know some pretty
good scouts. Your story about the Honorable David St C.E., H.S, etc is
quite amusing. But I'm not sure what you find amusing in my bulletins—said she in alarm. Wait until I show you Panton's introduction to
the O.S.A. catalogue this time.[5] Rather nice that Bryson looked you up,
but it is too bad that you have so little in common. At least that is what I
gather from your remarks.

By the way, how is your family? You haven't mentioned your mother or your father or Vera at all. Seven more months and Lismer will be back. Next October Douglas MacAgy will be going to the Barnes Foundation at Merion, Pennsylvania—world's finest collection of Renoir, Cezanne, Matisse, Impressionists, etc.[6] He will stay as long as old Barnes will keep him around, and one can't tell how long that will be. Douglas has been in the hospital again after a severe attack of 'flu, and they put him in to be sure he didn't develop T.B. again. I went to see him a few times and gave him all the news of the outside world. He's out now of course and we go off to shows and drink beer afterwards and talk until midnight. I'm very fond of Douglas. I haven't seen Dot Drever. I think I told you she was busy going to secret Communist meetings and is showing a few of Millicent's [Millicent Rose's] tendencies to lecture me, in a milder way of course. So I tell Douglas he is the last of the bourgeoisie. I suppose I might take on a party affiliation of some kind, and when the time comes all they can give you to do in a practical way is licking stamps in an office job, and I can't see what good that does. I may be just too smug, but there it is. I will not go in for all this secret meeting stuff behind locked doors and running around with red flannel shirts and a finger of scorn. Still, I suppose it *is* smugness. But Dot does irritate me when she begins on the art is propaganda subject, all of which I've heard before from Millicent and done far better.

I must go off to the post-box now. I'm afraid you'll be getting out your blue pencil and marking up this letter ¶ etc. I'm very sorry. But I am in a hurry and I've been talking breathlessly at you for over an hour and a half. It is the best I can do when you are so far away, just talk like a magpie. Three months until summer. Have you written to the I.O.D.E. people? Maysie found that they made their awards a long time in advance, so don't put it off too long.[7]

My love to you, my dear.

Helen.

1 The Scarborough Bluffs are spectacular cathedral-like cliffs rising as high as one hundred metres above Lake Ontario east of Toronto.
2 See Letter 186, n. 1, above.
3 The Coronation Picture Exhibition, organized by the Royal Society of British Artists, opened 16 April 1937 at the society's galleries in Suffolk St., Pall Mall.
4 HK is referring to travel guides. Russell Muirhead was an English editor and traveller (1896–1976); in 1930 he became editor of the "Blue Guides" and later the Penguin guides to England and Wales. Karl Baedeker was a German publisher (1801–59), best known for the guidebooks that bear his name.

5 See L.A.C. Panton's remarks on p. 5 of the *Catalogue of the Sixty-Fifth Annual Exhibition of the Ontario Society of Artists, March 1937* ([Toronto]: AGT, 1937). Panton reproduces an imaginary conversation from the past between the president of the Royal Academy and the Queen, written by a Mr. Titmarsh, in which the obsequious president feels obliged to describe to the Queen the paintings of the Royal Academicians. Panton then says, "The modern President [himself], relieved of the need of describing what may easily be seen by the ordinary observer, leaves the 65th Annual Exhibition of the Ontario Society of Artists to introduce itself."

6 Albert C. Barnes, who made a fortune from an antiseptic he developed, devoted his life to collecting art and to providing education in art appreciation; his greatest interest was in modern French painting, but he also collected old masters and aboriginal art. In 1922 he established the Barnes Foundation in Merion, Pa., to house his collection; his museum was closed to the public during his lifetime.

7 Maysie Roger had been awarded an IODE Overseas Scholarship for 1934–35. See Letter 86, n. 4, above.

188. NF to HK   Oxford

Postmarked 9 March 1937; addressed to HK at 84, Queen's Park, Toronto, Ontario, Canada.

Darling, Roy [Daniells] has just written to tell me to write [Walter T.] Brown and tell him what my plans for next year are. Now I expect to finish the Blake in Italy, or at least the general outline of it, and when I get back here I want to type three copies and send one to Geoffrey Keynes, one to Edgar, and one to a publisher. If I get a favorable report from Keynes—God knows how long I'd have to wait for a publisher—then the most logical move would be to sit down in the British Museum and proceed to write footnotes on it. I should do that anyhow. So I shall have to tell Brown that if he is willing to send money enough to keep me for the summer I should like to stay here: otherwise I shall return to Canada. If I were only taking schools, I could easily spend the summer at Gordon Bay; but with this Blake complication it might be suicidal. It all sounds as though I were hedging, but after all your mind isn't made up either, and everything is so much in the air now that you have no definite reason for coming over. I can't tell you anything more definite until I hear from (a) Brown and (b) Keynes. There's no way I can get the Blake ready for publication by the end of next term unless I do not work at all towards Schools, which wouldn't make my chances for a first very bright. I know it's infuriating not to be more definite, but I simply don't know whether I'm going to be here this summer myself or not. In any case I don't know how much money you've got, and how much I should consequently need. If I did come back I should probably have to borrow from you.

This is the fag-end of the term, when I feel irritable and depressed. We've had a setback—a cold spell lasting several days, and I'm getting sick of the eternal penetrating clammy cold and of this great barn of a room. I have an east and a west window, and consequently get no sun, which stays in the south. There isn't any sun anyhow. And this electric grate never really warms the room—I can't play the piano, I can't work except here in front of the fire, and I have to keep something between the fire and my face or else my eyes get sore. It's very subtle, but the room has me absolutely framed in every direction. And I hate the chilly and filthy W.C.'s so much I've been chronically constipated all year, and I hate that god damned bell that clanks every fifteen minutes. Another term of this will be all I can possibly stand. Oh, yes, and I have to keep all the doors and windows closed and live in a fug, and still the draughts blow up through the cracks in the floor. Small things, but they add up. Still, it's a big room, which is why the Bodley Club is having a sherry party in it at six tonight. I'm glad the centre of news in Toronto has shifted from death to pregnancy—my congratulations to Ruth [Dingman Hebb]. I was very much amused at Miss Manning's maidenly fears of being raped on Charles St.—she must have a curious idea of the sexual appetite of Charles St. Its reputation rests on the fact that it did have one red-light house about twenty years ago, but the lighthouse keeper moved. There isn't a male don in the college who does ten minutes of tutoring all year—I don't know about the women, but I wouldn't worry anyhow. As for travelling over here, my original idea was for you to write your exams and for me to work in the Museum. We could do things with bicycles, I should think—either South-West England or Ireland or Southern France or West Germany—lots of places.

Life uneventful. Elizabeth [Fraser] has had a trip to London and has landed a 30 pound job drawing carpet designs for some egg who has been twisting money out of Rockefeller to produce an epic on Persian Art. Also she's trying to sell Long's wall-paintings, or rather her drawings of them, to American museums, as [Ernest W.] Tristram seems to have cornered the British market. The Metropolitan Museum is building a new medieval wing, so a man she found in London is writing them. We had another walk on the Berkshire Downs, and saw the first real piece of medieval stained glass I've seen in England, but for the most part she's kept pretty busy. There's a 12th c. church at Iffley, about three miles from here, and we went to see it. We ran into a Rhodes man I know with his girl, and he held forth on the stone carving very learnedly—I was quite impressed until I went inside the church and picked up the source of his information in the form of a little booklet.[1] There was a round window in the west wall with a poisonous piece of glass inside it, and I remarked to the girl that it was a pity to spoil the window with such a sunburst, and she said, in a very brazen American voice: "I don't see why they had to put such gosh-awful glass when it woulda been so easy for them to have reproduced the patterns of the ancients." Miss Thorneycroft had me to tea again, and as her note had forestalled mine I asked her back. She came with Elizabeth and I showed her the Library. Elizabeth loved her—she is very nice. Also I took Elizabeth to my Oxford martyr for tea, whom I'm beginning to like very well. Elizabeth behaves herself all right, but is rather embarrassingly quiet.

I have heard the Lener Quartet[2] play—they played a Mozart—the one Hart House did the night I wrote them up for *Saturday Night*[3]—with a cloying, clinging, sticky legato tone like a beggar's whine, but they did the Beethoven A minor very well and the Debussy brilliantly. Also I heard Walter de la Mare say nothing at all to the English Club.

Mike [Joseph] and I have been winding up our plans for Italy. I think Mike should be a good man to travel with—he's quiet but has a keen sense of humor, he's a very liberal-minded Catholic, and although he seems to know little of art and music, he's interested in literary symbolism and I'm expecting him to be a big help on the Blake. He tells me that when the picture "Bottoms Up" was released in New Zealand, the censor blushed prettily and substituted "Bright Side Up." Somebody slipped out to a poster, substituted the original title, and put an asterisk after it leading to a footnote, "Bottom: an American expression signifying a tramp."

Blunden I've stopped writing papers for—we've become quite good friends. He was complaining yesterday that anthologists seemed to be interested only in his very early poems, and said that most people on meeting him expected to see a rustic of sixty-five. He's a shrewd lad: I told him I wanted to write an essay on the Piers Plowman poems after I got through with Blake, as they were the nearest thing to the Blake Prophecies in English literature. He told me I'd have to learn to edit texts, and said if I could prefix my essay on the Piers Plowman poems to an edition of them, however bad, I might make fifty pounds, but if I just published the essay I'd be "out three pounds nineteen six and several drinks."

The Senior Tutor,[4] next to Blunden much the brightest spot in the college, had me over for a sherry party Sunday morning. There was a vast and milling crowd there, but in spite of it I snitched three glasses of sherry, talked to the Senior Tutor about contemporary German painting, about which I know absolutely nothing, but he had one or two rather good things by a completely unknown artist—a Madonna, holding a bright red apple, for one. I made a little speech about contemporary German painting's being able to combine bright colors & get away with it, that German painting showed a vigour and vitality their political ideology only parodied, that the blue of the Virgin's robe & the red of the apple was a case in point, that the apple where one would expect a child carried the mind from the Virgin back to Eve. You should hear me when I have a glass of sherry dangling in front of my nose. I was in the library a little while ago and a child struggling with an essay on the Atonement—about which also I know nothing in spite of the combined labours of Jack Macleod & Hugh Moorhouse—asked me a question about it. I held forth for a quarter of an hour, whereupon he smiled doubtfully and said he was going, he was afraid, to write a very unorthodox essay. It would be a help if I knew something about Anglican theology, or what passes for it.

The Bodley Club had another meeting with Espey reading a paper on Norman Douglas. An entertaining paper—mostly bits from his autobiography, which is amusing in spots.[5] The Scottish Society met and asked me along to hear Renwick, who has written a book on Spenser,[6] talk about Gothic Revivals. A comparison of Horace Walpole, Scott & William Morris—ending up with a reference to contemporary painting—God knows why. Warren, who had also been asked, decided that he wanted to talk about Picasso in the following discussion, about whom he knows a great deal, but Renwick, who had composed his paper merely as an excuse to talk, as a Scotchman, about Scott to more Scotchmen, continued to talk about Scott. He said the art of Picasso's followers was an art of the cafe rather than the studio. This was too much for me, and I said that surely 18th c. Gothic revivalism was an art of the coffee house. Renwick continued to talk about Scott.

Vera says that a tough country kid was introduced to her room who immediately pulled out a plug of tobacco & spat on the floor. Vera said: "Get out your handkerchief & clean that up." He said: "Oh, yeah!" She got hold of his collar & threw him downstairs. He came back, looking very subdued, cleaned up the spot and got to work without a word. After school he said to her, "Boy, you sure can *teach!*"

That's all, apart from some phenomenally dull lectures. Mantegna at the Ashmolean by somebody from the Slade. I could have done the Hampton Court lecture better myself.

I love you.

Norrie.

1 The Norman church at Iffley, southeast of Oxford, is noted for the wealth of its orna-
   mental stone carvings, especially the zigzag patterns of its arches.
2 A string quartet from Budapest.
3 See Letter 158, n. 8, above.
4 The senior tutor at Merton College was Idris Deane Jones, M.A. 1924.
5 In his autobiography, *Looking Back* (1933), Douglas describes his life and his friends by
   taking up their calling cards and considering them one at a time, sometimes briefly and
   sometimes at length, depending on his mood.
6 W.L. Renwick, *Edmund Spenser* (London: Edward Arnold, 1925).

189. HK to NF   84 Queens Park
                                                                 March 17. 1937.

Postmarked 17 March 1937; addressed to NF at Merton College, Oxford, England, Via New York: Europa.

My dear: There is another fast boat leaving soon, and I can't resist sending you a note, even if a very small one. I have just finished my second cocoa-party, which was, I think, quite successful. I do fairly well with small groups of people especially as this sitting room is fairly small. Four or five people are about right for a well-rounded hour and a half. I had six to-night, and it meant that the conversation was much more general than I like. It kept going, of course, I can always see to that, but I liked my first party better. The girls were different, of course. Tonight I had two of the McMaster people in,[1] very nice but one is the loudest brassiest sounding woman I know. Did I tell you that Helen Millar is back?

To-night Bertram Brooker did his radio talk and I thought it was exceedingly good. A little too serious perhaps, but he warned us that he was no comedian. Baldwin is in Ottawa judging paintings for the Coronation show. Did I tell you that the committee was also to judge children's work for London and the Paris Exposition? Well, the committee, i.e. Baldwin, Southam, Eric Brown, Alford, Jackson—know nothing whatever about child art education. Norah [McCullough] thought it rather odd, but said nothing and this morning McCurry 'phoned long distance to get her to come to-night. So she will judge the work after all.

I have just written to Marian Higgs who lives at Charlton Kings near Cheltenham—she said before that she might look you up in Oxford sometime, so don't be surprised if someone turns up called HIGGS.

I dropped in to see Barbara [Sturgis] on Sunday and she told me she had been talking to Brooker lately and when the conversation flagged she spoke of you with admiration. He brightened up at once she said, and from then on they talked about you. She sends you her love, incidentally. She is coming here for dinner on Thursday night. To-morrow I am going to see a production at Hart House of Helen Waddell's Abbé Prévost.[2] Beatty had some complimentary tickets and Douglas [MacAgy] and I are going. I have spent the day reading Barnes' book on Matisse[3] as I am talking on Matisse and Picasso on Thursday and to a Vic group to-morrow afternoon. On Monday I played for Jessie Mac [Macpherson] at the University Women's Club and met some fairly unintelligent University women who cooed and said how nice it was to be able to keep up one's music etc etc. Jessie Mac has been studying with Emmy Heim—German Lieder. She sang Schubert and Hugo Wolf songs and I think she sings very well.

Norah [McCullough] had a letter from Edith [Burnett] to-day—Edith says very nice things about you and she and Stephen seem to be sitting back on the whole, having decided that you and I are quite promising, or something to that effect.

You should see my new lounging pajamas that Mother made—they're a plum colour with a pattern of jade green and blue and black and orange, and I have a grey silk kimono? ("o" I guess it is!)[4] I wore them to-night to my party.

I hope there will be a letter from you this week. There wasn't one last week. Oh, I almost forgot to tell you. John Jones [Harwood-Jones] was asking for you to-night. And last night I met Lois Hampson who had just come from an Alumni Executive meeting and she asked how you are. She also asked who was with me one night when she met me at Eaton's (it was Douglas [MacAgy]) as she thought he looked like your type—a little unintelligent. Anyhow, since you always used to swap insults she said to tell you that one. She has just seen Helen Rogers' trousseau—H.R. is being married in two weeks at T. Eaton Memorial.[5] I wished Lois all sorts of good luck as she and Gordie [Romans] have bought a ring or something of that kind, so she said the event wasn't coming off for years and years. I had the same answer for her when she asked me that question. Do you realize, my dear Frye, that I own several pillow cases and towels? ! Aunt Lily [Maidement] thinks something should be done, if I won't attend to it. Bless her heart. I hope the Blake is progressing and that you are very well, my dear—

Your

Helen.

1 Visitors from McMaster University in Hamilton, Ont.
2 Helen Waddell had translated Abbé Prévost d'Exiles's *Manon Lescaut* (New York: Dutton, 1935).
3 Albert C. Barnes and Violette de Mazia, *The Art of Henri Matisse* (New York: Barnes Foundation Press, 1933).
4 HK blotted out the last letter of "kimono" and then wrote an "o" above it.
5 Timothy Eaton Memorial Church on St. Clair Ave. W. in Toronto.

190. NF to HK   Roma

Postmarked 24 March 1937; addressed to HK at 84, Queen's Park, Toronto, Ontario, Canada.

Darling:

Still alive, but very tired, with tourist's neck and tourist's feet. We're in Rome and have been in Italy about five days. Term ended in Oxford uneventfully. In London I went to see Stephen and Edith [Burnett] again, and Stephen was quite helpful with addresses of pensions and so on. Then Mike Joseph and I left for Newhaven in the rain, crossed the Channel—Mike was a bit sick but then he'd had a hangover—with a few hour's sunshine, got into Dieppe in more rain, and arrived in Paris about dinner time. We got a bus across Paris, though we couldn't persuade the conductor to take our tickets for the trip we had bought in Oxford—luckily we had got some French money—left our bags in a cheap hotel near the Gare de Lyon and went out and had some dinner. Then we went for a walk down the Rue de Rivoli, but everybody had put up their shutters and gone to bed, possibly because there had been a big strike the day before. Anyway I've seldom seen a quieter town. Early next morning we left for Italy, crossed the border about six, changed trains at Turin, and got into Genoa, dead tired, at about midnight. We fell in with some very friendly Italians, some of whom could speak French, and asked them to recommend us a good cheap hotel. They mentioned the Colombie, which turned out to be the best hotel in Genoa, of course, and it cost us 116 lire to get out of it. Still, the bath we had was worth it. What particularly attracted me was a little switch at my bedside, with three buttons on it, one with a picture of an electric light underneath, one with a picture of a maid, and one with a picture of a butler. I produced a butler from it too, in the morning. We didn't stop to see Genoa, but left the next morning for Pisa, and spent the afternoon there, seeing the cathedral with the Cimabue mosaic, the Campo Santo with that magnificent Triumph of Death and the Gozzolis,[1] and making sure that the Leaning Tower really did lean. We landed in Siena that night, at a pension Stephen had recommended. A little more expensive than we needed, although he said it was very cheap. The management consisted of an old lady, her assistant, and a maid, all very cheerful, extremely friendly, and unable to speak a word of anything but Italian. We had long conversations with the old girl in the evenings, and if we'd stayed there a week we'd have learned some Italian. She was very clever—kept re-phrasing her remarks and shrieking at us until the central idea finally penetrated. Mike's room had Cupids on the ceiling: mine looked like a Gordon Craig gone wrong.[2] The house, like everything else in Siena, was an ex-palace, and my room had five enormous pillars with Ionic capitals in a semicircle across the middle of it, with a light shining down from between them. The maid tried to talk to me too, but with less success, perhaps because her points were subtler. She kept saying "Mi bacie," or something: it didn't dawn on me for a long time that she wanted me to kiss her. In the evening she came in and started pulling my hair, got her kiss and departed gurgling. Everybody wants to pull my hair in Italy. In the train to Genoa I caught the words "biondino inglese" and a woman's remark "com'una signorina."[3] Well, Siena is a lovely town—I forget whether you saw it or not. As we got in Saturday night, everything was closed up the next day, but we saw the Town Hall, climbed the tower as nothing else was open, saw the Cathedral, went into the little Museum beside the Cathedral where the Duccios are, stood around and looked helpless until the attendant finally let us in and showed us around.[4] Guides are a nuisance, though—we got let in for a lot of vestments and carved pewter and things. Next day we went through the art gallery[5]—the first part of it very good—and left for Orvieto. We spent the afternoon at Orvieto in the cathedral with a long speech about the Signorellis[6] from a sacristan who seemed to think I could understand Italian, and got into Rome at night. We hit a place called the Pensione Flavia, where some Rhodes Scholars we know were staying, and promptly moved. Yesterday we went through the Colosseum, Forum, and Pantheon, and today through churches (Santa Maria Maggiore, San Pietro in Vincoli[7] where the Michelangelo Moses is, San Clemente, probably the most interesting thing in Rome, and Santa Prassede) and the Lateran Museum. Tomorrow to the Thermae Museum, and the Capitoline if we have time. We're leaving the Vatican until after Easter. I don't like Rome much—everything is the biggest and loudest in the world, and the Mussolini mentality is stampeding everything. I wish I hadn't come to Rome—I'd sooner have stayed in North Italy. Still, it's all very good for me. Of course Mussolini came back from Libya the day we arrived and Rome was a riot of flags and soldiers, which may have prejudiced me.[8] Still, the same sort of mind put up the Colosseum and St. Peter's. And even Rome wasn't as patriotic as Siena, which must have had at least a thousand pictures of his ugly mug on the walls.

Keep on writing to Merton College, of course—I'll get your letters at Florence. I love you very much, stupid as this letter is.

Norrie.

1 Cimabue's mosaic, *Our Lord in Glory*, completed in 1302, is in the half-dome over the altar of the cathedral. *The Triumph of Death* is a fresco by an unknown fourteenth-century master; the frescoes by Benozzo Gozzoli, painted 1469–85, depict twenty-three scenes from the Old Testament.
2 Craig (1872–1966) was an influential British theatre designer; one of his innovations was to produce different moods by changing the stage light projected on large screens and flights of steps.
3 The Italian phrases, respectively: "kiss me," "fair-haired Englishman," and "like a young girl."
4 The cathedral in Siena, dedicated to the Assumption, is the earliest of the great Tuscan Gothic churches, built between 1196 and 1215. The paintings by Duccio di Buoninsegna NF saw in the Museo dell'Opera del Duomo were the celebrated *La Maestà* (1308–11), the *Triumphant Madonna*, and the *Life of Christ*.
5 The Accademia di Belle Arti, a gallery that housed a large collection of almost exclusively Sienese masters, including Duccio and Simone Martini; the paintings of this gallery are now in the Pinacoteca.

6 Luca Signorelli painted a large number of the murals in the cathedral between 1499 and 1504; they are one of the great fresco cycles of the Italian Renaissance.
7 For the drawings of San Pietro in Vincoli done by HK during her own trip to Rome in 1935 see illus. 17 and 18, vol. 1.
8 Mussolini had paid a twelve-day visit in March to Libya, where he had opened a new coastal highway to the Egyptian frontier.

191. HK to NF   Toronto, Ontario
                                                                     March 30. 1937.

Postmarked 31 March 1937; addressed to NF at Merton College, Oxford, England, Via New York: Bremen.

My dear: I am staying at Oaklawn[1] this week, since Helen Brown has gone home to Sarnia for the Easter holidays. I stayed in Wymil-wood during Easter—worked on Good Friday and on Saturday on a radio talk that was given to-night by Judge Denton.[2] On Children at the Art G. of T., the painting of Emily Carr, and events of the week. It was amusing, Baldie delivered the talk to the Judge on Saturday, and on Monday it came back for re-typing and all the quotations from Lismer were scratched and rearranged and re-worded—but in the main the judge seemed to like it. I forgot to listen to it to-night, but I could not have done so anyway as I was on duty and had to do the praying and pour thousands of cups of coffee. The don's sitting-room in Oak-lawn is huge, with striped hardwood floor, a chesterfield, large arm-chair, a big desk, a telephone extension, a fire place, a huge bookcase, a God-awful rug and high ceiling. I get a 'phone call and don't have to move from the desk!

Do you remember a big loud-mouthed girl in 3T2 who always spits when she talks, a friend of Eunice Noble—her name is Kay Russell, I think. She was in Moderns and after graduation she was in Paris for a year or maybe two. Well, the Ontario Educational Association is having the usual Easter pow-wow around the University and this mug way-laid me at noon to-day. But to-night, of all things, she was at Annesley for dinner—*I* had to lead in the procession, sit in the Dean's chair as she was out, and all that. And when I went to talk to her she was sitting with two Finnish girls from Sudbury—awfully good kids—and Eleanor Wainright also from Sudbury, a friend of Isabel Ricker's who has been teaching for several years and is back getting her degree finished up.

Well, the Russell sat there and said "Imagine your being a don! Why you graduated a year after I did! It reminds me of Bolton Camp when Helen Emerson was a counsellor and everybody thought she was so wonderful but I couldn't see it. Why she was in High School a year behind me! And the kids used to get crushes on her and say 'I wonder what Miss Emerson thinks of this or that!' 'They were all so silly!'" I put off that sprightly conversational tid-bit, remembering that she had always been noted for her subtle sense of the tactful,—when someone said something about Professor Hare. Then she was off again, of course, because she had stayed in the same pension in Paris a year after he had been there and madame had told her all about Monsieur Hare and the little boy had called him "Mon Petit Archie"—and so she couldn't imagine anyone calling him Professor Hare.[3]

By the way, getting on to a somewhat pleasanter reminiscence—do you remember someone who went to school with you in Moncton, called Tom Crawford? Well, he is in Toronto now and is a friend of Peggy Kidder's, and, oddly enough, is the one who is arranging our passage on the freighter! Peggy mentioned you because I have talked about an interest in the Maritimes, and so Tom said he went to school with you! We are not sure when we can get away, but at present we are trying to come over in June on a freighter carrying *coal*!! And we sail from Sydney, after having come from Montreal either by freighter or else being driven down by Peggy's mother and grandmother. I think I will drop in to see your aunt in Montreal and Hewie[4] and Fluffy, and I might even pay a visit to Moncton if I could. *Do* you think that would be too unconventional? With you not there to do the introducing? The freighter did cost Tom $30 to get to England last year, but the rates may have gone up this year. We hope to know soon at any rate.

Did I tell you I wrote to McCurry about the Courtauld exam, and he said I was under no obligation to try it again, that I'd probably be much better employed here and that things were very unsettled over there anyhow. I think I did tell you that but I can't quite remember, so you must forgive me for overlapping now and then.

Norrie, my dear, when you come back here we are going to give little parties for different staff members and we are going to invite the women and anyone who talks about babies and whooping cough won't be asked again. Do you remember what I told you about the *"Staff"* Common Room and how the idea was to have a men's sitting room at Burwash[5] and the reason for starting anything different from the Senior

Common Room in the first place was because they wanted to get rid of Currelly and a few others. But the women made an issue of it and poor [Joseph] Fisher was having a conference with Jessie Mac about it this afternoon. I was pretty annoyed earlier in the fall when someone said "wives are a blight!" but I see that the Victoria men seem to consider most women as such. Now why is that? Men should always have the companionship of other men just as women need other women, but in a professional way do they need to hate each other so? What a devilish smug place this college is sometimes—I can't figure what is the matter. The men and women surely aren't like this in other coeducational institutions,—but perhaps they are, and I just don't know about it.

I spent fifteen cents on a copy of Edmund Blunden's "Undertones of War"[6] yesterday. His picture is in it too. I imagine him to be fairly slight, medium height, slightly stooping and pretty diffident in his manner. I get that impression from his writing too, although I have not got far with my little Phoenix.

Douglas MacAgy and I went to hear the St Matthew Passion[7]—it was better than last year, I think, and I took Harold to hear the St. John.[8] Harold Sumberg is starting a small orchestra and asked Harold to play in it.

The picture committee was considering a Thomson sketch. Mellors[9] have had a very good show of Thomson's work, and Blair Laing gave a radio talk in his inimitable crooning way[10]—well, anyhow, there has been a good deal of interest lately in Tom Thomson. So Blair brought over a pretty feeble sketch and asked $200 for it, and I had to persuade the committee not to get it, Norah [McCullough] reenforcing me in that. Jim Lawson was called in and he advised them to get a Thomson at any price, which doesn't sound very discriminating to me. It was a pleasant thing, but slight, and an early sketch—1914, before he had developed that broad sweeping freedom that one expects. This was wiggly and hesitant in its going, though the colour was delicate and very pleasant.[11]

Norah has arranged a show of children's work from different places in Canada. Some of the best comes from Fritz Brandtner's class in Montreal where I tried to get your aunt to send the *Enfant Terrible*, who is now in boarding school I understand.[12]

I have been thinking of you in Italy for the last two weeks at least—I was not sure when you were going and you told me nothing of your plans, such as where you were going etc. I hope the man you went with was a good travelling companion, and that Italy was not too hostile to

Britishers, although I've been reading some pretty hot shots from Mussolini in the press.

Roy [Daniells] had a tea-party on Sunday and it was very nice. I kept counting back to see how long ago it was that you first came to see us and I gave you a raw carrot to eat. It is six years ago, and I'm always a little amazed at how strong-minded I was, my poor dear, you hadn't *much* chance, did you? I remember being sorry for you being so far from home, then scared to ask you to come to tea, then amazed that I had been so bold, and pleased when you were evidently shy and glad to come, and I was vaguely irritated and embarrassed (how many r's) when you made fun of me for playing Goossens, and perplexed at having asked George [Clarke] when I was obviously more interested in what you would do next. Six years. I love you very much and I'd like to tell you so here, to-night, now—My God! no. Not *here!!* Still, if you walked in the front door, for instance, and the girl on duty ushered you in to THE PRESENCE, I could manage a fairly conventional exterior I daresay. It's easy enough to say that at this distance, but even so far away I have some very queer sensations when I think of you. So I think of something else and they go away. And even if I did call you a mug the other day to Esther Johnson who was asking me where you were in Italy and I said I didn't know because you hadn't said—I didn't mean it and I apologize!

Helen

1 A VC women's residence at 113 Bloor St. W.
2 "Children in the Gallery"; a copy with HK's holograph annotations is in the HFF, 1992, box 4, file 9; another copy is in the Edward P. Taylor Research Library of the AGO.
3 Archibald Hare, VC 3T0, was instructor in the French department, 1930–33. He rose to the position of professor and retired in 1963.
4 NF's maternal aunt, Harriet ("Hatty") Howard. Hewie (Hugh Gordon) was one of her twin sons.
5 See Letter 186, n. 3, above.
6 A book of poems by Edmund Blunden, published in London by R. Cobden-Sanderson in 1928.
7 Properly, *The Passion According to St. Matthew*, a setting by Bach for solo voices, chorus, and orchestra of the passion narrative from Matthew's gospel; it was first performed in 1729.
8 Bach's *St. John Passion* (1723).
9 Mellors Fine Arts Ltd. was a Toronto art gallery, located at 759 Yonge St.; its name was changed to Mellors-Laing in 1940, and still later it became Laing Galleries.
10 The AGT radio talk scheduled for 30 March 1937 was the one written by HK and delivered by Judge Denton referred to earlier in the letter. Laing's talk is not on record;

he may have taken over one of the time slots assigned to Baldwin or given a talk independently. He was working at the time at the Mellors Gallery.

11 It would appear that both HK and Jim Lawson got their way. According to the minutes of a meeting of the Picture Committee held on 8 April 1937 it was unanimously agreed to purchase Thomson's *Autumn. Algonquin Park* from Mellors for $250 (rather than the original "feeble sketch"). According to a further memo from Alice Rathé, who refers to it as "Opulent October" or "Autumn Algonquin," it was offered to VC by J.S. Lawson in 1937 along with eleven other pieces. (Alice Rathé to Jean O'Grady, 1 June 1995). The purchase of the second Thomson sketch is mentioned by HK in Letter 194.

12 The reference is to Gloria Garratt, the adopted daughter of NF's aunt Dolly Howard; she was being raised by another of NF's aunts, Hatty Layhew.

192. NF to HK   Florence.

Postmarked 5 April 1937; addressed to HK at 84, Queen's Park, Toronto, Ontario, Canada.

I forget exactly when or what I wrote last, but I was doubtless in Rome, registering dislike. Rome is horrible. I wasn't quite prepared for the national monument to Victor Emmanuel II, but after I'd seen it it fitted in. Rome built that Colosseum barn, Rome built St. Peter's with its altar canopy a hundred feet high and its elephantine Cupids in the holy-water basin, Rome built that ghastly abortion already referred to, Rome produced a long line of tough dictators and brutal army leaders and imbecile Caesars and Mussolini. What Prussia is to Germany, what Scotland is to Britain, that Rome is to Italy—sterile as an egg and proud of it. Romans stare and peer at you hostilely and sulkily in the streets where north Italians are merely interested in you; Rome is full of Germans where Florence is full of English and Americans; Rome gave me a disease that felt like the seven-year itch but is gradually wearing off; Rome stunk; Romans gyp you; Romans break out in a rash of flags the day you arrive and welcome the return of their prodigal son Mussolini. History of Roman art: bastard Etruscan, bastard Greek, stolen Greek, bastard Oriental, bastard North Italian, bastard copies of bastard Greek, bastard Dutch, and various kinds of eclectic bastardy. Its one original art is the circus. By far the most interesting and genuine of the churches was San Clemente,[1] and I liked some of the mosaics—the Cavallinis in Santa Maria Trastevere[2] and the Torritis in Santa Maria Maggiore[3] particularly. The classical museums, the Thermae, the Vatican, the Lateran and the Capitoline being the ones I went to, were huge junk piles, but there

were good things in them, and I did get a vague idea of the development of Greek sculpture from superb archaic things like the Ludovisi
throne[4] to the Pergamene and Rhodian stuff. As for Rome—well, Rome
contributes tons and tons of sarcophagi with the Romans depicted in
relief as "conquering the barbarians," i.e., cutting unarmed men to
pieces, making their horses step on women's faces, burning houses and
stabbing yelling children. And a floor mosaic in the Lateran, covered
with pictures of broken bones, pieces of asparagus, fish heads and other
things that some filthy swine would naturally throw on the floor while
he was eating—that's the kind of idea that could occur only to a Roman.
More mosaics from the Baths of Caracalla, with the most brutal subhu-
man faces on them I have ever seen depicted in art.[5] There are fine
things in Rome, or would be if one didn't have to go to Rome to see
them, but some are over-rated. Parts of the Vatican are fine, though one
can't forget that one is in the Vatican, what with all their obscene fig-
leaves. St. Peter's certainly had to be seen to be believed—I knew it was
hideous but I didn't think so big a building could be so pitifully unim-
pressive. But the worst I have not told you. They have a pleasant little
trick in this country of "restoring" frescoes: i.e., of removing the whole
of the original fresco and substituting a modern copy, or what amounts
to one. They are doing that with the Sistine Chapel ceiling at this very
moment—when I was there about a third of it was covered up and a
great array of scaffolding built under it. They are doing that with the
Santa Croce Giottos here in Florence—the death of St. Francis is covered
up now, they tell me.[6] They are doing that with the Gozzolis in San
Gimignano,[7] a friend tells me who has been there. With that, with the
frightful cleaning of pictures in the Uffizi, and with all those sculptures
with the head from another statue and an arm from a third, about
twenty-five per cent.—so far—of the things worth looking at are fakes.
The rumor that they were putting pants on the Michelangelo figures
was denied, but they always deny everything, including the fact that the
frescoes are being restored. Still, the tin pants on the Cnidian Aphrodite
seem to have temporarily fallen off.[8] I thought the best thing in the Vatican was the little Fra Angelico Chapel.[9] I don't think I like Raphael
much—the Logge was terrible—mostly parodies of Michelangelo, with
Jehovah scampering around like a scarecrow in a high wind.[10] Of course
that had been restored too, and evidently quite recently—my Baedeker
was written in 1930, and it was amusing to compare the picture
described as "obliterated" with the travel poster leering down at you

from the ceiling. The best Raphael I saw was at the Villa Farnesiva,[11] I think—Raphael has a conventional Renaissance mind, and he seems to have no sense of organic form—that is, his big pictures are never the exact shape of the conception behind them. The School of Athens could have been painted a hundred ways. Michelangelo was magnificent but Beethovenish—the Adam is incredibly subtle, but I don't think any of him equals the Triumph of Death at Pisa[12] as far as impressiveness goes. The trouble with both of them is that they're civilized high brows— they're neither Christians nor pagans: they're just metropolitans—in short, Roman painters. The Vatican picture gallery had two or three fine rooms of early painting, including a Simone Martini head of Christ I liked better than anything else,[13] but most of it was just pure liquid, glu- tinous shit. So was the Borghese, bar a swell Titian and a copy of a Leonardo; so was the Doria, bar a Velasquez and a Breughel.[14] Lots [of] sixteenth, seventeenth & eighteenth century Italian painting also has to be seen to be believed. The Pantheon was magnificent—inside—one cat- acomb was thrilling, the other a dismal fake. Well, maybe I was unjust to Rome—there is supposed to be some good relief carving on the Petri- fied Penis, alias Trajan's Column, which Mike [Joseph] admires because it's sustained its erection so long—but I hated it, and so did Mike, and so did the two Americans travelling with us.

I probably told you that we picked up Baine and these two Exeter men in Rome. Baine we left there, and the four of us went to Assisi.[15] We got there at night and spent the next day there. Assisi was glorious. We liked everything there, and would have liked to stay longer. We spent the whole day in San Francesco, apart from a few hours wandering about the town—those Giotto, that Cimabue and what was left of the Cavallini kept us working hard for six hours. We probably missed some good stuff in Santa Chiara, but we got a lot out of our one day.[16] The view is gorgeous, and while I know the town is a tourist's museum, it comes off somehow. You were closer to me at Assisi than anywhere else in Italy, I think—I kept you in front of my mind all the time, stuck in so lovely a place with a fool like Millicent [Rose], and wishing you were there with me alone. It was a perfect day, and we made a bad mistake in leaving for Perugia that night. The next morning we went into a place called the Collegio da Cam- bio and looked at Perugino, some vaguely charming, some sickly.[17] Then the Art Gallery—very valuable historically, I suppose, as it gave the whole Umbrian school, but lousy. Rather a pathetic gallery, in fact,—it started off well and then faded out—the faces were all imbecile and vacuous, and the Perugino there—several rooms of it—was just a lot more like it.[18] Perugia was a bloody burg too—we could see models for those imbeciles everywhere we looked. We cleared out of there at noon and went on to Arezzo. I have nothing but pleasant memories of Arezzo—the Piero della Francesca frescoes, which we spent two hours on and which were well worth it,[19] and one of the best dinners we have had in a restaurant just beside it. It has one fine church too. Well, that night we got into Florence. Florence is frightfully crowded, and for the last two nights we've slept in one corner of a huge lounge room in this pension, but now we've got a room. I've had two days in Florence. Yesterday morning we went to the Uffizi.[20] The opening room contained a Cimabue Madonna, a Giotto Madonna, and a Lorenzo Monaco Madonna—three of the very loveliest pictures I have ever seen.[21] I stuck most of the morning in that room. Lorenzo Monaco was a big surprise—he had interested me in the National Gallery but I had no idea that he was in the top rank. There are three of his there, two absolutely perfect, one ruined by cleaning or restoring or something.[22] And I shall return with a profound conviction that Cimabue was the very greatest painter who ever lived, on the strength of two paintings.[23] Well, there was a lot more in the Uffizi—I'm going back tomorrow morning, when it'll be free, to look at the Mantegna and some of the Dutch.[24] In the afternoon—well, the Uffizi took most of the afternoon—we went around and looked at the Cathedral, which was a bitter disappointment—seen in black and white reproductions it's fine, but in its dirty pink and green pristine splendor it's a horror. I couldn't even get used to the Giotto tower, though I kept trying hard to keep it isolated from the cathedral by dodging around doors and things. Today we went to the Pitti Gallery, an experience I am very glad to have put behind me. Fortunately, Italian decadent painting is so bad that it's really extremely funny—we particularly liked the martyrdom of St. Agatha, where a huge blond sow was stripped to the waist and having her breasts worked on with pincers—"Fancy," said Mike, "a female saint's having breasts big enough to get hold of with pincers"—and there was something in the careful way the pincers were being fitted to the nipples that made us howl.[25] Then there was one of a cupid reaching up into the genitals of Hercules.[26] We call them the Teat-Twister and the Testicle-Teaser, and are extremely fond of them. This afternoon we went to the Museo Nazionale—two or three fine Michelangelos, including the Brutus, which I liked better than any sculpture of his I saw in Rome,[27] and a room full of Donatello. I'm having a good time. I'm glad I saw Pisa first—I got the impact of the Cathedral and the Triumph of Death straight away, and have never seen a better building or fresco since. One big improvement— the Americans brought a pair of field glasses, and I shall never again attempt to travel in Italy without them. What I missed with my myopic eyesight looking at the Signorellis in Orvieto[28] I shudder to think, and there was a Donatello in the Siena Cathedral[29] I couldn't see at all.

There is an amazingly penetrating sweetness about you—I would so much rather see you than the next town in Italy, whatever it is.

Norrie.

1 San Clemente, even after many restorations, still maintains the character of an early basilica; it was built by Pope Paschalis in 1108 on the ruins of a fourth-century church.
2 Pietro Cavallini's mosaics (late thirteenth century), between the windows and at the base of the chancel arch, represent scenes from the life of the Virgin. Cavallini may have been responsible as well for the mosaics outside, high on the façade of Santa Maria Trastevere.
3 The central theme of Jacopo Torriti's apsidal mosaics (1275) is the crowning of the Virgin.
4 The throne for a colossal statue of Aphrodite, an original fifth-century Greek sculpture decorated with reliefs that are among the masterpieces of classical sculpture, is in the Thermae Museum (National Roman Museum).
5 The mosaics, depicting athletes, gladiators, and their trainers, date from the third century; they are not in the Caracalla Baths themselves but in the Museum of Pagan Antiquities in the Vatican, a collection assembled by Gregory XVI in the nineteenth century.
6 All of the eleven choir chapels of the Santa Croce church contain frescoes by Giotto and his pupils; scenes from the life of St. Francis of Assisi, including one of him on his death-bed, are in the Bardi chapel.
7 The Gozzoli works NF is referring to are the frescoes in the Sant'Agostino Church. See Letter 195, n. 5, below.
8 A copy of Praxiteles's Cnidian Aphrodite is in the Museo Pio-Celementino at the Vatican.
9 The Chapel of Niccolò V, decorated by Fra Angelico in 1450–55 with frescoes from the lives of Saints Lawrence and Stephen.
10 The western wing of the Logge in the Vatican is decorated with stucco and paintings designed by Raphael, who supervised their execution; the paintings on the vaults— scenes from the Old and New Testaments—are known as "Raphael's Bible."
11 *The Myth of Psyche*, frescoes executed from Raphael's designs, in 1518–20.
12 See Letter 190, n. 1, above.
13 The Martini painting, *Christ Blessing*, originally crowned an altarpiece.
14 Velasquez's *Pope Innocent X* and Brueghel's *The Four Elements* are in the Doria Palace.
15 One of the four, Charles Bell, reported in his diary, "We were all glad to escape the noise and glory of Rome, and are in hopes of seeing tomorrow some really good art unmarred by Baroque alterations" ("The Imprint of Northrop Frye in Charles Bell's Poetic NOW," unpublished typescript, 4).
16 San Francesco and Santa Chiara are churches in Assisi. In the former are Giotto's first recorded paintings and the most famous of his Franciscan fresco cycles, along with

other works by him and his school; both transepts were painted by Cimabue; Cavallini and his pupils painted thirty-two scenes from the Old and New Testaments.

17 The Collegio del Cambio was originally a hall and chapel of the Bankers' Guild; the hall itself, the Udienza del Cambio, was decorated with frescoes by Perugino and his pupils, including those depicting the cardinal virtues, the Christian virtues, the Transfiguration, and the Adoration of the Magi (1499–1500).

18 The gallery was in the Pallazzo Municipio, the third floor of which is now the Galleria Nazionale dell'Umbria; it contains numerous works by Perugino and his school and by other Umbrian masters, including Pinturicchio and Bonfigli.

19 The church of San Francesco in Arezzo contains Piero della Francesca's masterpiece *The Legend of the True Cross* (ca. 1454).

20 Charles Bell wrote in his diary, "The four of us [Frye, Lou Palmer, Mike Joseph, and himself] who have come together to Florence spent the whole morning in the Uffizi. . . . We got to the first six rooms, but stood before the greatest pictures, Cimabue, Giotto, Simone, the Botticellis, over half an hour each" ("The Imprint of Northrop Frye in Charles Bell's Poetic NOW," unpublished typescript, 4).

21 Cimabue's *Maestà* was painted ca. 1285; Giotto's, ca. 1310; and Lorenzo Monaco's *Madonna and Child*, 1406–10.

22 In addition to the *Coronation of the Virgin*, the Uffizi houses Lorenzo Monaco's *Gethsemene* and *Adoration of the Magi*.

23 *Our Lord in Glory* in Siena and the *Maestà* in the Uffizi.

24 Among the Mantegnas in the Uffizi are the *Madonna in a Rocky Landscape* (ca. 1489) and his altarpiece, comprising the *Adoration of the Magi*, the *Presentation in the Temple*, and the *Ascension*. The Uffizi contains a large number of works by the Dutch and Flemish masters.

25 *The Martyrdom of St. Agatha* (1520) by Sebastiano del Piombo.

26 A fresco (1828) by Pietro Benvenuti in the Sala di Ercole.

27 In addition to *Brutus* (unfinished, ca. 1539–40), the National Museum contains Michelangelo's *Bacchus* (1497) and three additional unfinished sculptures: *Victory*, the *Holy Family* (a high relief), and *Apollo, or David*.

28 See Letter 190, n. 6, above.

29 A tondo of the *Madonna and Child*, over the door of the south transept.

193. NF to HK   Venezia

Postcard; postmarked 14 April 1937; addressed to HK at 84, Queen's Park, Toronto, Ontario, Canada. The letter NF says he is "writing tonight" is missing. In Letter 195 he explains that he wrote it as promised, but lost it in Florence, and whether or not HK received it would depend on "whether someone picks it up and puts a stamp on it and mails it."

We have just climbed this damned thing.[1] Writing tonight. Breathless. I love you.

Norrie.

1 The bell-tower of St. Mark's, on the southeast corner of St. Mark's Square.

194. HK to NF   Toronto, Ont.
                                                              April 18. 1937.

Addressed to NF at Merton College, Oxford, England, Via New York: Berengaria. *HK dated this letter "April 18," but she says she "went back to work to-day, being Monday," so the letter was written on 19 April.*

Dearest, your letter came last week, your first from Italy, and I felt quite out of breath with all the sight-seeing you were doing in five days. Your onslaught upon Rome was quite breath-taking. I hope you slowed down a little and took time off to go for walks in the hills around Florence. It is too heavenly to miss, the olive trees in bloom and wild flowers along the pathways and that glorious smell in the air. It was very odd, but on the anniversary of the founding of Fascism[1] I kept thinking of you in Italy and remembering all the Fascist songs we had to listen to on that day in Rome, and the weather here was very like Rome. Then for Easter it rained or was dismal and cold and I had a radio talk to write and stayed here for much of the time, and the weather did not remind me of Italy.

I am sure Stephen [Burnett] would be helpful for there is *nothing* he likes better to do than messing with railroad maps and keeping track of good pensions. I hope Mike Joseph is as congenial as you hoped. You don't say where you stayed in Paris—you were wise to make a stop-over, I think—we took the Rome express and hardly slept all night, with poor Millicent [Rose] trying to stay on the seat doubled up with a middle-aged Frenchman's carpet slippers pushing her in the stomach. You have already seen Pisa and Siena—neither of which we saw. I hope you walked around Orvieto, but perhaps you wouldn't have time if you left for Rome in the late afternoon. The Signorelli and Fra Angelico chapel is marvellous isn't it? Did you remember all the carvings on the front of the cathedral from the post cards I showed you? They are some of the loveliest things I remember. Before dark, Millicent and I walked around the crazy little streets inside the town wall, and I can still hear the sound of horses clattering over the cobblestones in the street outside our hotel next morning. You evidently did not go to Arezzo, or perhaps you were going to stop there on the way back to Florence—and what about Perugia? The museum at Perugia exerted an evil fascination for me—I look[ed] at those four later Perugino's so long that I paid more attention to them than I did to a lot of far better paintings, I was so annoyed with all the feet being turned out just *so*, and the eyes gazing heavenward with their glycerine tears ready to drop. At the rate you are travelling you will see a great many places—I was hoping you would go to Ravenna to see the mosaics there, but of course it is out of the way rather.

I feel as if I have just emerged from a long darkness. I spent all last week in the Infirmary. It began with a cold and then I went to the gallery on Wednesday and because I was simple enough to have walked down I had an emotional splurge and Marge [Boultbee] packed me into her car and back I went to the top floor again. I have been so tired that I thought I'd never crawl out but I went back to work to-day, being Monday. I still feel a little infirm but that will pass, of course. The nurse was awfully nice, and Kay Coburn came up nearly every day, partly to see how I liked various Tom Thomsons that she brought up for inspection. They are offering Mellors $250 for a Thomson sketch. The picture committee is a long story and a little boring so I shall dispense with it—more politics.

Last Saturday was the Senior Dinner[2] and I managed to get to it more dead than alive. Kay and I were the only dons who went. I had a very nice time, sitting at a table up in the balcony with Taylor Shore at the end, Mary Woodward on one side of him and Florence Wagstaff[3] on the other, a man named [W. Donald] Tweedell on my left and Les Vipond on my right. He and I had a very nice time, especially when we got onto a subject dear to us both—H.N. Frye. He was surprised that I knew you—but not impolitely so—and interested in hearing what you were doing. He said it was very odd that you were never at all personal with him and neither of you talked about your personal affairs when you were together, but only about D.H. Lawrence and all the rest of what you had so much to tell and he was so eager to hear. So that he did not even know what course you had taken. He wished me to give you his regards when I wrote to you, and I add that I like him very much. He said he had written to you and would do so again soon, that he learned more from you than from all his other courses put together and was sorry that you were away and that such a pleasant association had had to come to an end. He hoped that he would see you in the future and I made a special note resolving that he *should*. He is coming back to do graduate work in English, so that he will still be here when you return after another year, and I might have him in to tea. You see I am making plans for you already!

As I was leaving with Kay, Dr [Walter T.] Brown stopped to talk to me and asked if I hear from England regularly? I said I had just had one from Italy after an interval of three weeks. So they both took the opportunity of teasing me about letters every other day and such. Brown wanted to know what your plans are, I said the Blake was nearly finished, but I couldn't very well tell him it all depends on him or on the I.O.D.E. At any rate he was quite affable. Speaking of *my* getting myself thoroughly involved with you—if you ever came home to Victoria College with a Spanish bride you'd have to do a little explaining to Dr Brown. I seem to be firmly fixed in his mind, marked "Frye."

Eric Havelock buttonholed me and asked me whether I am interested in a job on The Forum. Pegi Nicol, as you know, got married, and is resigning, and they're looking for an art editor. I'd like the job. I'm afraid it might be a lot of work. I can do a better job than she did, at any rate. As a critic I'm very unsure, but I could farm out a lot of articles. It would be marvellous practice, I'd meet some very bright people ———— in spite of Dot Drever saying The Forum is all Trostsky-ites now and therefore anathema from her point of view. I am handing in another article to The School—that stuffy little O.C.E. magazine. On Children at the Art Gallery.[4]

I am making plans for coming over and I am not yet sure just when. I may come early in June or arrive about the 20th when you finish. I'd like to turn up in Oxford and see your rooms before you leave. Would it suit you better if I come then or for July and August, or August and September? I'll have to decide soon, and probably without your advice but I dare say you can fit in your arrangements to suit whatever plans I make. If not please let me know as soon as you can what you would like me to do. Peggy [Kidder] leaves on the first of June and I may wait and go on a fast boat later. Altogether I favour The Empress, for if I have only two months to spend I'd like to be with you as long as I can.[5] Barbara [Sturgis] will loan me one hundred dollars and I can collect another three hundred or more. That ought to do it if we're careful, but you'd better hurry and write to Brown! The Youth Hostel Association has an office in Oxford. You might investigate possibilities there with regard to sleeping places—Barbara says they herd the men into one end of the building and women in the other, so I would not need to worry about any embarrassing situations arising—this in answer to my question as to whether it was usual for men and women to travel together! I am wondering whether we might not find it easier to move about third class than the bicycle idea. It depends on how much money you can scare up, I suppose.

Marion [Kemp Harrison] is very happy with the infant, Harold started on Saturday playing in Harold Sumberg's orchestra for his advanced pupils—Roy is quite cheerful about exams, and Daddy is busy. Mother is energetic as usual, sometimes despairing about reducing the East York population. One woman with nine children and pregnant again complained to her that the Birth Control Clinic was no help, she went to them but they wouldn't help her at all. Of course she went about three months *after* she was pregnant instead of before. Mother says she thinks sometimes that these women are so dumb you almost have to live their sex life for them.

If you could dig up a secondhand copy of a Muirhead guide to Germany I wish you'd send it to me, but perhaps I can find out what I want at the German State Railways or from Albert Fuchs.

Tuesday night

I have just been out to the Park Plaza with Florence Smith. I had two glasses of milk and feel decidedly milky to put it mildly. If I'd been with Douglas [MacAgy] it would have been beer from the bar-room. Smitty, as Kay calls her, really is a good scout—she needs a good time, and some clothes. She can't have had much fun ever,—to-night Marge Boultbee and a gang including Douglas, Gordon MacNamara and Gordon Webber and several women trooped in to Murray's (they're running the Park Plaza restaurant now) and after seeing Trudy Schoop and Smitty said: "my you seem to know so many interesting people!"[6]

I must get to bed. This was my first full day back at work and I'm none too steady yet.

I shall be through here around June 10th, I asked Jessie Mac to-day, or I can leave earlier, but that seems a good time. Are you writing exams this year? Or does it matter if I show up a day or so before June 20th? I am getting terribly excited to think that I'm coming to see you soon. My dearest, my dearest man. Tell me what you think of The Forum—for *me*. Seriously, do you think I should attempt it yet?

Helen.

P.S. I have a whole stack of New Yorkers to send you soon. I'm sorry for the delay.

1 Mussolini founded the Fasci di Combattimento on 23 March 1919 in Milan.
2 An annual VC event at which the staff of the college entertained the graduating class in Burwash Hall. For the 1936 dinner, Prof. J.A. Surerus of the German department served as chair and Prof. E.J. Pratt of the English department proposed the toast. The dinner was followed by a reception at Annesley Hall and by dancing and other forms of entertainment.
3 HK must mean Doris Wagstaff, VC 3T7. Wagstaff recorded in her diary that on 10 April she attended the Senior Dinner, where she sat beside Prof. Shore (Doris Wagstaff Patterson to RDD, 10 November 1994).
4 The article was published later in the year as "Children at the Art Gallery of Toronto," *School*, 26 (September 1937), 10–13.
5 HK is referring to the time she would save if she sailed on the *Empress of Britain*, the fastest of the CPR's steamship fleet on the St. Lawrence service.
6 The context suggests that this remark should have been attributed to Florence Smith rather than Marge Boultbee. HK may have intended to write, "after seeing Trudy Schoop, Smitty said."

195. NF to HK   Oxford

Postmarked 28 April 1937; addressed to HK at 84, Queen's Park, Toronto, Ontario, Canada. Begun in Florence, this letter was not posted until NF returned to Oxford.

Sweetheart:

Florence remains the best town in the world. There are foul things in it, though. Santa Croce, for instance. Four of us went there one morning and found the Giotto Chapel[1] full of ladders and scaffolding, so we climbed the ladders and walked over the scaffolding. We were hurriedly informed that we would have to get a permit from every petty official in Italy to do that, but in the meantime ten or twelve other tourists had climbed up after us. Next day Mike and I hopped in again, and as soon as they saw my yellow mop heave in sight they took up the ladders. And no wonder. There was a fat pasty-faced swine there swabbing black paint on the Death of St. Francis as though he were painting the side of a barn. In Santa Maria Novella the big Cimabue or Duccio or whatever it is[2] was being carted off while we were there for just one more repainting. It was lying flat on its back with fifteen men all standing around, each with a different theory of how to move it—the only survival of democracy I saw in Italy. The light was shining on it so you could see it hadn't been touched except for the Madonna's robe, which was a sticky black mess. Wait till they improve it and make it all a sticky mess. The big surprise in the Uffizi was 2 Lorenzo Monaco, as I think I mentioned. After four days of Florence I got a bit stuffed and drunk, mentally—I was taking in so many painting-impressions, and I know so little of painting. Then I went to see the Masaccios in that hideous church across the river, and they knocked me as cold sober as a quart of black coffee.[3] I've never had anything make such a terrific physical impact on me in the way of a picture—I think it was because Catholic painting, with all its serenity and its conception of beauty as loveliness (I was thinking of something else)[4] was beginning to bore me a little, and I think I detected the individual in revolt in Masaccio—I may have been wrong. Anyway, the third time I went back to the Uffizi I went to the Flemish room first—previously the Flemish pictures looked so ugly and twisted after the Italians. As soon as they began to soak in I got a bit restless—the next time I go forth in search of paint it will be to the Low Countries.

We were in Florence for ten days and made two expeditions from there. One was to San Gimignano. It's a gorgeous town, even higher up and more picturesque than Assisi. I went chiefly to see the Gozzolis, as I had no idea of what sort of painting was in the Cathedral. Well, I saw the Gozzolis—Life of St. Augustine—and they were grand fun.[5] Also, the sacristan was the best in Italy—a fat old man who asked us if we were interested in architecture and showed us the cloisters, then picked out a postcard of them with two monks in the foreground and a pudgy little figure in the background to which he pointed with great pride, and presented it to us. But when I hit that cathedral! We went chiefly for some Ghirlandaios in a locked chapel,[6] but never got anywhere near them. We had noticed at Siena a painter called Bartolo di Fredi, because he seemed to have a passion for horses, and stuck them in everywhere he got a chance. Well, he'd done an enormous series of Old Testament scenes on the left wall—much the most complete we saw in Italy—he finished up with a Job series, for instance, curiously like Blake's in some ways.[7] He's a swell painter, but a completely secular one—his creation of Eve was a lovely floating nude, and his drunkenness of Noah was the funniest I saw, except a mosaic in Venice—Noah was fairly well clothed apart from his huge erect penis that stood up in the middle of the picture, but he managed to look as completely plastered as I've seen anyone look even in Oxford. And, of course, with the Ark or Pharoah's host drowned in the Red Sea, he just went to town on his horses. Apparently he loved animals of all kinds too. He'd obviously never seen a camel, so he just drew more horses, with impossibly long necks. On the entrance wall there was a Last Judgment—the Heaven was pretty perfunctory, but the hell was a Freudian riot—Lechery was a well-built naked woman with a fiend riding on her back and raping her with his tail; somebody else had a ramrod projecting from his mouth and his behind, and Usuria was lying on his back with an enormously distended belly and a devil squatting over his face and dropping a prodigious shower of turds into his mouth. The expression on that devil's face, half grinning and half straining, is something I'd go to Italy again just to see. The New Testament series, by somebody the guide book called Barna da Siena, was a very different matter. The lower row (the rest were more or less routine painting) was a passion sequence, ending with the Crucifixion, which was one of the most profound I ever saw. The man who did it was a genuine revolutionary—in every picture Jesus' enemies, whether Jews or priests or soldiers, were all huddled together in a lowering scowling mass, and the character study of Judas was amazingly subtle.[8] Well, there were other things in San Gimignano, and I certainly got a better idea of Sienese painting there than I did in Siena, where there were no frescoes to speak of. The other expedition was to Prato for the Lippo Lippi frescoes—great stuff, and I should imagine his best work.[9]

It was hard to get out of Florence, though not so hard after the stinkers arrived. I believe they refer to themselves as Alpini—a regiment of Alpine soldiers, mostly war veterans, who came to Florence to get drunk. Still, they were harmless enough. We went out with a girl in our pensione who spoke English very well and met one of them in the Boboli Gardens. They sell these huge bronze plaques in Florentine art stores—you can buy one of the Pope for 3 lire, one of Jesus Christ for 5 lire, and one of Mussolini for 10 lire. This man had one of Dante. She asked him if he liked Dante and he said no, he'd never heard of Dante, but he had to have *some* souvenir to take back from Florence.

Then we went to Ravenna—a swell town, where the mosaics are far better and easier to look at than the ones in Rome.[10] We had a very quiet day there, and went for a long walk under a blistering sun to a church about five miles outside the walls.[11] We got into Padua that night—Bell threw out the wrong bag at the station and my bag, with the Blake thesis in it, went on to Venice. It came back in the morning—Padua is St. Anthony's home town, and St. Anthony is the saint who finds lost things. Padua is an amusing town, with all its narrow streets and its rows of colonnaded loggias where people sit around at cafe tables. The

Giotto chapel was magnificent,[12] though I find Giotto, and still more Fra Angelico, don't quite connect as far as my personal likes and dislikes are concerned. Perhaps the next trip will affect me differently. The Mantegna was much the best fresco work of his I saw in Italy, too.[13] We spent a day and a half there and moved on to Venice. That, thank God, although it did pour rain once, gave us the best weather we'd yet had, and, as that's all there is to Venice, we got a lot out of the town.

It's a funny town. All the things you read about gondolas and canals and so on actually do happen, and it looks just as it ought to look, except that I didn't realize the "Bridge of Sighs" was bad grammar—it's only about twelve feet long, so there'd only be time for one sigh. Externally, Venice comes off perfectly—even its ugliness—St. Mark's, apart from some howlingly funny mosaics, is as monstrous in its way as the Imperial Hotel in Russell Square, and some of the church façades, which look as though they had been constructed entirely out of pigeon-shit, have a deformed and twisted hideousness that nothing in all the megalomaniac horror of Rome can equal. Still, that all fits in. But then other things fit in. It's the only real sucker town in Italy (except perhaps Naples, which I can't answer for); the only town in Italy where they charge admission to churches, where they charge admission on Sunday, where one pays a sojourn tax, and where the admission price to an outrage like the Doge's Palace would be 10 lire. The Italians are on the whole honest, and in Rome only sporadically not so: the only place where one gets systematically gypped and rooked and fleeced and hornswoggled is in Venice. Everybody speaks English there, as it's the place all the Americans go after Paris, and foreigners who speak English are dangerous. Then you go and look at their blasted painting. Huge crammed canvases stewing in an oily morass like the Slough of Despond each jammed all over its hundred square feet with people. And all the pictures express is the fact that they cost a lot of money. The only time somebody like Tintoretto or Veronese gets really emotional is when he can depict gods dropping gold and jewels and crowns on a broad-bottomed blonde sow with a smirk representing Venice. And when Carpaccio (who would have been a good painter in any other city) draws the martyrdom of the eleven thousand virgins of St. Ursula[14] or the crucifixion of the ten thousand martyrs in Armenia, you can see he was doing it for someone who would count his virgins and martyrs, and if he found one missing would demand his money back. Money, money, money. There are things about Venetian painting

I don't understand—I don't see why a Veronese Mercury should be as fat as the average Silenus, and look like a flying Oscar Wilde, and I don't see why Jesus in Tintoretto is always doing the Highland fling. But I can see that now that Venice has no money, she does nothing but grab it, because when she had money she had nothing else. I never came across quite so naive a worship of money before, except in some English eighteenth-century poetry, and I never saw the Communist caricature of the "bourgeois" quite so perfectly illustrated. I re-read the Merchant of Venice on the spot—I had never realized before how much money there was in that play.

I got the letter written I promised, but I'm afraid I lost it—I lost a lot of things in Venice, including some of the stamps Stephen asked me to buy for him—and whether you get it or not depends on whether someone picks it up and puts a stamp on it and mails it. Venice cured me in a day and a half of being a conscientious see-sighter. Of course all bourgeois societies have their escapists, and Venice had some curiously modern examples—the little row of Giovanni Bellini allegories,[15] for instance, were as near to intelligent sur-realism (if that isn't a contradiction) as I've seen, and the lovely Giorgione picture was just like the Rousseau pipe-dreams I like so well. Also there was one good Mantegna, one good Piero,[16] and there would have been some swell Hieronymus Bosches if they'd hung them where anyone could see them.

When I say "we," I mean sometimes Mike [Joseph] and me, sometimes two Americans from Exeter in addition. At Venice we rejoined Baine and one of the Americans picked up his mother, his very young (13) and very bored sister, and two American girls who had been living at Oxford.[17] The girls were simple souls but good fun. Venice requires a large party—it's the ideal town for anyone with lots of money and no brains—someone just like the Venetians, that is—and even if you have very little money you can relax. We went swimming on the Lido twice, went for rides in gondolas every evening, and each night Mike, one of the Americans, the two girls and I would forgather in the girls' room and get more or less amiably stewed. All but one of the girls—she has something wrong with her kidney and can't drink, so she looks on and suffers. She complained one morning that I kept calling her Miss Cold Sobriety (her name is Virginia) and had objected to her breaking up a bridge game and throwing me out at half-past one, and that I said I'd play honeymoon bridge if I only had the honeymoon. My thoughts seem to run to you even when I'm sozzled.

I picked up your letter at Venice, also an invitation to the opening meeting of the Society for Canadian-Italian Cultural Relations or something in Toronto. As for your coming over, I'm tied hand and foot until I hear from [Walter T.] Brown. The one thing I know is that somehow or other we've got to get together this summer—incidentally, I may have to borrow from you if I have to go back to Canada. I'm frightfully sorry about the [Herbert J.] Davis baby. Elizabeth [Fraser] works for a fat man called Long, who digs plaster off wall paintings—he can't do his own drawing like Tristram, so she does it. Tristram seems to have cornered the English market, so she's trying the Metropolitan in New York (secret, I think). Thanks very much for the addresses—we did pretty well, travelling with the Americans, who had been to Italy before and were going on Rhodes Scholar recommendations. I stayed in Italy five weeks on twenty pounds counting railway fare, so didn't do badly. I'm sorry too about Dot [Drever]—I don't think Communism fits her, somehow, though it was the obvious answer to her frantic dilettantism. I've seen so many Victorian evangelical consciences go that way I often wonder what the next stage is. Besides, Dot seems to be starting from the wrong end. No religion depends less on hero-worship and more on theory than Communism. Don't worry about your smugness—the whole point about the bourgeois is that he's worried, which is why the Communist despises him. It's too bad Dot takes to hectoring—it's not like her, and it shows a bad conscience. I'm sorry too she's not further left than she is—I prefer Trotskyites to Sunday-School Communists, and if I'm anything political I'm an anarchist. That is, I know that the world would be infinitely better off after it had an armed Communist revolution—there's no peaceful revolution possible, and there's no other way out of the destruction of civilization by war. But while that's all inevitable, I look forward to the revolution against *that*, which must follow, and cherish a wild hope that, as the impossible generally does happen in history, the second, complete revolution may actually come first.

Darling, do you suppose you could make an enquiry or two for me about the I.O.D.E.—find out who I have to write to, and so on?

I didn't learn much Italian. Mike's French is better than mine, and we got along. What surprised me was that one gets further with German than with English in Italy—not that I tried to get anywhere with it, but everybody took me for German and tried to talk it to me. It was funny the way an Italian would come up to a group of four of us, look us all over, fasten on me as the obvious racial type, and start off in German. In

Ravenna some youngsters yelled "Auf Wiedersehen!" after us on the street, and in Milan one of the hotel touts said "Sind Sie drei?" and when we said nothing continued "You are three persons, is it not?" They only decided we were English after they heard us talking, like the man in the train who asked us if we would be so friendly as to close the window because it was a few cold, yes? Or the waiter at Padua who undertook to talk English to us. He got "chicken" and "cheese" right, and then, as we were eating, he passed by, leaned over and said confidentially "Mercy me!", grinned at us, and walked off. We're still wondering where he picked that up. It was in Padua too that we decided we needed a better map of Venice than Baedeker provided, so we pushed Mike ahead to deal with the CIT man. Mike explained in fluent French that we wanted a "map" (he'd forgotten the word *carte*) and the man stared at him and then said: "Vat you vant—some pamphlets?" That enraged Mike, who is proud of his French. The Italians aren't supposed to like the English—sometimes a soldier's face would fall when I said "Non tedesco—inglese,"[18] but the average Italian doesn't care. One of the Exeter men, however, was getting his hair cut in Lucca when he noticed it was all going the wrong way, and that another barber was hissing (he knows a little Italian): "Cut it all off! Cut it all off! Inglese!" He was an American, so he got out of that. I'd have said American if I'd thought, but they generally want the language rather than the nationality. The rapprochement between Italy & Germany is being played up for all it's worth—you see pictures of Hitler everywhere, Italian & German flags beside each other in posters, and anti-Semitic books in bookstores. Of course the Italians made a great fuss over their Empire—Mussolini's title is now "Fondatore dell'Impero," the King is the King-Emperor, and they're frantically jealous of countries with bigger empires. There's a comic newspaper that had a big front-page cartoon showing a Union Jack over the Houses of Parliament with a big knot tied in one end. Now I've run out of paper and am going to the back of page one—the one that starts off with sweetheart—A spectator says, "What's the idea of the knot?" and his friend says "Oh, that's just to remind her of her great colonial empire." Every cat in Italy is pregnant. Well, maybe every other cat—there are an awful lot of cats. They're more loyal to Mussolini than the humans are—Mussolini announced in one of his speeches that Italians should drink more wine because it stimulates the begetting of children. Wonder why, if he's always having parades, he doesn't have one of pregnant women? When I got back to France, where Mussolini was allowed to have a mistress, who shot somebody else for some reason, the mistress was said to have had three hundred pictures of Mussolini in her room. She not only loved Mussolini, she understood him.[19] There are a lot of dogs too. You never eat a meal in a cheap restaurant without a dog staring at you and saying *"How* can you go on feeding that face with all this misery and starvation in front of it?" You're not supposed to notice he's so fat he can hardly waddle. Eventually, when he sees the dish disappearing and himself ignored, he comes up and pushes your hand away from your plate with his nose. He never barks or whines, he never eats spinach, and he never gets anything else, at least from me.

Where am I? Oh, yes, getting stewed in Venice. We went to Verona, which has a swell Romanesque church—San Zeno, with a lovely Mantegna triptych in it.[20] Not much else in Verona—a sprawling industrialized town. So we made an excursion to Mantua. That was a good idea. The Mantegna Gonzaga series[21] was in desperately bad shape—much worse than the reproductions would indicate—and we were rather disappointed. It was part of a gigantic palace, though, and what with that—it seemed nearly as big as the Vatican, though it couldn't have been—and Guilio Romano's Palace of T,[22] Mantua put on a superb show. It's full of sixteenth-century Renaissance at its best, and filled up a gap that had previously been represented only by the Villa Farnesina at Rome. The food at Mantua was ambrosial—about the best we had in Italy, and we had good food there. I'm no champion spaghetti-winder, but I like spaghetti, at least in Italy. Unfortunately, Mantua is away out in the marshes—it's practically an island—it was bitterly cold, and I got the sorest throat I've had since my tonsils came out. I got into Milan that night a very sick man. I was nearly broken-hearted. I had got flu in England at the beginning of last term, it had hung on all term and cut my working efficiency down to about thirty per cent., I had gone to Italy as much for my health as anything else, had struck as rainy and record-breaking cold a spring as there was in England, and here I was in worse shape than ever. Milan had a fair and was jammed with Germans—one of us had to sleep on the floor, but there was no question about who would get the bed. Next morning I was better—I couldn't have been worse—but still pretty bad, and I spent a gloomy day in the Brera and Last Supper refractory—I mean refectory.[23] That night we climbed into a big clean comfortable Dutch third class carriage, and woke up in Basel. We had breakfast, and then a long tedious ride through Alsace-Lorraine—we could see the Strasbourg spire from the train, but not much of it. Back of page two. Page two doesn't begin with sweetheart, but it ought to.

Sweetheart. On our trip England and Switzerland glanced at our bags but hardly touched them: France, Belgium and Italy wouldn't look at them at all. But the Customs Inspector for the Grand Duchy of Luxemburg, in whose territory we must have spent all of ten minutes, fished and poked and prowled around a long time. Luxemburg filled our compartment with Salvation Army heroes, including a woman who gabbled incessantly in a mixture of French, German and Flemish. Finally she announced that she could smell stale tobacco in the air, glanced up, saw the compartment was marked "Fumeur," and marched out with another woman, a very old rather senile man, and two small boys tagging after her. "It wasn't the tobacco they objected to," Mike [Joseph] said, "it was just the smell of Popery about me." We got into Brussels in the afternoon—Mike knows it fairly well. We got a hotel, a bath and some food—my throat was much better. In the evening we went to see Romeo and Juliet—in English, with French subtitles.[24] Scene Verona, in front of the church of San Zeno we had just been in. Very good show—Barrymore as Mercutio superb, though it's an obvious part to steal, and the dialogue was in places surprisingly intact—more so than the stupid little texts my freshies use. The female end sagged a bit—the Nurse wasn't too good and Norma Shearer was a pretty elephantine Juliet, but it's definitely two or three up for Hollywood. Against an orchestra of sentimental nose-blowing Belgians it was quite refreshing. The newsreel gave us another curious reminder of Italy—the King and Queen of Italy in some ceremony or other. The King is a bewildered, meek little man of about five feet four; the Queen a huge Montegrin Amazon of at least five feet ten. The Belgians roared. We got there just after the election in which the Rexists (Fascist) had been badly beaten. The Rexists are pro-German, which means that the left-wingers, war-veterans and patriots all ganged up on them—a funny combination, but it worked. We saw posters of a big red, yellow, and black boot kicking a backside labelled "Rex."

We thought we might see something of the town the next morning, but didn't get up till eleven and just had time to get away on the boat train, which annoyed me, as I wanted to see the fountain with the pissing boy.[25] At Ostend I had a neat trick worked on me—I wasn't prepared for tricks after Italy. The woman who gave us lunch and seemed very nice asked me if I had a pound for some change. She palmed off a Brazilian 200–reis piece on me for a half-crown—I expect it's worth about a shilling. Someday I'm going to go back to Ostend and spill beer all over her table. The Channel crossing was dull and the trip from Dover to London duller. Still, I'm not too sorry to be in England. From Brussels to Brussel sprouts is a let-down, everything in England is bad and expensive, except the few things that are a little better and a lot more expensive, there's not much good about general living comfort in England and nothing distinctively good. Still—one goes to an Italian church to see Giotto or Masaccio and doesn't notice that nine-tenths of the church is insanely ugly—ugly in that shrieking Catholic way that England at its worst doesn't seem to sink to. I would like to explore English villages and parish churches, though I know a good many of each would be hideous, but I should hate really to explore Italy—I just want to go and see what's there and come away again. Sometimes, as in Santa Croce, I felt that the people who ran the place hated the good pictures—back of page three and I'd better stop soon—no doubt you wish I would too—damaged them all they could, and if they didn't make money out of them would claw them all off the walls with their nails, tomorrow. I like the Italians, but impersonally—they're not my people—and though Florence, alone of all the towns I saw, struck me as a place one might live, five weeks was all I wanted—say seven weeks, to allow for places like Urbino and Cortona and to take things more easily than we did in Pisa and Orvieto.

I stayed the night at the Burnetts', and got to Oxford the next day. My sore throat has recurred, but I've been taking things easily and going to bed early. Blunden set us an exam when we got back—he told Warren he would—he didn't tell me. He seemed to like my paper, God knows why—it was written in a pretty bemused state of mind. Elizabeth, poor child, has moved to the other end of town, and is off to Lincolnshire this week copying wall paintings. I don't know if I give you a favorable impression of Elizabeth or not—the Burnetts don't like her much, but the Burnetts are not very tolerant people. She's a lonely soul with lots of courage, pride and sensitiveness, but she is a swell girl. She hits hard and rubs people the wrong way, in a way I think you understand, after six years of me, but she's more honest and straightforward than I am and has more guts. You'll love her when you meet her. Mother would be very distressed if you went through Moncton without seeing her—please don't do that.

I think I told you something about my impressions of Orvieto, Perugia and Arezzo—the only towns I remember your having been to were

Florence, Orvieto, Rome and Assisi. The Orvieto carvings were lovely, particularly the Genesis series.[26] I was not surprised to find Perugino bloody, though it was a shock after the Sistine Chapel thing, which I think is a swell picture, but I was surprised to find so much of the same stupidity in Raphael—things like the Sposalizio in Milan,[27] for instance. But Umbrian painters couldn't help painting imbeciles when they had Umbrians for models—everywhere we looked on the streets of Perugia we saw the same stolid vacuous door knobs. You'd better decide about the Forum yourself—your letters sound as though you were just about as busy as you could be, but you know best whether you could make room for it or not. There's no doubt that if you did the job you'd do it very well, and the Forum is in many ways a useful magazine to get printed in, I think. Also, I'd like to see you doing the job—actually, I don't think it will hurt you if it does mean overwork—there's always room at the top for things that interest you. Sure, go ahead—if I'm supposed to liven up Canadian music criticism, why not the rest of the family do the rest of the livening?

Mother lives such a quiet life, her letters come so regularly, and I'd be so lost without them, that I more or less take them for granted, I'm afraid. Vera is less quiet but equally regular. She has a ferocious bunch of brats that look like juvenile court cases on her hands, as no one else would dream of handling them. One came in chewing tobacco and spat on the floor. Dialogue: "Get out your handkerchief and wipe that up." "Oh, yeah?" Vera threw him downstairs, he came back completely subdued, and told her after school "Boy, you sure can teach." I cut this short because I think I told it before. Sorry. But it's typical of Vera, and of her letters.

I'm exhausted with this huge letter, my throat's sore and it's midnight. I want very much to see you, but, somehow or other, I think I'm going to see you. It's so absolutely necessary. But I must hear from [Walter T.] Brown first. And if you want to herd into one end of a Youth Hostel with a bunch of women you can bloody well herd—I'm coming down to the women's end, embarrassing situation or no embarrassing situation. {I MESSED THIS—SORRY—BACK OF NEXT PAGE}

I know what makes my throat sore—it's a lump.

Darling, you do write such lovely letters. And you grow up so fast you scare me.

I shall love you as long as I live.

Very truly yours.

1 See Letter 192, n. 6, above.
2 Apparently a reference to the large Cimabue Madonna (1285) in the Rucellai Chapel.
3 NF is referring to the Masaccio frescoes in Brancacci Chapel of the Church of Santa Maria del Carmine.
4 After "beauty" NF wrote "of ugliness" but then marked it out.
5 NF seems momentarily to have confused the two main churches in San Gimignano— the Church of Sant'Agostino and the Romanesque cathedral, known as the Collegiata. The frescoes by Benozzo Gozzoli illustrating seventeen scenes from the life of St. Augustine are in the choir of the Church of Sant'Agostino rather than in the cathedral.
6 The frescoes by Ghirlandaio in the Chapel of St. Fina depict scenes from the life of the saint.
7 The frescoes by Bartolo di Fredi on the north aisle of the Collegiata were painted ca. 1367.
8 The fresco scenes from the New Testament, on the south aisle of the Collegiata, are the best known works of Barna da Siena; he worked on them ca. 1381, and they were completed by Giovanni d'Asciano.
9 Lippo Lippi's celebrated frescoes in Prato (1452–66), which decorate the choir of the Duomo, depict events from the lives of John the Baptist and St. Stephen.
10 Charles Bell recalled that "what prompted Norrie's most irreverent outbreak was the old church of San Vitale in Ravenna, where the mosaics of Theodosius' choir yield elsewhere to a lush abandon of Baroque." Bell recorded the outbreak in his diary: "Frye says that when he gets to heaven his first request of St. Peter will be to let him rape a Baroque angel" ("The Imprint of Northrop Frye in Charles Bell's Poetic NOW," unpublished typescript, 4–5).
11 The Church of Santa Maria in Porto Fuori, noted for its frescoes of the school of Rimini. About the walk back from the church, Charles Bell says, "I can still see Norrie's platinum hair flouncing along, he wiping the sweat from his Canadian brow in a kind of fury" ("The Imprint of Northrop Frye in Charles Bell's Poetic NOW," unpublished typescript, 5).
12 The frescoes in the Scrovegni Chapel of the cathedral, depicting the history of Christian redemption, were painted by Giotto in 1303–5.
13 Mantegna began work on the frescoes in one of the cathedral chapels later named for him when he was only twenty-three; the chapel was almost completely destroyed in World War II—perhaps the greatest disaster suffered by Italian art during the war.
14 Vittore Carpaccio's *Legend of St. Ursula* (1490–95) is in the Galleria dell'Accademia.
15 NF is referring to the allegorical paintings of Giovanni Bellini's later period in the Galleria dell'Accademia.
16 NF is doubtless referring to Mantegna's *St. George* and Piero della Francesca's *St. Jerome in the Desert*; the Giorgione could be either *Old Woman* or *La Tempesta*. All four paintings are in the Galleria dell'Accademia.
17 The two Americans from Exeter were Charles Bell and Lou Palmer. The mother referred to was Palmer's; his sister's name was Nancy. The two American girls were Virginia and Mildred Winfree; the former was engaged to, and later married, an American Rhodes scholar, William S. Mundy, Jr.
18 "Not German—English."
19 The mistress was the French actress, Mlle. Fontanges, whose real name was Magda Coraboeuf. After she revealed her affair with Mussolini to the press, he forbade her to come to Rome; she thereupon shot and wounded the French ambassador, whom she thought was somehow responsible for her predicament, and served a year in prison as a consequence.

20 The triptych—the Madonna with angel musicians and eight saints—is above the high altar in San Zeno Maggiore.
21 Mantegna's frescoes (1465–74), his most famous work, are in the Palazzo Ducale, or the Palace of the Gonzagas. They illustrate the life of Lodovico II and his wife, Barbara of Hohenzollern.
22 The Palazzo del Te was a suburban residence of the Gonzagas; built of brick and stucco in 1525–35 by Guilio Romano, who designed its murals as well, it is considered his best work.
23 The references are to the Palazzo di Brera, which has a famous picture gallery, and to Leonardo da Vinci's *Last Supper* (1495–97), which hangs in the refectory of the Dominican convent adjoining the Church of Santa Maria delle Grazie.
24 A 1936 MGM film starring, in addition to those noted by NF, Leslie Howard as Romeo.
25 Mannikin Piss, the famous Brussels fountain at the back of the Hôtel de Ville; Mannikin is a diminutive bronze statue that continually waters the basin before him, even when he is dressed up in one of the hundreds of costumes provided on special occasions for him.
26 A portion of the bas-reliefs on the façade of the Duomo, designed in 1310 by Maitani, partially carved by him, and completed in the sixteenth century.
27 Raphael's *Sposalizio*, or *Marriage of the Virgin* (1504), the masterpiece of his Umbrian period, was painted when he was twenty-one; it hangs in the picture gallery of the Palazzo di Brera.

196. HK to NF   [*Toronto*]

                                                    A.G. of T. April 30. 1937.

My dear: I am sending you a note in a hurry to catch the boat again. I am trying to get my passage fixed up—at present I am sailing on the Empress of Britain, June 12th and I'm finding out fares in Germany but I can't tell you that yet. In case it is cheaper to buy tickets here for Germany, and I suspect it *may* be, as they give 60% reductions on all fares here, shall I buy your ticket here? I will let you know in a day or so about that. Third class everywhere—it will have to be if I'm to do it at all.

We have just had some trouble with Roy—he had a nervous crack-up and he isn't going to write his exams. We sent him up North to Lake Joseph with La Trobe—the scout master. He's been to Dr. Barnett and to a psychologist—I mean a psychiatrist and he certainly was in bad shape. It has been pretty tough on us all, but he will be better soon I think. The weather has been terrible, raining constantly, and cold. But everything is improving now—we are having a good deal of sunshine—just like spring in Rome—all bright and shiny with motor cars and new clothes and city noises. I've been to the Vic Chapel service and the Senior Dinner—Oh I told you about that. Gallery activities finish this week. Children's show next week. There is a concert this evening—Gwen Williams and Adolph Koldofsky. Barbara [Sturgis] will be in England this summer. You will have [Herbert J.] Davis there next year. Roy Daniells will be in Europe toward the end of the summer. I have forgiven Roy [Daniells]—I knew I would—he has been so decent about Roy—my Roy [Kemp] I mean.

I hope you don't think we're a family of quitters, even though we do seem to have a hell of a nervous system. Poor old Roy thinks all kinds of horrible things of himself—we have to keep him off that, of course. It is damned tough, after all the work he's done on his course this year, and his term marks have been high. [D.J.] McDougall's paper was the one that did it—when he got to work on that he cracked. And McDougall has been giving him firsts on his essays all year. Jerry [Riddell] went to the department and they said he was heading for first class standing. So what?

I will write as soon as I make out a list of expenses—this week end.

You *might* be more discreet on postcards—or did you realize that my mail is exhibited on the table in the front hall of Wymilwood and the whole house makes a grab for it in the morning? I loved it just the same.[1]

My love to you

H.

1 The reference is to NF's card of 14 April 1937 (Letter 193).

197. HK to NF [*Toronto*]
May 10. 1937.

My dearest!! Your letter came to-day, just as I was thinking it was high time that letter promised from Venice arrived. And I nearly had to take a half-holiday to finish reading it. I am terribly pleased that you saw so much of Italy—you covered a great deal more territory than I did, and you had pleasant companions evidently. And heavens above! to have spent only 20 pounds is miraculous. I'm beginning to think I am just a careless spend-thrift when it comes to money. Isn't there something that you've forgotten to count—not anything at all?

Now look here, you goose, if you think there is any earthly chance of your getting an I.O.D.E. this late in the season for *next* year, you must be hopeful—they usually award them about a year ahead, or so I have always heard. And they're a little vague, like the rest of these scholarship committees. Now, I'll try to find out—the woman I wrote to once was Mrs Detwiler, in Hamilton. Maysie Roger did all the business through her. And I can't do anything much until to-morrow, too late for this mail. But [Walter T.] Brown is coming through, I think. At the ~~Baccaula~~ how the devil do you spell it—baccalaureate—there ! sermon he said he'd heard from you, from Italy, but you did not give him your address and would I drop in and give it to him. So I told him it was just Merton College. Perhaps I'd better drop in now anyway and see how the money stands—or perhaps I could find out from Roy [Daniells]. If I go to see Brown I can give him another opportunity to make me blush as he teases me gently—as his generation rather enjoys doing. That might be a good idea—I'm such a nice quiet shy little thing and engaged to that fire-eater, all quite disarming.

As matters stand at present I've given up the freighter idea and I'm coming June 12th on the Empress of Britain, and I'm working out a scheme for seeing a *lot* of Germany—railway fares will be about $50 I should imagine from the inquiries I have made. I'll let you get your tickets in England as the reduction is the same I think for all countries outside of Germany. I have had a letter from Stien [Koetse] inviting me to see her in Haarlem. Now I'm not sure how to work that in—you complicate matters so. Of course you might go to Belgium and see Antwerp and Brussels and Bruge and Ghent and I could have my visit with Stien and meet you later. However, I'll probably have to leave the buying of my tickets until I see you, since I can't get any reply back in time unless you hurry & write by return mail. I'd like to know though, whether to get a ticket right through to Rotterdam allowing me to stop at Southampton. I'm told it would be cheaper. I would go to Oxford & London then return to Southampton and from there go on to Holland, Berlin, Leipzig, Dresden, Prague, Vienna, Munich, Salzburg, up the Rhine to Cologne, to Paris. This is tentative, with side trips to other towns. If you are coming home after all, would you send a deferred cable or let me know soon and I could send you the money right away. The family would be awfully glad to see you, and it would be especially good if you could be up north this summer with Roy being there. He seems to be better now. We had a cheerful letter from him to-day. I can't go over the whole business now, because I am tired of it, and besides I'm trying to get a cheerful note off to him to-night. He had a mental crack-up, and he is getting better, building a log cabin, and we don't give a damn about his college career. What's the use? We've got to see what turns up next, whether the history department will give him an aegrotat,[1] or what they will do.

I had lunch with Arnold one day lately and this time I was the recipient of his side of the Arnold matrimonial tangle. I came away thinking that I'd better be careful and not be too sympathetic, or else I might be another of his little maids—he told me I was a wonderfully good listener. I said I had to be. He went on to tell me a lot about myself. I can see he thinks I should be gracing some man's home, with all the——oh well, I won't go into that conversation. I'm not ridiculing him, I like him too well for that. And I can't bear it when Norah [McCullough] gets a bit gossipy about him. If he is over-sexed or suffering—and I know he is suffering from the tension at home, just as she is,—he certainly shouldn't be laughed at for that. Having heard his case, it is less easy for me to be as annoyed with him as I was when I wrote to you before. I'll tell you about it when I see you.

On Saturday I went to a shower at Jean Elder's for Ida [Clare]. She and Bill [Conklin] are being married at the end of this month. It was awfully funny—Mildred Millar brought her infant, and three others have one—Berna Langford, and expecting a second soon, Ruth Dingman, Dot Midgley. *Did* I feel the ancient spinster! Dot Darling is being married in August. Agnes Beatty is too, this fall. It is telling on me— you'd better be on your guard for I'm getting desperate and might run off and marry you some dark night when you're off guard. I'm warning you, that's all. Dot Drever is all right—I still like her very much—I just wish I could buy her clothes and make something of her looks, and get her to be a bit more constant in her hero worship. I was to send you someone's love—was it Jean Elder, or Florence [Clare]? I've forgotten, but I'm sending you enough of mine to do ten men.

Art Cragg is going to Cambridge next year.

Please let me know as soon as you can about the money question—I can just get $450 by borrowing $100, and I won't tie up next year any more than that. If you haven't enough then come back here and I'll send you the money—

My love to you

H.

---

1 An aegrotat was a passing but ungraded status accorded to students who, because of illness, were not able to complete their course requirements.

198. NF to HK   Oxford

Postmarked 18 May 1937; addressed to HK at 84, Queen's Park, Toronto, Ontario, Canada.

Sweet:

I didn't want to write until I'd heard from [Walter T.] Brown, and now that I've heard from Brown I still don't feel much like writing. This after he said "Earn as much money as you can so I'll have more left for the others," and "If the worst came to the worst we could put you on the staff and give you a leave of absence." I shall probably go to my grave believing what people say. Honest to God, he told me in his shuffling official way, that the college would finance my second year. I'm not a complete fool: I know he did say that. Well, I have £30 coming to me from Ottawa: when I get my bills paid out of it I'll have £10.

I see Blunden Thursday night. If he's encouraging, and has some possibilities of a job for the summer up his sleeve, I'll stay here. Otherwise—well, there are two plans. One is to grab Brown's six hundred, trust to God for the I.O.D.E. or something, and hang on. The other is to propose that if he has anything for me next year and will take me without a degree, I'll grab it. I feel nervous now that Brown has started to welsh, and I'd like to have that job cinched. I'm not getting enough out of Oxford to make sacrifices worthwhile to finish my course here.

And sweetheart, I'm fearfully sorry but I *still* haven't been able to decide about the summer. You can see my position. Germany I am afraid is impossible. Besides, travelling on your maiden passport in a Fascist country might be embarrassing. Not that I care. But if I came back to Canada, while I'd have to borrow about $100 from you, still I don't much relish living off the Burnetts until Victoria decided to come through with some of that dough.

Oh, God! I'm sorry to keep you in the air like this, and I hate having to scratch a note like this after keeping you waiting so long. The Blake—or most of it—will be in Geoffrey Keynes' hands in about two weeks, I hope, but it'll take ages before a publisher reports on it. Now you know as much about the situation as I do, what do you think?

I'll write again when I've cooled down.

Norrie.

P.S. I'm frightfully sorry about Roy—I do wish he wouldn't worry so over things.

P.P.S. A New Yorker would help my state of mind.

199. HK to NF   Toronto, Ont.
                                                           May 19. 1937.

Postmarked 20 May 1937; addressed to NF at Merton College, Oxford., England, Via New York: Bremen.

My dearest: I do wish your letters did not come in such fits and starts. I'm not complaining really, and I don't suppose you know yet about the money question. Roy Daniells met me the other day and said that [Walter T.] Brown or Currelly or someone had dug up another Trick Scholarship for you—$600. They all seem a bit jaundiced because you have not written a word to anyone, and Edgar grumbled that you might be a bit more observant of your social obligations. I think so too, and I'd scold you roundly if you were a little closer. Really—*I* can't write reports to these people about you. If only you'd write them a short note from time to time and keep them mollified. But there you are, and you send Brown a letter at last from Italy, after Roy [Daniells] has tipped you off—to say nothing of what I've poured forth by way of invective. Really, Frye, you *are* an idiot. I hope you will see Roy toward the end of the summer. He might lend you some money, for he seems to have more than he knows what to do with. But for heaven's sake, make arrangements in good time and don't leave it until you starve. Do you feel chastised? There, there, I love you just the same.

Roy has gone to Lake Joseph, and John Harwood-Jones went up last week with him. We had a pretty gloomy report last week, but a better one to-day. Last week he had a relapse, sleepless nights, and evidently a return of the melancholy and inertia. He was in a devil of a state nervously, but I think he will come 'round with rest and a good summer.

Norah [McCullough] gave a broadcast last night on children's work:[1] next week I'm doing one on the Permanent Collection.[2] Joan Fairley and John Hall are engaged and they are being married soon, before they go up to the Taylor Statten camp. H.J. Davis is giving a party for them this Thursday night. On Friday afternoon I am going to have tea with Gwen Williams. On Coronation day I had a big time looking at parades and paddling at the Island with Douglas [MacAgy]—as I have said, I am very fond of Douglas.

There isn't much news, and besides, someone is waiting here to go to Yonge Street with me to post this. Barbara [Sturgis] gave me a check tonight for $100, and we'll see her in London. She leaves the end of this month and may be in England all next year,—possibly in Oxford.

I hope there is word from you soon. I have just accepted our invitation to Suzanne Currelly's wedding. Now is the month of Maying—.

My love to you—

Helen.

P.S. I'm coming back here next year. I asked J. MacP. [Jessie Macpherson] and Florence Smith isn't, neither is Helen Brown.

1 Norah McCullough gave a talk, "Children in the Art Gallery," on 18 May 1937.
2 HK presented her radio talk, "The Permanent Collection," on 25 May 1937; a copy is in the HFF, 1992, box 4, file 9; another copy is in the Edward P. Taylor Research Library of the AGO.

200. NF to HK   Oxford

Postmarked 21 May 1937; addressed to HK at 84. Queen's Park, Toronto, Ontario, Canada.

Sweetheart:

I'm afraid I shall have to come back to Canada this summer and throw myself on your hands. I've been talking to Blunden: he says the college (here) can raise me about £20 if I write a good exam. for him in the fall, and I may raise some more in various prizes and things here. I'll wiggle through somehow if I get [Walter T.] Brown's $600, but I can't get through the summer too on that. England is a brutally expensive country, and I would spend all of the $600, counting the £50 I owe here for this term, this summer. I might make my fortune writing, in London, and I might not. Besides, I don't know if I can get the $600 for the summer or not, and it would take me till June 12th to find out. I'm sorry to spoil your trip, but the only excuse I have for staying here—getting the Blake published—would keep my nose in the B.M. all day while you were cooling your heels somewhere else.

This is gently leading you up and letting you down to a touch. Could you lend me £20 ($100) to get home on?

I hate seeing all the people I suppose I shall have to see, and want to avoid Toronto as much as possible. I've got another excellent reason for wanting to come back to Canada which you could trot out to any curious person, and that is my health. It's been frightfully bad all year—I don't know when my vitality has been lower—and I don't think I'd last the second year if I spent the summer freezing my feet in the B.M., or, for that matter, in Germany.

I'll try to write you a decent letter as soon as I feel more like it. Still, I'll soon be seeing you.

Until then, I love you inexpressibly.

Norrie.

201. HK to NF   Toronto, Ont.
                                                            May 23. 1937.

Postmarked 24 May 1937; addressed to NF at Merton College, Oxford, England, Via New York: Queen Mary.

My dearest: Sunday night. The Thornhills have been here for supper and Mrs. T. is reading Mencken's *Dictionary of the American Language,* Mother is knitting, Thorny is reading the Bible and Daddy is making remarks from time to time about the ancient Hebrews. I am waiting for the Ford Symphony Hour, and have given up the attempt to make conversation, for the time being.

I came home for the week-end but the residence is not closed yet, for the O.C.E. people stay on until June 11th, and by that time I shall be in Montreal, probably, seeing your Aunt.[1] Kay Coburn is going across on the Empress too, on Carnegie money, for she is getting the Coleridge papers photographed or something.[2] How about a little tea party for the troops? I'm coming especially to see your rooms in Merton, you know, for that was one reason I'm coming so early, to see you in your palatial retreat. I hope it won't interfere with your plans—if you are writing exams I can keep myself out of the way until you are finished, but I was counting on your not having any until next year. I had tea with Miss Dennison and her mother this afternoon, and they were quite interested in what you are doing and full of good wishes for my summer and

yours. Philippa and Howard have been in London all year. She is studying piano with Mr Howard-Jones and Howard is doing architecture in
London. Howard-Jones is coming here again this summer to give his
master classes to music teachers, which were very successful last year
according to any reports I've had. Gwen Koldofsky was very enthusiastic about them.

Last Thursday night I was at a party H.J. Davis gave for Joan Fairley
and John Hall, and had a lovely time of course, as one always does.
{Ormandy is conducting the Philadelphia Symphony—March from
Tschaikowsky's 5th which is to my mind the best part of it.[3] Douglas
[MacAgy] and I heard him do it here last Monday} Davis asked me how
you are, and I heard to my horror that you have not written to him yet
either. When I get to you you can prepare for a long time spent in writing
letters, for I'll stand over you with a hair brush until you get them done.
I understand how you feel about them of course, but you can't afford to
neglect some things, and keeping in touch with the English Department
here is definitely one thing that must be done. Davis is selling his house.
After his year in England he is going to Cornell, for good.[4] That made me
feel pretty low, you can imagine. On the other hand, all the more reason
for your keeping in touch with him, in case he ever has occasion to recommend some bright younger man for an appointment. All quite aside
from considerations of friendliness and gratitude for all that he has done
for you already. I hope you are sufficiently bowed low by now, and I'll try
not to preach any more. You must be tired of my nagging—two letters of
it. It is just anxiety on my part. {We've got another caller—just a minute}

Midnight

John Jones [Harwood-Jones] came in, and a woman from the church
who is crossing on The Empress too—slightly deaf, and I'm to meet her
on the boat-train because she's going alone. A teacher from Bishop
Strachan[5] will be on the same boat—someone I've met before. John has
just come back from Gordon Bay, had a good time and says Roy is much
better.

I think I will have to get to bed now after such a sprightly evening.
Heaven knows what's the matter with Mrs. T. [Thornhill] but she spent
most of the night reading and they didn't leave until fifteen minutes
ago. I must be on the job in the morning to finish that radio talk.

Love Helen

1 NF's maternal aunt, Harriet ("Hatty") Howard Layhew.
2 Kathleen Coburn had been introduced to the Coleridge family when she was studying in England in 1931–32, and when she returned to England in 1933 she was provided access to Coleridge's notebooks by the family; from that point on she devoted almost all her scholarly career to Coleridge's work, including the editing of his notebooks; her research elevated her to the highest rank among Coleridge scholars. The story of her lifelong devotion to Coleridge is charted in her *In Pursuit of Coleridge* (London: The Bodley Head, 1977).
3 HK is referring to the third section of the second movement in Tschaikowsky's Symphony No. 5 in E Minor, composed in 1888 and first performed the same year, with Tschaikowsky conducting, in St. Petersburg.
4 Herbert J. Davis resigned his U of T appointment in 1938 and accepted a position at Cornell, but he did not go to Cornell "for good"; he later took a position as reader at Oxford and still later became president of Smith College.
5 See Letter 173, n. 4, above.

202. NF to HK   Oxford

Postmarked 28 May 1937; addressed to HK at 84, Queen's Park, Toronto, Ontario, Canada.

Darling, I've been sending Edgar four of the 6000–word essays I've been producing every week here—four of my essays, remember—and I've told him my health has been frightfully bad for the last two terms, which is quite true, so that may give him an idea of what I've been doing when I haven't been fulfilling my social obligations. What you mean by saying I've blabbed to [Walter T.] Brown everything you told me after Roy [Daniells] warned me not to I don't know. I only know I'm very tired, heartily sick of Oxford, and want to take all your money away from you and come home as soon as possible and rest up. It's getting late—I don't know whether I should cable you or not.

My eyes have been bad since I came back from Italy, and I've slacked off work. I've been overdrawn ten pounds since then too, so have kept quiet. The most depressing event of the term was lunch with the Warden, who is a complete ninny.[1] The Warden doesn't know what to make of the university now that it's gone intellectual on him—he has a vague idea that the Rhodes Scholars are to blame. It was he who more or less began to feed me up with Oxford—he fitted so perfectly into the general pattern. And really, Oxford is incredible. I give one example. The Bodley Club generally holds a big dinner in the final term. I couldn't attend it anyhow as I haven't a soup and fish, but the point is they're not allowed to hold it in the college because the College—i.e., the members of the Senior Common Room—suspect them of atheistic tendencies.

I give another example. Merton is a very easy college to climb into, and where you climb in they've thoughtfully provided a pile of fresh new-mown hay for you to jump in. You jump, and find that the pile is camouflaged horse shit. Then you hand your shoes, all covered with horse shit, to the Boots next morning, which gives the officials a lovely chance to ask Awkward Questions. And at that Merton is quite adult compared to some of the colleges—Jesus, for instance, where you get your weekly accounts from the Principal, who inspects them to see how much beer you've drunk and how often you've come in late. Still, next year I'll be in what they call unlicensed lodgings, which will save me a great deal and will avoid all that sort of thing.

I've had two outings—one on a picnic to the Chilterns[2] with Miss Thorneycroft and Elizabeth [Fraser], which was grand, as we sat in a beechwood with a purple carpet of blue bells all around us. The other was to the Cotswolds[3] with Lou Palmer (one of the Exeter men we met in Italy), Mike [Joseph] and his (Lou's) mother, who has a little car. We saw several very lovely little villages and some wall paintings—the fresco tradition in England is spottier and cruder than in Italy, of course, but they have original ideas about symbolism one could travel all over Italy without seeing. The fragmentary ones, where they've just pried off the plaster and let it go at that, are nice; but the imaginative reconstructions of Professor Tristram give me a no doubt unjustified pain. They *do* look so lurid and so unreal, somehow.

Some female called Maisie somebody is opening an art gallery, and Elizabeth is putting up some of her drawings. She hopes Maisie may provide a showroom for her. Elizabeth has been the worst possible influence on me (though no one knows that any better than she, poor child) because whenever I visit her in a period of spiritual and financial depression, such as occurs frequently, I always find her with just as little money and even more depressed, so we work each other up to the verge of drowning ourselves.

I think wall-paintings are a mistake for her—she gets too excited and temperamental about them. Her field was in scientific (medical and archaeological) stuff, and if she hadn't fallen in love with this printer[4] and come to live in Oxford she'd have been better off. The Metropolitan turned her down—said they weren't interested in copies. I don't know what else they expect to get of frescoes, but Elizabeth said they probably thought that a spinster living in Oxford who copied wall-paintings was too awful for words.

Blunden came back from Germany full of enthusiasm for the Nazis. Poor Oxford always finds itself on the wrong side of a revolution—it gets more Fascist every day. Cromwell nearly wiped it out, and if, as I heard a Communist say recently, the fight in England will be the last and bloodiest in the world, there won't be much left of this place but a tangled mass of barb-wire. On May day the half-dozen radicals went to London to demonstrate, but the streets were full of policemen just the same.[5]

I'm sorry if I whimper and growl, but I shall keep on whimpering and growling until I get married and get a job. I don't much care what sort of job, at the moment, but it would be too bad if I got the wrong wife—perhaps you could help me pick one. I shall be seeing you shortly, which is really why I am a little impatient with Oxford.

Norrie.

1 John Charles Miles was warden of Merton College, 1936–47.
2 The Chiltern Hills, southeast of Oxford toward London.
3 A range of hills west of Oxford, in Gloucestershire.
4 See Letter 183, n. 1, above.
5 The demonstration was in connection with a strike of 25,000 bus workers that paralysed the London transit system.

203. HK to NF   Art Gallery of Toronto. Sat. May 29. 1937.

Postmarked 31 May 1937; addressed to NF at Merton College, Oxford, England, Via New York: 'Normandie.' The cable referred to is missing. In a note in the margin to the left of the paragraph beginning "I have cancelled my passage" HK has written "out of date," and she has put ditto marks in the margin to the left of the next paragraph, both of which result from her having received the news on 31 May that NF would not be staying in England.

My dearest: I suppose I shall soon be hearing from you in answer to my cable, but I'd better tell you what happened here. I went to get the situation clear, straight from the horse's mouth, and had an interview with [Walter T.] Brown. He teased me a little about absent minded professors, which was what I expected. I had to take in his side of the question, and here it is. You have not kept in touch with the English

Department, you have not made any request for money. The only thing that might have been done, which evidently could have been arranged quite easily was a renewal of the Royal Society award for a second year. But Pelham Edgar has been very much hurt at your lack of courtesy (Brown) in not keeping in touch with him and has done nothing about it. The word is the same all along the line: you haven't written to any of them but Brown and he knows that that was because Daniells told you to, and then you didn't even drop a line to Daniells. It is a bit thick, you know. So, the only thing Brown can do is get you $600 provided by Currelly for members of the staff,—they waive the point that you are a future member of staff,—and that on condition that you stay over the second year and find the money somehow. There is a job here for you a year from now, Brown says he's saving it for you, but the condition is that you have two years' graduate work at Oxford. There's no use coming home to see about it, he wouldn't take you next fall, not until the next one. And he won't unless you finish the Oxford degree. I cabled because I knew that you'd be needing some money soon. Also the committee which decides on this meets June 8. Brown will get them to agree to forking out the money on condition that you stay the second year, but while that may be passed on June 8, they won't fork out until they hear from you. The Royal Society met here this week, and Brown says he doesn't feel he can ask Edgar to do anything more. There was no mention of the promise he made about a year's leave of absence, and I couldn't drag that in—chicken-livered perhaps. After this we don't believe *anything* until we have it above a signature.

I have cancelled my passage on the Empress June 12, and am waiting to hear from you, for the money. I have $165 of my own in the bank and if I don't come over I will pay back Barbara's [Barbara Sturgis's] hundred because we can't afford to run into too much debt. You should stay there this summer, I think. Norah [McCullough] would rather have me here in June, so I am taking July and August off, and can come over then if you find some money. Please let me know—send me a short note *often* so that I can arrange my plans from this end. I leave Wymilwood on June 11, and I am not doing anything about the summer for the time being.

I went for a walk with Kay Coburn last night. We had everything fixed for me to go over with her, but that's out. Kay has just wangled $1500 from the Carnegie people to go across and photograph all the fifty-odd Coleridge notebooks in Lord Coleridge's library, to which she will have all rights of editing or publication. She may have to have some help at deciphering some of them—someone to transcribe obscure passages, and I suggested that you are a damn good typist. She knows the jam you're in and can't at the moment think what to do about it. It is pretty tough having to borrow that much—after four year's she has just finished paying back what she borrowed to finish her second year at St. Hugh's. What about asking Daniells? And what was the result of your interview with Blunden? And have you found out what prizes you are eligible for according to the Oxford calendar? I'd prefer to have you ask Daniells for a loan. I thought of going to try and mollify Papa Edgar, but I think that would put you in a worse position, *my* doing your talking.

God help us, what a gloomy letter! You have been in worse jams than this before now, or at least about as bad, and we got through them somehow. I do wish you could get a job over there, when I think of how impressed Victoria would be, it seems the important thing to do, rather than coming back here where they know all about your financial troubles, and now and again have a tendency to remember how much money they've spent on you. You must not let me interfere with your plans my dearest, I can leave my feelings in cold storage for another year, that is, if I don't think about it.

The radio talk came off without any difficulties last Tuesday. Had a bad time convincing the family that I did it, Daddy being convinced that it was Norah [McCullough] after all. He thought I must have gone to pieces from nervousness and Norah had to read it for me. Can you beat that! But his faith in his family is pretty badly shaken after Roy's [Roy Kemp's] brief excursion off the rails. Walking around with a son talking casually of dropping off bridges is no fun. However, Roy is much better now, he and La Trobe have built the log cabin—are building it, rather. It is three feet above ground now, and they both seem to be enjoying the whole thing immensely. Mrs Arnold may go up to Gordon Bay this summer, renting one of Hamer's cottages, taking the three children and a nursemaid, leaving Bert as usually to his own devices. I'm not too keen on getting involved with that family, in case I am up there for the summer, but I suppose it will be all right. She wants to go somewhere where she knows someone, and John Jones [Harwood-Jones] suggested Hamer's cottage.

Norah is having a picnic in Caledon[1] for the whole gang, this afternoon. She is away this morning and I have spent most of it answering 'phone calls about getting out there. I wish you were coming along too.

Barbara [Sturgis] is moving, and some of my stuff is going to Dot

Drever. I'm terribly glad I didn't live with Barbara, I'd hate to live in such a mess,—and she hasn't thought of sending the rugs and curtains to the laundry—rugs with a year's dirt on them. Oh well.

Ida [Clare] and Bill [Conklin] are being married this afternoon, and Suzanne Currelly next week. I've been out buying wedding presents at the Sea Captain's Shop—good fun, but expensive. Has to be done, I suppose. Next year you'll have Arthur [Cragg] at Cambridge. And [Herbert J.] Davis will be in England toward the end of the summer, I'll find out where—but it would be much better if you wrote to him. I told you they were going away.

I'll finish this later, I must go to lunch now, and the picnic, passing up Ida's wedding.

Monday night

Norah's picnic over, moving over. Spent Sunday paddling at the Island with Kay Coburn who has given me a suggestion or two. I 'phoned the IODE office and found out where to write. Their conference is on now, so there's no time to lose—hence my letter, a copy of which I enclose.[2] Kay suggested seeing Pratt and asking for advice but he's in Bermuda. I may go to see Robins, although Pratt would have been much better. Your letter came this morning, saying you were coming home, and I thought that all our difficulties would be settled. Certainly it is the cheapest thing we can do, and probably by far the pleasantest, for the family will be awfully glad to have you, and Harold keeps hoping you'll be back. Roy will be there—he is improving rapidly, and we could all be healthy and happy together. Grand idea. The only thing is—you'll miss seeing [Walter T.] Brown.[3] I'm sending back his letter[4] in case you haven't a copy. He read me what he said anyway, from his carbon copy. Kay [Coburn] says if you haven't life insurance you can take out a thousand dollars and will it to the person who lends you money. You ought to be able to pay it back in two years or so, with economy, if they give you an $1800 job, which is the figure Kay mentioned. I will send you $100 by the next fast mail after this, as I did not get to the bank to-day. I'll nose around, and see what else I can do here, will see Pratt in three weeks when he gets back from Bermuda, but he is going to Vancouver almost immediately after that. Most of my friends are in a curious state about my trip—they still think I leave on June 12th. So I'm having some important changes of plan which make it necessary that I stay here. You don't need to feel afraid to see people—it is quite natural that you should come home this summer and it will be cheaper for both of us. And a lot healthier. I am quite sure we can dig up money from somewhere, so just you write a nice little letter to Brown. And I love you very very much, and want to sit in the sun and watch you get freckled. My dear.

H.

1 A town located about fifteen kilometres northwest of metropolitan Toronto.
2 HK sent the following holograph letter, dated 31 May 1937, to the IODE office.

Miss W. Gordon
106, St. Ann Street,
Quebec City.

Dear Miss Gordon:

I am writing to ask you if there is any possibility of your being able to give financial assistance to a student who is now in Merton College, Oxford. Mr Herman Northrop Frye is a graduate in Philosophy, English and History of Victoria College, a graduate in theology of Emmanuel College, and last year he was given the Royal Society Award in English Literature to enable him to continue work in Oxford. Mr Frye now finds it necessary to borrow money for next year, and as I understand your committee is meeting at present I hope this request will reach you while the Maritime Educational Secretary is still with you.

Mr Frye comes from Moncton, New Brunswick, and if there is no loan fund available for him in Ontario I thought there might be a possibility of some help from New Brunswick. He will need one thousand dollars ($1000) and can offer life insurance as security with the assurance of an appointment the following year to the English Department of Victoria College, University of Toronto. I have written asking Mr Frye to get in touch with you but as I am much nearer and am trying to help Mr Frye in this matter, I decided to lose no time in writing to you directly.

I hope that you will feel that you can give his case every consideration, and I will send you any further particulars about his scholastic record that you wish.

Very sincerely yours,

(Miss) Helen G Kemp.

After June 10th my address will be c/o The Art Gallery of Toronto, Grange Park, Toronto.

3 Principal Brown was planning to be in Oxford 12–26 July for a "Life and Work" Conference.
4 HK enclosed Principal Brown's letter to NF, dated 29 April 1937, advising him to stay in England for the summer: "The cost of maintaining yourself in London for three months would not be much greater than the cost of returning to Canada and maintaining yourself here." Brown also confirmed what HK has reported in the first paragraph of her letter—that Charles T. Currelly was willing to recommend that NF be given $600 in scholarship aid for the 1937–38 academic year, that the college had no loan fund to assist him, and that he would have to raise the additional funds for another year at Oxford himself.

204. NF to HK   Oxford

[*1 June 1937*]

Telegram; addressed to HK at 84 Queen's Park, Toronto=. Although "1937
May 1" is hand-stamped very plainly in blue ink on the telegram, internal evi-
dence clearly indicates that the telegram was received on 1 June. In her letters of
10 and 23 May (Letters 197 and 201) HK is still proceeding with plans for her
trip to England, and in his letters postmarked 18 and 21 May (Letters 198 and
200) NF says, first, "if I came back to Canada . . . I'd have to borrow about $100
from you," and then asks outright, "Could you lend me £20 ($100) to get home
on?" In her letter of 29 May (Letter 203), HK indicates that she is expecting an
answer to a cable she has sent and writes, "I cabled because I knew that you'd be
needing some money soon," and then, finally, NF gratefully acknowledges
receipt of the money in his letter of 8 June (Letter 205). Evidently the clerk in
the telegraph office changed the date on the stamp according to habit, but forgot
to change the month at the same time.

MUST COME HOME CAN YOU LEND ME SOME MONEY=

NORRIE.

205. NF to HK   Oxford

Postmarked 8 June 1937; addressed to HK at 84, Queen's Park, Toronto,
Ontario, Canada.

Darling, it's perhaps as well that somebody has some idea of how to
manage my affairs, as I obviously haven't much idea of it myself. I suppose I have been a complete fool with Edgar, although he talks as
though I had never sent him a word. I did write him at Christmas,[1] telling him how I was getting on, how the Blake was going, and something
of Elizabeth [Fraser], who is a close friend of his wife. I also said I would
forward some of the Blake in three weeks, and the rest at the end of the
following term. Well, in three weeks' time I was down with the 'flu, and
although I slogged and slogged at the Blake for weeks, it just didn't add
up to the right answer. However, the first two chapters—half the
whole—are getting their final draft now. Blunden has considerable hope
of publication, and suggests Faber & Faber as the first move. I have written Edgar, sending him the first chapter of the Blake,[2] and explaining

that I'd see him for suggestions when I was in Canada, and that if the book were published I'd want to dedicate it to him. I hated to write and just put him off with more promises—I wanted to deliver the goods. That's the best I can do to mollify him—the book, if it comes out, will be a damned important one, and when Victoria College sees H.N. Frye splashed over the Times Literary Supplement they may be less worried about my correspondence. Not that I'm trying to defend myself particularly. In the meantime the Royal Society has to have his O.K. before they send me the last £30, and they probably won't get it, so I may have to borrow still more money to pay for my piano here. Edgar did nothing whatever about my Christmas letter, and the Royal Society, after a delay of several weeks, finally sent the second instalment without him, so perhaps there is more than one angle to this lack of courtesy business.

Well, I'm more grateful than I can say for all your work with the College and the I.O.D.E. and the money. Your own job, Roy and me must be a terrific combination for your small shoulders. I'm so glad the radio talk came off all right.

As you see, I'm not feeling very well yet, and I'm beginning to feel about you as I feel about the rest: I must get that book out first and listen to complaints about my bad manners afterwards. Bless you, darling. And if you can get a typewriter up to Gordon Bay you really won't have to scramble around cleaning up the messes I make much longer. Don't lose your faith in me.

Norrie.

1 NF wrote to Edgar from London on 28 December 1936, telling him that he had written about 80,000 words on the first part of his Blake thesis. NF's letter is in the Pelham Edgar Collection, VU Library.
2 NF did not actually write Edgar until 10 June, saying that he was sending the first chapter under separate cover. NF's letter is in the Pelham Edgar Collection, VU Library.

206. NF to HK   Oxford

Postmarked 9 June 1937; addressed to HK at 84, Queen's Park, Toronto, Ontario, Canada.

I'm sorry about my last letter: I don't sound very pleasant at the moment, I know. The point is: the Blake is the only thing I can do now to recoup myself. I am sure it will be published, and that it will attract a lot of attention when it is published. Things will look different then. The whole story looks very different to me than it does to you, but you'll understand much quicker if I don't go into explanations or excuses. I'm damned sorry about spoiling your trip this summer, much more grateful than I can possibly say for what you are doing, and I concede that I have spent the year sleepwalking, oblivious to everything, with my sense of proportion, perspective, good manners and common sense totally atrophied. The only things that can be rescued from this are the dreams that come to me in my sleep.

And, unless sea air can perform miracles, I think that when you see me you will also see why I'm coming to Muskoka, throwing myself on your hands, making no effort to stay over here, and looking pretty ignominious generally. In the meantime you can look at my handwriting. I'm planning to sail from Southampton on June 24 on the Empress of Australia.

Blunden says he'll give me an introduction to Faber & Faber. I'm a little afraid of them, though the advantages of having them publish the book are so obvious that it's worth a long chance. Cambridge Press will come next, and I think I should land them all right. Or somebody after them.

But I can't start protesting about how much I love you until I have the Blake to point to.

207. HK to NF   [Toronto]
                                                         June 11. 1937.

My dearest: Graduation house party is in progress; I went to the Vic tea-party and talked to Pelham [Edgar] and his wife—she is really very nice, and I like her immensely. I didn't mention you, of course. There was no opportunity,—Pelham introduced me as Hazel Kemp again, remembered seeing me in Ottawa and the map etc. He toasted the bride at Suzanne's [Suzanne Currelly's] wedding so I complimented him on his speech. Dr [Walter T.] Brown has got the 600 for you from the Board of Regents—he is not sending you a letter because of the lack of time— you leaving there and he being tied up with sitting on platforms while people graduate. I went to the reception and prize-giving last night. Of all the dowdy, stuffy affairs,—oh well. Roy got his aegrotat all right and is still north making the log-cabin. I have wind of what looks like a good job for him with Mr Matthews who does our slides, who also sells all kinds of scientific equipment.

Let me know what boat you're coming on and I'll try to get to Montreal. As it is I don't know when you arrive, when you are leaving or anything. Do let me know, for I want to meet you.

[Herbert J.] Davis has gone to Chicago but the Wookey[1] will be here all summer, and we're going up to see her. You are also going to drop in to see Pelham (orders from your business manager!)—the old fossil—I can't understand what is the matter except that a personal note would have interested him probably more than all your brilliant essays. There is just a chance of a very interesting shift here—Peggy Roseborough told me about it. E.K. Brown is coming to Toronto and Roy Daniells may go to take his place.[2] It isn't definitely decided yet and John Creighton is after the Vic job, but Kay [Coburn] doesn't think he'll ever be given one there. How that affects you I don't know.

Kay leaves on the Empress to-morrow—the boat I was going on. Maybe I can come over next year—I hope so. Victoria is a bit nauseating at times, and I'd like to see some pictures. If I think too much of you I feel terribly queer—I'll be so glad to see you, oh my dearest! Tell me when and how you're coming.

Helen.

1 Gladys Wookey Davis.
2 E.K. Brown, who had taught at the University of Manitoba, 1935–37, joined the English department at UC in 1937; he left in 1941 for Cornell University. Roy Daniells, who was a member of the department at VC, left for Manitoba in 1937, where he taught for ten years before going to the University of British Columbia.

208. NF to HK   Oxford

Postmarked 20 June 1937; addressed to HK at 205 Fulton Ave., Toronto, Ontario, Canada.

Thank you, darling. I think I said I was sailing from Southampton on the *Empress of Australia*. I want to get back as soon as possible—I may return to Europe on a freighter. I want to stay in London long enough to look up Geoffrey Keynes. The boat sails June 24 and is supposed to arrive in Quebec 8 a.m. July 1. From there I take something else to Montreal. I've already bought my ticket for Toronto. Please don't bother to come to Montreal unless you really want to—I have a bad conscience about the amount of money you can spend on me. I got the Blake off—the first half—to Faber & Faber today, which is the reason for this type of note. I love you very much—far more than I can attempt to say in my present state of mind.

209. HK to NF   [*Toronto*]
                                         Friday June 25, 1937.

Addressed to NF at an unknown location in Montreal.

My dearest: WELCOME HOME! WELCOME HOME! WELC—my typewriter sticks!

I can't find out exactly when the boat-train gets in, sometime in the morning of July 1st, at Windsor Station, Montreal. Very well. I'll be there.

I hope you've had a marvellous crossing. I am sure you will have because the weather here has been perfect for days. But you never can tell about the ocean.

I'll save all my news until I see you.

                                         July 1st.

Helen!

210. NF to HK   Toronto

Postmarked 21 July 1937; addressed to HK at Gordon Bay, Lake Joseph, Ontario. After arriving in Toronto from England, NF joined HK at the Kemps' cottage in Gordon Bay. In July he took the train to Toronto, where this letter was posted, to discuss his teaching position at VC for the 1937–38 academic year.

Fifteen hundred. At least, I think it'll be that. The Chancellor didn't want to discuss money until the Principal told him how much he could jew me down, but I said I had orders from my fiancée to get more definite information. He said in an injured way, "You're not thinking of getting married, are you?" I said I was. He said "Do you think that's wise?" I said I did. Then he said something about our being separated for the following year, and I said I thought we'd hold out, or words to that effect. He still looked injured—the college could exploit me with less strain on its Non-conformist conscience if I remained celibate. My year at Oxford will be the following one if at all possible, but he can't promise. No leave of absence—I still just get Currelly's $600.00 for my second year at Oxford and that's all, with what I can save: "the two of you" says the Chancellor with a leer—this year. And of course I can't go on the permanent staff because "for your sake and our sake" I should have at least two years' training abroad, "Principal [Walter T.] Brown thinks and I think" and for the same reason I don't get the Lecturer's salary of eighteen hundred, but the Chancellor will take the responsibility of saying fifteen hundred.[1] They've got me where they want me and they know it. But I do a Lecturer's work, all right. I probably get Roy's [Roy Daniell's] three biggest courses—first year 16th c., which I know pretty well, the Milton course, where I have to compete with Woodhouse,[2] for 3rd. year, and 4th year 19th c. thought. The Chancellor phones Edgar to get that confirmed and lets me know tomorrow (Thursday) morning, so I can't leave before Friday. On the other hand I want to leave then, as John Jones' [Harwood-Jones'] frau moves in Saturday. The Chancellor has visions of my reading frantically all the rest of the summer, of course, and is fussing like blazes to find out exactly what I'm to do. I'll have groups besides that, doubtless.[3] They sure picked up a bargain. I shall remember it when the time comes to discuss my "obligations" to Victoria College.

Roy says he'll come up Saturday if he doesn't go to camp Onawaw, where Jessie Johnston wants him to take moving pictures. Otherwise he doesn't know. He and John do some giggling about a "blonde" in 4th year U.C. whose picture Roy showed me and who seems to be an attraction to Toronto. I made it as clear as I could that we wanted him at Gordon Bay.

John and Sallee Creighton are going to Bennington, a small college in Vermont, with Sallee doing part-time work. I saw Miss Ray and she looked vague and shamefaced. I told the Chancellor that you would keep your job as there wasn't yet so much prejudice against married women in the Art Gallery as in other places. He winced.

1 NF was appointed "special lecturer" and actually received a salary of $1600, "less 5% cut," which Ayre describes as "an obligatory cut to remind the staff of the Depression" (143).
2 A.S.P. Woodhouse, a Miltonist who had been a member of the English department at UC since 1929 and who had already become a central force in English studies at Toronto; he eventually became chair of the department at UC, a position he held from 1944 to 1964. Three months after NF's letter, the combined English departments, at the initiative of Woodhouse and with the support of E.K. Brown, completely revised the English undergraduate course. In the late 1930s the graduate program in English was also revamped, and Woodhouse chaired the graduate department of English for almost twenty years. Woodhouse's national reputation was considerable by the time NF arrived on the scene, and it became more so during the next two decades.
3 NF ended up teaching Joseph Fisher's course in the eighteenth century (Fisher had enlisted for military service), the Milton and Spenser course for honour students, seventeenth-century prose, and nineteenth-century prose.

1938–1939

Before the final group of letters there is a fourteen-month break in the correspondence, and, once again, the details of the Fryes' lives during this period are sketchy. Frye had told Chancellor Wallace, as indeed he and Kemp had told a host of others, that they were to be married, and exactly a month after he left Toronto for Gordon Bay, they returned to Toronto, where, on 24 August 1937, classmate Arthur Cragg performed the ceremony in the Emmanuel College chapel. When Frye sends news to Elizabeth Fraser of the impending nuptials, she replies curtly, "Good. But see that your marriage doesn't get in the way of finishing Blake by Sept. 1st.[1] Returning from their honeymoon at Gordon Bay, the Fryes set up housekeeping in the University Apartments at 6 St. Thomas Street, near the Victoria campus. Ayre reports that they "settled into a genial round of parties largely centred on the core of voluntary staff of *Canadian Forum*" (144). Still strapped for money, Frye appeals to Daniells early in the term for a loan to pay off his Oxford debts. "Can you lend me seventy dollars ($70.00)? The Bursar of Merton wants to be paid twenty-five pounds for last term. I've got it, as far as salary goes, but not now; I can pay you back in two months. I wrote that bastard explaining that I had been recently married and would like to be let off battels until next year, when I returned to Oxford. He said he had every sympathy with married couples, but that a year after marriage events frequently transpired which proved even more expensive, so I have to pay up. I hate Oxford, but, like war, one has to be in it to realize how awful it is.[2]

Frye had begun writing for the *Canadian Forum* in 1936, and during the 1937–38 academic year he produced several more pieces before he headed off to Oxford the following fall—an article on music, another on surrealism, and a review for the *Forum*, as well as a satire for *Acta Victoriana*.[3] Helen Frye herself wrote brief essays on two artists, Yvonne Williams and Fritz Brandtner, for the *Forum*.[4] Ayre notes that in February 1938 Frye read a paper on the techniques of modern writing to the University of Toronto Press Club and recycled several of his Oxford essays for the Graduate English Club (146–7). They both lecture on art to a group organized by Barker Fairley, professor of German at University College and a painter in his own right. In late March Frye learns that he has been awarded a $750 Trick Travelling Fellowship to complete his studies at Oxford. On the whole, Frye writes to Roy Daniells in July, the year was rather successful, adding that his best experience was with the music group of the Women's Literary Society at Victoria, composed mostly of his first-year honour students. He and Helen spend June at Gordon Bay, after which he teaches a summer school course on nineteenth-century poetry and prose before gathering himself together for another year at Oxford. "The Blake," he tells Daniells, "is in good shape, except for the recasting of some of the work on the major prophecies. I couldn't have picked a subject calling for more exacting writing and arrangement of material. It takes its own time."[5] On 23 August, Frye, having returned to Gordon Bay, writes to Chancellor Edward Wallace: "At the moment I am resting from the summer school, escaping the worst of the heat, and feeling generally rather poised and hovering, with all my possessions packed away and ready to take off for England as soon as my boat sails on the 24th of September. I am feeling a bit let down without anyone to teach here in Muskoka; the woodpeckers and bluejays catch a didactic glint in my eye and uneasily get out of the way."[6]

   In late September Frye leaves Montreal on the *Empress of Britain*, visiting briefly with his aunt Hatty Layhew before he sails. The spectre of war haunts the letters he writes on the voyage over, and the signs of a nation preparing for war greet him as he enters the English Channel. He stays in a London boarding house for a week, goes to a sherry party thrown by Elizabeth Fraser, and on 6 October (Helen Frye's birthday) leaves for Oxford. For his second stint at Merton, he takes up residence in a boarding house some distance from the college, sharing a suite with Rodney Baine and Mike Joseph. The day after he arrives he goes to see Blunden, and he gets to work immediately, writing papers first on Crashaw and Herbert and then on Vaughan, Traherne, Herrick, Marvell, and Cowley, all of whom, he writes his wife, he has "ideas about."

Blunden advises him to postpone his Blake thesis and to study for the "schools"—examinations for the degree.

His first week back Frye attends lectures by David Nichol Smith, the Merton Professor of English at Oxford, and J.R.R. Tolkien, but finds little to recommend either. "Nichol Smith," he says, "wouldn't be bad for my sort of job: getting one point per lecture hammered home, but to me he's prolix & dull. Then there's Tolkien on Beowulf, dealing with a most insanely complicated problem which involves Anglo-Saxon genealogies, early Danish histories, monkish chronicles in Latin, Icelandic Eddas and Swedish folk-lore. Imagine my delivery at its very worst: top speed, unintelligible burble, great complexity of ideas and endless references to things unknown, mixed in with a lot of Latin and Anglo-Saxon and a lot of difficult proper names which aren't spelled, and you have Tolkien on Beowulf." Frye reports that he is writing a paper on the Dark Ages, apparently for J.N. Bryson, his Anglo-Saxon tutor, and in late October he grumbles that he has tied himself "in fearful knots over a paper on the character book." "That drew a suggestion," he adds, "for exploring 17th c. scientific works, so I'm quitting work for the term, as far as extras are concerned." Frye does, however, give a talk on "A Short History of the Devil" to the Bodley Club.

Frye's circle of friends expands to include three more Rhodes scholars—Alan Jarvis, from the University of Toronto; Charles Bell, from Mississippi, who has set up a ménage with Mildred Winfree; and Tom Allen, from Queen's University. Allen has a piano, so Frye, Stephen Corder, and an unnamed cellist, form a trio and frequently congregate in Allen's room to play Haydn, Brahms, Ravel, Mendelssohn, and Schumann. "The trio and the dark beer," Frye reports later, "will be the only two things I'll miss next year." He actually sends back more detailed reports of his musical activities and gallery tours than of his literary studies. In October he goes with Alan Jarvis to see Sir Michael Sadler's art collection, sending Helen what amounts to a gallery guide. He also meets the artist David Jones at Campion Hall, and writes a review of the Canadian exhibition at the Tate Gallery for the *Canadian Forum*. Helen wants Eric Newton, art critic of the *Manchester Guardian*, to review the show as well, which he eventually does after Frye serves as intermediary. In November Frye takes a day-trip to London with Mike Joseph to see *Guernica*, a Chirico show, and another exhibition of modern paintings. *Guernica*, which was shown along with its preliminary drawings, especially impressed Frye.

Back in Toronto Helen Frye continues to work at two jobs, serving as staff lecturer at the art gallery and as a don in a women's residence at Victoria. One of her ongoing responsibilities at the gallery is to schedule talks for CBC radio. She reports that she is "doing a lot of new things this year and getting away with it," including voice instruction from Sterndale Bennett, a local theatre director and actor. Bennett's lessons help build her confidence as a speaker, and she prepares a radio talk entitled "Art for Everyman," which is broadcast on 1 November 1938; she also arranges loan exhibitions, labels lantern slides, and lectures to Victoria College students. But she complains that she is "disgruntled about things" because the art gallery is lifeless and the residence life "isn't nearly as tolerable as it was two years ago." She grouses about the provincialism of Victoria College—in fact, she and Frye both grumble throughout the letters about Victoria's Victorianism. But her active schedule at the gallery leaves little time for sustained complaining. The first week of November, for example, finds her speaking on mural painting for the League for Social Reconstruction, lecturing to 180 members of the Women Teachers Association, giving two other talks, and organizing various teas and breakfast parties for the students at Oaklawn, a women's residence at Victoria College. Her group of friends, like Frye's, expands to include the Faculty Women's Association, the staff of the *Canadian Forum*, and members of the art community. She continues to record disheartening episodes in the ongoing saga of Magda and Bert Arnold.

Meanwhile in Oxford, Barbara Sturgis, Helen's friend, stops by for a visit toward the end of the term, and Frye attends plays by Monk Lewis and Henry Arthur Jones. When the term is over on 3 December he goes to London, where he stays, as a guest of Mike Joseph, at New Zealand House. He equips himself with a new suit, visits the Burnetts and their two German refugees, goes to three art exhibitions, and pays a call on Elizabeth Fraser. "I very much admire Elizabeth," he confides, "but I confess she puzzles me. I'm afraid, too, that she's getting to be my maiden aunt, whom it's something of a duty to see. But that's unfair. I do like her very much." Frye then sets out for Paris by way of Rouen with Rodney Baine and Mike Joseph. They take in the usual Parisian sights, and although Frye writes that he is not living a life of dissipation, he does record a number of drinking bouts. After Baine has left to tour Normandy, Frye and Joseph take a side trip to Versailles: "when you get in the dead centre of all the algebra and sit down there the sheer monstrosity of the scheme *does* get you, all right, like Hitler's voice." They meet Baine in Chartres, where, with the bitter cold, Frye "thought more about [his] toes than about the medieval soul"; and the three of them return to Paris for Christmas. The frigid weather (it is the coldest winter since 1879) makes sightseeing difficult even for a Canadian, and the short days compound the problem: "it's nearly dark at three and the economical French would sooner die than turn on a light." Still, Frye manages to see Saint-Chapelle, Notre Dame, the Louvre, the Musée de l'Homme, a number of gallery exhibitions, the Jeu de Paume, the Musée de Luxembourg, and the Musée de Cluny. The paintings he catalogues consist mostly of modernists—Kandinsky, Klee, Chagall, Despiau, Borés, Kisling, Masson, Soutine, and Utrillo. He hears concerts by Yves Tinayre and Jacques Thibaud as well.

Helen spends "a grand week" after Christmas in Chicago with Frye's sister Vera, and in her first letter of the new year she begins to wonder whether their vague plans to meet in England for the summer will materialize, and if so, how they will pay for the trip. "I wish you'd start thinking about finances after March," she writes in early January, "and let me know what you are planning. I need a new coat just now and if I get it I'll be starting from scratch again by the first of February, so that it will take some time for me to save much. I thought of going to New York and New England if Europe is out of the question, and of course I'm expecting to do it with you, or at least some of it. But *how* are you getting enough to keep you there in the summer, even if I do? Or if I came over in the spring—what then? You figure out something and if you can borrow enough perhaps I can come."

Frye returns to London by way of Amiens, where his brother Howard had been killed in World War I. "I don't know whether he's buried near here," Frye writes, "or in the Canadian cemetery at Vimy. Or rather, I don't know where his cross is: I suppose the bomb that hit him did the burying." He is struck by the sculpture of the cathedral at Amiens ("the symbolism is better organized and more completely worked out" than that of Chartres) and by "the terrific reaching for height and those superb flying buttresses" of the cathedral at Beauvais. What most affects him, however, is a particularly nightmarish wooden statue of the crucifixion at St. Etienne's Church in Beauvais. "It caught my eye," he reports, "because that's a very bad and very rare medium for a crucifixion, and as I looked at it it got worse . . . . It's one of the most wilfully grotesque things I've ever seen."

Back in London, Frye again visits the Burnetts, who now are harbouring two additional refugees, sees Elizabeth Fraser, and heads back up to Oxford. Meanwhile Helen repeats her admonitions for her husband to settle his plans for the summer, and she hints that Martin Baldwin is pushing her to apply for a scholarship at Yale. When she learns that Frye has about £60 left for the rest of the term, she suggests that if she can scrape together enough money she may be able to sail for England in June, arriving there about the time he finishes his exams. In late January she predicts she can save about $300, but a few weeks later she announces she is "insolvent again," and she seems to hedge about going abroad: "You know, if we really were sensible, I suppose I'd be saving to buy furniture or something to fill up space when you come back." Frye's accounts of his tutorials are sketchy: "Blunden continues vague and complimentary. He says things like 'I wish you'd write these things down, just as you say them: I think there's something to be said for a book of table-talk,' or 'I don't care about a paper: it's enough just to get you talking.' But he doesn't seem to remember what I've told him particularly." In early February Frye reports on doing a paper on *King Lear* that "Blunden seemed to like," but adds, "otherwise I've done little work." Two weeks later, however, he does write a paper on the history of the language for J.N. Bryson.

Frye worries about his appointment at Victoria for the fall of 1939. He expects to have a staff position, but in late February he has received no official confirmation, and this puts him in an especially dark mood: "I'm hoping for the best. At the worst I can join the Chinese army. I think I can pile up more concentrated misery in this place than I could in hell. I detest England and I loathe Oxford: I think I always have done." But "the coming of spring," he says, "has lightened my misanthropic soul very considerably," and just before the end of the middle term he plays the part of a professor in a farce staged by the Merton Dramatic Society. After taking the first week of his Easter holiday to prepare for his exams in Old English, Middle English, and Chaucer, he spends two weeks of his vacation in Blackpool at the home of fellow student Bunny Mellor. Eager to return to Canada, Frye writes, "Wait till I get back and we'll make things hum in that hick town of ours. My lectures next year will be twenty-five times as good as they were last year, and I can lecture on anything from Beowulf to Beverley Nichols at a moment's notice. Once these silly exams are over—but I won't lay plans yet. Reading Latin and Greek, either original or translation, is the next thing I have to do. And then, when I hit a PMLA conference they'll think it's an air raid, or the Martians." In late March Frye visits his Oxford classmate Jack Mason at the home of Mason's aunt and uncle in Preston.

At the beginning of April Helen is still uncertain about the summer trip: "I spend my time alternately counting days and counting money—the one side still comes out too much, the other too little, but I'm still hoping." But financing the trip is not the only problem: the menace of Hitler's despotism is now more threatening than ever. "I don't know whether I'll be seeing you there or here," she writes. "I simply cannot read what is to happen in the next three months." But Frye, who has left his boarding house and moved back into residence at Merton for the spring term, remains sanguine about his wife's coming and their taking a trip to the continent. In April he feels that war is not imminent, but by the middle of May he writes that he feels "a little more apprehensive about war scares lately."

Helen, meanwhile, is searching for an apartment in Toronto for the fall and begins to envision their life together in the community: "I'm looking for a coach-house apartment or a separate flat or an apartment or a very small house. It certainly will be private for I want privacy! For a few hours a week anyway. I'm beginning to feel that you and I have got ourselves involved in a public career that we'll find hard to kick over. I don't think that I shall want to stop working at the Gallery next year: I'm getting ideas about it. And now that I'm learning to speak to crowds is no time to stop. I'd be home shouting in your poor defenceless ear and driving you crazy. Anyway, I'm thinking of a house to live in." She eventually gets a second-hand report that Principal Walter Brown is expecting Frye back in the fall, and she passes this information along to him in her letter of 15 May—information that, of course, relieves the major anxiety they have both had.

During the second week of June, Frye writes his examinations and sits for his viva voce, earning a first, the only Merton student for the year to achieve such a mark in English literature. In mid-June Helen sets sail on the SS *Georgic* from New York, and she is met by Frye at the Waterloo station when she arrives in London. His telegram to her aboard ship is the last piece of correspondence in the present collection. They do get to take a hurried trip to the continent, leaving London for Paris in late July and meeting Mike Joseph in Florence for a two-week tour of northern Italy. On 12 August they sail from Southampton on the *Empress of Britain* and arrive back in Montreal on 23 August, thus bringing to a close the last of the separations that have generated this exceptional body of letters.

1 Elizabeth Fraser to NF, 7 August 1937. HFF, 1991, box 3, file 1.
2 NF to Roy Daniells, undated, but written in November 1937. RDF, box 3, file 8.
3 "Music and the Savage Breast," *Canadian Forum*, 18 (April 1938), 451–3; "Men as Trees Walking," ibid., (October 1938), 208–10; "Lord Dufferin," ibid., (April 1938), 458; and "Face to Face," *Acta Victoriana*, 62 (March 1938), 10–12.
4 "Yvonne Williams," *Canadian Forum*, 18 (June 1938), 80; and "Fritz Brandtner," ibid., (December 1938), 272.
5 NF to Roy Daniells, 20 July 1938. RDF, box 3, file 8.
6 NF to Edgar W. Wallace, 23 August 1938. UCC/VUA, 89.130V, box 26, file 286.

211. NF to HKF [*Montreal?*]

Postmarked 24 September 1938; mistakenly addressed to HKF at 131 (rather than 113) Bloor St. W., Toronto, Ont.; presumably posted from Montreal or from somewhere along the St. Lawrence. The date on the postmark is clear, but the place of posting illegible.

I seem to have missed Aunt Hatty [Layhew] or Aunt Hatty me, but as Montreal seems to have inherited Toronto's rain I don't wonder. My cold, if not much worse, is certainly no better, and the front page of the morning paper is a mess.[1]

N.

Heavy pressure on pen, indicating a strong sex nature and a leaky nib.

1 NF is referring to the Czechoslovak–German crisis. Prime Minister Chamberlain had met with Hitler on 23–24 September in Godesburg, the Czechoslovakian army was mobilized on 24 September, the French cabinet ordered partial mobilization the same day to defend the Czechs, and Mussolini remained in firm support of the plan to partition Czechoslovakia. The "mess" NF refers to may also include the aftermath of a severe hurricane that swept across the northeastern United States, leaving five hundred people dead in its wake.

212. NF to HKF Camp Lévis Ocean Limited

Postcard; postmarked 25 September 1938; mistakenly addressed to HKF at 131, Bloor St. W., Toronto, Ont. Dashed off after NF boarded the Empress of Britain, *and apparently dropped off for posting at Lévis or somewhere else along the St. Lawrence. Someone has marked through "131" in the address and written "113," the correct street number, above it. HKF records in a postscript to Letter 216 that the mistake has resulted in some delay in the arrival of both of NF's postcards and also of a letter, which is missing.*

I hope it's 131 Bloor W. I saw Aunt Hatty for 15 minutes. Train full of bright young men with ideas about Central Europe.

N.

213. NF to HKF   [*Aboard the* Empress of Britain]

Postmarked September 1938; addressed to HKF c/o Art Gallery of Toronto, Toronto, Ont. The postmarked date is illegible; however, as NF left for England on 24 September, the letter was probably posted a day or so after that somewhere along the St. Lawrence, as the postmark is "Camp Levis Ocean Limited."

My dear:

I phoned Aunt Hatty and she came down just as I was about ready to start. One of her mistakes was going to the Bonaventure Station—there was a chapter of accidents I don't remember—and she gave me some fruit and two magazines. She discussed magazines with me, saying the New Yorker was clever but awful, that Wilbert [Howard] read the Coronet, also clever but awful, but generally an English one called For Men Only. I said it was a dirty rag, which it is. She said the magazines were Coronets—or I thought she did—but one of them turned out to be a Men Only. I must write her and apologize. I asked her what Hew [Hugh Layhew] and Flo were short of and she said she'd write you.

The trip along the St. Lawrence has been lovely—bright sunshine through heavy massed clouds, rolling country and whitewashed buildings spotlighted in the sun. The trees are superb. It's pretty cold, and the E of B[1] has energetic ventilators that blow your hat off and it's almost impossible not to sit in a draught and get a stiff neck, but there it is.

There are a lot of Rhodes fellows on board—they have two full tables at dinner, though, so I don't eat with them. I'm at a table of four—one intelligent chap, an old boy with a whisker, one boy in the R.A.F., who knows Jack Harris only by name.

The boys are all right—one is going to Merton for English[2]—I haven't met him yet. I'll send the lecture notes from Southampton—this boat moves faster than most boats & this letter had better go right away. Sorry for all this inconsequential babble: some moronic ladies are insisting that Whiskers has a young lady sharing his stateroom. I love you.

N.

1 *Empress of Britain;* see Letter 82, n. 4, above.
2 Tom Allen. See Letter 214, n. 2, below.

214. NF to HKF   Southampton

Postmarked 29 September 1938; addressed to HKF c/o Art Gallery of Toronto, Toronto, Ontario, Canada.

My dear:

Well, it's been a bit dull, after all. The food on the Empress is bad. Damned bad. English and bad. Or at any rate I can't eat it, and that combined with a cold put me rather off for a day or two. The cold is better, suspended, though the asthma came the first night. Yesterday I slept solidly from two to seven, in the afternoon too, and felt a lot better. The lounge has a gramophone, a very noisy one, and the music has that elephantine heave peculiar to the English music hall. The Empress also has an elephantine heave which I should assume to be peculiar to it. It rolls a bit, but considering the weather, with the spray soaking you if you venture out on the top deck (the lower one is closed), it rides quite well.

I have now retired to the Drawing Room, where there is no gramophone. This is where the few women congregate—there are only two under forty-five, so the dances aren't up to much. But they leave you alone pretty well.* I haven't been able to locate this Bradford woman— it's practically impossible to find anyone you don't know by sight when they're not in their staterooms. But I'll make further attempts.

Of the three men at my table, one is a silly but harmless old buzzard who seems to be a sort of English schoolmaster. He spends half breakfast-time telling me just why he always takes bran.** Another is a farmer and an M.P. from Alberta—Liberal, I should judge—a man somewhat like the Yale man I met on my field.[1] He's very pleasant. Told me I'd brought back a wonderful accent from Oxford with me. I don't know how often I've been told—by Canadians—that I have a thick English accent—it must be because I have an academic one. (The ladies, having got through "nahthin loike wot is on the Quehn Mehry," are now working on one of the female's gangrened toe, and branching out from there to other cases. Women seem to be fond of mutilation—we'd better hand over the next war to them). The fourth is a young chap in the Air Force. I got opposite him in a bridge game, and quickly got out of it. The Rhodes

---

* i.e., the management of the ship
** it keeps his insides regular. Sounds like a grandfather clock. I restrained an impulse to
  ask him if it kept his pendulum swinging.

men are a bit green. One—Allen—is going to read English at Merton[2]—
he's blonde and quite naive—I guess Blunden will get along with him
all right. He's from Queens, and is a piano-player, of the Prelude in C#
minor variety. He has a book of 4–hand stuff, and I helped him out one
evening with the piano when he seemed to be stuck, so now I'm stuck.

The shows on board aren't bad. The first was Zola,[3] just as good as the
last time, the second a poorish one on the life of Garrick, which I think
was English, and certainly had the English anemia. ("She was so weak
she couldn't stand up, but she didn't vomit." "The least little thing will
upset my stomach.") They cut it off before it was over. The one today
was that Leslie Howard comedy[4] we saw at the Uptown on Mrs. Blair's
pass.

Aunt Hatty's *Coronet* advertised a middle spread of Velasquez's
Rokeby Venus,[5] but it had been removed—I wonder if by Aunt Hatty. If
so, it might explain her opinion of it. There are some Renoirs I'll send
you if you want them.

The ladies are now a bit vociferous on the relative merits of electric
washing machines and "the English way," so I'd better leave.

I went to church Sunday morning, and some illiterate ship's officer
mumbled the morning prayer. The one thing a religious service, or the
reading of the Bible, does to me is to give—sometimes—the emotional
intensity that a dream gives an experience, and for the same reason—
that your conscious mind is asleep.

I bought a Penguin—Richard Jefferies' "Story of My Heart"[6]—you
have the book at home. I'm torn between the desire to save my six pence
by reading the book and the utter impossibility of reading it. So I moon
around, and occasionally fish it out of my pocket and stare at it.

But Richard Jefferies improves on acquaintance—as a matter of fact I
think he's written one of the significant books of his time, which is later
19th c.

I've just heard Chamberlain's speech.[7] He makes it sound a lot like
war—it may be partly bluff, of course, to tell Hitler he means it. I can't
understand Germany at all—the Nazis seem absolutely determined to
make the rest of the world gang up on them and smash them. By the
way, there was a book written in 1912–3, by Norman Angell, which you
also have, called *The Great Illusion*, proving that a complete financial
breakdown would follow a war.[8] But I still think there's something in it.

Everybody I've talked to seems fairly indifferent to war. They all
think it's a bad idea, take support of it by all classes of people to be inev-

itable, have no conception of any of the underlying motives of war except the immediate political situation, and simply shuffle the countries of Europe around like pawns. There are no strong feelings. They say Hitler's drunk with power, but there's absolutely no smash-the-dirty-buggers feeling—they understand, I think, the distinction between a government's will & what the people want. It's a saner attitude than the 1914 one, if that's any consolation, and however long it lasts.

But in the meantime the passengers are worried, depressed and anxious—there's a gloom over the whole ship. If Germany mobilizes—Russia's air force—Hitler wants the Ukraine—you young men it is who'll have to go—that's what they said in 1914—I guess Dorset will be out of danger—will you go back to Canada—over and over, on and on, round and round. God, I hope it blows over. Everybody seems drifting so helplessly and pitifully, and most of them don't even know it. But there's a 24–hour postponement, which may be the first of a series of stalls designed to save Hitler's face—I hope so.[9]

I attended my first ship's concert tonight. I had felt rather like a piker for not volunteering, but I was glad when I heard it I didn't. Apparently it's mostly the crew—in 3rd, anyway,—who have a trusty and ancient repertoire, doubtless all from a book called *The Sailor's Friend* or something. The very cute little girl who runs the kiosk said she'd heard the concert over and over.

I may not get the Artist in Society done in time,[10] but I've been working at it. Of course you're in no hurry for it till after Christmas, but I wanted to send a thick packet this time.

The crew, I understand, is practising a blackout drill tonight. The boat has every berth taken for its return voyage. But several people have made tentative arrangements for the next one. If I go back, I'll see you again soon—that would be a very bright silver lining on a very big and black cloud. If you get really scared, cable me saying you're dangerously ill or something. I don't think I'm a coward—I think really I'm less of one than some people who don't do any agonizing. But war is imbecile, patriotism and duty to the state is a silly idea, and will soon look so, and my love for you is very, very real. It's a moral love too, or is so long as morality isn't challenged, but the violent murder of millions of innocent people to support a stupid blunderer against a bullying lunatic so that a few millionaires can become multi-millionaires doesn't strike me as a moral issue. That sounds like Kay's argument rather than mine, of course.[11] We were both right.

But if war comes, will it be a Marxist or a Spenglerian one? Will it lead at once to socialist revolutions all over Europe and help destroy capitalism, or will it start brutalizing people to the level at which they accept indefinite series of annihilation wars as part of the scheme of things? Both points of view have so much truth in them.

This morning it begins to look as though Hitler was not only getting the Sudenten territory he asked for, but the four-power pact he wanted. A four-power pact with Italy his stooge, Britain his protesting but effectively bullied fag, and France isolated. If Chamberlain's hatred and fear of Russia is as great as his policy would seem to indicate, I'm very much afraid there's no permanent peace that way, and I shall be going through all these ruminations again in six months.

The old boy stuffed with bran I mentioned is really something of a trial. He will tell jokes he doesn't remember—very feeble ones, of course—forgets the point, and hauls it out of his subconscious ten minutes later when you've mercifully forgotten about it. Then there's a girl who affects a wisdom beyond her years, or her intelligence. She's among other things a caricature of what a woman ought not to be during a war-scare—flag-waving and brave-boys-going-to-defend and wish-I-could-help and so forth. I told someone she'd be useful as a sand-bag—she's a very pudgy damsel—but she turned out to be a barbed-wire entanglement. I find a judicious reference to a wife very useful at times. A Rhodes man was discussing with me the possibility of getting married to diminish the possibility of conscription, not too seriously, in her presence, and she said: "Yes, but don't get married just for the sake of being married. I've seen more lives wrecked as a result of getting the wrong woman" . . . as I say, it's good to be married in the abstract, let alone to you in the concrete.

I've met the Bradford—she gave me half an hour this morning, but she's very friendly with a Lt. Col. in the 3rd who monopolized her. She may improve at tea, to which she's invited me, but so far she's pretty awful.

I'd better finish this before I pack. I love you, I love you, I love you. Nothing else seems permanent in the way of peroration.

Norrie.

1 Clarence Bonfoy.
2 HKF's note to this letter indicates that this "must be Tom Allen." Although Thomas John Allen, educated at Peterborough College and Queen's University, was at Merton on an IODE Overseas Scholarship for Ontario in 1938–40, he was not a Rhodes scholar.

3 *The Life of Émile Zola*, a 1937 Warner Brothers film, based on a book by Matthew Joseph-son. It starred Paul Muni and Gail Sondergaard and was directed by William Dieterle.
4 *It's Love I'm After*, a 1937 Warner Brothers film starring Olivia de Havilland and Bette Davis in addition to Howard.
5 Also known by several other names, including "Venus and Cupid," "Venus at Her Mirror," and "Toilet of Venus." The painting is at the National Gallery, London.
6 Richard Jefferies's autobiography (Harmondsworth: Penguin, 1938). This was the "Penguin Illustrated Classics" edition of Jefferies's spiritual autobiography, first pub-lished in 1883.
7 On 29 September, the day NF's letter was posted, Neville Chamberlain, the British prime minister, flew to Munich to attend a four-power conference arranged by Musso-lini. The agreement reached by Mussolini, Daladier, Hitler, and Chamberlain was that the German occupation of the Sudenten territories would be spread over ten days and that the existence of Czechoslovakia would be guaranteed by the four powers. As Chamberlain did not return to London until 1 October, NF is apparently referring to remarks Chamberlain made before his departure to Munich. Thinking that Hitler had been appeased at the Munich conference, Chamberlain returned to cheering crowds in England to announce "peace in our time." The optimism in England was short-lived: within six months Hitler had invaded the rest of Czechoslovakia.
8 Angell's book, *The Great Illusion: A Study of the Relation of Military Power to National Advantage* (London: Heinemann, 1912), was first published in 1909 under the title *Europe's Optical Illusion*.
9 Chamberlain had persuaded Hitler not to invade Czechoslovakia until the two of them had had still another meeting—the third within fifteen days.
10 This seems to be an article HKF has sent to NF for his comments. Though no known article by HKF with that title exists, she did give a radio broadcast on 1 November 1938 entitled "Art for Everyman," one of the major themes of which is the artist in society (see Letter 220). The text of her presentation was published in *Curtain Call*, 10 (January 1939), 13–14. It could be, on the other hand, that "The Artist in Society" was an article that HKF had asked NF to write for the *Canadian Forum*, but, again, no known article by him with that title exists. NF is not referring to his review of Cana-dian art at the Tate Gallery, as that show did not open until 14 October. The only other article he wrote about this time, "Men as Trees Walking," was published in the Octo-ber issue of the *Canadian Forum*; as we learn from Letter 216, that piece had already been published by the time she wrote.
11 The reference is apparently to Kay Coburn.

215. NF to HKF   London
                                                         Sept. 30. [*1938*]

Postmarked1 October 1938; addressed to HKF c/o Art Gallery of Toronto, Toronto, Ontario, Canada.

My dear:

This is my first day in London. I haven't done anything yet except look around: I can't get at my trunk which has the map which has the streets Elizabeth [Fraser] and Harold Taylor live on, and I'm much too dizzy and stupid to talk to anyone anyhow. Except you, of course.

Well, European politics have entered another phase, I think. I don't know what the phase is, but the four-power capitalist pact is its basis, and it may be the beginning of a transition from national to international Fascism. I got up the Channel seeing war all around me and yet knowing it was all over. Cherbourg first, full of submarines and submarine nets and enormous breakwater walls with round towers at regular intervals, anti-aircraft guns built into the rock of the coast, airplanes roaring overhead, and a general feeling that the *real* defenses were being camouflaged. A steward assured me that I couldn't see much.* Then Southampton, with searchlights practising on an airplane—seven of them were trained on it, making a huge star-shaped pattern with a gleaming white plane in the centre. Then London. I stayed at the Imperial Hotel, Russell Square, overnight, and when I got up the agreement had been reached. The newspaper posters carried practically nothing except the word "Peace." Everybody took it very calmly—I was surprised that there were no demonstrations, even when it was a nice sunny day.† But there were notices everywhere about issuing gas masks and a long notice about what to do during an air-raid—a rather silly document adding up to zero. There isn't anything to do in an air-raid, except get off the streets, and leave town if you've got the money. I tried to get a tube to Waterloo for my trunk, and found that a lot of important stations, including it, were closed for "structural alterations," i.e., construction of the only sort of air-raid shelter there is in London. I dropped in to the Nat. Gall. and found a large section of it locked away in a "safe" place, including the first picture I tried to see, Piero's Baptism.[2] The parks have been torn to pieces to make trenches. All of which equals forty million pounds. Rather an expensive six months' lease—possibly a year's lease—but cheaper than war, and it gives the taxpayer a healthy idea, if he needs one, of what a war would cost. Of course peace may last indefinitely if Hitler finds the 4-power pact easy to work.

We heard a broadcast on the boat to the effect that Cambridge was postponing opening of term "until further notice," and I heard a rumor from a Rhodes man here that Oxford was doing the same thing, though he later had it contradicted. I'll find out definitely tomorrow, but I'm

---

* He explained that Cherbourg was a mawnor nyvol byse.[1]

† Fifteen minutes ago.

going up Friday anyhow, as my money won't last two weeks. That means that the Universities will close down altogether in the event of war, which would give me an air-tight excuse to go home . . . I wonder if they'd close down for any other reason, not involving so much murder?

I stayed overnight at the Imperial Hotel, a thing I don't think I'll do again. Somebody started vacuum-cleaning the room over my head at two in the morning. Then I got a room on Bernard St., just behind Guilford, for 25/ a week, a room exactly as horrible as that would imply. But I can stand anything for a week. When you're not sleeping in my bed other hardships don't matter much. But a good and cheap French restaurant is functioning on Southampton Row.

It's really true about the Penguin slot machines—each book rests on a chute with a plunger beside it, but as there's only room for one copy of each book, unless they want to stuff the whole machine with two or three, they're all practically empty. Otherwise the bookshops are just what they were. The appetite for books on sex, ranging from historical and semi-erudite studies to Marie Stopes, and from scientific studies of perversions to pornography, is as strong as ever, if not stronger. And Bloomsbury believes just as firmly in the imminent revolution in human imagination as it did two years ago. And Hilaire Belloc is revising an already infamous book on the Jews[3] because of the Spanish war, in which Jewish Communism is trying to smash the Christian (i.e. Catholic) Church . . . . Posters and advertisements are on the whole a little bit brighter, I think. I've never seen a good poster that didn't have an abstract design: it seems to be inevitable.

The Bradford woman invited me to tea—she's pleasant, but she's a commonplace young Englishwoman, and there isn't anything more commonplace than that. Tourist on the Empress of Britain gets all the engine vibration—teacups rattle in their saucers. 3rd was in the bow, and got no vibration. She lives in Winchester, and I may look her up.

I may as well get this off, I suppose: no use letting it lie around to accumulate more news. I'm tidy about the news litters (no pun) I drop on you.

Norrie.

1 NF is calling attention to the steward's pronunciation of "minor naval base."
2 Piero della Francesca's *Baptism of Christ* is among the paintings of the Umbrian school in the National Gallery.
3 Hillaire Belloc's *The Jews* (London: Constable, 1922) appeared in a third edition in 1937.

216. HKF to NF   [*Toronto*]
                                        Saturday night Oct. 1st. [*1938*]

My dearest: I feel rather queer writing to you. I shall have to get my hand in, I can see that. I have just had a long bath and washed my hair (still long!) and climbed into my swanky pajamas, and here I am in the don's sitting room at ten-thirty surrounded by notes from youngsters who say they have gone home for the week-end. *I* don't know what to do about it, but they keep on signing the leave book and filling out little cards the way they've been told, and I dare say I shall get it all through my head in the end. But when they come to ask permission I always give it to them, on the theory that they couldn't have any *very* wild ideas as yet, and that when they ask permission it's usually something that's permitted. So you get the picture: don keeping up a bold front, but a little vague as to what it's all about. The whole thing is ten times easier than before: I'm older, the kids are younger, and I'm the big Banshee in this house. There are still some notes from Peg Roseborough on the notice board—Herta [Hartmanshenn] says Peg used to rise up and thunder at them periodically, something I can't just see myself doing.

This week has been hectic. You can imagine, after [Martin] Baldwin left me with the bulletin on my hands, as you saw, and there have been exhibitions and groups to talk to and all sorts of interruptions from people wanting to know about loan material etc etc. Charlie Comfort and me is friends—he and I went to have our voices tested for radio. I read part of my first radio talk[1] and Mr Harvey called from the receiving room—give it more *umph!* more from the chest! give it a kick over, keep it out of the mud! All of which being translated means:—when the voice is resonant enough it sends a needle vibrating widely and that means it will carry to Vancouver. If it is down in the mud it's flat and the needle hardly moves and the result is a monotone that's very dull and can't be heard very far or even stepped up with their instruments. They call that "favouring" a voice. Radio jargon lesson no. I. Anyhow they say I'm all right. Comfort read a passage out of the University Calendar on the great advantages of Hart House, with great unction. He really has a swell voice I think, for radio.

Douglas MacAgy is just back from a flying trip to Cleveland where Thomas Munro offered him a job, but he feels he is obliged to go back for another year to Barnes.[2] However, Munro may hold it over a year for him and is expecting him later, in any case. I had dinner with him and his mother to-night at their apartment, and then he had to go out to Carl Schaefer's where Caven Atkins and Paraskeva [Clark] were going to be. I told him to be careful of Paraskeva, citing last year's Artists Forum. Marjory King wants me to read a paper on mural painting to an LSR group she is organizing. Douglas says that there's nothing being done in Paris among the younger artists. Utrillo is selling a lot of pictures all over Paris and London and they're all tripe. He thinks that there are very few artists anywhere who are doing much these days,—we didn't really get enough talk on this. Civilization rocking with bigger issues than a nationalist art is the general drift. He has just seen a lot of recent Milnes and thinks they're very poor, that Milne is over-doing his lone-genius act living in the wilderness.

The papers here had us in a fine state all last week. I went in to see Miss Farrell the milliner, and before I left she was nearly in tears, poor dear. I told her you were on your way over, and then we both got onto the young men we knew etc. It was impossible to keep off the subject and as for Hitler's speech—! Every radio in town carried that screech to a group of scared people.[3] I finally decided after half an hour that I'd spent enough time on that lunatic. Besides, his voice gets into the blood and does queer things to you. I gather that they made a few million pounds worth of mess in Hyde Park and other places. And now, as Charlie Comfort says, we've been sold down the river. Cody, the bloated jackass, got the poor innocent freshmen all assembled in Convocation Hall and gave them the usual address of welcome and told them all to go to war and fight for a lot of abstract nouns. As somebody said, Cody is a great fighter,—he'd get up and fight to the last undergraduate!

Monday evening, 10 P.M.

I am about to go to bed. To-morrrow I do an extension lecture on Canadian art to the nurses of St. Michael's Hospital. Thanks to your help I'm getting the hang of this lecture idea, and I'm going to go ahead and talk about what I like. Your Surrealism article[4] looks swell and they're sending you the Forum out of good feeling etc to Merton this year. Your mother sent a copy of the Moncton paper which had the note in, word for word! I'm going to try that publicity some more! So did the Toronto papers.

They've roped me in on the art group again of course, and I had to talk to two separate seekers after truth tonight—I mapped out the scheme for the study group and then they want also to have a practical group. Gordon [Webber] has gone to Chicago to-night to see if he gets his job or not. The bulletin went to press. Don Buchanan told me the result of our voice tests—Comfort is best, Baldwin next, Marge [Boultbee] has good volume but reads badly, I read all right but nature didn't give me much volume. I've put myself down for a talk and D.B. said to go ahead—but I think I'll get some coaching from Sterndale Bennett anyhow. Maybe I'd better keep to writing instead of thinking of radio.

I love you like everything and I hope I'll do you credit with the nurses.

Helen.

P.S. I'm at 113 Bloor West. I got your letter and cards after some delay.

H

1 It is not clear what talk HKF is referring to here; according to Letter 220 she has not yet completed her first known radio talk of the year, "Art for Everyman," broadcast 1 November 1938.
2 MacAgy had an appointment at the Barnes Foundation in Merion, Pa., where Albert C. Barnes had amassed an extraordinary collection of modern French paintings, Old Masters, and primitive art.
3 Which of Hitler's speeches HKF is referring to is uncertain. Hitler did not begin his bitter verbal attacks on the British until a speech at Saarbrücken on 9 October. HKF could be pointing simply to Hitler's response to the Munich accord, or to one of the speeches Hitler made in mid-September demanding the succession of Sudenten German territory.
4 NF's article on the development of surrealistic painting, "Men as Trees Walking," was published in *Canadian Forum*, 18 (October 1938), 451–3.

217. NF to HKF   Oxford
                                                                       Oct.7/38.

Postmarked 10 October 1938; addressed to HKF c/o Art Gallery of Toronto, Toronto, Ontario, Canada.

My dear:

I haven't had a letter from you yet to place opposite my devoted five letters and two postcards, but perhaps the boats haven't started to come in. I'm at Oxford now, settled in with Rodney [Baine] and Mike

[Joseph].[1] I found out that Mike was across the street from me at Bernard St., so I took him up to the Burnetts' for dinner. He was in Southern France during the crisis, like the Burnetts. They liked him very much, I think. He also found the French less frightened and jittery than the English. He said he saw one man who was called up during the mobilization kiss his dog, wave goodbye to his wife, and leave with his wife calling after him: "Take care of thyself! Take care thou dost not catch cold!" Edith is simply worrying herself into a decline over air-raid precautions and gas masks and the rest of it, and is more interested in the news than she's ever been before.

I spent most of your birthday,[2] I regret to say, reading Middle English, instead of going with Mike to what I gathered was a perfectly swell modern version of *Troilus and Cressida* on the general pattern of the *Julius Caesar* we saw. I had an idea there'd be a lot of exams when I got back. There were, but I deliberately skipped the first (well, I overslept) today, and when I went to see Blunden today he told me that things like collections[3] didn't exist for me. He was very friendly and complimentary all round. I really wasn't ready for anything like a test, so I was relieved in one way, though I'd rather have liked a chance at a £20 scholarship, not that it could have been awarded to me on the strength of what I could write at the moment. Blunden said I'd made a big hit with Geoffrey Keynes, which astounded me—I thought I'd made a complete fool of myself. Then he rambled on to the incredible amount of work some people managed to get done, Hitler being an example . . . the year is going to have its difficulties. Then I went to see Bryson, who ignored exams too, and is getting me to come with a New College scholar, and says he's going to push me ahead rather rapidly, starting with the *Pearl*.

The more I think of Oxford Schools the less I care about a first. The examining board is dominated by two bloody fools, [M.R.] Ridley of Balliol and Fletcher of St. Edmund Hall. Ridley has written a miserable book on Shakespeare[4] and his wife started a B. Litt. thesis on Keats which was simply a writing up of the notes to the definitive edition: Ridley pinched it and produced a perfectly useless book called "Keats' Craftsmanship"[5] as a result. No intelligent student can agree with anything he says, and as he has a childishly bad temper and jumps on anyone who disagrees with him, he's pretty bad. It was he who got Mike [Joseph] his second and Rodney [Baine] his third: Rodney had defended his hated rival in Shakespearean criticism (Stoll: that fool who provided me with the Cody story I wasted on Olive) and Ridley's comment was concerned only with his "ill-mannered" writing. Doug very nearly lost his first by disagreeing with him on the viva, but made it up later.[6] As for Fletcher, he thinks he knows something about the 17th c.: he doesn't, but I do. However, I'll work ahead and not worry.

We have a sitting room which is quite comfortable, and a bedroom apiece. My bedroom is quite useless for reading in bed, which is no doubt a good thing. The landlady, Mrs. Grylls, is silly and fussy, but if the others can endure her I suppose I can. We talk so much we haven't done any work yet, but we'll doubtless quiet down.

I think I'll spend the Xmas vac. in Paris with Mike—I want to take a good look at the Louvre, make side trips to Chartres, and live cheaply. Apparently France is cheaper than Italy.

I got back an answer from Miss Whinney, but we couldn't connect this time: we'll do it in December, I suppose. I went to a sherry party Elizabeth [Fraser] was having—she'd invited the Burnetts, but they misunderstood the time. Elizabeth is very nervous and keyed up, and I'm really very glad that she's to be in London this year. It's possible to be friendly with her only on her terms, and while I'm glad I met those terms for a year, I'd just as soon not see her too often this time. I'm very fond of her, and don't want to lose patience with her over trivialities.

When I got here I found a huge pile of sandbags outside the buttery. They were going to turn the colleges into hospitals in event of war—a supremely silly idea—you know what their sanitary facilities are, and we're near railway centres and at the big Morris factory.[7] Besides, as Haldane's book on air-raids points out, the moral effect of wiping out Oxford in the early stages of the war would no doubt be considerable.[8]

I love you.

Norrie.

What town is DePauw University in?[9]

1 NF, Baine, and Joseph roomed at Mrs. Grylls's boarding house at 18 Polstead Rd., just north of St. Hugh's College. They shared a combination living room and study and had separate bedrooms, something Oxford authorities insisted on for all students. Rodney Baine to RDD, 12 December 1995.
2 6 October.
3 A term examination.
4 M.R. Ridley, *William Shakespeare: A Commentary* (London: Dent, 1936).
5 *Keats' Craftsmanship: A Study in Poetic Development* (Oxford: Clarendon Press, 1933). Ridley explores Keats's verbal "carpentry" as revealed in his manuscript revisions.

6 HKF's note to this letter indicates she thinks the reference is to Doug LePan and that
   NF, whom she has asked about it, "says it's quite possible." According to Douglas
   LePan the reference was quite likely to him, but he did not remember the episode
   occurring in quite the way NF has reported it.
7 The Morris automobile assembly plant was in Cowley, about two miles southeast of
   Oxford.
8 J.B.S. Haldane, *How To Be Safe from Air Raids* (London: Gollancz, 1938).
9 The answer, which HKF did not provide, is Greencastle, Indiana. Perhaps NF wanted
   to write to Peggy Roseborough: six months later HKF sends along Roseborough's
   address in Greencastle (Letter 259).

218. HKF to NF   113, Bloor St. W.
                                                                    Oct. 12. 1938.

My dearest: The most amazing thing has happened—on Tuesday a
letter came from you, written from the boat, and on Wednesday, to-day,
the next one came, written from London. I am so glad that that week is
over, at any rate, although the spectacle of England now, pulling up her
socks, isn't going to be very pleasant. I take it that Oxford opened and
that you and Mike [Joseph] are in your flat by now. I went in to see Jerry
and Kay [Riddell] one evening in desperation and realized that after all
you need not have gone that week, that you could have waited. But I
had to get into this place I suppose. I was thinking to-night that in
another twelve days a month will be gone already, and after that there
will only be nine more. To-night I think this was a crazy idea, my voca-
tion isn't students etc etc. Well I'm tired out, so I had my hair waved
and had dinner by myself in with the dismal Rogart family, and read the
Toronto Daily Star. Forest fires are now making the headlines, with
pregnant women burning to death.[1]
    To explain the hair-waving: to-morrow night I go to a reception at
Browns' to meet the new faculty members. I didn't know whether I was
invited as a widow, or what, but as Ella Martin has also been asked I
guess it's the don. I 'phoned Henry Noyes but have not seen him yet. He
was to be busy all this week, and of course to-night the *male* members of
staff are having a dinner to look over the additions. Last week one night
I went to see Magda [Arnold] who had the curse very badly—we finally
called a doctor to get it eased off a little, in spite of her protests that Bert
[Arnold] doesn't believe in pampering oneself. I said this wasn't his line.
(He wasn't home, as usual, and when I left at 11.30 he still had not
arrived.) Well, Magda of course told me about Plotinus and in that big

dark cheerless room she was all alone stretched out on the sofa when I arrived, with Plotinus open on her desk. She had to tell me what Line thought of it and then she told me of her great admiration for MacCallum—"I *do admire* that man!"—you can hear her chant it. This time there is something unfortunate happening in their family. Mrs. MacCallum, who had pleurisy in the summer, developed T.B. and is in Weston Sanatorium having treatment. She may be better in a month, so that is at least encouraging. Magda said "Would you believe it, that man MacCallum goes out to see her *every* night from seven to nine—the visiting hours. He gives up everything for her, when people ask him out in the evening he says he'll come, yes,—at nine-thirty. That's an awful lot for a man to give up,—there aren't many men who would do a thing like that!" Poor Magda. I didn't like to disagree with her—if her marriage has turned out a lemon it is a shame, but we've been over that so often. Long wails about the kids who have been in bed since coming back from the north. Colds. I had to keep firmly practical and cheerful. Mlle Rièse asked me if the Arnolds were getting a divorce, some friends were asking. So I told her no, I didn't think so at all.

MacDonald disappointed us badly about the trip north for Thanksgiving weekend. We had counted on it so much but nothing came of his promise as he had to take the rugby team to Kingston. I went to a show with Rièse who is a very agreeable cove and much more fun than Herta [Hartmanshenn] who is very lumpish at times. Grace Workman is the new don, a nice girl, but I don't find her very interesting. In fact, to tell you the honest truth, I'm not awfully keen about this widow's life and I've never been in such a boiler factory as the Annesley dining room at dinner. I'm sorry, there I am complaining again.

Roy [Kemp] is going to the opening of the *Paintings of Women* show with me on Friday.[2] I asked Henry Noyes but he has a *two-hour* extension class to give each Friday! He will be making a fair amount at that rate. Sounds quite pathetic about his wife.[3] I guess there's just one thing that would make our situation worse and that is if you were in a sanatorium on the Isle of Wight, with T.B. Poor Henry is trying to get her into the country and put her into a hospital here.

I have been reading Eve Curie's *Madame Curie*,[4] which is charming in spots and the early part especially. Later on she re-iterates the wonder of their married happiness and the unique genius of her mother to an extent a little hard to bear. Magda's reaction to the book was one of rejoicing that here indeed was one woman who had amounted to something—women are so much more stupid than men etc etc. Women here in Canada are stupid, or something. Oh well, she did have the curse.

I'm going upstairs to my single bed now and I guess I'll go to sleep. I love you so much. I'll tell you all about the reception and that will make your news despatch a little less grumpy.

I kiss you good-night.

Helen.

1 The headline in the *Toronto Daily Star* for 12 October 1938 reports "Another Family of Four Dead in Flames, 1,000–Mile Area Ablaze in Northland: Expectant Mother's Body Found Beside Husband, Son, Sister." The fires were in the Dance township of northwestern Ontario, near the Minnesota border.
2 "Paintings of Women from the Fifteenth to the Twentieth Century," at the AGT 14 October–14 November 1938.
3 Henry Noyes's wife, Gertrude, had contracted tuberculosis; at the time, Canadian regulations required a five-year waiting period for people with tuberculosis to enter the country. Knowing of this regulation, she had no plans to leave England in 1939. But after Britain entered the war, the Canadian regulations were altered, and in September she was given permission by the Canadian embassy to travel to Canada with her husband (Henry Noyes to RDD, 20 December 1993).
4 Trans. Vincent Sheean (Garden City, N.Y.: Doubleday, Doran, 1937).

---

219. NF to HKF   Oxford

Postmarked 21 October 1938; addressed to HKF c/o Art Gallery of Toronto, Toronto, Ontario, Canada.

My dearest girl:

I suppose I have settled down by this time, but I still feel I haven't. At first I thought I simply couldn't live in this place. Mrs. Grylls is fundamentally all right, but she hasn't a brain in her head, and her stupidity is of the flustered, hen-crossing-a-road variety. However, after one terrific row which was based on the fact that a lawyer had told her she should be getting more than she agreed on for Rodney's [Rodney Baine's] room, she's settled down and is quite amiable. I don't spend much time here, except on Sundays. I've finally got used to coming down about nine on the 'bus and staying down for the day, which means that I do a good deal of work, as about the only place to stay is in the libraries. On this arrangement I seem to be spending more money on lunches than two years ago when I sat in my room more, but you can't work if you're weak inside. But the difficulty of manoeuvering from a home some distance away to one's work is a difficulty I'd better get used to if we get a house in the near future.

I've had one tutorial with Blunden and everything seems O.K. I did so little writing last year that now my sentences creak and groan when I try fitting them together. It takes incessant practice. My handwriting is if possible even worse than usual. But if I write & write & write all this year maybe I'll be able to write schools with fair glibness. Blunden—or did I tell you?—was quite firm on my shelving the Blake and getting to work on schools. I still don't like the idea, but I'm docile. My first paper, on Crashaw & Herbert, was badly written, I thought, but Blunden said he saw no falling off in skill, and that if anything my exegesis had improved. This week I'm slaving away at an epic on Vaughan, Traherne, Herrick, Marvell & Cowley, all people I have ideas about. I got a terrible shock when I saw my Forum article,[1] as it's nowhere near my standard of writing, and am getting down to business.

You mention Herta [Hartmanshenn], so I suppose she's back. I hope so.

I had tea with Alan Jarvis a few days ago and he looks flourishing: very nice rooms in University College. He had several copies of the Varsity there, and they looked as funny as hell: Cody being interviewed about Communism in the University, for instance: "There used to be a few Jews with that idea."[2] And then there was a Huidekoperkempnnott advertisement[3] and an interview with Roy about Fort Henry[4] and an interview with a certain Mrs. Helen Frye about who's going to carry on after Lismer? "We are," said Mrs. Helen.[5] I suspect that the we is pretty editorial. Anyway, I began to feel homesick, or rather, my homesickness got worse for a bit. Alan [Jarvis] had been driving all over Europe with Douglas Duncan. He saw the approved German art show, and showed me an illustrated catalogue.[6] Mostly portraits of Nazi gangsters, sentimental evening-on-the-farm pictures intended to illustrate the romance & dignity of the peasantry, and ripe, juicy, luscious nudes—the coming mothers of the race, you see. One of the lousiest of them was bought by Hitler and became the most popular piece in the show.

I started attending lectures the first week—you know what I am. All pretty awful. Nichol Smith wouldn't be bad for my sort of job: getting one point per lecture hammered home, but to me he's prolix & dull. Then there's Tolkien on Beowulf, dealing with a most insanely complicated problem which involves Anglo-Saxon genealogies, early Danish histories, monkish chronicles in Latin, Icelandic Eddas and Swedish folk-lore. Imagine my delivery at its very worst: top speed, unintelligible burble, great complexity of ideas and endless references to things unknown, mixed in with a lot of Latin and Anglo-Saxon and a lot of difficult proper names which aren't spelled, and you have Tolkien on Beowulf.

II

Alan got in touch with me again and we went to Sir Michael Sadler's place to look at his art collection. Sir Michael was former Master of Univ.[7] and Alan had an introduction to him from Bickersteth. He has one of the best collections of modern art there are. A lot of sculpture: things from Sierra Leone and Papua besides Despiau and Maillol and Skeaping and Henry Moore (three lovely things in his garden) and Barbara Hepworth and two lovely Zadkines. Of paintings, there's a lot of Segonzac (whom I don't cotton too much), a bad Signac, a very unusual Matisse, 3 Picassos (one rather messy and one a cubist portrait of a young man, very fine), one Klee (curious: a lot of incisions on a heavy blue and brown background) two SUPERB Cézanne water-colours, the best Bouvard I've ever seen, three grand Rouaults, about a dozen David Jones (the man Fairley's interested in), and a lot of English people: a vulgar Vanessa Bell, two good Nicholsons, a fairish Wadsworth (Alan liked it better than I), the best Sickert I've ever seen, a mediocre Christopher Wood and a lot of other things I can't think of just now. There were a lot of Henry Moore things: drawings of a single theme, like Mother & Child, pasted on a larger canvas. Somebody called William Roberts I didn't know but was impressed by, some Frances Hodgkins, quite like David Jones but heavier, two Duncan Grants, one good & one bad, some good Paul Nashes. Then there were several Kandinskys of the explosive firework period, a dull Léger, a good Monet, an early Utrillo, a glorious Marc drawing, and, of earlier things, some Guercino etchings, fine vigorous Baroque stuff, a 14th c. Spanish woodcarving of a Madonna, a Monticelli (average: Alan didn't like it) a Courbet (curious: brilliant green trees & blue sky), a big collection of Cotman drawings and a room full of Constable, mostly early. And two Dufys which were great fun, two big Noguchi drawings on the staircase, some Dorn carpets. And a sur-realist object by Calder: balls hanging from wires in a complicated way so that if you touched it it formed a lot of different patterns. Alan said the last time he was there Sir M. stood in front of it and said: "It reminds me of Dons arguing. They also feel that they have volition." We saw about half the stuff, I guess. Sir M. burbles a bit & his wife is trying, but I had a grand time.

There's a bye-election coming off in Oxford City soon. The Tory is someone called Hogg, and opposed to him is an Independent with Liberal and Labour support, A.D. Lindsay, one of the greatest philosophical scholars alive, author of countless books, Master of Balliol and just-resigned Vice-Chancellor of the University.[8] It's risky for an Oxford man to run in Town. If he gets in Mike [Joseph] has promised me all the beer I can drink, and as I'd promised him all the beer he could drink if N.Z. went Socialist again, and it did, I guess we're in for a souse. (Vice-Chancellor means boss: the Chancellor is the Duke of Devonshire, just a stuffed shirt). This has caused a terrific flutter in reactionary dovecotes. The Warden of Merton & his wife explain earnestly to all undergraduates that Lindsay is really an awful man: "You should see him eat!" "Fancy anyone voting Labour!" says Lady Miles, grinning around the table.

I went down to London Saturday & saw the Canadian show. I'll send the article along as soon as I get some of the intelligent weekly comment on it, if any, and you can see what I've said then.[9] They'd put all the shits in one room—Grier, [Kenneth] Forbes, [George A.] Reid & the rest of it—which I found amusing. Skimpy French carving, good Jobins however, skimpier B.C. totem stuff (better in the B.M.), good [Cornelius] Krieghoff, one amusing Walker, a remarkable 18th c. primitivist "Negro Slave" portrait by some Frenchman, two Kanes. Then the shit room—only one good picture in it, Dorothy Stevens' negress. Then a sculpture gallery—Betty Hahn had something in tin which was amusing and there was good stuff by a Montrealer named Trenka. Loring & Wyle as usual, Jacobine Jones had a good bull, Mannie Hahn a rather impressive horse's head. Then a room with average Group of 7 stuff, & a room with two average [David] Milnes, and so on and so on—everybody I could think of was there except Brooker & Muhlstock, & Brooker was in the calendar. And a spotty water-colour room. Will Ogilvie, Prudence Heward, Milne (water-colours especially), Thomson and Varley and Pegi Nicol are our best bets, I think. Fairley wasn't there either. I stayed with the Burnetts as usual & they had Elizabeth [Fraser] to dinner.

You remember young Corder, whom I used to do violin with? Well, apparently there's now a 'cello in the college, and they had a trio with a somewhat inadequate pianist last year. So I've seen Allen (we're all out of residence & have to have a residence piano) and he says it's all right to use his. The pianist in question is also a boy I know quite well, a Lancastrian named [Bunny] Mellor, who had me to tea the other day and whom I asked up later—he was writing a paper on Blake. He said he was tired of getting papers back from Blunden with the note "see H.N. Frye about this" scribbled on them—it's happened twice already.

My favorite water-dropping haunt, near the Market, has bullseyes painted on the standing urinals. I love you to the verge of monomania.

Norrie.

1 "Men as Trees Walking," *Canadian Forum*, 18 (October 1938), 208–10.
2 See "Cody Denies Charge Communism Rampant in University," *Varsity*, 5 October 1938, 1, 4. H.J. Cody, president of the U of T, is quoted as saying, "There used to be a few odd Jews inclined that way. But they saw that Russian communism was as totalitarian and repressive as the totalitarianism in Central Europe. I think even in the city there are comparatively few Jews who have communist tendencies. They know they receive pretty fair treatment in British countries."
3 NF is referring to the advertisement, which ran for several weeks in the *Varsity*, announcing the opening of a photographic studio at 24 Harbord St. by Roy Kemp, Christina Huidekoper, a 1935 graduate of the University of Southern California, and Herbert I. Nott, like Roy, a 1938 graduate of the U of T. The studio, which opened 6 October 1938, specialized in portraits and group photography. Perhaps NF runs the three names together to affect a German compound.
4 See "Kemp Photographs Old Fort Henry," *Varsity*, 3 October 1938, 1, 4. Roy Kemp had photographed the restored fort at Kingston during the summer.
5 HKF was interviewed for an article in the *Varsity* (30 September 1938, 4) about the resignation of Arthur Lismer, who had become professor of fine art at Teacher's College, Columbia University. The *Varsity* reports HKF as saying, "No one will replace Mr. Lismer, but children's Saturday morning classes at the Art Centre will continue as usual. The educational staff has been reorganized to enable us to carry on without him."
6 This show—the *Grosse Deutsche Kunst Ausstellung*—was held annually from 1937 to 1944. Hitler made five trips to the 1938 show and bought 202 works of art. See Jonathan G. Petropoulos, "Art as Politics: The Nazi Elite's Quest for the Political and Material Control of Art" (Ph.D. diss., Harvard University, 1990, 277).
7 Sadler was master of University College, Oxford, 1923–34.
8 Lindsay was running for parliament on an anti-Munich platform against Quintin Hogg, a passionate Conservative supporter of Chamberlain's policy of appeasement. Lindsay argued that Europe was being betrayed into the hands of Hitler. Although NF reports in Letter 222 that Lindsay lost by 3,000 votes, the majority was not overwhelming. Not long after his victory, Hogg recognized the Nazi threat, and when the war began he joined the army.
9 NF's review of the Canadian exhibition at the Tate Gallery, which opened on 14 October, includes a critique of reviews of the exhibit (see Letter 222, below): "Canadian Art in London," *Canadian Forum*, 18 (January 1939), 304–5. For a complete list of the works exhibited in the show, see *A Century of Canadian Art: Catalogue* (London: The Tate Gallery, 1938).

220. HKF to NF   113, Bloor St. West. Toronto.
                                                        Saturday, October 22. '38.

My dear:

I have never written to you before on a typewriter, and I have no idea how it may turn out. I have been sticking somewhat closely to one lately as I suddenly decided to give Henri Masson a note in The Forum[1] and I have been writing letters for future articles,—I asked Blunt to do the one on the London show and I am hoping to get Eric Brown to come to life again in the Magazine (that cap was a mistake).

I am sorry that my letters were late in reaching you, I did try to send you news as often as I could, and you will just have to blame it all on the Paintings of Bitches Show. We are getting along fairly well at the A.G. of T. There is certainly enough to do, but I think we will manage nicely. I have Allan Armstrong, the graduate in architecture to help me with loan exhibitions and to label lantern slides,—he looks like a tremendous help, even after one week's trial. I am in the midst of two articles,—the one for The Star on murals, advertising the Prog contest,[2] and my radio talk for Nov. 1. I am trying to get that last one done this weekend because I have to go over it with Sterndale Bennett on Tuesday, and just now my head is so clogged up that I can't think of even a good way to begin. I called it, "Everyman Looks at Art."[3] I am learning how to breathe with my diaphragm and how to talk as if I were in Massey Hall,—he says there's hope even if I am only 5'1" with a small chest expansion, that doesn't matter. Anyway he does help my self-confidence. And the voice.

I blew myself to two season tickets to the Music Masters Series at Eaton's Auditorium, the first concert being by Lhevinne.[4] Two groups of Chopin, one of Debussy, and the last was all Liszt. Can you beat it? I phoned Henry Noyes and asked him to go with me. We went out to dinner at the Babloor[5] first and wound up there again afterwards which did a lot toward consoling me of the lack of a better programme. Henry had just had a card from you, in which you mentioned Donald Ewing, who is not in his classes but we did meet him at the concert. He tells me that the music group starts this Monday. Mine started last week, with some twenty kids down at the Gallery to see the show. There are about thirty-five people signed up for the music group. Donald is still firmly on the look-out for monologues. Mary Winspear was down the other day with

65 girls from her school,[6]—she is doing her extension lectures on Monday and Tuesday evenings, and I think I will go out beering with her afterwards. So far, I find Mlle. Rièse the most fun to do things with, that is amongst the dons, excepting Kay [Coburn], of course.

Last Tuesday at noon, the Faculty Women's Association luncheon was held at Wymilwood, and I went just to keep on keeping the home-fires burning. I sat beside Kay Riddell who told me about their difficulties with Gordon Webber who announced to the class that they would not do any drawing or painting this year at all, but that they were going to make constructions in three dimensions out of all sorts of materials. None of the women want to do it, but none of them would tell him so, but just went off in corners, grumbling to themselves. I told Kay to talk to him about it because just because he was hipped on Moholy-Nagy's ideas[7] is no reason why they must all make wind machines etc. for the rest of the year. On my other side was Madame Lasserre and we talked about Tecton[8] and the buildings they are doing. Also about Eurythmics. Magda [Arnold] and I got out after they had introduced the two new wives,—Mrs [T.C.] Young and the new man in English.[9] A lot of pretty speeches were made, of course, trust Mrs. [Walter T.] Brown for that. Magda and I left them to the rest of their meeting. She said she had much more important things to do that afternoon. She had been sitting beside Mrs. Grant Robertson. Someone asked her how she liked her job, and before she had a chance to answer at all some old woman across the table said "Oh yes she liked her job all right, a lot better than her children do!" Magda looked around in amazement at anyone saying such a thing, and it was not until Mrs. Brown made a speech about the recent degree given to our dear Dr. Robertson, with several pretty sallies in the direction of Mrs. Robertson that Magda realised that the old girl was Mrs Grant's embittered mother-in-law.[10] Magda is getting into a lather again, she says Bert [Arnold] is always accusing her of neglecting the children, and that is what she hears every night when she goes home. Bert and Magda are pretty exasperating to their friends. Mrs [H.R.] MacCallum is at home again now, I was told.[11]

Sunday night. 6:30.

The people in this house have just had another Sunday tea with men—last week it was the freshies, and this time the juniors had their beaux in. I have just left them to entertain them by themselves: they don't seem to be doing a great deal, but I'm sure they're happy. The head of the house is a fool—Jean Wells. I forget now whether I told you before that I was talking to her one day in the sitting room when the maid knocked on the door. I wasn't sure which was wanted and bounced out to find King Joblin waiting there. He made some loud and facetious remarks about my being the don, that he is don of Middle House, and I expected him to slap me on the back at any moment. Anyway, he was taking Jean out somewhere. She is quite soft in the head, and the sort of girl who can't say anything without grinning up at you coyly, baring her front teeth, sucking in her breath and rolling her eyes in a fluttering sort of way. She is anxious to be liked, so can't possibly be firm on any point—just one big lump of dough. Blonde, with fluffy hair, overweight, and all those mannerisms backing up her stomach. She came into my room after she had been made head and told me she didn't want to *enforce* anything,—big time ahead. The rest of the house is swell.

I really don't like writing to you on a typewriter. It doesn't seem like talking to you, not right to you, it is more like giving you an official report on my official life. Norrie, I'm doing a lot of new things this year and getting away with it. I'm developing a voice, for instance. I was practising reading at home this afternoon—booming at Mother from the kitchen to the front room. She is quite interested, and helps me. I have some exercises—aforementioned—which are helping, and I can do them almost anywhere. I think I'll go after a course on University Extension sometime. Graham McInnes of course went in for it this year but I'm not sure that he is back. The show at the Tate lasts into the middle of December. One month ago to-day you left, and I am so glad there are only nine more at most,—besides I may get there before that. Do you need money? I can send you some if you do—I have saved $30 this month and should be paid this week. Do you want me to send you your stories submitted to the Atlantic Monthly? They were left behind. Do try to start the Blake on its rounds. And although I do understand about the damned Oxford first and those stupid examiners, yet I still think a first a matter of good politics, surely you can put up with the morons for nine months. It isn't a matter of working hard so much as pulling the right brand of wool,—oh well, use your own good judgment. I played the piano most of the morning,—it sounds better in this room. I am going to hear the Hart House Quartet to-night with Roy [Kemp]. My best to Mike

[Joseph] and Rodney [Baine]. I found your Varsity pin in the desk drawer: I am wearing it to show I'm engaged.

Love

Helen.

1   "Henri Masson," *Canadian Forum*, 18 (November 1938), 241.
2   HKF's article on murals appears not to have been published.
3   "Art for Everyman" was given on 1 November 1938. A copy of the talk is in the HFF, 1992, box 4, file 9, and also in the Edward P. Taylor Research Library of the AGO, A.3.6.8., File: Radio Talks, 1938–39.
4   Josef Lhevinne's concert, which featured Chopin's Sonata in B Minor and Impromptu in F-sharp, was performed at Eaton Auditorium on 26 October.
5   A hotel and dining lounge located on the east side of Bay St., just below Bloor.
6   Mary Winspear was a teacher at St. Clement's School, a private school for girls.
7   László Moholy-Nagy was a Hungarian-born Constructivist artist, sculptor, and photographer (1895–1946) whose avant-garde techniques were based upon what he called "vision in motion."
8   An architectural firm, founded by Berthold Lubetkin, that received recognition for its imaginative use of reinforced concrete.
9   Kenneth Maclean, who had been teaching at Yale, joined the VC faculty in 1938 as Pelham Edgar's replacement.
10 Grant Robertson was a member of the classics department at VC; his father, J.C. Robertson, was an emeritus member of the same department, and the "embittered mother-in-law" was his wife. The "dear Dr. Robertson" HKF refers to was the distinguished medical doctor, Elizabeth (Bessie) Chant Robertson, or "Mrs. Grant," who received her Ph.D. in 1937.
11 Here the typing ends; HKF wrote the rest of the letter in ink.

221. HKF to NF   113 Bloor St. [*Toronto*]
                                                            [*27 October 1938*]

My dear: It is eleven o'clock and I've been plunking away all evening on my radio talk for next Tuesday,[1] but I've just seen in the paper that the Bremen is leaving soon, with this for you, I hope. I get so disgusted: I wrote some of the WORST DRIVEL for that talk and scrapped it, and I now have a fairly straightforward piece of writing but it may have too many ideas in it: I don't know. I read some of the DRIVEL to Mr Bennett and it sounded pretty lousy to me—I was trying to be chatty about what people think of art and I packed in all the worst clichés I could think of. Now that I have got that off my chest I hope that I'll *never* start anything that way again. I've been working darned hard,—for me. I've got this article still to finish for the Star, and the radio talk, and my Thursday lecture on the Devil was today,[2] also a talk to the Vic kids in the college with a lantern. About 25 or 30 turned out, and I think it went off very well—I gave them the "What's Beautiful" talk again.

I gather that there were about 35–40 people out for the music group and Marcus [Adeney] talked but there wasn't much discussion. Elizabeth Proctor who is in Oaklawn (sister of Dave Proctor now in Emmanuel) said that Marcus spoke so low that she went to sleep in a corner. I asked Eleanor Dillon about it and she seemed fairly pleased about it, but said he'd been pretty vague. Invited me to a supper meeting but I said I wouldn't go as they have such large numbers already for Wymilwood. She tended to quote Mr. Frye on the subject of mass hypnotists when I said I'd heard Lhevinne.

Pelham Edgar was in the Gallery to-day talking to Baldwin about the speech he's going to make to open the R.C.A. show next month. I had a chat with him: he said he was glad I was down there, and I was taking Lismer's place wasn't I? I told him I was, at any rate for the time being. He asked what was the news from you and patted my shoulder when he left. You'd better send him a card—*definitely* one at Christmas. Baldwin thinks my idea for the Chinese show is swell—go ahead. I've got to start on that right away. I've decided to do some talking to a large group too—150 women teachers one evening. No use getting my voice all trained if I don't practice.

Kay Coburn has someone typing her Coleridge ms. in my room during the day on the typewriter I rented. Kay still talks of moving out of residence, so does Rièse, a sort of Utopian dream of theirs. Rièse and Herta [Hartmanshenn] are both sore at Grace Workman who is SCIENTIFIC and rapidly learning all Norma Ford's worst mannerisms. She is so damned much of an earnest seeker, too, and belongs to the SCM among other blights. To-night she had an IMPORTANT date and got Rièse to take her duty for her—she was just busting to tell us that she was doing it for a worthy cause. Without being asked she went on to say she was addressing a Presbyterian CGIT group on sex education—with a long-drawn-out ed—u—ca'—tion,[3] if you get the idea—sing it. With diagrams of the organs on a black-board. She told Herta this: Herta looked at me and I dared not meet her eye so I solemnly nodded at Grace's ear. But she wouldn't have got any idea. Rièse consigns all scientists to the devil. And I just think of Phyllis Oughton at camp that summer. Still, maybe my radio talk for the general public will be just as funny to a scientist.

I haven't any news except dinner last night with Agnes Beatty at the

Babloor—radio talk etc all evening then a short walk with Herta. Guess I'll go to bed. I sometimes dimly imagine that I used to go to bed with you, but maybe I'm dreaming. I don't let myself think of that very often, or else I might get unhinged. It would never do for a don to get the weeps, and my jaw is getting stern. I love you *so* much.

Good-night my dear

Helen.

1 See Letter 220, n. 3, above.
2 "The Devil: Ugly Pictures in the Middle Ages." For an outline of the lecture, see HFF, 1993, box 4, file 6.
3 HKF has written the word slanting upward to "ca," then downward to "tion."

222. NF to HKF   Oxford
                                                    Oct. 28/38.

Postmarked 28 October 1938; addressed to HKF at 113, Bloor St. West, Toronto, Ontario, Canada. Enclosed with this letter is a holograph manuscript of NF's "Canadian Art in London." See Letter 219, above. The picture of the purple dress referred to in the second paragraph appears not to have survived, but recalls the drawing of an amethyst satin dress, borrowed from Norah McCullough, in Letter 155.

My sweet pet: I've been working quite hard this week because I got two letters from you Monday morning. I got up feeling restless and not wanting to work, and I knew there'd be a letter for me. So I went on revising the Dark Ages. I like the Dark Ages: even the simplest books on it sound fearfully erudite.

That dress looks pretty overwhelming, but you know my weakness for purple, and I'd be sure to like it. I keep it on the mantelpiece to remind me that even the English winter can't last forever. I've been here a month now, and there can hardly be more than eight more before I'll be seriously thinking of going back. Oh, my dear! The curious part of it is that I'm lonesome for Toronto as well as you—I hardly expected that, but there it is.

I'm completely disgusted with the way the English mags wrote up the Canadian show.[1] There was some damned good stuff in it as well as a lot of tripe. But nobody seemed energetic enough to get beyond the tripe room. *The New Statesman* was the worst as usual—they made me so furious I wrote them a letter, which they won't publish. They gave it (the two "historical" rooms was of course all they looked at) five sentences and said something about "Morris"—obviously Morrice.[2] I picked that one up and suggested that the critic was wrongly directed by the attendant to the pre-Raphaelite room.

I've seen one cinema which wasn't bad: *Le Puritain*—all about a Roman Catholic, however, and you know how I dislike calling prudes Puritans. It's a Liam O'Flaherty picture.[3] He didn't like the way Hollywood did *The Informer*,[4] so he went off to France to get this one done to his liking. A fanatical young prude, member of a vice society, murders a girl in his boarding-house because he thinks she's been immoral and deserves to be punished. Then he tries to punish her lover by foisting the crime on him. Then he feels he's done wrong and should make amends by giving another prostitute a good time. As he gets drunk, he debates the question, whether God rules everything or has man (i.e. himself) a divine destiny. He's caught in the end. Good & brilliantly acted, but duller than *The Informer*.

Mike [Joseph] had some New Zealand friends in for the week-end. They're all good-natured Catholics and their conversation is an incredible saga of drunkenness, venereal disease and "affairs." They tell, for instance, of a friend who dashes in asking if he can have a bath. He's hungry, too, but he's in a big hurry, so his host and the girl he's living with go into the bathroom while he makes the water very soapy, for reasons of decency, and feed him spaghetti, squatting the meanwhile together on the only available seating accommodation. And they have very disreputable relatives, which abashed me, as I haven't any except an uncle who burned his house and tried to burn his wife (dad's sister) for the very sordid rewards of insurance. But Devon had an aunt who ran a bawdy-house, an uncle who was hanged and a grandfather whose handlebar whiskers kept getting in the soup. The last was the only one who really repelled him. The hanged man was subsequently proved innocent, and when I expressed horror and sympathy Devon said: "Oh, well, he deserved to be hanged anyway." New Zealand Irish proletariat, Joyce's material transplanted. Then an Englishman joined the party: his name's Sitwell & he's connected with the Sitwells, but hates them like hell, and he spent most of his time telling us about his last dose of syphilis and brooding over the fact that I was married. He was pretty drunk, and as I had had a lot of beer and a gin and a sherry and some whiskies and still felt fairly sober I thought I was doing well. As he went he said:

"I'm disappointed to hear that you're married, but you're not a bad chap." It's curious that Mike himself is never drunk and never looks at or thinks of a woman. I may say that you did not personally appear in the discussion: it was merely mentioned by Devon that there was a married man and a priest present.

The priest was a New Zealander named Father Blake, who got through the Moderns school last year and now lives at Campion Hall, a Catholic institution here. He showed us through it. They've got all kinds of money and have some early Catalan paintings, a lovely Donatello wood-relief, a big Murillo, medieval vestments, [Frank] Brangwyn murals in the chapel (not very impressive), the famous Eric Gill St. Martin of Tours relief, and in the lecture-room a Henry Moore drawing (collage, I think), a rather Braque-ish Ben Nicholson, and some David Jones. David Jones lives there as a guest, just recovering from a nervous breakdown. I met him. Very Welsh, fattish with hair over his forehead, shy and sheepish, obviously a devout Catholic, with copies of the Criterion[5] around and a huge picture of Chamberlain clipped out of the *Illustrated London News* pinned on the wall. He showed us a copy of the Ancient Mariner with his drawings.[6] His very fantastic, crowded outlines are effective for that poem in a curiously wrong way. I think he's a remarkable artist, but I'm not completely sold on him. I'll write to Barker Fairley and tell him I've met him.

Recital of old music at Brasenose one evening, with some versatile blighter playing the virginals (Byrd, Bull & Handel), the recorder (Handel), the "viola d'amore" (six strings above the bridge and six below), and singing in a choir which did Gibbons, Campion and Byrd. Swell fun. And the trio is really functioning. We did two hours in Allen's rooms and did six Haydns, including the three you did. The more enjoyable the things I do here, the more homesick I get. The cellist is a good lad—has an uncanny ability to count measures.

I think I mentioned Charlie Bell, Mississippi, Rhodes Scholar at Exeter. He's doing a B. Litt.: printing Chaucer's *Knight's Tale* with a translation of the Boccaccio poem Chaucer got it from. As he doesn't know any Italian he's got a job ahead of him. Or at any rate not much Italian. Well, he's not quite living with a very pretty little widow he's engaged to—her former husband's death was a good idea, I gather—and he has a piano and a collection of records and she's in the Bach choir. She also bought herself a recorder, on my advice. So I think the Bell ménage is likely to be something of a retreat for me this year.

Odi et amo,[7] as Catullus would say. I love you and I hate not being able to. Bless you, darling.

Norrie.

Lindsay lost, of course, by 3,000, cutting the Tory majority in half.[8]

1 The Canadian art exhibition was reviewed in the *Times* (15 and 26 October), the *Sunday Times* (16 October), the *Daily Telegraph* (15 October), and the *Manchester Guardian* (15 October). In the review in the *New Statesman and Nation* mentioned by NF, the writer remarked that "quite certainly there are pictures here too worthless to represent a Dominion or to hang in a public gallery" (22 October, 610).
2 The reviewer in the *New Statesman and Nation* had said, "Much the best works are by a sensitive and accomplished artist called Morris" (22 October, 610).
3 A 1938 Les Films Derby movie, starring Jean Louis Barrault, with story and dialogues by O'Flaherty.
4 A 1935 film based on an O'Flaherty story; it won three Academy Awards, including best screenplay.
5 A literary journal founded in 1922 by T.S. Eliot; *The Waste Land* appeared in the first issue.
6 Jones had illustrated a limited edition of Coleridge's poem; 460 copies were printed by Walter L. Colls at the Fanfare Press in London in 1929.
7 "I hate and I love"; Catullus, *Carmina*, lxxxv.
8 See Letter 219, above.

223. HKF to NF   [*Toronto*]
                                                    Friday, Nov. 4. 1938.

My dear: I have meant to write to you all week, but this has been one of those weeks—thank goodness it is about over. The bulletin is about due and I am debating about speakers for the R.C.A. show,—I'm putting in the "What Does the Artist See?"[1] series for my talks, which, by the way, need a good deal of pushing again. We haven't done anything about it and I've only had ten people out to each of them so far. We expect Lismer up to do a talk toward the end of the month and I've sent him a telegram as to *when*, but so far, no answer. My radio talk was all right,[2] Baldwin liked it,—my voice was a little high was his one criticism, but clear and with more variation. So I'll have to bring it down some. W.G. Constable was here this week and gave a typical Constable lecture on 18th Century British Portraiture—suave and aristocratic and all the rest. It took me back to that year at the Institute with such a smack that I walked home through the park and blew up on the Rièse doorstep. We went off and had some beer and reviled everyone we could think of, quite cheerfully. We think we'll take a trip, maybe to Hamilton, maybe to Cleveland or somewhere. What made me mad was the way Baldwin ignored all of us when W.G. was here, and took him to Band's for a party afterwards, but didn't ask me, or any of us,—he had the Alfords, the Lyles, and a few other of the really worthwhile people in town, all dressed up for the occasion, and they entertained the great man. He spoke to the university students and the Empire Club and saw the local millionaires. I went down twice to hunt him up and do a private bit of gushing but he had just departed both times. To my great relief, I must say. It still takes an awful lot out of me to salute a BIG GUN, even though I'm getting used to Alford—the porpoise.

I'm getting disgruntled about things lately. There isn't any life in this organization, at least I don't think so. And I get fed up with the residence too, it isn't nearly as tolerable as it was two years ago. I guess I'm getting aged. Sometimes I think I'll clear out, but I know I won't. Twenty more days until the twenty-fourth of November and that will be two months gone. Here's a compliment for you—Alice Eedy told Elizabeth [Eedy] that you were the best lecturer she ever had. Elizabeth says she's always coming home and complaining about this guy Maclean. You mustn't mind when I grouse about staying here, it helps me to put it on paper, and you're the only one I know who will take it for what it's worth. Besides, the other night I got so mad because someone asked me AGAIN how it feels to be a grass widow and I said I'm having a grand time etc, and then wished to hell I'd let her have the works and told her. It was Louise Comfort, and Brieger was there in one of his Germanly masculine moods—he said how nice for you—to be in Oxford. So it must be swell.

Herta [Hartmanshenn] and Maysie [Roger] and Christine Graham and Frances Russell and Mildred Redmond and I all went to Chinatown last night and to Wilson Knight's performance of *The Tempest* afterwards.[3] The meal was grand; the play was lousy,—the performance I mean, naturally. Some dame named Miss Koenig, a teacher of dramatic art in this city (phone number in brackets) had directed the show and given Ariel to herself to do. She had a heavy posterior and legs shorter than they should have been in proportion, and she hopped around gracefully landing flat on her feet like a leaping toad. Dressed in a short tunic affair and gauzy wings which would have been swell if she'd kept her legs covered. The cast was very dull. Prospero was slow and heavy and there wasn't much to be said for any of the others except Wilson

Knight who did a very good job, I thought, on Caliban. Caliban dressed in a fur jerkin and had green make-up, with greyish green on his arms and legs—red knees—red eyes—and a matted brown wig. I always feel vaguely motherly about Wilson Knight—that must be his appeal to women—and I transferred that to Caliban, the poor thing. I'd like you to have seen his Caliban, but the rest of the show was very disappointing.

There was a sale of Swedish glass on in Eaton's and I bought 8 water glasses. They're smoked glass with rings around 'em, handmade. I hope you like them. I decided to start collecting this and that in hopes for next year, which no doubt will finally come 'round. I also bought a French embroidered nightgown to keep me company for this year! Have just been sent the moving bill from Pattison which is again $11.00, with now $2 a month to pay for storage. If I can find a place for the rest of the stuff I'd move it out too. I sent a beautiful little wooden plate and wooden turtle for sausages to Mary Carman & Mac [Mackay Hewer] from you and me.[4] So that's one off the list, but I haven't done anything about Art & Florence [Cragg] yet.

Tell me if you need any money and I'll send you some—let me know right away or else you may be stranded without anything from Little. Because I may go off on a trip somewhere and spend a lot if you don't warn me. I wrote you a letter last week to go on the Bremen but I lost it—I hope someone posted it.[5] Tell me whether it arrived or not. I'm so glad you saw Sir Michael Sadler's collection. Mellors[6] have a good one here just now—French Painting—with two swell Modiglianis, some good Pissarros etc.

Guess I'll go to lunch, it's one-thirty and I'm completely empty.
With love

Helen

1   The series consisted of five talks entitled "What Does the Artist See?" "Seeing Land-
    scape," "Seeing People," "The Visionaries," and "The Development of Social Satire,"
    given on Thursday mornings from 17 November to 15 December 1938. HKF's notes for
    the talks are preserved in the HFF, 1993, box 4, file 6.
2   See Letters 220 and 221, above.
3   Wilson Knight's production of *The Tempest* was performed in the Hart House Theatre
    3–5 November 1938.
4   A wedding gift; Mary Carman and Mackay Hewer had been married earlier in the year.
5   The "lost" letter is apparently Letter 221, which HKF says she intends to send by way of
    the *Bremen*.
6   See Letter 191, n. 9, above.

224. NF to HKF   Oxford
                                                                  Nov. 8.

*Postmarked 8 November 1938; addressed to HKF at 113, Bloor St. W., Tor-
onto, Ontario, Canada.*

Darling:

Oh Boy! At last I've found a pen with a really fine point. I'm writing
this in the J.C.R. and as all the pens have disappeared and I've left mine
at home I've borrowed this. I can see why it's available, though.

It's been a long time since my last letter: I must get down to business
and write oftener. I don't miss you so much when I write often, and I'm
rather gloomy just now, this being November, the nadir (I hope) of the
English year. Christmas cards are already being advertised in the windows. I like thinking of Christmas, because when it's Christmas it's only
a week from 1939, and 1939 is the year I see you again. And hear you
again. Your voice seems to have been expanding steadily ever since I
left, and I'm looking forward rather nervously to my encounter with a
blinding glare of purple and a stentorian roar of: *"HOW ARE YOU?"*

I've been working like hell on my papers for Blunden, who seems
delighted with them and suggests a harder one each week. Last week I
tied myself in fearful knots over a paper on the character book which
expanded to the size of a minor Legouis & Cazamian,[1] only more
detailed. That drew a suggestion for exploring 17th c. scientific works,
so I'm quitting work for the term, as far as extras are concerned.

The trio goes on merrily. Yesterday we tried to read a Brahms—simple for them, but I couldn't do it at all—and a Ravel, which wasn't simple for anybody. I bought the Haydn minuets. We can play the Haydn C
major (the hard one) with quite a flourish now.

I spend quite a bit of time at Charlie Bell's, whose ménage I think I
described. His fiancée Mildred [Winfree] registered Bill Sitwell's reaction when I told her I was married, and was rather irritably told to shut
her face by Charlie. It developed that she had a girl in mind for me. As
Rodney [Baine] said she tried to match him with a very good-natured
but very wide young woman, I seem to have had an escape. Charlie has
a lot of good records, including the first five of the *Zauberflöte,*[2] and I
think I'll take Alan Jarvis over tomorrow night. He also has a complete
set of reproductions of Jacopo Bellini's sketch-book drawings.[3]

I went to the first meeting of the Bodley Club. A paper on "The English in India" by an Anglo-Indian, breezy and bawdy—a typical Bodley Club paper. Answered by an enormously erudite but rather ponderous and humorless Hindu. Developed into a dog-fight between them. For me who doesn't know a nabob from a cheeroot, pretty dull. I rather rashly volunteered a paper: my idea about *A Short History of the Devil*.[4] I haven't much time, but I've more than I shall have later on.

Last night there was a total eclipse of the moon on a beautifully clear night. We looked at it through field-glasses. They were swell, because they made the moon look really round—a huge deep orange globe with cold green shadows and a blue penumbra, stars all around it. I haven't seen anything so lovely for a long time.

Now, sweetheart, there's more to write about than that, but I've just dashed this off until I can think of something more. I had a nightmare yesterday morning. I dreamed I was living with you again, and then I woke up.

Thank you, dear, but I don't need any money yet, and I hope I shan't for a few months. I love you.

Norrie.

Last Sunday night the J.C.R. had a meeting and as usual voted down the *New Yorker*. I said I didn't care because I got it anyway. But I don't.

I've just got the new *Forum* and I think your little Henri Masson article is nice.[5]

I think you're nice.

1 See Letter 132, n. 8, above.
2 Mozart's opera *The Magic Flute*, first produced in Vienna in 1791.
3 Bellini's drawings, most of which are in the Louvre and the BM, reveal his interest in architectural and landscape settings; he was the father of the Venetian painters Gentile and Giovanni Bellini.
4 NF had seen Defoe's *The Political History of the Devil* as "a possible influence on Blake. What interested Frye was the way society threw up huge conspiratorial theories focussed on putative bogeymen like Jesuits or Jews. Although it [NF's talk] took in the complete range of European history, it had manifest relevance in the age of Nazis" (Ayre, 152).
5 See Letter 220, n. 1, above.

225. NF to HK   Oxford

Postmarked 9 November 1938; addressed to HKF at 113 Bloor St. West, Toronto, Ontario, Canada.

I don't know why I forgot to tell you in my last note (I remember saying there was more to tell if I could remember what it was) that I went to London with Mike [Joseph] last Saturday to see the Picasso *Bombing of Guernica*. All the studies he'd made for it were there too, studies of bulls, murdered horses, and weeping men and women mostly. The *Weeping Woman* we saw at Toronto was there.[1] I was glad to see those: I couldn't have got much out of the picture itself without them, and they had a vivid impact and a unity I wasn't sure about with the big one. If I'd had more time, though, I think the big pattern would have got hold of me. It's the best contemporary work I've ever seen, I'm quite sure of that. Then we went to see a show of early Chiricos, the clapboarding and egg-face period, before he got to the horses and the Classical stuff. Above were some quite lively and amusing things by an Englishman called (I think) Harvey Jennings.[2] Then we went to another art dealer and saw a lot of assorted modern things, including a Rouault and two very fine Soutines. Then we went to a show—one of Hitchcock's, the man who did the *39 Steps*. I liked it even better than that: I think it was called *The Lady Vanishes*.[3] Then we went along with Father Blake and had some whiskies, and had dinner with Stephen & Edith [Burnett]. They've done so much for me I'd like to get them something for Christmas, but don't know what to get except books, which they have too many of now, unless you could get Edith some silk stockings, which are in great demand in England. Her size is 10, but perhaps you'd better look up her mother.

The next day a string quartet came and played at Merton—a Haydn and a Beethoven. There was a Dvorak I didn't stay for. They did very well, as well as any quartet playing I've ever heard.

Joe Reid, the Winnipeg-man-with-the-room-over-mine-two-years-ago-who-made-the-Oxford-Group-confession, dropped into our place on Sunday. He's got a job with the Eastman Kodak people in London, making instruments. He came over on the boat with someone who told him, he thought, that he was going to study geology at Cambridge. He mentioned my name, and the chap said, "Oh, yes, I know Frye: I married Frye." Joe said he didn't look like a sodomite and he didn't think I was one, so he asked again what he was studying at Cambridge and Cragg said "theology." Otherwise he seemed quite normal. He lives at Harrow, where the school is, near London.

There's a funny chap in Merton called [Bunny] Mellor, who cultivates me a bit. He's a good example of Mike's remark that all you need to do to become the centre of a cult in Oxford is walk down the High Street with your pants on backward. His particular idiosyncrasy is a beard. He plays the piano, badly, and runs one of the Oxford magazines.[4] Nice kid: my description isn't hostile. He had a 21st birthday last night,[5] and was sent about 30 complimentary pints of beer: his table was a sea of amber. Then we adjourned to his room and we really started drinking. A contemporary of LePan's, an enormously erudite philologist and quite good pianist named Brooks,[6] passed out around 10:30, practically disappearing in a fog of puke, which broke up the party. Largely because he kept pouring port into his beer, and drinking the mixture. I went home comparatively ignorant of philology but quite safe inside, knowing more about fruit and grain alcohol.

I love you and I miss you horribly. I keep on dreaming about you and waking up again. I wish I could just stay asleep and wake up in July.

Norrie.

1 Picasso's *Weeping Woman* was on display at the 1938 CNE in Toronto, which featured representative surrealist paintings. NF reviewed the exhibit in *Canadian Forum*, 18 (October 1938), 208–10.
2 NF must mean Owen Jennings, who was principal of the School of Art, Tunbridge Wells; he exhibited widely and his works were owned by the BM, Victoria and Albert, Art Institute of Chicago, Albertina, Brooklyn, and other museums.
3 A 1938 British film, released by Gaumont; it starred Margaret Lockwood and Michael Redgrave and was directed by Alfred Hitchcock.
4 Mellor was editor of *Cherwell*.
5 Mellor was born on 8 November 1917.
6 Kenneth Robert Brooks was a student at Merton College, 1933–40. He helped with music, as a composer and pianist, in productions by the Merton Floats and the Oxford University Experimental Theatre Club in 1936–40.

226. HKF to NF   113 Bloor Street West.
                                                         Toronto. Nov. 10. '38.

My dearest: The Normandie goes off with this to you on Saturday, I hope. The last letter I sent you had to be taken right down to the main post-office and I was so rattled that I put New York: 'Empress of Britain' on it, but the man said it would go all right.

I don't know what to do about that fool Canadian show—I wrote to Anthony Blunt for an article and nothing has happened: I've had no answer. I might write to Eric Newton, but in the meantime please send along yours so that we will have at least one article on it. Probably the best one, but you know how it is with people—an English critic would be a good idea if he had anything worthwhile to say. I met Fritz Brandtner last Saturday at the Picture Loan and got enough for an article on him for this issue.[1] Speaks very well, another of these revolutionary artists—but very full of vitality and pleasantly sure of himself. I liked him very much. Poor old Douglas Duncan has had to carry on practically alone because his committee is away—like Peggy [Kidder] and Norah [McCullough] or else busy with other things and have just left him holding the bag.

Norm Endicott was there and asking for you. Their kids have all had colds.

I have had a busy week, but get a holiday to-morrow—Armistice Day—and hope to get caught up on some things. I have a talk to give Marjory King's LSR group on mural painting, and a short article for a school magazine on the value of art to the individual or some damn thing, and this note for the Forum. This week I gave various talks in the Gallery—I went to Mr Bennett on Tuesday for a lesson, at noon, and it was a terribly rainy day. I *was* low, and I couldn't get any pep into a talk at all. I practiced making a speech to him—since the radio talk was over we were trying this other thing. He spent all the time making me snap out of that and remembering that I'm top dog in my field so far as those teachers were concerned. Those teachers were the Women Teachers Association that came on Wednesday night. I was scared, for some reason, as I haven't done one of the evening groups so far. Sterndale Bennett worked hard on my ego, though, and by the time I had to talk I made a good job of it, of course. There were 180 people there last night, and they could all hear me, and I talked away about the exhibition and had a good time. Dot Drever was there and we walked home and had a beer together. She is having another stage now, I think. Has come to realize that in her zeal for organization work she has had to neglect a little of her teaching possibilities, so now she is concentrating on her school. She says she has done an awful lot of stamp-licking in the last year.[2]

I didn't give the Libido talk to-day although it was listed for to-day, because I didn't have time to get new slides.[3] So I talked about pictures in the show, and it went over very well. There were eleven out—my devoted followers! It is getting much easier for me, this talking, but I do get flustered sometimes without you to keep me in good shape. I had to dash up this afternoon and talk to the Vic kids on the Ugly Pictures in the Middle Ages—they seemed quite interested. Sixteen out. It still is not up to your crowd. I gather that there were twenty who signed up for the supper meeting next Monday. Betty Mihalko (sp?) said she hated to speak to Marcus [Adeney] so she hasn't done anything about his fourth dimensional talks, and is just waiting to see what happens at this one.

There is a big news item in the Kemp family. Harold is on the Junior Rugby team—and they won the city championship. So he feels that he is a big hero—first time in seventeen years, or something like that.

The house is very quiet to-night. Janice Welsh is on duty, the second of six which were imposed on her for various offences, and she has to answer the door and 'phone until twelve-thirty. They are having another tea on Sunday, for men, and a breakfast party in the morning which rather gets me down. And our house party comes off in two weeks—I don't know whether to ask Henry Noyes to it or not—I haven't heard from him since we went to the concert. Perhaps I'll take Roy.

Mike's [Mike Joseph's] friends sound pretty overwhelming, and in spite of the Sitwell's objections I'm glad you're a married man. I'm glad you saw Sir Michael Sadler's collection, and Campion Hall. I'm likely to go to Fairleys' on Saturday, to a cocktail party in aid of *The Clarion*,[4] so I'll tell Barker [Fairley] you met David Jones. Douglas Duncan agreed with you about his illustrations for *The Ancient Mariner*.

I seem to be a bit soggy to-night from giving talks—guess I'll post this and go to bed with a book to freshen up. Haven't had a chance to do anything at the piano. I'm glad you have a trio and Charlie Bell's ménage sounds like a blessing. Betty Mihalko says last year she enjoyed her work but she is bored this year. I don't know whether that has anything to do with you or not. But I know this year lacks something pretty fundamental as far as I'm concerned. Two more weeks and two months are gone. Every day I count it up but the time doesn't go fast enough.[5]

Nov 10

$$\frac{24}{14}$$

. I love you. H.

Well. Here's a long P.S. I've just phoned Grube and he suggests that you get in touch with Anthony Blunt and ask him whether he can do the article for us, and if he can't then ask Eric Newton, who is I think art critic on the Manchester Guardian.[6] McCurry suggests asking him and I think that is a good scheme. Would you mind? I know it is a nuisance but it takes so long from this end, and to get an article for the January issue we'll have to have it *here* by Dec. 10th which is the date for going to press. I can't ask for a Newton article if Blunt is doing one, and if you have any luck tracking down Blunt you can find out where we stand. I'll enclose my letter to Blunt which you can send back later.

I walked down to the Gallery with Fred Haines one morning lately, who was full of complaints about "intellectuals" and went on about the sur-realists who were just poseurs. He is about the most poverty-stricken man spiritually that I know of, for one in his position and with his responsibility. I felt depressed after half an hour with him and had to talk it over with Baldie [Martin Baldwin] for consolation!

Again about that article—please send yours along as I said before.

I'm trying to get an article on Lismer. Jackson is going to write it on him as a painter,[7] and I guess I'll put in an editorial unsigned on his educational work and get in a sly crack somehow. He's coming up here to lecture on the 28th of November—did I tell you?

(These women in the common room have got a jazz band going on the radio—guess I'll go out.)

P.S. Had a letter from Barbara [Sturgis]: do please look her up next time you're in London. Sturgis: 56 Scarsdale Villas. W8.

1 "Fritz Brandtner," *Canadian Forum*, 18 (December 1938), 272–3.
2 The reference is to Dot Drever's activities on behalf of the Communist party.
3 The talk was to have been the fourth in a series called "Why Do Artists Paint Ugly Pictures?" The first talk, given 20 October, was entitled "What Does Beautiful Mean?"; the second, on 27 October, "The Devil: Ugly Pictures in the Middle Ages"; the third, on 3 November, "The Sot: Ugly Pictures in Bourgeois Painting"; and the fourth, scheduled for 10 November, was to have been "The Libido: Ugly Pictures in Modern Times."
4 A Communist party magazine.
5 In the numbers that follow HKF means that in fourteen more days it will be 24 November, two months after NF sailed for England.
6 Eric Newton, in fact, reviewed the Canadian exhibition at the Tate Gallery in the *Manchester Guardian*, 21 October 1938, 336.
7 If HKF was successful in getting A.Y. Jackson to write an article on Lismer, it was never published in the *Canadian Forum*.

227. HKF to NF   113, Bloor West, Toronto.
                                                     November, 21, 1938.

My dear: I was terribly sorry to find that I was too late last week to
catch a boat, and then I put off writing to you until the end of the week
because there was so much to go to. Audrey Stewart[1] was quite shocked
to-day to find that I don't write to you every night, and that I had
missed last week. So I'll try to give you a news bulletin of the week's
events.

Sunday: met Herta [Hartmanshenn] as I was going home to dinner at
noon and she did not need much persuasion to come along too, then
Roy came for a walk with us in the Don Valley. I hurried home to tea at
Oaklawn as I thought that my people were having men in to tea again,
but when I arrived I found that they had changed their plans without
telling me so I spent a quiet evening talking to the kids. When the head
of the house informed me that the guests were to come the next Sunday,
I said that so far as I was concerned they had come last week and that
there would not be guests two weeks in succession. We withheld our
permission. (!) Anyhow, my house is too sociable. That morning they
had a breakfast party and I was invited, of course, and I went with them
to the service in Convocation Hall where the Victoria Choir was singing.
The sermon was fairly lousy as it was given by a Y.W.C.A. secretary
who had just returned from China.[2] An American with a terribly hard
accent, and much too long-winded. Kay Riddell met me and asked if I
would address the Vic Alumnae one afternoon on some undetermined
subject like modern movements in art or something. So I said I would be
delighted. I talked to a gang of school-teachers last week one night, or
maybe the week before,—the night that I met Dot Drever. Yes, that was
the week before because I remember telling you about it.

Tuesday: I talked to a group of the L.S.R. on mural painting. There
were only about fifteen people there, and they straggled in half an hour
late, and the leader of the group was a very nice woman who ran in all
out of breath and told me she had had such a time getting there because
she attends a dress-making class that night from six to eight and then
has to go to the study group after that. She is called Mrs. Pincoe and is a
friend of Mrs. Robins, who incidentally, did not come out. Not that I
blamed her, for I understood that the Faculty Women's Association had
another of their famous meetings that afternoon. I don't know what the
project is this year, I think it is the subject of a long series of debates,

judging from what Kay [Coburn] says. That night I was feeling fairly exalted, for I had dinner with Mrs. MacAgy at the Babloor before I went to the talk. She was asking for you, of course. She thinks Douglas [MacAgy] is rather lonely, this year, and he wasn't very well, after his active summer.

Wednesday night was the Vic Alumnae dinner in the Round Room at Eaton's, but I didn't go. Mrs. Bennett spoke on Canadian literature,— and they said it was a very good evening, but it would have cost me 1.50.[3] Besides, I had a new development that day in the shape of a row with Gwen Kidd. Peggy [Kidder] and Gwen had been together at the staff meeting the night before and aired all the things they did not like in the general management of educational work, and Gwen accused me of trying to horn in on children's work and grab more power (!) and she thought I should not have been called Assistant Ed. Sup., and she wrote a long list of complaints down for Peggy to talk to me about the next morning. It had started in the first place by Audrey [Taylor] who had met Mr. Band in the Centre on the Monday morning when Gwen was not back from her week-end in New York. Audrey told Band something that I had said without malice re Gwen's general attitude of running things and Audrey got all emotional about it and took it far more seriously than I ever intended it to sound, and we had the funniest tempest all round. Gwen and I had a talk all morning about the different points on her list, and I assured [her] that I had no intention of making her consult me on points to do with the Art Centre but that I would like to know occasionally what was going on. Well, we patched things up, and then I trotted around to see if Audrey bore any resentment about my title, which Gwen had insinuated, and found that that wasn't right, and then I asked Dot Medhurst, and she didn't either, but thought the whole thing was a great joke, and so I guess we all love each other now. I am going to be careful, though, to go out with Gwen now and again, because I think that will help. We haven't had any social affairs this year at all, and that is a wonderful way to work up suspicions and hatreds. I am getting quite fond of having Marge [Boultbee] around,—believe it or not, and I find that she has her points, at least she is not suspicious of everybody the way Gwen is naturally, and she has been doing a much better job this year,—for her. Well, on Wednesday night I felt so exhausted that I couldn't face the Annesley Dining room, so I phoned home and bolted out to Danforth. Harold [Kemp] pulled out his whole bag of tricks and we had a grand time, eating dinner in the kitchen, as it was a cold night, and there were just four of us at home. Presently Roy [Kemp] called up in a weak voice and asked if there was anything left to eat, and he trailed home too, after another hard day with Herb Nott acting up. Fortunately Roy had stopped off to collect a case of beer, and so we all cheered up very soon, but Harold would not hear of such a thing. I still looked doleful, he insisted, and so he and mother and I went to a show (on me) and then he would admit that I showed some improvement. Herb Nott is an awful fusser and puts Christina's [Christina Huidekoper's] nerves on edge when he helps her or just by being around. He is rather dirty⁴ at times and full of cracks about the time Roy takes out for lunch, for instance, even if he has a business appointment. They think of getting rid of him, but it will take time. The house that they are working in is a fine old building set far back on Harbord Street, and there is a family living there,—a family on relief. That arrangement is not satisfactory as the family has a tendency to sit on the front steps and tend babies with customers getting photographed inside the front room, and then the baby will squall. However, Huidekoper, Kemp and Nott pulled a fast one and are renting the whole building from the end of this month, subletting two rooms upstairs to a couple of dress-designers,— which will be enough to pay all but four dollars of their rent per month.

Thursday: I went to dinner at the Havelocks—the Briegers were there and Marcus Tate from Trinity. We had lots of cock-tails and Havelock was quite rude to Brieger and told him he had had too many, and we were all very hilarious and the dinner was excellent. After dinner and coffee we drove over in Havelock's ramshackle car to hear Harold King give a lecture on Art and the L.S.R. at the Heliconian Club. I had a swell time. They asked for you, and there was a lot of joking about the fact that Marcus Tate thought I was married to Roy [Daniells] the last time he saw me at the Hart House musicale. I called on the Grube family to deliver my stuff on Fritz Brandtner, one night, and was fed some gin. I guess we had better explore the subject of cock-tails,—you find out all about it. I think you and I are very much in the good graces of the L.S.R., I am certainly beginning to feel admitted to a charmed circle.

Friday: completely exhausted and went to bed—not without a good deal of wishing you were on this side of the water. But there, I can't tell you how much I love you and how much I miss you,—not on this damned clanking typewriter. I had a notion on Friday night that I was slowly going nuts, but I thought I would wait until the next day to be sure. And I had a good sleep, p- that is,[5] when I finally decided that I wouldn't think about you any more and how far away you are, and in spite of the fact that I have counted six months in the last week, and it is still only nearing two since you went away. Still, two months are a nice thing to have behind us, aren't they?

Saturday: Santa Claus Parade, which I went to see, and ran into Alec MacDonald who inquired very kindly about you. He calls me Mrs. Frye, but he does at least refer to you as Norrie. In the evening I went to the first meeting of the Artists' Forum which met at Harold King's. He spoke on Daumier and Cezanne, and gave an exceedingly interesting talk. Unfortunately the Erickson-Browns hit upon that day to give a party at their country home so Audrey [Taylor] and Gordon [Webber] and Graham [McInnes] were not able to be out. The committee this year is Rik Kettle, Harold King and myself, with Jean [Lennox] as secretary again. Graham, incidentally, was married when he was in London, to a beautiful Australian girl. He said he was in Oxford one day and saw you from a cab, walking at your usual high speed along a road. He shouted at you but you didn't hear, and he had to go on because he was having lunch with Sir Michael Sadler or something.

It is now long past eleven, and I hadn't better bang the typewriter any more to-night.[6] I went out with Ella Martin in between times and ate at the Park Plaza Murray's, where Ella told me some of her troubles and there were some elegant women and some wonderfully handsome men just in from a posh party.

Let's see. I had got to the end, practically, of Saturday. Tillie [Cowan] and I walked home from Kings, and we thought of you while we were doing it, and Tillie thinks you're wonderful and must be a great person to live with and sends her love and misses you a lot. Well, we gassed away and wound up at the new Honeydew[7] at two o'clock still talking.

Sunday: slept in until eleven, skipped the Chancellor's sermon at chapel on the present situation, went home for dinner to find Roy had brought Doug Butler home to sleep with him the night before. He and Doug went to a dance with Christina [Huidekoper] and somebody else, wound up late, and turned Harold [Kemp] out of bed. Next morning Doug had disappeared with a perfectly new pair of socks Harold had bought for himself—because Doug had only his evening clothes and had to go back to the studio to change. He and Roy turned up again for dinner and we had a most hilarious time. Did I tell you Harold's rugby team actually won the city championship? First time Riverdale has ever won a city championship. Harold is a big hero and got his name on the sporting page and a lot of invitations to parties from admiring females. Harold and I practiced Haydn trios all afternoon while Roy worked at the studio taking a picture of that wonderful dog of Smith's. The photography business is being done on the barter system—Fred did the plumbing and Roy returns it with pictures of the dog. He has to photograph the carpenter's baby etc etc. Then I went to Fairleys' for the evening and met the Wilkinsons—he is the new medieval history man and his wife is one of the jolliest women I've met. They are thrilled with Canada and anxious to learn all about it. The Fairleys—Mrs Fairley especially—is very tired because Bill has been sick all fall and she has been very worried. He is very delicate, and caught cold after the summer in the north. Is somewhat better now. Mrs Fairley first sent you her respects, and Joan worked around to something less respectful and Mrs Fairley said she'd been wanting to send her love anyway—so she did and she does.

Monday: letters at the gallery—reminding everybody in town to come to Lismer's lecture next Monday. I gather he's going to blow the lid off, but I'm going to have a good audience there for whatever sort of combustion it turns out to be. We have had to let Eugene Alliman go, as his work in the supply cupboard was never well organized and we were tired of superintending him at every step. It is horrible having to fire anybody but Baldwin did the talking to him, and I had a little chat with him before he left—told him he wasn't cut out for this sort of work and he'd better try to get something more in his own line. He was looking for something else anyway as there wasn't any hope for a better job here. Allan Armstrong is a big help and awfully nice. You'll like him. Knows a good deal of music—makes pipes and plays a clarinet. Do you know any music for trio and clarinet or flutes etc? I'm hoping Roy can get busy soon with the trio. I'm so glad yours is functioning so well.

I will phone Mrs Manning re gift for Edith [Burnett] and will try to send it off soon. Had better get something less personal than stockings if you're to give it—or perhaps something from the Sea Captain for them both would be nice. I'll shop around.

I'm turning a bright green at all the exhibitions you're seeing—but never mind, I'm developing a VOICE. To-morrow night I talk to 300 women from the Settlement! Art for the char,—in words of one syllable, but loud.

I have started to interview students re courses. It's quite fun. We met Dorothy Redmond at Murray's to-night—she said Dot Dawson or Thompson or somebody who went to school with you was asking for you. D.R. is a SWELL GIRL.

It is queer—to-night I feel all practical and business-like and like covering half-a-dozen more pages to you. And on Friday and Saturday every inch of me was ready to scream that I wanted to touch you and be beside you, and I couldn't put up with this any longer. The psychologists can have it,—I don't give a damn. I'm married to you and therefore I can surely admit that I want to be with you so badly that sometimes— Oh well, I expect you know what I mean.

I like your article on the Canadian show[8] and I think we'd better run it along with the other which I do hope you can dig up. And soon.

What do you want me to do for Christmas for your mother? Shall I send a box from here or are you sending something from England—do get her something amusing and I'll send a box again too.

My love to you

Helen.

P.S. Am sending New Yorkers soon.

1 The Audrey referred to later in this letter is apparently Audrey Taylor, an instructor at the Art Centre of the AGT. The context in the present paragraph seems to be the art gallery, and as no one else named Audrey was on the staff of the gallery, HKF may mean Audrey Taylor rather than Audrey Stewart, or one of the names may have been a married name.
2 The service was held in Convocation Hall Sunday morning, 13 November 1938. Lyman Hoover, student secretary of the International YMCA, gave the sermon.
3 The annual dinner of the Victoria Alumni Association was held on 16 November 1938 in the Round Room at Eaton's. The special speaker was Mrs. John S. Bennett.
4 Above the word "dirty" HKF has written "mean."
5 HKF seems to be referring to her typing; even though the "p" in "sleep" is typed perfectly, she has skipped a space between "sleep" and the comma.
6 With this sentence the typing ends; HKF writes the rest of the letter in ink.
7 A grill and coffee shop located at 204 Bloor St. W. in Toronto.
8 "Canadian Art in London." See Letter 219, n. 9, above.

228. NF to HKF   Oxford
                                                          11–24–38.

Postmarked 25 November 1938; addressed to HKF at 113, Bloor St. W., Toronto, Ontario, Canada.

Sweetheart:

I've done no work today, and, though I have no news, I thought if I dropped you a note the day wouldn't be altogether wasted. I'm working fairly hard on the devil for the Bodley Club: my idea is a book long, so it *does* have to be boiled down.[1]

Blunden came to tea the other day: Mrs. couldn't, or at any rate didn't. Mostly shop talk about the 18th c.: I tried to prevent it becoming a free tutorial, but Blunden seemed to like it, and as politics is out it's just as well. Blunden told me that if I got a fellowship at All Souls' I should jump at it and bring you over: this after he'd just finished telling me what stupid mugs they were at All Souls' and what bloody books they wrote. Poor old Blunden: I think he really does hate Oxford, but he feels he oughtn't.

I don't get letters from across the Atlantic so often this year. I expect putting the *Queen Mary* and the *Normandie* on the same day slows down the mail service. Mother's last letter said that Lew Layhew, Hew's twin brother, just got married in British Columbia. I got a note from Barbara [Sturgis] to the effect that she might drop in and see me this week-end.

November 24—two months gone. Winter has started in earnest with a howling gale yesterday. I love you.

Norrie.

I've got the first issue of *Acta* and find it rather mediocre. Alice Eedy writes too fast.[2]

N.

1 See Letter 224, n. 4, above.
2 NF is referring to Alice Eedy's short story "The Trees Are Lifting Up," *Acta Victoriana*, 63 (November 1938), 9–10.

27. Roy Kemp and the Fryes, 1937 (courtesy of Susan Sydenham)

28. The Fryes, 1937 (courtesy of Susan Sydenham)

29. S.H.F. Kemp, Helen Frye, Roy Kemp, Frye, Gertrude Kemp, 1937 (courtesy of Susan Sydenham)

30. The Fryes, ca. 1939 (courtesy of Susan Sydenham)

31. Frye, ca. 1938 (courtesy of Susan Sydenham)

229. HKF to NF   [*Toronto*]
                                                                Dec. 1. 1938.

My dearest: My friend at the Post Office tells me that mail closes for the Queen Mary this afternoon so here goes:

I'm at home with the curse and a cold and feel very luxurious. Kay Coburn brought me a huge chrysanthemum yesterday to cheer me up and worked here in the evening while I caught up with my Forum correspondence.

Lismer had us all thrilled and up in the air for the week-end—you can imagine. Looking well, but not liking New York, wishing he were back here, but all being friendly with Baldwin etc. He turned up unexpectedly on Saturday—I had been told that he was coming late on Sunday— and was there to staff meeting, and had to be interviewed by *The Star* and the *Telegram* and the *Globe and Mail*. We had a staff party on Monday after his lecture, which increased considerably when we asked others who had not as yet had a chance to speak to A.L. Graham McInnes and his wife were talking of you—telling me more of how sorry they were not to have had more time. The Briegers are entertaining Dr. Jastrow, a German woman archaeologist who is working here for a few weeks with Prof. [H.A.] Thompson. Lismer's lecture *Art and Democracy* you can imagine, a summary of world conditions with great energy and highly elaborated, with cracks at fascist dictators and warnings to us to sweep our own doorsteps—then three quarters of an hour's slides rushed through quickly with little comment. The whole thing took an hour and a half and somebody may have got a clear impression, but I doubt it. Baldwin said next morning to me that A.L. gave a fine lecture, but it was a shame that it wasn't written and read better,—that he somehow summarized all the things we'd been talking about this year, and that he agreed with all of it. Lismer's coming did not clear up any of our problems and it was just as I expected,—that we'd have to carry on with our own ideas and meet new situations as best we can. Lismer doesn't think Norah [McCullough] will be back at all,—but then that is just a guess. Her family expect her in July.

Just back from dons' meeting at lunch—plans for the Christmas dinner were discussed.

Norrie my dear, I'll write you a better letter when I feel better,—but here's a joke. Miss Maitland, the nurse, is always inclined to put the worst interpretation on any symptoms you happen to have—and I told her I'd had a slight fit of the weeps yesterday, something like what happened when I got stuck in the Infirmary two years ago. And she said "you *did*?! I thought your marriage would have stopped all that!" So now I gather, medically speaking, marriage for me is a wash-out, if my tear glands still work!

I sent you that night letter re Canadian Forum article[1] because I would like to get it for January, as well as yours. I hope you can dig it up. I'm trying to find out from Mrs Manning whether there's anything else beside stockings that Edith [Burnett] would like—Mrs MacAgy is 'phoning but had to wait until after noon as Mrs M is never out of bed before twelve.

My love to you

H.

1 HKF sent NF a telegram (missing from the correspondence files), asking him to request from Eric Newton a review of the Canadian art exhibition in London. See Letter 226, above.

230. NF to HKF   Oxford
                                                     1938 Dec 2

Telegram; addressed to HKF at Art Gallery of Toronto, Toronto.

WRITTEN NEWTON CARE GUARDIAN BUT NO ANSWER YET CHRISTMAS IN PARIS LOVE

NORRIE

231. NF to HKF   London

Postmarked 6 December 1938; addressed to HKF c/o the Art Gallery of Toronto, Toronto, Ontario, Canada.

Sweetheart:

Term's over, and I'm in London. I'm sorry if I was remiss about the Forum article: you've got mine by now, of course, but I thought Blunt was your first choice. I didn't know where he was, but took your word for it that Newton was on the Guardian. I'll wire again if I get an answer from him. The show lasts here till the end of December, so there's really no hurry.

I stopped work for Blunden this last week, but was kept busy writing this paper on the devil for the Bodley Club.[1] It turned out fairly well, although I didn't get the exact quotations I wanted. (If nothing I say makes any sense it's because Mike's [Mike Joseph's] great-uncle and grandmother, very reactionary R.C.'s and anti-Semites, are trying to start an argument about the next war with Rodney [Baine] and me). It was one of my breath-takingly erudite efforts, and everyone was terrifically impressed. Mike answered it, and was very intelligent: condensed and summarized the whole paper extempore, when he hadn't heard it before. Considering that most of the members were half tight, it being the last night of the term, and considering the terrific speed at which the paper had to be read in order to get the discussion through by midnight, they were quite bright about it.

Barbara [Sturgis] dropped into Oxford in course of a hike. She seemed to be quite well: I took her to dinner and to the Playhouse,[2] although of course she would insist on paying her own way. The play was a melodrama by Henry Arthur Jones, quite the best dramatist, except Shaw, of the 1890 period. The play had obviously been doctored to make it a typical melodrama and the actors burlesqued it. The undergraduates, who have got it firmly wedged into their foolish little noodles that no melodrama is to be admired, joined in enthusiastically. I was rather sorry, because the play really had guts, and there were plenty of really bad & much funnier plays of the period they could have done. The next day she came to lunch with Rodney [Baine] and Mike: Mike she liked but Rodney I think said something she didn't like: I didn't catch what it was.

The following Monday Mike and I went to Magdalen for much the same thing: a burlesqued Gothic horror 18th c. play by Monk Lewis.[3] This play was really hokum, and I enjoyed it thoroughly. All about a haunted castle and a helpless heroine in the clutches of a loathsome villain who had murdered her mother & imprisoned her father—he was her uncle & a resentful younger brother to her father. There were the usual echoes from Hamlet & the usual dark hints about those awful Catholics ("But she is your niece," says the horrified father; "I have influence at Rome," snarls the villain).

Breakfast with the Chaplain[4] with three other undergraduates. I talked to him about my devil paper afterward and, although I still don't think he's any great shakes, I got a slightly higher opinion of his faculties, & his conversational powers have improved. I'd like to get at him again. I'm told I terrified him so much two years ago he kept saying all last year: "Oh, well, of course, *Frye*—" with a deprecatory smile whenever my assaults on the citadel of Anglican smugness were mentioned.

I seem to be carrying this letter all over London and writing at it everywhere: at the moment I'm the guest of New Zealand House, where I'm to meet Mike. This morning I dashed around to Barker's store[5] in Kensington and bought a brown suit and a pair of brown shoes. I think I always look better dressed in brown than in blue & the shoes will do for the Oxford uniform. I dropped in on Edith & Stephen [Burnett] but their refugee is still with them.[6] His English is much improved and he's opened up a great deal. He told me a bit about his term in prison in Germany. He was visited by a Storm Trooper who beat him up every day— the procedure seems to be according to the German conception of humour. They asked him each day if he were a Communist, and if he said no (he isn't one) they beat him for lying, and if he said yes they beat him for admitting it, if he said he didn't know they beat him up for impudence and if he didn't answer they beat him for sulkiness. Then the "prison teacher"—a sort of chaplain—came around to explain that all culture had been destroyed in Russia and that Marxism was only a primitive form of National Socialism. Then he was summoned before the Warden, who asked him if he had been convinced of the truth of Naziism: Ernst told him a prison wasn't the place to be convinced of anything. There was a Jewess there too—Irma somebody—the Burnetts have known her for a long time. Beautiful girl—actress and ballet dancer, allowed out of Germany on a domestic permit—she's cook to a Jewish family she knows. They let her out only after hours and hours of questioning & going through all her letters & papers & writing a dossier about her the size of the Oxford Dictionary. They pointed to the word "Ophelia" in a letter to her & asked if that were a code word. She said no, but after she got through with her dancing she took that part in a play and the name was just a nickname. Oh, what play was that? Hamlet, by Shakespeare. The dossier said ". . . given her as a nickname when she danced the part of Ophelia." She tried to explain but they said "Oh, we can't be bothered with all those details." She said they were decent but crushingly thorough.

Look here, I have a bit more to say, but I never seem to be able to get this letter finished, so I'll post it and start on a new one. I love you.

Norrie.

1 See Letter 224, n. 4, above.
2 The Oxford Playhouse, located on Woodstock Rd., north of the university.
3 *The Castle Spectre* (London: Bell, 1798), first performed at the Drury Lane Theatre on 14 December 1797.
4 Rev. Arthur Hubert Couratin.
5 John Barker's, a large department store near the Town Hall on Kensington High St. W.
6 A twenty-seven-year-old German Social Democrat from Prague named Ernst; he spent thirty-two months in a Nazi prison and a year in Prague as a refugee. See Edith Burnett's letter to HKF, dated 20 December 1938. HFF, 1993, box 3, file 7.

232. NF to HKF   Paris

Postmarked 11 December 1938; addressed to HKF at the Art Gallery, Toronto, Toronto, Ontario, Canada.

Sweetheart:

I think I told you about everything that happened in London except that Mike and I, as usual, went to three art exhibitions. The first was in Tooth's,[1] Epstein's drawings to Baudelaire's *Fleurs du Mal*[2] and some rather indifferent Paul Nash, who I think does landscape and semi-abstract things very well and out-and-out surrealism not nearly so well. The Epstein things I liked very much: very sophisticated people were telling each other to go if they liked Epstein but not if they liked Baudelaire, but I thought they were quite swell whatever one thought of Baudelaire. Some of them very Blakean. He'd stressed the symbolism and ignored the cheap sensationalism, and made a very good thing of his subject. The second, at Lefèvre's,[3] was mostly an Englishman called [John] Armstrong, who turned up in the town to show. One room of straight surrealism, very good, strong Chirico and Dali influences, another of imitations of Greek, Minoan, and Egyptian stuff—mainly vase-painting. He went in a lot for Ruins of Time and Waste Land symbolism. Interesting man. The third at Leicester,[4] Snow White drawings, water-colour on celluloid, and two painters, both jackasses.

I went to see Elizabeth [Fraser] my last night. She'd just had some money from home and was feeling quite cheerful. She was in a very much better temper than the last time I saw her and I didn't have so long to stay. So I came away feeling better. Her news was much the same: half-starved for a couple of months, a new job she's on the point of quitting, but with her chin still up. I very much admire Elizabeth, but I confess she puzzles me. I'm afraid, too, that she's getting to be my maiden aunt, whom it's something of a duty to see. But that's unfair. I do like her very much.

I crossed the Channel without mishap, although it was rough. A Chinaman from Merton and his girl friend were on board, and I was pleased to see them both violently seasick within ten minutes. It sounds awfully mean, but it does give me profound satisfaction. Besides, I'd sat beside the girl on the bus ride from Oxford and we'd had a fight. Our first stop was Rouen. (I'm travelling with both Mike [Joseph] and Rodney [Baine]). France is a bit awkward at the moment because all the stained glass has been packed away in boxes during "le moment critique," and we may have to postpone Chartres till after Christmas. We saw the cathedral, though, and St. Ouen,[5] and several minor churches, and the Art Gallery. I'm glad I'm not doing too much sight-seeing this vac., because nobody has any field glasses and without them there's no use breaking my neck to look at glass and Gothic and gargoyles. We had a fine morning the second day in Rouen, however, and some of the glass really came through.

This is our first day in Paris. We got in last night,[6] and couldn't think of much to do except drop into a newsreel. One of the features was one in a series of debates on various subjects. The proposer had an idea of building dams at Gibraltar and the Dardanelles and drying up half the Mediterranean. This would give more land for excess population, and the surplus water could be turned south to make the Sahara blossom like a rose. An objector pointed out that not only would the displacement of water put the earth off its axis, but the dams would be very vulnerable in the event of war. All beautifully illustrated with maps and diagrams, and apparently intended to be serious.

I forgot to mention the Art Gallery at Rouen—there was a Despiau show on—mostly heads, and three full-length nudes.[7] It's part of an organized attempt to show Parisian artists in the provinces, and provincial ones in Paris. French Art Galleries are irritating: you have to go on and on to the very latest Impressionists and the stuff keeps up its quality to the very end, while in Italy you can always quit at the 16th century.

Today we went to see Saint-Chapelle and Notre-Dame. That took us till 3, and as everything closes at 4 in the winter time, when it gets dark, there wasn't much to do but poke around in some smaller churches. Then we went to a big bookstore and ran into a couple of Oxford Canadians—Jack Garrett and a Balliol man—and had a drink with them. Rodney is discovering one of the disadvantages of being brought up in a Prohibition country, that all the medicines given to children taste very similar to the stuff we drink in cafés in Paris, so that the latter evoke the wrong associations.

Oh, darling, I want so much to cover all this ground with you: England, France, Italy: I don't care so much about Germany until they throw the Nazis out. Italy's bad enough, but it's so incredibly rich a country. But I want you with me, and the more I see the more homesick I get. And *don't* spend all your money on a trip with Rièse or somebody—not yet. I still have hopes you may come over. I could put in a very pleasant month or so—however much money we may have. Still, we won't worry about it. If we can't make it this summer, we can put the money aside until next. No matter what we do, we're no more reckless than Europe itself.

Practically everyone in Paris is English or American.

I love you.

Norrie.

1 Arthur Tooth and Sons, a London art dealer on Bond St.
2 Jacob Epstein's illustrations appeared later in a special edition of *Flowers of Evil*, edited by James Laver and printed for the members of the Limited Editions Club (London: Fanfare Press, 1940).
3 A London art gallery on Bruton St.
4 A gallery in Leicester Square.
5 A beautiful Gothic church, superior in extent and style to the Rouen cathedral (Notre Dame).
6 NF stayed in the Jeanne d'Arc, a Left Bank hotel on the Rue de Buci (Ayre, 153).
7 The sculptor Charles Despiau (1874–1946) was best known for his portrait busts.

233. NF to HKF   Paris

Postcard of Picasso's Guernica; *postmarked 11 December 1938; addressed to HKF at the* Art Gallery of Toronto, Toronto, Ontario, Canada. *The reference in the first sentence is to the postcard itself.*

I bought this in London, of course: I've carried it around in my pocket till it looks the way it does. Second day in Paris. I've had my first look at the Louvre—painting. Also I've had an Amer-Picon and a Mandarin-Curasol and a Lune-Citron and a Byrrh and a Cointreau and I feel like kissing a policeman and my head spins and I'm quite sozzled and I love you very much. Don't worry: I'll settle down in a day or two and reopen the subject of Eng. Lit.

Norrie.

234. NF to HKF   Paris
                                                                           1938 Dec 19

Telegram; addressed to HKF at the Art Gallery of Tor.

NEWTON WILL DO ARTICLE MERRY XMAS LOVE=

NORRIE.

235. NF to HKF   Paris
                                                                      [*25 December 1938*]

Postmarked 27 December 1938; addressed to HKF at the Art Gallery of Toronto, Toronto, Ontario, Canada.

Sweetheart:

I've neglected you shamefully since I've come to Paris: part of the reason is about ten New Yorkers, which I got, and thanks. I also got the Forum with your article on Fritz Brandtner,[1] which I liked. Newton sent me a very decent note: I think he'll pan the show, so it'd be just as well if his article and mine about imbecile English critics were printed in separate issues.[2] By the way, say "we should like," not "we would like." In the article.[3]

Also, Mike [Joseph], in his quiet way, has kept me going about 24 hours a day. Rodney's [Rodney Baine's] been away a week, touring cathedrals in Normandy. I'm very fond of Rodney, you know: I just feel that I need a holiday from him occasionally. We went to the Louvre several times, including one night show: they're too tight to turn the lights on these dark winter afternoons, but they floodlight certain exhibitions at night. So medieval ivories and Limoges enamels really came out where we could see them. And the Musée du Luxembourg,[4] dullish except for the Bourdelle Hercules and a superb Rouault vernicle.[5] I was disappointed in the Seurat. And contemporary modern painting at the Jeu de Paume—some lovely Kandinskys and a Klee and a Chagall. Notre Dame of course: the famous gargoyle has had his face lifted. And the huge ethnographical Musée de l'Homme in the Trocadéro: anthropology: primitive and peasant work. No more material than is in the B.M., but beautifully laid out. Strongest on French colonies, of course: not so good on Benin, which is British. Another equally well laid-out wing is the Museum of Comparative Sculpture, which has casts and originals from all the big cathedrals and elsewhere: grand big instructive show, with very useful maps. Two concerts: one a small orchestra playing four Bach piano concerti and a Pergolesi, the other the Pro Arte Quartet[6] playing the Ravel, Franck and Debussy Quartets.

That's a few of the things we've been doing. We met Rodney in Chartres. It suddenly turned freezingly cold—about zero weather, and the coldest since 1879, I understood from the papers. As you can imagine, looking at the sculptures outside Chartres was no fun at all. Inside there was a warm register in the north transept we stood on most of the time. But they were taking out a couple of windows beside it, and digging in the floor of the nave and kept opening the big west door, so it was pretty barn-like inside too. They were tuning the organ too, just to help concentration. I'm afraid I thought more about my toes than about the medieval soul, but then I was too short-sighted to see the glass properly anyway. However, I know pretty well what's there to be seen. Darling, we simply must cover Europe ourselves within the next year or two. If we can't make it this summer we'll meet in New York and see it instead, but sometime very soon you and I are going to see everything I've already seen and a lot more too. I don't know why I feel so strongly that I have to see things with you before I feel I've really seen them—probably just because I'm terribly lonesome for you and have never done any travelling with you. But I do, and I'm never really happy no matter what I'm seeing.

This is Christmas night. Last night, the 24th, another month went by. Next week will be 1939, and I think time will go faster then. Last night we went to L'Eau de France, a place the Burnetts had recommended, for dinner: the sort of place where chefs come around with huge alcohol lamp affairs and serve the food on the table. Then we went to Midnight

Mass at St. Eustache: a very good choir, with a lot of Bach and several carols. The first part of it wasn't too good, as we got seats away back in the north transept and the faithful kept pushing in and out and whispering and falling over chairs. We edged up later to the nave and saw the high altar with the candles.[7] We were fairly well lit ourselves by this time too, and got home about 2:30.

I hope you found something amusing in the stuff I sent you. That's another reason I want you here: so we can go shopping and I can get you the things you really want. Also, your presence on the streets would discourage pimps. They are quite subtle at times: one introduced himself as an anti-Nazi German and asked us to have a drink with him, so nicely we still aren't absolutely sure.

I gave Rodney and Mike a volume of Émile Mâle apiece,[8] and they gave me a French "History of Contemporary Art"—one of the Cahiers d'Art, and a huge tome, awkward to carry.[9] I was very enthusiastic about it at first, but it really follows pretty stock lines: starts with Cézanne, follows with the later impressionists, and from there on is Picasso, Braque, & Matisse, with variations. About 400 reproductions. Introductions the vague general variety that would fit anything. It's dated this year, but is really about fifteen years old, I think. Still, it will be good fun for me and probably useful to you when the much-wished-for next year rolls around.

Rodney and Mike are fond of movies and drag me around to a lot of them. I've seen the French version of Snow White,[10] which gave her a better voice. The thing that's wrong with that show is the 19th c. music: it's expert, but Offenbach-Sullivan-Herbert-Gounod stuff.

There was a London episode I forgot to record: we went to a pub in Whitechapel[11] one night with a New Zealander Mike had picked up and he introduced us to a minister who runs a Presbyterian church in Whitechapel and does social service work. He's Barthian and militant socialist-pacifist. Name's Miller. He'll be through Toronto next year and we'll have to feed him.

I'm quitting now; I'm sleepy. I'll resume in a day or two. Oh, Mike and I spent a day at Versailles. We sort of felt we had to. The Doge's Palace at Venice was perhaps bloodier, but lustier: the Venetians really believed in money and gloated over bad taste and vulgarity: amusing barbarians, in short. Versailles—well, I had to see it, of course. And when you get in the dead centre of all the algebra and sit down there the sheer monstrosity of the scheme *does* get you, all right, like Hitler's voice. Also we went to St. Denis, but we need a ticket there to see anything properly. Lovely 12th c. glass, with a light blue you don't see much of at Chartres.[12]

1 See Letter 226, n. 1, above.
2 They were: NF's in the January issue (see Letter 219, n. 9, above) and Newton's in the February issue (see Letter 240, n. 2, below).
3 NF is referring to a phrase HFK had used in the first paragraph of her article on Brandtner.
4 A museum of contemporary artists whose paintings and sculptures were purchased by the state; works in its collection deemed worthy went to the Louvre or provincial galleries about ten years after the artist's death.
5 The two works were Émile-Antoine Bourdelle's large statue of *Hercules Drawing His Bow* (1909), which was purchased by the Musée du Luxembourg in 1922, and Georges Rouault's *St. Veronica's Veil*, a 1921 etching.
6 A Belgian string quartet formed in 1912 by Alphonse Onnou, violin, Laurent Halleux, violin, Germain Prévost, viola, and Robert Mass, cello; the quartet became known as an exponent of modern music and achieved its greatest recognition in the 1920s and 1930s.
7 Saint-Eustache, opposite Les Halles Centrales, is one of the largest churches in Paris.
8 NF had read Mâle's *Religious Art in France of the Thirteenth Century* (New York: Dutton, 1913) when he was at Emmanuel College (see Ayre, 109–10). The book was later published as *The Gothic Image* (New York: Harper & Row, 1958).
9 Christian Zervos, *Histoire de l'art contemporain* (Paris: Éditions Cahiers d'Art, 1938).
10 Walt Disney's 1937 film, the first full-length animated feature ever produced.
11 A section of London on the left bank of the Thames; the chief Jewish district of the city.
12 NF is referring to the church at St. Denis, where Abbot Suger gave birth to the Gothic style in church architecture.

236. HKF to NF [*Toronto*]
January 4. 1939.

Addressed to NF at Merton College, Oxford, England, Via St John: Duchess of York.

My dear: I've just got back to work, to Oaklawn and to Toronto, not terribly reconciled, after a grand week with Vera in Chicago. I do wish I'd seen Chicago years ago before I ever thought of Europe, then London need not have knocked me flat so completely: it was my first big city, after all, wasn't it! You can imagine all the things we did—we went to the Art Institute and the Oriental Institute, the University, and the Bauhaus,[1] Marshall Fields, the Museum of Science and Industry, the Aquarium. The Field Museum and the Planetarium were closing just as we arrived so we missed them. We went to two WPA productions—

"Copperhead"—a badly dated, rather silly play about revolutionary times in the USA—and a glorious nigger production of *The Mikado* with costumes meant to be the unsophisticated nigger's idea of Japanese elegance.[2] They had a grand swing orchestra and practically stopped the show with "The Flowers that Bloom in the Spring." I can still hear it. I met several of Vera's friends—Gladys Adair at the Art Institute, and Marvel and Margaret Wilson. And Peg [Craig], of course, was there for most of the week.* We talked of a great many things, Vera and I, and we got on together beautifully. She said she was glad I thought of coming, and I don't know when I have had such a good time. She took me to *Little Sweden* and we had a drink of glug—their Christmas drink of heated wine in which raisins and almonds have been cooked. When I got back to Toronto it seemed to have shrunk badly, but now, as usual, it is settling into its usual routine, and so am I. Only I don't feel like it at all. For two cents almost I'd take a boat to England next week. I have all sorts of amusing ideas like 'phoning you Long Distance some Sunday. It would cost fifteen dollars,—but by the time I got you convinced who was speaking and asked you if your winter coat was warm enough the time would be up. I hope you weren't too cold in that trench coat in Paris, I gather that the weather is much colder than usual.

Douglas MacAgy has been in Toronto this week and leaves to-morrow. He stayed over a few days longer and doesn't want to go back very much. He says he's tired of Americans and Barnes and Philadelphia.[3] I begin to feel deserted all over again—how *do* you spell *desserted*? Anyhow, I *am* very fond of that lad, and I wish he weren't going away. He tells me that Alford is beginning to look with longing eyes toward the States. Well, after I've been to Chicago, I don't wonder.

Doug LePan was here too, and has just gone back. I missed a tea-party there by going to Chicago—asking for you of course. A card came for you from Lou Palmer.

I wish you'd start thinking about finances after March and let me know what you are planning. I need a new coat just now and if I get it I'll be starting from scratch again by the first of February, so that it will take some time for me to save much. I thought of going to New York and New England if Europe is out of the question, and of course I'm expecting to do it with you, or at least some of it. But *how* are you getting enough to keep you there in the summer, even if I do? Or if I came over

---

* Peg sent you her love.

in the spring—what then? You figure out something and if you can borrow enough perhaps I can come. The year has begun, anyway.

I had a crazy time getting your magazines out of Customs. I'll tell you about that later. But thanks so much, it was sweet of you Norrie and I liked them very much and I love you very much. Two damned freshies have spent the past half hour gurgling on the phone over some fool who won't tell them who he is. I'm tired of this place even before I start the term. I got examined to-night by Dr. Barnett who remembered you and settled up both our bills for a dollar. Nice.

Love

Helen.

1 László Moholy-Nagy's School of Design at 247 E. Ontario St.
2 The Works Projects Administration, established under President Franklin D. Roosevelt, combatted unemployment during the Great Depression by employing artists and writers as well as manual labourers. *Copperhead* was a 1918 play by Augustus Thomas, based on a story by Frederick Landis, about a northerner believed to have southern sympathies.
3 See Letter 216, n. 2, above.

237. NF to HKF   Paris

Postmarked 5 January 1939; addressed to HKF at the Art Gallery of Toronto, Toronto, Ontario, Canada. *The letter from HKF referred to in the second paragraph is missing.*

Sweetheart:

Still in Paris. It's now 1939, which is the year I go home. I can feel the time going faster already now that I can say "last fall," and "this spring." I got a sweet little letter from you at the American Express the other day, and I opened it when I was drinking an apéritif with Mike [Joseph] and a Rhodes Scholar Merton Freshman named Weismiller who has published a book of poems—not bad Robert Frost stuff.[1] But I shut it up quickly because I didn't think I could face both it and the other people at the same time. Any one of your letters can give me a choking feeling that interferes with a Cinzano, but this one seemed to live and breathe you so much that the bottom just dropped out of Paris, and there was I, homesick and miserable. I can't let myself get that way, though, and I don't as a rule. You're so sweet you must be all a dream. You often are.

I understand from your letter that you've sent me a photograph for Christmas, which Merton is probably holding. At this point I go all gruff and grim and say: well, I was hoping you'd have the sense to do that, but I never thought you would. There are times when you show the instincts of a perfect lady. Then I relax and say bless your heart. You know what I mean.

But I mustn't talk about you, must I? You want to hear about me and about my impressions of Paris, don't you? Well, I've been trying to cut down on sightseeing and stayed home while Mike [Joseph] and Rodney [Baine] went to Reims today. I had lunch alone and when the waitress said: "Etes-vous seul?"—we always eat in the same place—I explained and then heard the man across from me order his lunch. I said to myself: "There goes the only man in Paris who speaks French with a thicker English accent than I do. But he'll place me by our friend the pink mop."[2] He leaned over and said: "Excuse me, but I think you must be an American by your accent." He turned out to be quite a decent reporter from California.

New Year's Eve Mike & I went to a Montparnasse cafe full of Americans, and stayed there until six in the morning. Some friends joined us and we had a fair time. But that afternoon I'd drunk several apéritifs on top of practically no breakfast and no lunch and got a bit unsteady. I was conscious of everything I was doing, including the fact that I was making obscene remarks about Chamberlain at the top of my voice, but I was dizzy. New Year's Eve is fun, with everybody lit and good-natured and trying to sing the Marseillaise and God Save the King without knowing the words. About four we sobered up and went out for breakfast. I had another party with Mike a few nights before, and we collected an American who was doing a thesis on Stravinsky's latest work and his wife, who was ugly but pleasant. She got maudlin and kept trying to hold my hand while on my left a Negro kept expounding Negro music to me. He was a very earnest man. All I know, or thought I knew, about Negro music is that the Spirituals are English folk-tunes, and after he'd trampled over that offering like a mad elephant he started on the musical possibilities of jazz: Negro jazz. Finally I swallowed another brandy and got going on German composers of the later 17th century.

I seem to have found my pen.[3] I don't feel that I have enough French for a haircut, so I've just let it grow. I told the boys it was because I liked being conspicuous: people look at me: it's true that they laugh, but they look. I made this remark in a restaurant, and had barely made it when a whore came over and started stroking it—my hair, I mean, not the remark or the restaurant. Mike and Rodney roared, and the whore, who had missed the context, was quite annoyed. However, she recovered, and said that after she'd seen her "cousin" (the man with her) off at the station she'd meet me in some café or other "pour en faire des bêtises ensembles." Hideous hag. I suppose there are good-looking whores, but heaven knows where they are—they probably don't have to get out of bed.

Well, I seem to have told you all my good stories and here it is two o'clock and I go to Amiens tomorrow. And I've told you about nothing but dissipation, whereas I only dissipated Christmas and New Year's and remained cold sober the rest of the time. So please discount accordingly: the serious part will follow tomorrow night.

Well, now I'm in Amiens. This is the town my brother was killed in: only I don't know whether he's buried near here or in the Canadian cemetery at Vimy. Or rather, I don't know where his cross is: I suppose the bomb that hit him did the burying.[4] We went through Beauvais too, which turned out to be much better than I expected: it was thrilling with that terrific reaching for height and those superb flying buttresses.[5] I sometimes think that some of these cathedrals are much more effective with plain glass: you don't want pretty colours when you're concentrating on height. We have no guide-book and are probably missing a lot, but we stumbled over another very interesting church in the same town called St. Etienne. In case you didn't see it, there's one thing in it that's been giving me nightmares. Just as we were going out of the church, I saw a big wooden statue of a crucifixion. It caught my eye because that's a very bad and very rare medium for a crucifixion, and as I looked at it it got worse: the lines were all out and the face was awful and everything was all wrong, but wrong in a curiously subtle and direct way. Finally we got a book on the church and found it represented a legend of a Christian betrothed to a pagan who prayed to the Virgin to make her ugly, and woke up the next morning with a beard. Her father was furious and had her crucified. It's one of the most wilfully grotesque things I've ever seen.[6] Amiens is a grand cathedral too: I like the sculpture better in some ways than Chartres: anyway the symbolism is better organized and more completely worked out.[7]

I've seen some smaller museums in Paris: the Musée de Cluny is the best of those—a big junkpile with a lot of very good stuff in it like V and A.[8] Sightseeing in winter, where it's nearly dark at three and the economical French would sooner die than turn on a light, is uphill work. There were a lot of medieval household objects which were interesting—the guidebook advertised a chastity belt but we couldn't find it—and there was a crucifix with levers behind it to make the head nod and, I think, the eyes roll. Clever people, priests.

I don't know if I told you about Yves Tinayre's concert. He's a baritone—I heard him in London. He can sing anything, and is a scholar who digs superb stuff out of manuscripts besides. He gave a long talk to a very small audience and followed it with a programme of 17th c. music. The high spot, as far as I was concerned, was a six-part fugue with two subjects by some Italian contemporary of Bach. The more I think of what the average musician knows the more sick at my stomach I get. And there was a big fashionable well-attended Ravel concert, on the anniversary of his death. A woman everybody paid great attention to was there—probably Madame Ravel.[9] Everybody and everything absolutely first-class—I can't imagine where such extraordinary artists come from. A singer, a violinist, a pianist, a harpist, a conductor, any one of whom would have been a sensation at home or in England. Why don't they travel? Ravel just doesn't write dull music, and there's a caustic biting humour to his stuff which will keep it from dating, I think.

We made a tour of exhibitions one afternoon—Mike and I. One was a grand show with a lot of Klee and some Laurens sculpture.[10] I'm beginning to get the hang of a lot of people like Borés and Kisling and André Masson I didn't know much about before, and I've seen a lot of remarkable Soutine, whom I was interested in anyway. Utrillo seems to me a consistently dull stick, but he turns up everywhere.

But what's the good of it all when I can't have you? Six months more of my sentence to work out. Oh, darling, I think I'll bust if I don't see you soon. I wish I could fly.

I could fly as straight as an arrow,
To visit my wife over there,
If I could excrete my marrow,
And fill my bones with air.

God bless you, sweetheart.

Norrie.

1 Edward Weismiller, *The Deer Come Down* (New Haven: Yale University Press, 1936).
2 NF seems to mean that the American would be able to identify him by his hair. Eleven years earlier, after he had placed second in an Underwood typing contest, his photograph had appeared on a pink advertising blotter circulated by Success Business College (Ayre, 52). The "pink mop" is perhaps a reference to that photo.
3 Here NF changes from pencil to pen.
4 Howard Frye was killed on 18 August 1918, by artillery fire near Amiens.
5 St. Peter's Cathedral in Beauvais is one of the finest Gothic buildings in France and one of the largest: it has the highest of all Gothic arches, and its vaulting rises to 257 ft.
6 The statue was a sixteenth-century wood carving of St. Wilgeforte. The strange legend that NF recounts is an erroneous explanation of earlier crucifixes that represented Christ as fully clothed and shod, wearing a beard. The legend arose to explain the image, which was wrongly believed to be a woman. Wilgeforte was said to be the daughter of the king of Portugal, who wanted her to marry the king of Sicily. Another statue of Wilgeforte is in the Henry VII Chapel at Westminster Abbey.
7 NF is referring primarily to the sculpture on the west façade of the Cathedral of Notre Dame in Amiens, the largest Gothic church in France and one of the most imposing in all of Europe.
8 The "good stuff" includes the Musée de Cluny's extraordinary collection of tapestries.
9 Ravel died in Paris on 28 December 1938. Ravel never married; the person NF thinks may have been Madame Ravel was someone else.
10 NF is apparently referring to the exhibit of Paul Klee's work at the Louis Carré Gallery in Paris. The show opened on 7 July and ran for twenty-three weeks, so NF would have seen it in December of 1938. The other Parisian exhibit of Klee that year, which opened at the Simon Gallery on 14 January 1938, would have already closed by the time NF was in Paris. Henri Laurens had a 1939 exhibit of his sculpture in Paris at the Pierre Loeb Gallery. The two artists did not exhibit together during this time.

238. NF to HKF   Paris

Postcard, postmarked 9 January 1939; addressed to HKF at 113, *Bloor St. West, Toronto, Ontario, Canada.*

I love you. Owing to the cosmopolitan nature of this silly card that's all I've got room to say.[1] But isn't it a swell picture?

Norrie.

1 Because the title of the painting on the postcard, *The Last Communion and the Martyrdom of Saint Denis* by Malouel and Bellechose, is given in five languages, there was little room for a message.

239. NF to HKF   London (ugh!) Jan. 12. [*1939*]

Postmarked 14 January 1939; addressed to HKF at 113, Bloor St. West, Toronto, Ontario, Canada.

Sweetheart:

Not much happened in Paris after my last letter. I went to another concert: Jacques Thibaud's 40th anniversary of his Paris début. Another social event, well-attended. Funny concert. The conductor started with the Figaro overture, which he conducted with little jerks of his forearm, like a nervous tic. Still, the orchestra knew it. On came the maestro, shook hands with the conductor and concertmaster, bowed profusely, played a Mozart concerto impeccably, took a great deal of cheering and bravoing but didn't give an encore, was ceremoniously kissed by the conductor, shook hands all round again, and finally disappeared. All through the concerto his relations with the conductor had been amicable but strained: the conductor's idea of the speed was a degree or two slower and he kept dragging the orchestra while the maestro kept pulling it on. When he finally left I could almost hear the conductor's gasp of relief: he turned to his orchestra and they pounded the hell out of Till Eulenspiegel. The nervous tic disappeared and the conductor jumped and farted around like a colt: he didn't know the score very well and got several entries wrong, trying to haul the guts out of the violins when the brasses were taking the theme away across the stage—but he had a grand time.

On my last night in Paris we all drank a great deal, of course, and discovered among other things that a lighted match, dropped into an empty Chartreuse bottle, produces a lovely blue flame. I remember begging Mike [Joseph] to go down to the Dôme[1] again, realizing in more sober intervals that I didn't at all want to go and would be horrified if he took me up on it.[2] Fortunately, he didn't, and next morning we were on the train, which was packed with very callow Englishmen. There was a large skiing party there, exuberant and athletic, with one girl showing off proudly with a broken ankle: "I wish I could show them my liver," Mike grumbled. I ran into a very decent Balliol American, philosophical, earnest, and full of that half-angry resentful disillusionment with Oxford that generally lasts a term or so before it becomes mere soul-weariness. Guy Nunn came back with us: you'll hear more about him. Merton, Dan Devon's roommate, American, with Trotskyist leanings.

The Trotskyists have the political situation figured out far better than the Sunday-schoolers, not having to befog their minds with this democracy *versus* dictatorship claptrap.

So now I'm in London. I thought I might as well rub that fact into myself, so I went and had a steak, kidney and mushroom pudding and a pint of beer. It came to a little over two tons—sorry, I meant two shillings. Britannia, sitting in the midst of the sea with a millstone in her stomach, must at one time have done something perfectly awful to a child. Then I went, for the first time, to St. Paul's Cathedral, but got involved in a subtle theological speculation and had to leave. That speculation concerned one Major-General Mountstuart Elphinstone, who was somebody big in Bombay. There are a lot of marble tombs in St. Paul's, with life-size statues of people reclining on them in restrained English attitudes, awaiting an English Last Judgement. Major-General Mountstuart Elphinstone's statue is erect, full of a kind of expectant dignity. Speculation: when the last trumpet shall sound for the soul of Major-General Mountstuart Elphinstone, will the mouldering skeleton in the tomb get up and start adjusting its skull, or will the marble statue arise gracefully to heaven to pay the Major-General's respects to his Lawdship?[3]

I brought some cigars and some Cointreau to the Burnetts. The customs inspector had a degraded, debased mind: a Jewish mind. Making a career out of suspicion doubtless causes it. He asked me if I had anything to declare, and I expanded in a radiance of priggish virtue and said I had a bottle of Cointreau in my pocket. All he said was, "What's in the other pocket?"

I went to see the Burnetts last night. Ernst has gone to Manchester,[4] but a couple of other refugees are busy painting the kitchen. Apple and Pumpel, believe it or not. I haven't met Apple, but Edith says he's a huge powerful giant of a man with a baby face—very broad, with dimples and blue eyes, and very shy and easily embarrassed. The first time he met Edith Ernst was his interpreter, and distorted what he said into extravagant personal compliments. Apple realized what was happening and got very embarrassed and squirming, finally producing and thumbing through a pocket dictionary until he found the word "liar," and handed it to Edith saying "Ernst."

Don't miss a Pelican Special called "Design."[5] The bookstall seller I got it from was in a busy Tube station and was saying "Pelican Special; new Pelican Special just out," as though it were a newspaper. They're doing a tremendous amount of good, those books. H.G. Wells is so impressed by them he thinks they'll start a wave of liberalism that will help send Chamberlain out on his brown-stained arse at the next election.

Elizabeth [Fraser] was gloomy again: on the point of quitting her job and of breaking with one of her few remaining friends. She's so straightforward that each individual quarrel she has simply forces one to believe that the other person is a so-and-so: it's only when they pile up that one realizes that she's either very unlucky in her friends, or that she brings out the worst side of them, or that there's something very wrong with Elizabeth. She's got great stuff in her, but it's all going to waste. She's simply too introspective to get it out.

This place on Bernard St. is cheerful, cheap and clean, but Mike's great-uncle is a trial. I may have told you before that he keeps telling Mike, who gets up around ten but at that much earlier than he does, that a vigorous young chap like him should arise at six and bathe in the Serpentine.[6] He's one of those awful pseudo-Tories who feels that everybody should be cut off relief and made to work. Etc., etc.

I must run off to Oxford now, where I hope there will be letters from you. Bless your heart. I love you.

Norrie.

1 A church built by J.H. Mansart to complement the buildings of the Hôtel des Invalides; commissioned by Louis XIV, the Dôme stands as one of the great examples of seventeenth-century religious architecture in France.
2 Regarding this last night in Paris, NF gave a similar report in a card to Roy Daniells, postmarked 8 February 1939: "I spent the vac. in Paris, as I think I told you, with a very steady New Zealander who drinks like a tank. On the last night I got very drunk and maudlin and begged him to stay with me indefinitely in Paris, but I came back to my Nonconformist self and returned." RDF, box 43, file 11.
3 Elphinstone (1779–1859) was governor of Bombay; his statue is in St. Paul's, and he is buried in the cemetery behind the church.
4 To pursue his studies in science.
5 A book on industrial design by Anthony Bertram (Harmondsworth: Penguin, 1939).
6 An artificial lake in Hyde Park, laid out by Queen Caroline, the wife of George II, in 1730.

240. HKF to NF   [*Toronto*]
                                                  January 15. 1939.

Dear Norrie: Sunday night at home. Harold has gone off to church again to be crucifer, Mother is there and will be at a meeting afterward, Roy is going over for more business or something which leaves Daddy and me to stay home and drink beer. I seem to be suffering from a hangover or lack of sleep: I maintain that I'm in the same state as a man whose wife doesn't look after him, so I go out every night and stay out as long as I can. To-night somebody is talking about music among the South Sea Islanders or something at Rik Kettle's but I'm not going. I may not have written to you for some time, but it is the middle of January and there is a good deal to do if you look for it,—as I am firmly looking for everything I can that will keep me from remembering that you are away I am managing fairly well. Hell of a sentence, that.

There are one or two things I wanted you to turn over in your mind before it gets very late. Have you written to Currelly at all? If not, please do as soon as you can—just on general principles. I have no definite reason for thinking of it now except that I remembered the fuss we had about Pelham [Edgar]. Did you drop him a line at all, by the way? It counts for so much when people do get a note from you—Kay and Jerry [Riddell] keep asking for you and tell me that they had a card from you before Christmas. I dropped in to see them the other night and they told me Roy Daniells had been here at Christmastime on his way to New York. They liked your Forum article[1] and Jerry cordially said he could wring your neck for knowing everyone else's repertoire in addition to your own! Kay looked extra charming in a beautiful hostess coat that she had been given for Christmas, and I enjoyed myself no end. {By the way, Eric Newton's article[2] came just in time—quite good and exactly what I expected: you'll see it soon so I won't describe it. Did I tell you I had a letter from McCurry saying he liked your article?}

The second thing I wondered about was next year. How'd it be if you wrote to ask Johnny Robins (a) if he is expecting you back next year and if so what to do, and (b) if the answer to (a) is "yes" could they advance you enough salary to see you through the summer? I gather that the salary would not begin until August and the most I can save will be $300 by good luck and staying home. If the college won't come through that leaves me and Roy Daniells: I can't think of anyone else just now, and I *would* like to come over this time! Please let me know what you plan to do and how you stand for money just now—i.e. how long it will last. We thought you had enough until March or thereabouts—don't leave this off until the last minute.

Is there any news at all about the Blake ms? I suppose you have had to forget it in the rush of other things.

Marcus Adeney gave a çello recital last Sunday at Wymilwood and I took Harold and Roy with Willa Dole. We went to the dean's room after for coffee. Harold behaved beautifully and hauled coffee around and lit cigarettes and talked to various people like Prof. Lasserre as if he were quite an old hand at affairs of that kind. I was very proud of him. Betty Mihalko told him that they like Marcus but not nearly as well as you. So Harold told us that to make me feel busting with wifely pride. {I've just had two glasses of beer—does my writing look that way?} Daddy says to thank you for your card: they liked it very much, and of course I thought it was very nice.

I went to hear the Toronto Symphony on Tuesday—Mendelssohn, Emanuel Feuerman doing the Dvorak çello concerto, and Strauss: Till Eulenspiegel. I took Gwen [Kidd] up to see "The Lady Vanishes," a grand film by Hitchcock, the man who directed "Night Must Fall,"[3] on Saturday. Last night, I went with Maysie Roger and Marjory Tucker (the girl who won a scholarship to England in Modern History, Ernie Gould's year) to see Professor Mamlok—a Russian film about Nazi persecution of the Jews.[4] Very well done, good photography and a very powerful set of characters, propagandist of course, but one with which I sympathize more than the other side. It may interest you to know that one George McCullagh started a series of broadcasts to-day in the interests of democracy. I gave a gallery talk on Friday on American painting, a subject about which I could hardly know less.[5] Baldwin, Comfort, Frye and Graham McInnes were the speakers for this month. It went off fairly well, except that I gassed about Thomas Benton when I meant Grant Wood. Nobody noticed it, probably, but Marge Boultbee who said it was a good talk. I'm advertised as speaking to the Victoria Alumni on trends in modern art, soon.[6] Frye, Boris Berlin & Howe Martyn is the list for the present. Douglas Bush is up to do the Alexander lectures next week:[7] I'll go to see that man and lay plans to put you somewhere in line for those one day.[8] Vera, of course, has you slated for the University of Chicago, but I'm just trying to see you through Oxford at the moment. We've got Yvonne Williams talking to the Artists' Forum next week.

I feel a little scatter-brained and I think bed is the place to fix that.

Guess I'd better go back to Oaklawn. Please answer the various implied questions I've put to you and I'll start making plans for the summer if you get money from somewhere. Did I tell you I was getting a new coat? Did you like my picture?

I love you

Helen.

1 See Letter 219, n. 9, above.
2 "Canadian Art through English Eyes," *Canadian Forum*, 18 (February 1939), 344–5.
3 NF has already mentioned seeing *The Lady Vanishes* (Letter 225). It was billed in Toronto as "best directed picture of 1938." *Night Must Fall*, a 1937 MGM film based on a play by Emyln Williams, was directed by Richard Thorpe, not Hitchcock.
4 A grim, anti-Fascist, and melodramatic film, directed by Adolph Minkin and Herbert Rappaport; released in 1938.
5 The records of gallery talks given in 1939 have not survived.
6 HKF spoke to the VC alumni on modern art on 25 January. The Executive Committee minutes for this period record that the talk was part of a tea-lecture series on music, art, and books; on 31 January the committee passed a motion to send flowers to HKF.
7 Published as *The Renaissance and English Humanism* (Toronto: U of T Press, 1939).
8 Twenty-seven years later, in March 1966, NF did deliver the Alexander Lectures, which were published as *Fools of Time: Studies in Shakespearean Tragedy* (Toronto: U of T Press, 1967).

241. HKF to NF   [*Toronto*]
                                                               January 29. 1939.

Norrie my dear—I've neglected you rather lately, but I'll tell you what has happened since I wrote to you two weeks ago to-night. I gave a gallery talk on American painting for one thing—that had me worried but I think it turned out fairly sensibly. The Wace Lectures in Victoria College were all about bits of pottery they'd found in Crete, and proved something or other different about the trade routes of the Greeks.[1] Ella Martin had it all figured out but then it's in her line. I just went to one and then I drifted over to hear Douglas Bush the following night at Hart House. Humanism in the Renaissance.[2] He's a big brawny square-headed creature with a flat middle-western accent, and he sidles onto the platform and begins a lecture in a monotone which keeps on with no variation except an upward half-tone inflection, or a downward half-tone, at intervals as if he arbitrarily put in a comma every eight inches in his typing. He is swell at witty cracks, and if his manner had been more lively his lectures would have been wonderful. As it was, he held his audience right to the end of the series. They had various entertainments for him, but as Kay [Coburn] said, the women on the staff weren't invited. But if you can't make a better appearance and give as good a lecture as that bird—then I'll take in washing. When you come back I think I'll drag you to see Sterndale Bennett too, so that will take care of some of your machine gun fire.[3] Oh yes, I've got plans for bossing you around, my lad, once I just get hold of you again. However, I think you're going to like it. Hen-pecked husbands complain, but they seem to take it. You've always been fairly docile anyway.

Last Sunday we had tea at Oaklawn with guests and I invited Henry Noyes who is a perfect lamb and one of the best people I know for holding up a limping conversation. Two shy first year SPS men were the cause of this. We had the Artists' Forum meeting after that at the Aldersons,— Yvonne Williams had slides on glass up from Boston, and so it was quite good. Bitterly cold night and there weren't many out. Henry told me that he'd been talking to Dr. Brown about possible jobs, and Walter T. told him he'd be glad to give him a recommendation when he wanted it—but as Henry says, that's about all he would give him. Brown met me at one of the Bush lectures (one of the reasons I'd gone, I must confess!) and said he'd just had a letter from Paris. I said, that's funny, so had I. Exchange of pleasantries re life in Paris. I'm going on the theory that it's a good idea to get around. I'm sorry about Henry [Noyes] though, I do wish they'd get rid of [Florence A.] Smith, and of course Marion Hamilton is going back next year to the coast to finish her degree as her beau is going there. So that leaves one other woman with a small job on the staff—Ruth or Beth Jenking—doing graduate work, and I imagine she's very good, judging from just meeting her a couple of times. It is really a crazy place, though. Henry had never met her or heard of her even—in the same department! You and I are going to give some parties for those mutts— beer parties—and get 'em oiled. Well, anyway, it sounds to me as if they still mean to have you there next year, and any little thing you happen to er—uh—find out,—you might let me know? Speaking of next year, Baldie [Martin Baldwin] has just had another letter from that guy in Yale asking for candidates for their damned scholarship and he's anxious to push me into it again. I said nothing doing. I thought I might send you a night letter, but considered I might as well save the money for all you'd do would be to blow me up I suppose. If you're thinking of getting a job at Yale next year then I'll apply, but I can't see anything whatever to recommend next year at Yale for me. If *you* can, cable!

Last Monday we had a concert—Tudor Singers—better than ever. Healey Willan has reduced the choir from sixteen to ten and the balance of tone is much more delicate. He has a great nostalgia for the Elizabethans—says they knew how to live, and their music and their social grace is ninety percent forgotten now. It was a grand evening, and I took a couple of students to usher,—it was quite a lark for them. Tuesday afternoon I gave a talk on modern art to the Vic Alumni—I guess it was all right. It went on just for an hour as they said, but was late because we'd had trouble with the lantern. I went up to see Jack Oughton and Phyllis afterward, and their little Elisabeth. Lovely child—fair and plump and sweet-tempered. I felt like a very unfruitful piece of humanity and didn't know what to do with her, especially when Phyllis let me hold her. You can get the picture. Phyllis is working half-time at the museum, and has a girl to look after the baby. Jack is going on a expedition to the Arctic this summer.[4] Wednesday night was zero weather and I played sonatas with Roy [Kemp] over on Harbord Street—our piano is there now. Thursday I had the Vic students down seeing the American show and went to a meeting of the Allied Arts Council. I guess I won't go to another, they're still out for large undefined objectives and there's much talk. Speakers on platform were Henry Noyes, Lorna Sheard, Alison Sutcliffe, Norman Levy, Leo Smith and Margaret Gould. Speeches from the floor were poor, and the meeting finished with a resolution about something or other railroaded through, and I went home thinking that if I heard anything more of the word "enthusiasm" I'd spit. So many earnest souls like Jean Lennox and Rik Kettle. Baldwin went and was furious, and came up and wasted half my morning next day, getting cheered up. Besides, he was in the midst of one of his fits of impotent fury at Alford, and I had to hear about that.

On Friday night I had a grand time—went to Betty Endicott's for dinner and Mary Campbell who teaches at Harbord was there.[5] I'm taking her to hear Poldi Mildner on Thursday. Norman [Endicott] will be in England by now, and I hope you see him. He'll be in London, of course, I don't know where yet. And then last night Earle Birney phoned and I trotted up to see them—drinks and several pleasant people. Marion Hamilton and her beau was there but I didn't talk to them much. Esther [Birney] has a cousin named Madge, a Polish Jewess who plays the piano well, and is trying to get a job here, without much success, as the local boys are being frosty and discouraging. I'll try to introduce her to some people, but I don't know what the chances are. Esther sends you her love. I had a swell time with them last night, and I told them (after the rest had gone) your story about the whore in the café, stroking your hair. Incidentally, I was on the point of cabling FOR GOD'S SAKE GET A HAIR-CUT, but just let it pass.

I loved your letters and have been laughing ever since, and wish I could show 'em to some of our more Rabelaisian friends. Anyway, Earle and Esther [Birney] enjoyed the one about the two Americans—the woman and the poor man.⁶ I had lunch with Arnold in Chinatown one day and told him that one. He got to ruminating about the nature of American women then, and their sex life matter-of-factness. We had a very jolly lunch that day, and only mentioned Magda once—that she'd been in Chicago. So that I felt much better, not being the recipient of more marital confidences.

You must have seen an awful lot of Americans—are they the only ones with any money this year? I'm just asking because I was talking to Mrs Boris Hambourg and saying that you were having a gay time in Paris and she said she didn't think it was possible now, that Paris was so sad and down at the heels—or something.

I'm glad you took something to the Burnetts. Edith liked the stockings and dropped me a note, telling me about Apple and Pumpel (!)⁷—please find out if she had to pay duty.

Yes, I've got *Design* also *Art in England*.⁸ They are very good.

I'm sorry about Elizabeth [Fraser]. You don't seem to find her in very good humour when you turn up. Perhaps it's the great depressing dead weight of being alone in London that's affecting her. Then I suppose the fact that you actually are married makes a difference now,—anyway, you haven't had much chance to see her this year have you—and people sometimes have to get used to each other again after a long absence. Anyhow, I won't speculate at this distance, not knowing Elizabeth.

I do hope you like the photograph and that there was a letter waiting for you. I was sorry that you missed the Musée Condé, because there's some lovely stuff there—heavenly illuminations done for the Duke of Berry, a Leonardo, a lot of fine Clarets. It is a charming building anyway. I'd love to have heard the Ravel concert and the Yves Tinayre concert, and I love your crazy verse.

I'm bursting to know what is to happen re finances, as I've written checks and got *all* my debts paid to-day and start next month from scratch with about $65. I hope there's a letter from you to-morrow but that's probably too much to ask as the one from London arrived on Friday. But I'm insatiable.

Helen.

1 The Armstrong Lectures at VC were given by Prof. A.J.B. Wace of the Department of Classical Archaeology at Cambridge. The series consisted of two lectures, "A Survey of the Aegean World Down to the Fall of Troy" and "The Coming of the Greeks," delivered on 16 and 17 January 1939.
2 See Letter 240, n. 7, above.
3 Bennett had been giving HKF speech lessons for her CBC radio broadcasts.
4 It was not an expedition, but the annual run of the *Nascopie*, an Arctic supply ship; Oughton went along as a supernumerary and collected specimens for the ROM (Jack Oughton to RDD, 1 December 1994).
5 Harbord Collegiate Institute, located at 286 Harbord St.
6 See Letter 237.
7 See Edith Burnett's letter to HKF, dated 30 December 1938. HFF, 1993, box 3, file 7. Apple and Pumpel were the German refugees the Burnetts had taken in. See Letter 239.
8 For *Design*, see Letter 239, n. 5, above. *Art in England* was a 1938 Penguin book by Richard Stanton Lambert.

242. HKF to NF   [*Toronto*]
                                            Monday, Jan 30. '39.

The letter from NF that HKF refers to in the first sentence is missing. As references in the present letter suggest, he apparently wrote the missing letter after 12 January, saying that her photograph had not arrived and telling her about his "financial state."

Norrie darling! I finished writing to you last night hoping there'd be one from you to-day—and there was! It is just mid-night and I've only now got home from Mimico where I spoke to a study group of friends of Muriel Code—people who had gone to school with her and who meet now as a sort of reading group and review books and occasionally have speakers. I was a bit peeved at being roped in for this but then I was in good form and the girls were nice and some were really keen—so I quite enjoyed it. Sometimes my dominating personality really gets to work and produces something—it seemed to anyway, to-night.

So you begin your letter without any excuse of writing to me, and I quite gaily have no excuse for writing to you,—but I am anyway.

Darling, I *am* so sorry about the photograph. I phoned Roy [Kemp] to find out what the devil happened to it. He had it mounted and packed by a man who was doing that work for them, and it was supposed to be sent off about Dec 10th or even earlier. But Roy is awfully put out because this is the second package this man sent, which has not arrived and another one framed with a glass cover was smashed to blazes through careless packing. All this just adds to the joy of photography. He will find out right away. I am so sorry for I had counted on your getting that when you came back from France. It is exasperating.

The next *Forum* is out and we ran Newton's article[1]—it arrived just in time. I probably told you that. I'll send on the stories and more New Yorkers right away.

I'm so glad to hear about your financial state, it gives me something to go on. If you aren't able to borrow the 20 pounds then I can send it of course, but if you can then we certainly must arrange a little expedition of some sort. I thought that if you can't afford to stay much longer than the middle of July then I might come about the middle of June when your exams are finishing then we could go about a little until you had to be back for the viva. Of course if the college would advance you some money—enough to stay longer—then all would be rosy. We could find out which would be the cheapest country just now with exchanges as they are and that would help too. I think I said that $300 would be about the most I can hope to collect just now.

George McCullagh is broadcasting on Sundays—urging youth camps for vocational & army training, a national coalition government and amalgamation of railways. He made Daddy rather sick yesterday— Daddy said it would have been a fairly decent speech if it hadn't come from McCullagh. This is a bad piece of blotting paper I'm using. Sorry.

Daddy is very much cheered up and very busy organizing a federation of lip-reading and hard of hearing and totally deaf organizations.[2] The government is pushing it and there's to be a national secretary appointed as a permanent official—with a salary—and Daddy is the logical man in line for it. We are holding our breath.

Guess I'll have to go to bed, for want of anything better to do. Let me know if you have any trouble and need money and I'll send it.

I wish I could think of three hundred and sixty five different ways of telling you I love you—I hope it doesn't get monotonous. Anyhow, it sure does soak into this paper permanently.

Helen

P.S. Muriel Code is really a peach!

1 See Letter 240, n. 2, above.
2 S.H.F. Kemp, whose own deafness prevented him from entering the ministry, took an active part in the National Society for the Deaf and Hard of Hearing, serving on the board of that organization; he later became president of the Federation of the Hard of Hearing and editor of the *Hearing Eye*.

243. NF to HKF   Oxford

Postmarked 2 February 1939; addressed to HKF c/o Art Gallery of Toronto, Toronto, Ontario, Canada.

My pet:

I keep wondering if you get all my letters and postcards and things. I haven't seen a sign of your picture yet, and can't imagine what's happened to it. I got the New Yorkers though, and thanks very much.

It's some time since I've written, but nothing whatever has happened. I wrote a paper on *King Lear* that Blunden seemed to like, but otherwise I've done little work. I don't know exactly what I have done, in fact. That silly bastard Little hasn't sent my money yet, so in the meantime I'm living off overdrafts and borrowed money. That accounts for some of the slackening in activity.

Darling, you'd better make up your mind whether you're coming over here or meeting me in New York. I've told you the financial news: £60 to do me till June. What I think I shall do—shall have to do—is not take my degree after my viva, but take it *in absentia* in the fall, when, I hope, I shall be able to pay the fees. That isn't exactly regular, but I think it's legal. That will mean that I can leave the summer term's battels over, as I did two years ago.[1] It depends on how much money you can raise whether you can come or not. If I run short I don't think I'll run too short not to be able to borrow from Mike [Joseph] or Rodney [Baine].

I'm expecting Victoria to take me back, of course. I've written to most of the people you mention,[2] but there's no use asking Robins if I'm going back because he doesn't know. There would be only two things preventing my going back. One, they may prefer Henry Noyes so much as to keep him and drop all their connections with me and lose all the money they've invested in me. Two, they may go so broke they won't be able to pay an additional salary, which will mean letting a man go and dropping their standing as a college. See?

On re-reading your letter, though, you have a point about the college's advancing money. I'm planning to write the English Department this week. I shall ask my questions of Joe Fisher rather than Robins, though, I think. The difficulty will be putting off the college here and travelling around Europe instead. In the meantime I'll send back your passport, which for some curious reason I've acquired, doubtless through some devious Freudian method of my unconscious.

Really, nothing's happened. As soon as Little sends my money I'll take a trip somewhere and make something happen. Rodney & Mike keep working hard & steadily on their theses. Bryson has switched my tutorial to nine in the morning. I turn up at 9:15, he turns up at 9:40, we quit around 10:50 and leave a girl who was to come at 10, and did, blaspheming in the corridor.

I love you. Write me often. A postcard will do.

Norrie.

1 "Battels" refers to the tuition and room and board expenses NF would owe on his Oxford account at the end of the summer.
2 On 13 January 1939, after he returned from Paris, NF wrote to Chancellor Edward W. Wallace, saying that he was going to follow Edmund Blunden's advice to concentrate on his exams and postpone trying to get his Blake manuscript published. NF ends his letter by remarking, "So it's a good year, but no matter what sort of year it was I should still be lonesome for Helen and anxious to get back home." See E.W. Wallace's General Correspondence (89.130V, box 26, file 291) in the UCC/VUA.

244. HKF to NF [*Toronto*]
Monday. Feb 13, 1939.

Dear Norrie: Your letter came this afternoon—I was beginning to wonder whether I should send you a night letter to see whether you had pneumonia. I'm glad you haven't, and I expect I let a week or so go by without writing to you, back there awhile ago. Yes, I think all your cards and letters came, and I loved them all,—sorry I didn't seem to be clear about receiving them.

I've just phoned Jerry [Riddell] about the cost of taking your degree *in absentia*—he thinks it will be five pounds extra, otherwise no difference, and he said he took his *B. Litt.* after about four years. Only objection is that it comes hard paying the fees later when you're away off from Oxford with other places for your money. Well, if you can't borrow from the college I think you've a good idea there.

I think I've answered some of the arguments you put up re the job in Victoria next year—that is—they seem to be expecting you and not Henry [Noyes] and they've launched a campaign for one million dollars. Head-line in *Vic News Flash*. No news of its success at present.

I'd send you some money now but I suppose by this time Little has come through. As I say, I'll send it at once if you say so, but if you don't give me an SOS then I'll hoard it.

I've got another picture wrapped up securely this time by Downard, and I'll send it off to-morrow.

I've been running around at quite a rate. One week-end I spent in the Infirmary with a cold. Then I started out into the world again on Monday full speed ahead. Symphony concert—George Enesco came and swooned over the Beethoven Concerto. They did his Romanian Rhapsody and the Sorcerer's Apprentice.[1] Then I took nine kids in the house to dinner at Chinatown, our old friend Charlie Wong looked after us. Played with Roy [Kemp]. Gallery opening on Friday—I went with Yvonne [Williams] and Esther [Johnson] and Gwen [Kidd] and her flat-faced sister—gave them sherry first. Come to think of it, the opening was Feb 3, the day after your letter was post-marked, and I scuttled to the Infirmary the next day. Not that it matters. Betty Endicott and I went to hear Poldi Mildner on Saturday night—we had a swell time but Poldi was a great big beautiful Viennese blonde who pounded hell out of Brahms, (Variations on a Theme of Handel), Liszt, Chopin, and did the Octave Etude and some Mendelssohn as encores. Complete wash-out, musically. Sunday morning I took some kids walking in High Park, went home for dinner went with Roy to a concert at the Granite Club,[2] came here for tea where the kids were discussing original sin and revolting against their parents. Then I went to the Artist Forum meeting— Humphrey Carver on Housing. Excellent discussion. Whew—*that* was a day! The original sin idea, incidentally came out of the sermon Earl Lautenslager preached in the chapel yesterday. I didn't go, but Jessie Mac [Macpherson] was fuming at breakfast time. Earl has evidently gone in for fiery oratory and hell and damnation of the sort that used to go with revival meetings. Kay Coburn said she thought it was almost grounds for divorce if a man developed such ideas. I don't know whether it's Barthian theology or not—they tell me that John Line is spreading some of the same doctrines and that every sermon this year in the chapel has been practically the same to a greater or less degree. When you get time you might tell me about these things. I really don't know what you think and I'd like to, you know. You said you wouldn't force your opinions on me, but I have never thought about it at all,—that is what you disagreed with Norman Langford about, wasn't it? The main impression I got from these reports was that Earl had gone in for a very emotional kind of sermon, and in his talk to the students he kept repeating that he was not one of the clever ones in his year, but that the others—Rhodes scholars and such—were now pagan but he is a Christian. This doesn't make sense, because I just heard scrappy reports.

Poor Henry Noyes—Gertrude was to have sailed February 4th but they cabled from Ottawa to keep her out and she was turned back at the boat.[3] He's going to Ottawa to see if he can do anything but it is really an awful mess just now. Had an apartment and all. I asked him to go with me to the Annesley At-Home on Friday but he couldn't so I'm taking Alan Armstrong who will be quite a help. You'll like Alan,—I'm very fond of him.

Fairley was in New York lately, and on the way he saw [Herbert J.] Davis and the Gordiers and Victor Lange and Pegi Nicol and a lot of shows and exhibitions. I've had a dismal letter from Lismer—he hates New York and not knowing people.

I'm sorry this paper is such a hunk of blotter but it is all I have just now—I'll get some new paper and write you a long letter on it. I'm a bit on edge—I put myself down for a talk on *furniture*!—and now I've got to tuck in and do it. Really, I don't know how much longer I'll last on the meagre amount of information I have—I've been getting along this year on blarney, mostly. It really will be nice to have one person in the family who knows what he is talking about. However, everything's fairly rosy. We're having a marionette show at the Gallery on Friday, so I'll have to go there first before the party.

I hate to stop writing to you but I really haven't any more to say.

My passport is no good now. I'd have to get a new one this summer even if I hadn't married you.

I'm not making up my mind about Europe yet, waiting to see about money—and I'll go on a moment's notice if I can. I think I talked about time in my last letter.

I love you very much

H.

1 This concert of the TSO with Georges Enesco as guest violinist took place on 7 February at Massey Hall. On the program were the Beethoven Violin Concerto, Enesco's

Rumanian Rhapsodie No. 2, Dukas's *Sorcerer's Apprentice*, and Healey Willan's *Marche Solonnelle*.

2 An exclusive private club located at 63 St. Clair Ave. W.

3 See Letter 218, n. 3, above. Gertrude Noyes was finally able to leave for Canada in September 1939, sailing with her husband on the *Aquitania* (Henry Noyes to RDD, 20 December 1993).

245. NF to HKF   Oxford

Feb. 14. [*1939*]

Postmarked 14 February 1939; addressed to HKF at the Art Gallery of Toronto, Toronto, Ontario, Canada.

I don't need St. Valentine's Day to remind me that I love you, but I do need it to realize that it's the middle of the middle term, and I'm halfway to Helen. And the sun's coming out, and it's stopped raining, and I got my money from Little this morning.

It's because I haven't had that money, and I didn't like borrowing, that I've stayed in Oxford and haven't done much, so there's really no news. Norman Endicott dropped in yesterday, bless him. I was very glad to see him. Working on aspects of 16–17th c. prose: he didn't stress the details much. Sunday is a dull day for a call, but I introduced him to Mike [Joseph] and we went out to lunch together. We talked mostly about literature, and disagreed as usual. He tells me Woodhouse's new book is out, in a beautiful orange cover.[1] Woodhouse sent his publisher the orange box his favorite cigarettes come in, and said one like that. Norman will be up later, working in the Bodleian, so I'll see more of him then, and have him meet Blunden.

Blunden continues vague and complimentary. He says things like "I wish you'd write these things down, just as you say them: I think there's something to be said for a book of table-talk," or "I don't care about a paper: it's enough just to get you talking." But he doesn't seem to remember what I've told him particularly. He gave me a book last time: a translation of Keats' Hyperion into Latin.[2] I think it may mean he feels I should be reading more Latin: I actually do think he's oblique enough for that. Neither he nor I have expressed any particular interest in Keats. I haven't done much for him lately: I've been working on a history of language paper I'm worried about, and I think I've broken its back.

I've caught cold, but I'm getting over it, and the weather's drying me out gradually. Thanks for the New Yorkers. The Forum didn't send me the issue with my article in it, but they did send me the one with Newton's article in, which I liked: I hadn't realized he'd been in Canada. I think I'll drop him a note and thank him. You've probably done the same.

I got a cool but more or less adequate letter from the Chancellor, answering every point in my letter to him in turn. The Chancellor lacks the gift of torrential spontaneity, I sometimes feel. I still believe he hates me, but probably his brain is too befuddled to remember why.

The trio doesn't function so often now, so I get less practice. We read a Mendelssohn one sometime ago in which he burst into the doxology in the last movement. Uplifting man, Mendelssohn. I went to a Dolmetsch concert too, and had a good time. Norman says the harpsichordist is no good, but he gave me ideas about Handel and Scarlatti I could never have got from a piano—or, of course, from any Toronto harpsichordist. Wanna harpsichord. Then they did trios with recorders: the purest counterpoint I ever heard. Everybody in Oxford seems to have bought a recorder except me: even Mike's [Mike Joseph's] thinking of getting one. Charlie [Bell] and Mildred [Winfree] each have one. Charlie bought a book of Byrd's music and after I played it through for him he gave it to me and said he'd get a bigger one. He's bought an enormous number of Anthologie Louvre records.

Rodney [Baine] has just been to Winchester, where Warton was headmaster, and came back with a lot more information about that extremely dull poet.[3] Mike went to London: same purpose re Falconer, same result. Same kind of poet, for that matter.[4]

Darling, if I get Victoria's appointment for next year in writing, I think I can borrow from anyone here who has the money with a clear conscience. And Victoria should start paying me in July anyway, so a month's advance wouldn't hurt them.

As soon as I get my stories and my picture, in reverse order, my confidence in the efficiency of the postal services will be restored.

Four months more.

Norrie.

1 *Puritanism and Liberty* (London: Dent, 1938).
2 *Keatsii Hyperionis*, trans. Carolus Merivale (London: Macmillan, 1863).
3 Baine was writing a thesis on Joseph Warton (1722–1800), brother of Thomas Warton and headmaster at Winchester College, his alma mater, 1766–93; Warton was best known for his critical essays, especially those on Pope.

4 Joseph was writing a thesis on William Falconer (1732–69), known chiefly for *The Ship-wreck* (1762), a poem in three cantos that was quite popular in its day.

246. HKF to NF   113 Bloor St. W. [*Toronto*]
                                                              Feb. 18. 1939.

My dear: The Annesley At-Home was last night, so I'm feeling slightly seedy as a result of a long hard week. Lectures, bulletin going to press, too many things to attend to all at once. Then in the midst of a day full of dealing with next month's programme and trying to extract a lucid statement from one Frank Carmichael as to whether he will or will not review the OSA when Panton has already consented to do it—and I have to do some political lying—Alan [Armstrong] developed 'flu and couldn't go with me to the dance, so all afternoon I had to 'phone Roy and Ross Silversides and Rik Kettle. When I finally got Rik he was delighted to come and so I had a very good time and so did he. Then there were arrangements about the marionette show we had at the Gallery—Muriel Heddle and Mrs Keogh's outfit. Capacity house and a grand show. They did Moussorgsky's 'Pictures at an Exhibition' and Ravel's 'Mother Goose Suite'[1] and Reg Stewart playing the piano with some fool of a singer—one of the men had to rush up with a basket of flowers and a bouquet and present them to Madame Whoosis. It really was funny, and just when Earl [Ross] reached the front Downard switched on the lights and Earl blushed—and Downard thought he had a wonderful joke on him. They did 'Danse Macabre' too—we saw them do that at the Christmas symphony,—they also did 'The Mosquito'[2] which I don't like. Next week there is a Town Planning Conference with several meetings at the Gallery—I hope they get somewhere with their plans. Did I tell you that the Hart House Quartet had to cancel their European tour after Christmas? Engagements cancelled in Austria and Czecho-Slovakia, and so they are getting engagements on the radio and are giving a series of popular concerts for students on Mondays at 5:15 at Hart House Theatre, and concerts for children at the museum on Saturdays, and concerts for the public at the Art Gallery on Sunday afternoons. Music for the masses sort of thing.

To-day I *finally* acquired that new pair of glasses, I do hope you like them because now I'm insolvent again. But *from now on*—I'll try to save some money.

I will really try, I mean it. And then we'll see if I can get over to see you. You know, if we really were sensible, I suppose I'd be saving to buy furniture or something to fill up space when you come back. It might be an idea for us to try a glorified rooming house—oh well, there's no use talking of that just now. I'm completely disgusted with this pen, the ink, and this paper, so I'll stop for the time being. I'm going up to see Magda [Arnold].

Sunday morning.

Well, I did. I went to see Magda. Jessie Macpherson was singing in a recital last night but I thought I was too tired to listen all evening so I didn't go. That was a tactical error—because I had to listen all evening and make adequate responses as well. I started off by saying I'd heard that Magda was in Chicago at Christmas too,—and she hadn't known that I was, and she was furious to think that we'd missed each other. Of course I had quite deliberately not let her know that I was going—anything worse than a journey with Magda I can't imagine. I weathered Millicent [Rose]—but I will not attempt that sort of thing again! Well, she was waiting for me in that bleak front room of theirs, with its two small lamps lit, and the horrid little reproductions hung thinly on the walls and the general air of having been put together by someone who just didn't care. I hate that house of theirs, it always begins to make me brood as soon as I walk inside the door. I think I told you that Magda left for Chicago on Christmas day. Here is how it happened. All one of the greatest triumphs for herself, you understand. Upon my word, I do think she's getting worse. I may do her an injustice, and so you can discount my remarks if you like, but I'm going to make them anyway—and tell you about Magda the way I see her. I can't tell you about the way *you* see her or the way she must seem to Bert [Arnold] or to Line or MacCallum. Last summer she had a huge book on the theory of insanity or sanity, a new theory propounded by a Russian count,[3] and she very likely showed it to you. At any rate she read it through and this year she gave a paper on it to the philosophy club. Incidentally, the philosophy club is a very special club to which only very special people are invited, and as Magda says, it really is amusing—she is the only woman amongst thirty or forty men. I mentioned Jarvis MacCurdy and said he was a lamb—Jessie Macpherson borrowed him for the Annesley At-Home, and he made good use of his time getting people to sell tickets for an LSR theatre night. Magda said, oh yes, quite nice, nothing very profound of course. Magda read her paper—or maybe it was in a seminar, but no matter,—and no one else has read the book so it was a riot, the whole affair. Neither Line nor MacCallum or Bert have read the book, and Line teased her, and she attacked him on a book he had recommended which she disapproved of and there was a regular free-for-all, with Line finally getting red in the face. Heaven knows what the other students were doing while this combat was taking up the arena, but it was a big sky-lark. After that, Magda thought that was no way to treat one of her professors so she went around to see him and he said why did you attack that book and she said why did you have to tease me, and they decided to have a weekly seminar to discuss the Count's book—Line and Magda, and then MacCallum is in on it now. Magda wrote to the Count when she was writing her paper and asked whether she could get a research fellowship to study with him next year. He runs an institute of psycho-therapy and is vaguely connected with the University of Chicago.[4] He wrote back saying that at Christmas time he was having a course—six hours of lectures per day, and gave her free tuition and travelling expenses. So she hiked off to Chicago. The people were lawyers and economists and graduate students, five women and a lot of men who took the women out to lunch and they all had a grand time. The count (I have to call him that because I've forgotten his name) diagnosed her case right off, she said, and told her that what she needed was peace and happiness. She said all right,—but how—and he told her how. That she did not divulge and naturally I didn't ask her. But the 'how' of that riddle would certainly have me up a gum tree. Magda seemed terribly annoyed when I told her I'd seen the Oriental Institute because she had seen it just the day before, and we might have done it together. Oh lord!

Let me see, inevitably the monologue got to Magda's plans for next year—she's applied for a travelling fellowship, and has outlined her plan of research. Then as inevitably it got to the charms of William Line and the attributes of MacCallum. Charm, it seems, is something that Magda fights against. Line has charm, and Bert, she thinks, has charm, but MacCallum hasn't. Now let us think of women who we'd say have charm. So I volunteered Emmy Heim, and then Mrs [Walter T.] Brown. Well, people our own age—so I said Kay Riddell. Yes—well, exactly. Charm, but nothing very deep. I began to feel rather green by this time because I am extremely fond of Kay, and not interested much in

Magda's brand of depth, so I began to make a move toward home but even then I had to smoke more cigarettes and listen for ten pages more. If that conversation had been typed I think Bill Line would have appeared at half-inch intervals all the way down the page. Charm, in this discussion, is evidently something superficial and a power of attraction between the sexes, which people of the same sex cannot recognize. I thought that fair enough, because I know damn well that if ever at any moment I may be charming it is certainly to Bert, but not to Magda. I walked home for air, away after midnight, and wished I'd meet Bert on his way back from perhaps visiting Peggy de Reeder or some of the other attractive women he knows. But I didn't. I just came home and found two of my kids saying good-night to their beaus on the doorstep. Oh yes, Magda finished up by asking about you, and she said she missed you this year. Point blank, like a gun. So I guessed she does. Norrie, I don't know why the devil I am so patient, listening to that woman all night, and letting her fan her ego the way I do. It is probably because I suppose she needs a listener, but I'm getting over being such a docile professional listener, and it's about time I made her realise that what she doesn't know about colour and beautiful surroundings and how to choose her clothes and cut her hair, would make quite an evening's talk on my end. Let alone music and pictures and jokes, and entertaining and getting on with a husband and enjoying people, and all the annoying smackings and clucks and scratchings of head that she makes when she is talking. She showed me a coat she'd bought—Bert lent her the money until the summer when she may get a job.

{This does sound bad-tempered, and I'm sorry}

To-night Jessie Mac [Macpherson] is coming in for tea and we're going with some students to see a play at the Casino.[5] Last Tuesday the art group went through the Globe and Mail building in the evening.[6] I think I've been quite devoted to students lately. I'll have to start interviewing them soon and make out a report on the work of each, or their personality or something.

The other night Kay Riddell phoned and asked me to come over and talk to her while she ironed. So I did. Jerry came in later and told me that the Chancellor had been worrying lately about all these young women in residence, out on the streets at night. Why, there are so many men around, and sometime one of them may *speak* to the girls. So Jerry thought he'd better have something to report to the Chanc next time, that he'd done his duty and taken Mrs Frye home.

This letter seems to be over-loaded with Magda, and I didn't tell you about the party on Friday. But I didn't have much conversation with the Chancellor or Dr. [Walter T.] Brown, when I had to talk with the patrons. They left early and when we went in for our second duty call, the only one left in the room was the redoubtable Archie Hare, comfortably smoking a pipe! It was grand, so I told Rik to go ahead too. Some of the women students smoked and nothing was said to them. There is smoking in all the houses but it's still against the rules.

It's about time for me to go home and have a little music with Roy and Harold [Kemp]. Did I tell you Harold is on a fencing team and was in a tournament lately? He says he's not going to fence when he comes to college, but he is going to be a boxer because it's more useful, because when you get into a fight you can't run home to get your foil.

I'm just rambling on and on as usual because I like gossiping to you. I'm really looking forward to marrying you next year, my dear, I really think that it is my duty to be in the home and not in Yale. Now don't you? Of course if I should feel it my duty to help get on with the solution of the women's rights problem then perhaps I ought to be taking my career more seriously. I'll have to have a long talk with you about it one of these times. I've got a job. That is good fun just now, but didn't I more or less promise to live with you? And maybe we'll be leaving Toronto sometime for somewhere like Chicago where I can get some new ideas about pictures. But at the present time I'm counting the days until June. About four months.

I sent off the picture and I hope you like it. I sent one to your mother too.

Helen.

P.S. The rest of this page and all of the back one would be about how much I love you but I can't think of different ways of saying so. If I were Vera Brittain I might do it with other people's poetry but I'm not and I won't. And besides this letter sounds too much like the minutes of a clinical meeting.

I hope you see Norman Endicott some of these times. Irene sent a card at Christmas and asked you to 'phone her—her phone number is Flaxman 5919 and she lives at 29/25 Cheyne Place SW3. She said they're hoping to come here in the spring—do get in touch with her next time you're in London. Have you dropped a line to Art and Florence

[Cragg]? I've never sent them a wedding present yet—do you think we can leave it until you come back?

H.

1 Moussorgsky's *Pictures at an Exhibition*, an 1874 suite for piano, later orchestrated by Ravel; Ravel's *Mother Goose Suite*, which depicts characters in fairy tales by Charles Perrault and others, was also originally written for piano and was later orchestrated by the composer.

2 *Danse Macabre*, a symphonic poem by Saint-Saëns, op. 40 (1874), based on a poem by Henri Cazalis; "The Mosquito" was apparently either Ludwig Mendelssohn's *The Mosquito Dance*, op. 62, no. 5, or Carl Mueller's composition of the same title, op. 10, no. 2.

3 The book was Alfred Korzybski's *Science and Sanity: An Introduction to Non-Aristotelian Systems and General Semantics* (Lancaster, Pa.: International Non-Aristotelian Library, 1933). Korzybski was Polish, rather than Russian, though born in Russian Poland in 1879.

4 Magda Arnold attended a workshop at Korzybski's institute in Chicago in 1939, which she reported was "one of the more memorable and useful workshops" she took in her professional life. Korzybski had worked out a method of "vascular relaxation"—a gentle shaking of various muscle groups that turned the muscles, as he said, from "rubber" into "cotton wool." Korzybski never published anything about vascular relaxation (Magda Arnold to RDD, 21 March 1994).

5 The Casino was a combined movie and "vaudeville" theatre (more popularly known as a strip joint) located at 87–95 Queen St. W. The movie showing on screen that week was *Strange Boarders*, a British comedy-thriller in the Hitchcock mould, based on the novel *The Strange Boarders of Paradise Crescent* by E. Phillips Oppenheim; on stage was *Stocks 'n' Blondes*, with "Comedy Star of Film and Screen" Phil Silvers and a cast of thirty-five, including fourteen "Glorified Girls."

6 Located at 110 King St. W.

247. NF to HKF   Oxford
                                                                  Feb. 24 [1939]

Postmarked 24 February 1939; addressed to HKF c/o Art Gallery of Toronto, Toronto, Ontario, Canada.

Sweetheart:

Your letter of Feb. 13 just came. I'm sorry if I wrote you a snappish letter a month ago, but I'm apt to take a gloomy view of things during an English winter. I'm badly worried, in that automatic and unreasonable way one does worry, about Victoria: I expect them to take me back, but I've nothing on paper, no replies from anyone (except the Chancellor, who was so non-committal I could almost hear his boots shuffle) to all my letters, and I just have to sit and wait and hang around until they feel like appointing me. So when you said to write to Robins to see if I was going back I thought Christ, they've got a new idea, and Henry Noyes is trying to grab my job, just as I was afraid he would, and of course he's on the spot and a handsome man. You see, my money hadn't come and I'd caught cold and was getting steadily rained on and was studying initial palatal diphthongization in Old English and had just got that News Flash thing. And Roy [Daniells] used to keep telling me that the Victorian brass hats were no more rational creatures than the glacier rock in front of S.P.S., and couldn't be trusted as such. So I thought anything might be happening. And I've made no alternative plans. However, I'm hoping for the best. At the worst I can join the Chinese army. I think I can pile up more concentrated misery in this place than I could in hell. I detest England and I loathe Oxford: I think I always have done. Whether it would be any better with you and some more money I don't know, but I'd like to try it and see.

Assuming I get a job at Victoria next year, my salary would start in July. With that, and with this *in absentia* manoeuvre, which I'll talk to Blunden about, I think we could manage a trip all right. I don't think I shall have to borrow more than ten pounds, if that, to finish the year with. You'll come, I suppose, as soon as we get some money amassed. I'm not sure I want you before exams: exams to me are rather nerve-racking and humiliating besides, and it'd be difficult to get away from Mrs. Grylls before the end of term. Diarrhea is not a social disease, and I'd sooner empty my pot on my examiners' heads by myself. On the week following exams, however, there'll be a ball it would be nice to display you at. In between exams and ball I may be drunk, but I'll try not to have a drunken and dissolute bum meet you at Southampton or London. According to the plans being bruited about among my friends, you may be met by eight or ten drunken and dissolute bums: not at all the sort of thing for a seasick woman. However, come when you like: I'll send you the exact timetable when I get it. But I'd like to give you all my time when you do come, and then again I'd write a better set of papers if I knew you were on the way. I think that little space between exams and ball would be best. Then we'll go somewhere cheap and close to England (with Mike [Joseph] in Paris?) until viva. Then Germany perhaps, for another month. Then you go back to work and support me, and I come trotting along to keep house. Where shall we live next year?

(Sorry about this pen: that word was "where"). Shall we have a baby? I think I'd be jealous of a baby.

I'm terribly sorry about Henry's wife: I was talking to Saul Rae last night and he said he was pretty sure she wasn't in Canada. What was the trouble, quarantine regulations? I haven't heard from anyone except, as I say, the Chancellor. You might point that out to people who say they heard from me last fall and would like to hear again. Apparently, not writing letters is a less unnatural and monstrous procedure than I thought in my unregenerate days.

Work goes on. The College has finished Toggers.[1] Torpids. Intercollege boat racing. Merton has two boats on the river and both of them did fairly well. The Canadians met last night and discussed immigration. Very dull. Mostly Rhodes men, square-jawed historico-politico-economico people. They said Canada's population would disappear by 1971 at the present rate of decrease. Fortunately there was beer. I drank five bottles and recommended letting in a lot of Jews, because I didn't like a fat shiny orang-utang who kept saying we ought to take a leaf out of the totalitarian book. Orang-utangs being hairy and muscular, that sentence doesn't hang together very well.

The trio has discovered Schumann, and he's swell. The trio and the dark beer will be the only things I'll miss next year. Blunden is quite worked up about Kay [Coburn] and her Coleridge: he wasn't very coherent, but the general idea was that she didn't know enough to edit a man like Coleridge, and ought to enlist the aid of some Oxford men. Perhaps he, or his wife, or a friend, had been angling for them and were annoyed at a foreigner's getting them. Or he may simply want to read the stuff within the next five or ten years. Anyway, he seems quite annoyed. I hope Kay isn't trying to do more than just transcribe them: she'll get massacred by the English reviews if she does. And he's right: she doesn't know enough for any editing: she read a paper to the English Club in which she got Plato mixed with Aristotle and I tore it to pieces in about fifteen seconds. This is private, I need hardly say.

I went to London the other day with Mike [Joseph]. We saw some surrealist shows: nothing particularly good. One of them had an umbrella made of sponges and a chair covered with ivy, called "Nature takes the chair." And a French movie, called *Quai des Brumes*,[2] very good.

I hope your picture comes soon. I hope you come soon. Lent has started. In a few days the calendar will be purged of the last taint of

February.	September
March.		October
April.		November
May.		December
June.		January

I love you.

1 See Letter 185, n. 7, above.
2 A 1938 film, based on a novel by Pierre Mac Orlan and directed by Marcel Carné and Jacques Prévert.

248. HKF to NF								[*Toronto*]
								March 1st 1939.

My dearest! do you see the date? I am so happy: the weather has changed and we have a sunny day, and I am taking the morning off. There isn't much of it left though, just enough to send you a note and then lunch at Wymilwood.

Everyone has been down with the 'flu—Jessie Macpherson has had it for two weeks. Rièse was in the Infirmary with torn ligaments in her leg, and then Kay Coburn caught cold, but is better. I went up to get meals for Maysie [Roger] on Saturday and Sunday because *she* had 'flu. I didn't catch it this time, fortunately. Sunday was an exciting sort of day—it snowed and blew about, a sharp driving sleet that stung you in the face. I went over to breakfast, then got Maysie's, and went home for dinner. I was to visit the Fairleys but they were all sick too. Lismer came up from New York that morning to see us, and I thought it was a pretty desolate kind of day for him to arrive, but I think he was pleased to be here no matter what the weather. He saw a lot of his friends—mostly art centre and Jackson and Isabel McLaughlin on Sunday. On Monday he was to turn up first thing at the Gallery so I practically ran all the way to the Gallery and then he didn't show up until ten-thirty, and then only for a minute or two. The Centre people were very possessive, as usual, especially Gwen [Kidd], who couldn't be more mother-hennish if she were married to him. So that I got fifteen minutes talk with him on Tuesday, that was all,—about the work we've been doing. But on Monday night there was a meeting of the New Education Fellowship—you'd better come to that too when you come back,—it certainly needs pepping up,—in the Arts and Letters Club. 75 cents for dinner. I nearly wept. There was a very small group made up largely of middle-aged teachers and Art Centre admirers of A.L. [Arthur Lismer]. Gwen and the gang made their way to head table. Gwen sat on his left like a consort. I couldn't see that. I hadn't paid a membership fee and seventy-five cents in order to talk to Tillie Cowan or the rest, so I plumped myself down beside Gertrude Metzler who teaches weaving at Northern Vocational School, and talked to her and a Miss Miller from the same school. On the other side was a sweet-faced teacher who asked me if I'd had experience with grade work, next to her was an Ontario small town woman who'd probably been teaching ten years and makes enough to wear coy hats and keep her hair mar-celled. Across from her was a queer dried up old monkey-face who's been to China three times and goes somewhere every summer. I couldn't get much conversation going with those people—partly because Marga-ret Wilson was next [to] monkey-face and she had gone the limit with prettifying herself, and was telling her troubles in her own inimitable fashion. The styles this year seem just made to bring out the worst ten-dencies in someone like Margaret Wilson: she's gone in for hair in curls on top of her head, a hat that perches over one eyebrow, with a large vel-vet bow at the back, and a taffeta dress with ruffles all 'round the neck. Her mouth is all sweetly pasted on, and she looks too sweet for words, except when she talks—her talk is a mixture of treacle (in public) and wormwood off-duty. We were talking about an article recently in Reader's Digest on the evils of smoking,[1] and monkey-face said "women have always smoked!" and I volunteered that there certainly had been a change of outlook on the use of drugs,—for instance in Coleridge's day they used opium almost as now they use aspirin. Miss Milk and Water beside me said oh yes, and now—do you know I have the greatest fond-ness for poppy seeds in rolls—I just can't get enough of them—and so on. I thought it was à propos of the opium subject and went on but she told me of all the shops where you couldn't buy poppy seed rolls—she was eating one just then and I suppose that was nearest to her thoughts. I gave up trying very hard with them, but was interested in hearing their crab-bing about the new curriculum which, it seems, forgets the fact that chil-dren are children, after all. They say also that there is a great unrest among their children,—I thought because of the hard winter, but she meant the course of study. No discipline. Lismer was the speaker of course, and although I may have been off-colour after a long day,—I think he gave one of the worst rambles I've ever heard him do. Really,

Norrie, I feel a little concerned about him,—I feel that we are doing quite a good job here and I am seeing the gap close up. And I hate to see him come back and bring out his worst tricks of rambling incoherent sentences, and a talk with no organization, in which if he has ever thought out his central idea, at least he has never defined it. And it is certainly time that he did. After this ramble, with accusations thrown at the heads of everyone on the subject of art education, fascism, etc, we got into Isabel McLaughlin's car and drove to the Art Centre, where he had arranged to have a meeting of the Saturday staff. *That* was certainly superfluous, to my mind, for instead of talking of business matters, he chatted away vaguely again, with Dot Medhurst mostly. About principles of education. I can't remember any of it. He apologized to me afterward, but there went my evening just the same. A bunch of young kids there—and he and Dot talked—she and Gwen had just been to an NEF conference in Detroit.

It's twelve o'clock—I'll have to go to lunch now.

Ten o'clock.

The stuffing seems to have gone out of me completely. I'm so tired and depressed. The first of our spring lectures was this afternoon. The series is "Significant Living Artists"—and Baldwin did *Architects* this afternoon. It was dull as *hell*, and there were about thirty-three people there. If you were here I'd like very much to borrow your shoulder for a good cry, but as it is—here I am. And I sent an exhibition to a guy in Elk Lake and he wouldn't accept it—and it'll cost us $19 for express charges. Gulp again. That isn't my fault really—we've got all the correspondence—but it is depressing. And after I got back from Baldwin's lecture, late for dinner, Grace Workman was in a state, terribly nervous, and was being interviewed by a huge inspector, because she had been accosted in Queen's Park by some poor devil of an exhibitionist who couldn't keep his pants done up.[2] I'm trying to find someone to have a beer with but nobody seems to like it.

I was about to finish telling you of Lismer's visit. There isn't much really. On Tuesday we had a chat, but there's so little a man can do about supervising a job from such a distance.

Thursday night.

At that point I went over to see Janet Murray and talked to her about my troubles and had some sherry and cheered up. Lismer addressed the teachers' class on Tuesday night—the usual jollying along, and caught his train to New York. Then I went over to the Gallery and talked to two hundred women from the Settlement and had a good time. My voice is much better, and I can be heard quite well in the long Gallery. At noon I'd been to see Sterndale Bennett and he'd put me through my paces on the opening speech, line by line. I made a mistake—it's the chorus of Henry V, not Henry IV. It's perfectly magnificent anyway, and I'm awfully happy trying to do it. Bennett is a grand soul—his brother is a musician—the one who was mentioned as organist in Oxford in Vera Brittain's book. And another brother married one of the finest actresses in London. You'll like him. That night after talking to the Settlement women I walked home late, up around the Crescent, and it was terribly wet and icy. As I came up past Burwash two men were behind me, one was George Affleck (!) and the other was Dr Stephenson. Dr Stephenson saw I was having trouble on the ice and he said he needed help so he clung to me. When we got outside his house I said here's where you live isn't it? He said "Oh, you know me, then do you?" I said "I'm Helen Frye—you know Norrie—" I had to tell him I was your wife, *not* your sister, and he was so pleased he took me in with George and fed us cocoa and asked all about you and I had a grand time. I told him I'd have to tell you about my adventure with two strange men and a mud puddle.[3]

Tonight Harold [Kemp] and I went to hear Piatigorsky who was as marvellous as we had hoped.[4] We worked hard, and managed to get *four* encores!

I must post this now. The girls have been making candy, it's midnight and the place is still noisy. I'll be glad to get back to a certain amount of quiet living one of these days. I met Donald Ewing to-night, who told me to tell you that he was coming around to certain of your views on Wagner.

I love you

Helen.

1 Henry C. Link, "So You're Going to Stop Smoking," *Reader's Digest*, 33 (July 1938), 17–20.
2 When she got back to Annesley Hall for a pre-dinner gathering, Grace Workman recounted her experience, and Kay Coburn, the senior don, insisted that she report the incident to the police; Workman later identified the man picked up by the police following her description (Grace Workman Scott to RDD, 7 October 1994).

3 For a life of Dr. Stephenson, see C.C. Love, *Frederick Clark Stephenson, 1864–1941* (Toronto: Ryerson Press for VU, 1957). The Stephensons lived at 77 Charles St. W.
4 Gregor Piatigorsky was featured in a cello recital at Eaton Auditorium on Thursday, 2 March 1939.

249. NF to HKF   Oxford

Postmarked 8 March 1939; addressed to HKF c/o Art Gallery of Toronto, Toronto, Ontario, Canada.

Sweetheart, I have been neglecting you shamefully, but I'll promise to reform and write regularly, or I couldn't expect you to, and I'd get pretty dismal without your letters. I've got your picture,[1] and that along with the coming of spring has lightened my misanthropic soul very considerably. I think it would be a swell picture of anybody—that firm will make money if they do work like that. And with you as the subject—well, I look and look at it for hours. I never dreamt it would be so fine a picture: all I could think [of] was your horrible graduation photo and I just assumed no picture could do you justice. Well, it doesn't do you justice, of course, but it's a beautiful picture just the same. It just takes the part of you that will go into a picture: at first I thought it was a bit statuesque and Duchess-of-Kentish, but I don't think so now. I'll have to frame it, because things warp so easily in England, but I can't decide whether to frame the whole thing or have the border cut down. I don't like cutting the border: it spoils the proportions, but on the other hand I'd like to use it as a desk photo next year. What do you think? You are a lovely girl, you know: you take my breath away sometimes. I wish I could tilt that head just a bit, to see that round little occiput on the other side, and then move it back again. It was so nice of you to think of getting it for me, too.

The Merton Dramatic Society, known as the Floats because it goes back to a time when the footlights were chunks of tallow floating on grease, has functioned. There weren't any plays the first year I was up, because somebody always howls about obscenity just as they do in Toronto and stops them going for a while, but now they're supposed to do one big play every other year and there are actors alternately. Last year they did the Ascent of F6,[2] and this year they did a very bad play, badly acted and villainously produced, about witchcraft in a coast town, & a Shaw play about Shakespeare and Queen Elizabeth which was an appeal for a National Theatre.[3] Fortunately they had an extremely good farce sandwiched between them which saved the day—at least that was what everybody said. And even that would have fallen to pieces if one character in it hadn't been so extraordinarily good—at least that was what a lot of people said. The producer enticed me into it by saying I wouldn't have anything to do: once I was in I discovered the Merton Floats have a bigger reputation than the O.U.D.S. itself. Our play was lifted from a Conan Doyle story by a Merton man who wrote it in a sort of Victoria-and-Albert German Romantic style. It was subjected to several layers of modernization and then was all right, except that the Senior Tutor didn't know what the Warden would say about the swearing (the word "bastard," inserted by me). The plot was that a professor (me) is experimenting with mesmerism. He works on a student in front of an audience and they exchange souls. The professor, as the student, goes home & is greeted with rapture by his daughter, who loves the student, & very coolly by his wife, who doesn't. Then I come on, very drunk, as the student. The experiment is repeated & the student & daughter this time exchange souls. Mrs. Blunden was my wife: dons' wives have to take all the female parts. Blunden's respect for me has gone away up, I can see that. If only I knew something about cricket I think Blunden would be quite fond of me.

So last week was full of rehearsals and those two performances. I really did make a good professor: you should have seen me. This week I've inherited a lot of sherry parties. Elizabeth [Fraser] blew in yesterday. She came to see the printer,[4] but as she loves just jumping on trains, she hadn't written & she found him in London. Then she came out to my digs and phoned the College. In about an hour I got the message, by sheer luck, passed up Hall and took her out to dinner, and then discussed her next book with her. I suggested Browne's Urn-Burial or else Chaucer. At ten Elizabeth decided she'd better find out about trains, and as there was only a 2:30 a.m. one left she went off armed with my books (which she'll post back) to wait for it. She hadn't a cent left, having taken a taxi to the printer's, and would only borrow twopence from me for bus fare home in London. That's Elizabeth for you. Not to mention sundry insults, glowerings and gloomings about her job. But I can overlook everything for the sake of her first comment when she saw your picture: "Hasn't she a nice face?" Exactly the right thing to say.

Can you keep a bag packed, sort of? The minute I get my reappointment at Victoria, or a definite promise of it, in writing, I'll start seeing about an advance and in the meantime will borrow money here—from

Blunden if necessary. If you're broke now I don't suppose you'll have much. I've heard from Joe [Fisher], but to no purpose, so to speak. Also from Cragg, who is over his ears in work.

I think I'll post this or I'll be getting a cable saying are you dead, I hope so. Stop talking about going to Yale: if you want a career that bad you can bloody well go and live with Magda. Thanks for sending your picture to Mother: it was very like you to think of that, and it meant a lot to her. Exams here are June 8–14, Commemoration Ball June 19. Hope you can make it. I'm reading Anglo-Saxon again & finding it fairly straightforward. The time really is going fast now. Term ends this week.
March
April
May
June.

I love you.

1 This is the second copy of the photograph of HKF taken by Roy Kemp that she had sent NF in December; the first had got lost in the mail.
2 A play by Christopher Isherwood and W.H. Auden (London: Faber & Faber, 1936).
3 George Bernard Shaw, *The Dark Lady of the Sonnets*, first produced at the Haymarket Theatre, London, 24 November 1910.
4 John Johnson.

250. HKF to NF   [*Toronto*]
                                                              March 10. 1939.

The second half of this letter, dated 12 March, may have been originally intended as a separate piece of correspondence. But before the letters were catalogued, it was found folded together with the letter of 10 March, giving the appearance of having been mailed in a single envelope.

My dearest: Your letter of Feb 24 just came this morning. By this time surely you will have had my letters telling you all I know about the situation at Victoria, and you must have received the picture at last. I am quite sure you are perfectly all right so far as Vic is concerned. I met Joe Fisher one night on my way over to dinner and he said he'd answered your letter. I didn't ask what either of you said but hoped for the best. And Henry Noyes is still looking for a job—I'd like to find him one if there was anything anywhere, not your job, naturally. And Henry is not trying to grab your job, and I know he wouldn't try anything of the sort. The English climate is making you morbid, and a little uncharitable. Believe me, Henry is fine, and I repeat,—I'm very fond of him. Do you know what you need? You need me to tell you what a handsome man you are, and you need Donald Ewing and Phyllis Rutherford and the rest of your bright students to make you feel happy. I didn't mean to worry you when I kept urging you to write to people, but I'm afraid the distance lets you imagine all sorts of things. I've had a tough time lately scraping up enough news of you to answer all the people who've asked for the latest reports, when my latest was written on the 14th. Mr Hay and I picked up Pelham Edgar yesterday on St George Street, returning from the funeral: he said he was going to answer your letter last night. I hope he did.

The funeral above mentioned was Robson's. He died on Monday afternoon and there was a public ceremony at the Gallery. Sclater performed the service which was much better than I expected. They couldn't have got a better man to conduct the whole thing, simply and with dignity. Baldwin had a bad time with Mrs Robson who wanted the casket open and people to give a last look. But when I arrived it was closed up, and I felt greatly relieved. What happens to us next is on the lap of the gods.[1] I had lunch to-day with Barker Fairley and we hatched a little scheme in which he and MacCallum and perhaps Jackson are going to write an article for *The Forum* criticising the policy of the Gallery and recommending the purchase of more Canadian pictures and more one-man shows of contemporary artists. I'll publish it in the summer[2] so that if I'm fired you can feed me occasionally. I've just been talking to Jessie Macpherson and she wants to get started on the picture committee again. I recommended that Jackson and Fairley be put on it to advise, and I think she will. She thinks of getting a Lismer, which I will push for all I'm worth.[3]

I had a grand time on Wednesday, for I had to entertain Robert Davis from Buffalo, who gave a lecture on Wednesday on contemporary painters. Baldwin was preoccupied with funeral arrangements so I had to gather a gang together for lunch, and then I went to dinner with him at the University Club and then we went to the Skating Carnival.[4] Awfully nice, he is, and we had a great time talking about gallery problems and stuff. He tells me that Mussolini has sent over a lot of Renaissance painting including Botticelli's Birth of Venus to the San Francisco fair;[5] that there's to be a show of contemporary art including Canadian,

and of Pacific art—Japanese & Hawaiian and goodness knows what—
and north American Indian art. They've had committees working on all
these for the last two years.[6] Davis says it will be much better than the
New York Fair[7] which is too huge—besides, their art section is poor in
New York. They've got about 10,000 entries and are only accepting 800
in the painting section, and the artists were sore at having to pay the
costs of sending their pictures in to be judged and then home again
when they were refused. Davis thinks the San Francisco fair will be one
of those things you'd regret having missed—like the Chicago Fair. And
there are special rates—from any point in the US you can go to both fairs
and back for about $97! There's a big Blake show on in Philadelphia just
now—I'll send you a catalogue perhaps.[8] And in the fall, when the new
Museum of Modern Art opens in New York there's to be an exhibition
of three hundred Picassos![9]

Now after your letter comes with mention of a ball at the end of term
I'm not sure how the hell I'm going to work in all of these things and it
has me quite in a dither, and I realize that my plans are based on an
income about the size of Sir Joseph Flavelle's. Incidentally, he is being
buried to-morrow, and Sir Henry Pellatt died this week too, along with
stray grandfathers of students etc. Oh it's been a grand week!

I think your idea is *really* grand and I'm holding onto the purse strings
like everything. I spend my time alternately counting days and counting
money—the one side still comes out too much, the other too little, but
I'm still hoping. Ella Martin wants me to go over with her. Graham Spry
is here, Irene is supposed to come next month, I believe. Did I tell you
about *The Forum* dinner last Saturday? I think I wrote to you earlier this
week but it is so long ago I can't remember. Besides all the deaths the
weather has been foul and I've been catching 'flu and escaping it by
turns. I was worried for fear you'd caught it when I didn't hear from
you. About fifteen weeks to go. Had a report from Norah [McCullough]
of her Centre in Pretoria.[10]

I love you so much. And sometimes I wonder whether I did live with
you. I did, didn't I. Oh Norrie!

H.

Sunday evening March 12.

My dearest Norrie: I've got one or two amusing things to tell you and

I'd like to be spending this evening sitting beside you by the fire. I'd like you to read to me, and I'd like to be able to kiss you when I wanted to,— just about all the time—and that would interfere with the reading. But you might not mind very much, especially since I haven't been very close to you lately. It is just the right sort of night to stay in with you close to the fire. It has been snowing hard all day, and there is a strong wind. Drifts are a foot deep out on Bloor Street, and we are quite surrounded. I am not in Oaklawn at all, but somewhere where you and I are living together. I have a new blouse—a deep mulberry colour which you will like. My new glasses are nice too. And my hair is long enough to wind round my head. I think you'll like that. But I don't know what you're going to think of me underneath the clothes. I'm just a little afraid to take them off, because I'm feeling awfully thin. Sometimes I think I'll go off and do a lot of exercises so that I'll be rounded out more and there'll be a little more of me for you to hold onto. Sometimes I feel thin and small and bloodless and a little apathetic, and I hate being like that—I want to feel warm and strong and I want to love you in a million different ways. When I think of being with you again I do feel hot and cold,—you will look at me all over—but I won't be shy anymore. I'm too proud of you, and happy because I am married to you.

Well, anyway, I was going to tell you about something else. On Saturday night I went with Gwen Kidd and her aunt and her moron sister to see the Theatre of Action[11] production of Sklar's *Life and Death of an American*.[12] It was amazingly well done, with a ramp used like the Julius Caesar production—just the one set for the whole thing, and quick episodes following swiftly one after the other, and a chorus commenting on the action, and a voice offstage as Jerry Dorgan's conscience. They used mass formations and strong spot-lights, letting the rest of the stage remain in darkness. There is a horrible deadness about being with Gwen—her aunt is awfully kind and I like her very much—but those Kidd women are hopeless together. I'm thinking of her other sister now too.

This morning I came on deck for breakfast and thought I wouldn't go to chapel: Walter T. Brown was preaching. Then I remembered your letter and thought of my wire-pulling schemes, so I dashed over and sat in an aisle seat so he couldn't help but see I was there. I just don't seem to remember sermons, so you'll have to forgive me for that—and the choir sang very well. They have improved greatly, and there are about forty or fifty coming out now. I met [Wilmot B.] Lane on the way out so I went over and greeted him gaily. He said he'd had a letter from you in which you'd said you couldn't stand all the Anglicanism around you on every side. I stifled my impulse to say you'd married one. Then we edged over to the wall, and he told me *very* confidentially that you were missing me, too, and that you were just counting the time until THE END. He said, "you know it's *very* hard for a young man to be away from his wife,—I know,—I've been through it. It's a hard struggle." I made some sort of remark, to which he replied "No, no, it's not likely that he'd tell you about it,—but of course I'm different,—he would tell *me*." Now look here Frye—none of this man to man stuff with Lane, if I hear any more of this I'm going straight to the Chancellor and have a grandmotherly talk about *my* feelings as a female! I wish I'd stop blushing long enough to insert into Lane the story about the whore who liked your blonde mop, and the one about the two Americans at the Dôme.

I went back to the Gallery this afternoon and backed up Baldwin in the business of carrying off the Hart House Quartet concert. Did I tell you they're giving three free concerts for people of the neighborhood, on Sunday afternoons. We had about five-hundred people there to-day—with the storm and all. We felt it was a huge success—in the Sculpture Court.[13]

People are coming back from church and men are calling for the girls, and the house isn't as peaceful as it was. I'll have to come back to Oaklawn.

Norrie, darling, the spring term will be starting soon, the flowers will probably be out even now,—where are you going for Easter holidays? *Do* have a good time with the rest of the year in England, and I'll come as soon as I can. Go and see Gertrude Thorneycroft. I hope you'll look up Miss Whinney this time.

As soon as the weather improves I shall go hunting for a place for us to live in next year. I suppose you will agree to any bargain I happen to chance upon? I'll try to get a separate place, *not* in an apartment building, and will keep the rent as low as I can. There is, of course, the possibility of just a room somewhere—but I don't think so. We haven't much furniture for a house—that's the catch.

We'll see.

Helen.

1   Albert H. Robson, who was vice-president of the AGT from 1927 until his death, had
    been a leading force in raising acquisition funds for the gallery, and it was largely

through the subscriptions of gallery members, which he enthusiastically cultivated, that the gallery was able to make a number of important purchases. Robson was the author of *Canadian Landscape Painters* (Toronto: Ryerson, 1932), as well as volumes in the Canadian Artist Series on Cornelius Krieghoff, A.Y. Jackson, Clarence A. Gagnon, and Paul Kane, all published by Ryerson. HKF reviewed the last two of these for the *Canadian Forum*, 18 (December 1938), 286, and (February 1939), 354.

2 If McCallum and Jackson wrote their articles, they never appeared in the *Canadian Forum*; however, Fairley's article, "Canadian Art: Man vs. Landscape," which was about the Canadian painters at an exhibition at the AGT that opened in November 1939, was published in the *Forum*, 19 (December 1939), 284, 286.

3 The minute book of the Picture Committee was kept up only until 1937, so there is no record of the purchase, but there is a painting by Lismer called *Northern Lake* hanging in the reading room of the VU Library.

4 The annual gala performance of the Toronto Skating Club, held at Maple Leaf Gardens 6–10 March, billed as "The World's Finest Extravaganza on Ice."

5 In addition to Boticelli's *Venus*, the Italian exhibition at the Palace of Fine Arts at the Golden Gate International Exposition included works by Verrocchio, Michelangelo, Donatello, Raphael, Bellini, and others. The exhibition ran from February to December of 1939.

6 The Palace of Fine Arts exhibition was planned and executed by Grace Morley, director of the San Francisco Museum; Charles Stafford Duncan, a well-known California painter; Langdon Warner, director of the Fogg Museum in Cambridge, Mass., who was in charge of the works from the Pacific Basin; Roland J. McKinney, who resigned as director of the Baltimore Museum to put together the contemporary American collection, including Canadian and Mexican artists; and Dorothy Liebes, who mounted the works of decorative art.

7 The New York World's Fair was opened by President Franklin D. Roosevelt on 30 April 1939.

8 The show, which included more than four hundred of Blake's works, opened on 18 February 1939 at the Philadelphia Musem of Art, and remained on view until 20 March. The catalogue for the exhibition, prepared by Edwin Wolf II and Elizabeth Mongan, was *William Blake, 1757–1827: A Descriptive Catalogue of an Exhibition of the Works of William Blake Selected from Collections in the United States* (Philadelphia: Philadelphia Museum of Art, 1939).

9 HKF is referring to the opening of the new building of the Museum of Modern Art on 53rd St. (the MOMA was founded ten years earlier); Picasso's huge retrospective exhibition, which opened in November 1939, attracted wide attention and subsequently toured three other cities in the United States.

10 In January 1938 Norah McCullough had taken a leave of absence from the AGT to work in South Africa.

11 A drama group in Toronto in the 1930s that was committed to ideological theatre and strongly Marxist in its orientation.

12 A play by George Sklar (New York: John Day, 1900).

13 See Letter 182, n. 2, above.

251. NF to HKF Oxford

Postmarked 14 March 1939; addressed to HKF c/o Art Gallery of Toronto, Toronto, Ontario, Canada.

Sweet:

There isn't much to say this time. Term is over, and I'm staying up a week, reading Old and Middle English. I'm doing three exams a month, and am starting on these two and Chaucer for March. I'd rather like to get £5 worth of books, which I can if I get a first: it would set me up in texts for next year.

I shall be less gloomy with each letter now. March is half over: I can hardly believe that the time really is going, but it is. Next Monday I go to Blackpool with [Bunny] Mellor. I expect to stay until Easter, and perhaps later if I find we get along and I'm doing some work and drinking only a moderate amount (his father runs a brewery). Both Bryson & Blunden took me aside and told me to knock some sense into his head: the S.C.R. has a violent prejudice against him because he wrote an article for a Cambridge paper in which he described Oxford in terms which any Cambridge man would instantly understand, but which made the S.C.R. furious. He wanted to stay here and work during part of the Vac. and they managed to amass enough petty spite to tell him he couldn't. In Oxford, as in Toronto, the undergraduates are all right and the professors and dons mostly turds, but Oxford is far worse than Toronto because the dons have too much power, and don't have to curry favour with the undergraduates. Mellor is young and silly and takes himself far too seriously, but he's a very intelligent kid, and when he gets knocked around a bit more will be all right. I don't know when or how long I shall be in London.

I've heard from Lane and from Cragg. Cragg has "155 families to visit, 3 church services a week, 3 young people's meetings a week, 4 Ladies Aids & 2 W.M.S.'s monthly, besides social evenings, concerts, annual meetings, etc." I ask you! When does he call his soul his own? Lane's letter was rhapsodic: Lane imagines himself to be a poet, and he was trying to match me. Joe Fisher also wrote. Everybody non-committal. If [Walter T.] Brown writes me a non-committal letter I shall scream. I think it's a good sign that he hasn't.

Darling, I do wish you felt better—you seem to have had a pretty tough winter. Wait till I get back and we'll make things hum in that hick town of ours. My lectures next year will be twenty-five times as good as they were last year, and I can lecture on anything from Beowulf to Beverley Nichols at a moment's notice. Once these silly exams are over—but I won't lay plans yet. Reading Latin and Greek, either original or translation, is the next thing I have to do. And then, when I hit a PMLA conference they'll think it's an air raid, or the Martians.

I had a silly don-rag, as usual. Bryson reported somewhat vaguely that I was a very competent person doing things in my own way. Blunden said I was Merton's No. 1 chance for an English first, and then the Warden said, "Well, he's a good actor," and I started to leave. Just as I was leaving he said "You musn't laugh when you're acting," Mr. Frye. I said "I apologize, sir," and walked out. I think he was slightly lit. I had a hangover. I hate people who are facetious when I have a hangover.

I don't know that there's any more news. Very little seems to happen to me these days, which is the way I want it for a bit. I love you very, very much.

Norrie.

I've moved into residence: Mob Quad again.

252. NF to HKF   Blackpool, Lancs.
                                                           Mar. 28. [1939]

Postmarked 28 March 1939; addressed to HKF c/o Art Gallery of Toronto, Toronto, Ontario, Canada.

Sweet Pet:

This hideous paper is because I couldn't get my own stationery into my bags at Oxford. I'm at Blackpool, Lancashire, staying with young [Bunny] Mellor. I think I told you that both Blunden & Bryson asked me to "knock some sense into his head," but he actually makes a very pleasant host and I'm having a quiet & very enjoyable time, doing a certain amount of work. He *is* an infant in many ways: three pints of beer and he dashes off to phone up his old headmaster and tell him he's an old bugger, which for a senior at Oxford seems like vengeance beyond the grave, and he loses his head so often and so easily that I feel a good deal more than four years older. No, hell, I'm six years older.[1] His parents are all right: father a very small and John Citizen looking sort of man: mother cheerful and good-natured but not very well and on a special diet. I think having a guest in the house probably gives her the willies. His father has something to do with a brewery: the first night I arrived we went on a free pub-crawl. It's funny to be with a kid still under parental discipline: tomorrow I'm going to Preston to visit Jack Mason and Bunny isn't allowed to go because it would cost him too much money. His parents aren't mean, but he's extravagant, and they feel that he ought to understand the value of money. It just struck me that I haven't asked my parents for a cent since the spring of 1930. Blackpool is one of the biggest seaside resorts in England, but it's pretty quiet now. Nice town, somewhat smaller than Toronto. North England is very like Canada, except that all the houses are the same colour of brick and the trains are slower. The accent is different, too. I'm told that Edinburgh is almost entirely Canadian. Well, Elizabeth [Fraser] told me. The people seem to be very friendly. We haven't done much except see a few of Bunny's school friends, but Bunny has a piano and a lot of music. It's cold and rainy and I don't think I shall try the Lake country this time: haven't any hiking clothes anyway.

March is practically over: then two months. My worries over Victoria are just the exasperation of waiting. Until I get their appointment I can't make any arrangements to bring you over or get a salary advance. I shall be a few pounds short during the last term anyway and I shan't want to borrow money from anyone except you unless I get a definite security: and I don't want to take your money again. And they've got two months to make that appointment, and I don't know anything about their Boards of Regents and things. They moved fast enough last year, when they had to. Of course my remark about Henry was the result of a morbid state of mind: the context of it made that obvious. I'm sorry he's out of a job: I thought he had some sort of arrangement with Queen's.[2]

Darling, why wouldn't a flat be all right for next year, until we save up enough for some furniture? I'm mystified by your references to separate rooms and roominghouses: anything not absolutely self-contained is *out*. I have a mortal horror of sharing bathrooms or kitchens or walking through other people's hallways, and we want to do some entertaining next year. Outside of that one condition, however, you can pick what you like. A separate house would be swell, if it didn't require too much outlay.

As usual, this is a dull letter, but I'd better get it sent off. The faster the time goes, the more impatient I get at having to write instead of talk. I love you.

Norrie.

Good old Lane: he reacted just as I wanted him to.

1 NF was actually a bit more than five years older than Mellor.
2 Queen's University, in Kingston, Ont.

253. NF to HKF   London

Postmarked 4 April 1939; addressed to HKF c/o Art Gallery of Toronto, Toronto, Ontario, Canada.

Darling:

I'm back in London again. Somehow or other I never got to feeling at home in Blackpool: all I wanted to do was sit down and read, and Bunny [Mellor] got fits of trying to entertain me and kept going around seeing people who obviously did not want to see either of us. He's a very nice kid, and I like him a lot, but two weeks among adolescent Englishmen is enough for anybody. Nothing much happened: I did some work, not as much as I should have done, did a lot of beer-drinking (I've drunk more this last year than I ever expect to do in the next ten years: if I'm ever separated from you again, which God forbid, I shall become a sot), saw some boring movies, played on Bunny's piano (Bunny has an enormous library of exceedingly difficult romantic music, bought after hearing it played by professionals, and which he tackles with disastrous results) and ate my meals. Mrs. Mellor's health is not good—semi-diabetic diet and so forth—and she was probably glad to see me go. I hope I don't sound too much the ungrateful guest, but you get what I mean. (I'm in the same digs in London I always go to, and am in the common room now trying not to listen to all the conversation, which is why I sound so addled and parenthetical.) From the money that silly kid spends at Oxford I thought his father was a millionaire, and was quaking for fear my pitiful little bags would be unpacked by a servant, but actually the money represents a lot of parental belt-tightening.

I went over to Preston to see Jack Mason and went to a B.B.C. concert with him. His people have gone to New Zealand and he lives with an uncle and aunt, quite young, who lost a beautiful little baby boy (to judge from his pictures) some time ago. It's pretty grim, because she can't have another. Jack I don't think has any feeling for English literature and will probably not do too well;[1] he has far more sense than Bunny but far less sensitivity. I liked him much better when I got him on his own ground: he's a cynical left-winger and described all the streets we walked on, pointing out private enterprise and cooperative houses, commenting acidly on the architectural ineptitudes of the former and the dullness of the latter, giving me corner-of-the-mouth life histories of the inhabitants, and generally making a hideous industrial town come alive and interesting. If he could write as he talks, he'd make a good novelist. I think he'd be well-fitted for journalism. You'll probably meet him in the fall, as he's coming through America on his way to N.Z. And then of course you may meet them anyway. I got a letter from Robins, which seemed to assume I was coming back: he said he'd be glad when I got back and the Department "settled down": he spoke of Kay's [Kay Coburn's] going away and of having to absorb her work, and generally wrote quite a reassuring letter. The B.B.C. concert, by the way, was Wagner & Tschaikowsky, but three pints of beer can do a lot for the Pathetic Symphony, and we were sitting directly underneath a superb blonde among the first violins. Then later on in the week Jack came over to Blackpool, and brought two very decent men with him, who brought two apple-cheeked girls bursting out of their dresses who claimed to be nineteen. Bunny led us all into a ninepenny dance-hall and Jack and I had a cosy evening drinking coffee in a corner.

The English are jittery again: they can't believe Hitler will really back down. They have a superstitious fear of him, I think: they feel he's a man of destiny or something. And nobody, including myself, wants to fight or spend money defending POLAND. The Poles are even bloodier swine than the Nazis, if possible: more anti-Semitic, just as sheeplike and less efficient.

Mike [Joseph] stays here, and we went out to a newsreel theatre last night and saw some Mickey Mice. Not as good a lot as usual. Mike's just discovered a book his man Falconer contributed to which exists only in the Bibliothèque Nationale in Paris, and he's writing Blunden to see if Blunden thinks he ought to go and look at it, hoping he'll say yes. I shall have to drop Blunden a private note on my own.

I'm awfully tired: slept on a mattress last night that was like a suet pudding. I complained about it this morning, so you can imagine how bad it was. I didn't sleep, as it happens: not a wink. Thrashed around and tried to pacify myself concentrating on you. It wasn't hard to do, at that. Every once in a while I have a horrible claustrophobic feeling as though I were shut up in a cage of air and couldn't even rattle bars. That means I'm missing you again. But it's April. Oh, darling, I'm not much of a hero: I do a lot of whimpering and whining, but I won't dare realize what a nightmare this year has been until it's over. I hope the association between English literature, your absence, and Hitler doesn't remain permanent in my mind, or I shall have to take up pharmacy or green grocering for a career instead. But it won't, of course.

I love you.

The Mellors used to have a cat that once tore up a plant set in earth in a wash tub, brought it in and laid it on the dining room table, in the exact centre, dirt and all.

I love you.

Mike and Dan Devon were caught pissing in the gutter outside Balliol by a very embarrassed policeman, and were fined five shillings each.

I love you.

Bunny has a cousin who carries her baby around in a sort of cradle with hooks, and hangs it on a tree when she's playing tennis.

I love you.

Cambridge won the boat race, very easily.

I love you.

"Those Aryans in Germany," says mother's last letter, "are not marching *forward*."

I love you.

All the way from Blackpool to London on the train I saw sheep and little baby lambs, some hardly bigger than squirrels.

I love you.

Norrie.

1 Jack Mason received a third in his Oxford exams in 1939.

254. HKF to NF [*Toronto*]
April 5. 1939.

My dearest: I've just come from looking at a show of Massons put on for my special benefit. Douglas Duncan brought out all the canvases he'd exhibited some weeks ago. They are amazingly good and I'm certainly going to see him next time I go to Ottawa, whenever that may be. André Biéler was in town last Saturday and we had a great sort of chat: I'm invited to stay with them when I go to Kingston. If I weren't saving to come to England I'd make several trips right this spring. Mrs MacAgy is going to New York to-morrow night and she asked me to go along. Our summer is going to be good—it must be, after all the temptation I am withstanding!

I don't know what Hitler is doing at the moment: I gather he is just sulking. Papers are running news of Albania. It was also announced to-day that Iliffe was shot and killed by Arabs in Jerusalem.[1] Did I tell you about lunching with him in Brussels? He was a very nice man and very well liked here—he came here from Cambridge and worked in the museum with Currelly and married someone in Toronto who worked in Hart House when Marge Boultbee did. He left here around 1933 and went to Jerusalem as curator of the museum.

The Senior Dinner was a great success and I had a very good time. Didn't get a chance to drop that hint about next year in the right quarter. Robins asked when you'd be back. Joe Fisher said he'd written to you lately again. Fairley told me on Saturday that Henry [Noyes] has been offered a job out west.[2] I'll send Peggy's [Peggy Roseborough's] address as soon as I can find it. I hope you have a good time in Blackpool. I don't think I shall be leaving town for Easter at all. I really haven't any plans and I have to be here for another Hart House Quartet concert on Easter Sunday.

I haven't anything to say tonight but I thought I'd better send you a line. Mother and I went to the St. Matthew Passion last night.[3] I think it was the best performance I have ever heard. Bill Morton was narrator instead of Eisdell—and he made a glorious job of it. George Lambert was better than last year but that still leaves something to be desired. The choirs were splendid. It seemed to me there was a greater precision and greater control everywhere. I wish you'd been there.

Well, our children's pageant will soon be over and Lismer's visit too, for that matter. He arrives on Monday. I suspect, from what Norah

[McCullough] says—in a letter to her sister, that she won't be back until February. The awkward thing about that is, that I'm afraid we will have learned to do her job by that time, and it won't be much fun stepping down. But we do need her, badly.

Good luck with the work, and enjoy yourself. I don't know whether I'll be seeing you there or here—I simply cannot read what is to happen in the next three months. But take care of yourself, my dear. I am really amazed that it is April, and I love your crossed-off calendar. And I love you.

Helen.

P.S. This is a dull scrawl: I'm all tired out from walking around all morning with an Indian student from Bombay who is visiting here, a girl named Faleeta Coomerappa. I took her round the Gallery and back for lunch to Wymilwood and I did too much standing I guess. So to bed. I'm also looking for houses.

1 H. John Iliffe, British curator of the Palestine Archaeological Museum in Jerusalem, was shot on 5 April; the story was reported the next morning in the *Toronto Daily Star*.
2 Noyes was offered and accepted a job at the University of Manitoba, where he taught for one year.
3 This particular performance of Bach's *St. Matthew Passion* took place at Convocation Hall on 4 April 1939, with "about sixteen soloists and the Conservatory Choir of one hundred and fifty voices" (*Varsity*, 13 March 1939).

255. NF to HKF   London

Postmarked 8 April 1939; addressed to HKF c/o Art Gallery of Toronto, Toronto, Ontario, Canada. The letter mentioned in the second paragraph, which HKF wrote toward the end of March, is missing. Here NF responds to two items in it: $400 for their summer expenses and her remark about Kenneth Maclean.

Sweetheart:

Not much news this time. This is Easter, and I'm full of reminiscences. I can remember an extremely pleasant week-end in Hamilton last Easter, with a beautiful woman who somehow seemed to be the very spirit of spring. She went a little dim in the autumn: some of the radiance is missing—but we old men have our memories. Two years ago I can remember standing in Santa Maria Maggiore, listening to a rapid mumble which Mike [Joseph] said was a Paternoster going by in a cloud of dust. Then I got very heavy in the guts, dashed home at a speed the boys said they had never seen equalled, and shat for two hours.

My chief news is a letter from you. I can't imagine where $400 is coming from, but I have great faith in you. Mike [Joseph] is going to be free between schools and Viva, and I thought we might go to Paris, then to Italy, to see Florence again and take in the Pisa, Siena and Ravenna you missed, then go to Vienna and Munich. Then I could dash off to Oxford and plug for my Viva, leaving you and Mike (whose Viva will be later than mine) to come more slowly up the Rhine, answer my two statutory questions, dash back to Cologne or the Low Countries or wherever you want to be, and go somewhere else. If I take my degree that last week in July I shall have to be in Oxford then too. I don't think Mike would mind going on that trip. As for Rodney [Baine]—well, I've seen his thesis and I suspect it may be keeping him busy, though I hope not. From Ravenna to Vienna takes us through Padua (Giotto and Mantegna) and Venice (gondolas). Oh, darling, I hope it all works out. But every time I get an idea like that somebody like Mussolini gets a very different sort of idea.

Mike keeps working: yesterday we were stuck with Good Friday and couldn't do anything. We tried to go to Canterbury, but there weren't any trains. We've seen a few movies: a lovely ballet-like French thing, with hardly a word spoken, called Sous les Toits de Paris.[1] Blockade,[2] which was pretty hard to take, was on the same programme. Then we saw Disney's Ferdinand,[3] swell but too short, and a grand piece of Hollywood hokum, so obvious it was really funny: Gunga Din.[4] I've been here a week and haven't got in touch with anybody yet. But Henry's [Henry Noyes's] mother-in-law sent me a letter and I shall go to see her. I'm very glad Henry is going to Manitoba. Sorry Maclean is a frost: it'll be impossible to fire him now, owing to [Walter T.] Brown's shrewdness in giving him a permanent appointment right away. It looks as though Joe [Fisher] (who I think really can teach) and I will have a lot of messes to clear up. Wish Henry was staying. I love you.

Norrie.

1 A 1930 French film, directed by René Clair and starring Albert Préjean and Pola Illery.
2 A 1938 United Artists film on the Spanish Civil War, directed by William Dieterle and starring Madeleine Carroll and Henry Fonda.

3 *Ferdinand the Bull*, a 1938 animated short directed by Walt Disney.
4 A 1939 RKO film, directed by George Stevens and starring Cary Grant and Sam Jaffe.

256. HKF to NF   [*Toronto*]
                                                          April 11. 1939.

My dear: It really is grand,—about the date, I mean. I think I wrote
you a measly sort of letter last week and this may not be much better but
I hope you'll forgive it. We're both getting apologetic about letters,—I'm
sure it is a sign that we need to get together a little oftener! It is, suppos-
edly, spring at this point, last Sunday being Easter, and *would* you
believe it? Last night we had a driving snow storm which messed up
traffic everywhere and left the streets slushy and dripping—six inches
of water in the gutters. Ella Martin was quite furious and lost her temper
about the weather. It was so funny we all had to laugh at her. But it has
been a queer Easter week-end. I didn't go anywhere at all, because I had
to work. Thursday night Laure Rièse and I went to see a crazy film
called *Midnight*[1] with Claudette Colbert wearing lovely gowns and having fantastic adventures in Paris. Friday morning I cast about for something to do and someone at breakfast mentioned Henry Noyes. So I
beetled home and 'phoned him up. I went walking in High Park with
him and wound up at his house for lunch. We had a grand walk in the
wind, and looked at the animals and made speculations about the camel
and the llama, and talked about his experiences with the Victoria
League and the Daughters of the Empire in England.[2] His new job is settled and he is very pleased to be going west. He'll be working under
Roy [Daniells] and as he says there is hope for the future since the other
members of the department are nearly retiring age. I told him your
future was by no measure settled and he said he was sure it was—that
when he had gone to see [Walter T.] Brown about a job Brown had said
they'd like very much to have him here but they were expecting you
back. I suppose I should nose around a bit but I'm sure they'll write to
you in their own good time. Hepburn is cutting University grants right
and left this year, which will result in higher fees next year I suppose.
Henry [Noyes] said he thought Maclean a good man, but that he had got
off to a bad start this year with the class which was kicking about him,
that he is more of a recluse than is understood here, and isn't quite used
to the Canadian student. He was doing a number of new courses too.

Mary Louise Clarke told me the other day that she has been thinking fondly of you lately: she'd just finished an essay on Aristotle on the strength of lectures you gave in English to first year. They expect you to take the music group again—in fact Betty [Mihalko] said at the tea that it was *your* group! Betty will probably run it again. Henry goes to England in May. By the way, you might look up his wife if you can—she is in London now. I think you said you had some sort of address.

You mustn't be alarmed about what I say about rooming houses, I won't do anything rash. I was writing out loud, so to speak, and then the idea sounded crazy. I'm looking for a coach-house apartment or a separate flat or an apartment or a very small house. It certainly will be private for I want privacy! For a few hours a week anyway. I'm beginning to feel that you and I have got ourselves involved in a public career that we'll find hard to kick over. I don't think that I shall want to stop working at the Gallery next year: I'm getting ideas about it. And now that I'm learning to speak to crowds is no time to stop. I'd be home shouting in your poor defenceless ear and driving you crazy. Anyway, I'm thinking of a house to live in.[3]

Let's see. On Saturday I wrote letters to people urging them to come to the children's show to-morrow (O.E.A. convention again) I worked until nearly two o'clock and found Mr Hay still adding up columns so I proposed lunch. We went off gaily together in a pouring rain to Angelo's and had beer and those good omelettes they make. And he talked a lot and we're very good friends. I'm getting on very well this year with the men at the Gallery from Baldwin up and down—feminine wiles etc! I went off and had my hair curled then, and that brightened me up too. After dinner I was sitting down to a quiet evening when Earl Birney 'phoned. Said he'd been sick at home with pleurisy and was bothering all his friends. Would I like to come up? So I came up and drank cock-tails with him for the evening and we played the piano to each other—very badly. Esther [Birney] was out and Madge turned up late after a party—did I tell you about Madge? She's a Polish Jewess, a pianist, who is visiting the Birneys this winter, looking for a job here and keeping house for them. She's Ken Johnstone's wife but they are divorced or separated or something. Anyway, she says Ken's mother is very good to her. I came back to the house to find the few remaining students were staging a ghost party. I read them *Lost Hearts*[4] and got them duly scared.

On Sunday afternoon the Hart House Quartet gave its second concert at the Gallery in the Sculpture Court—and we had thirteen hundred and fifty people there!! I was thrilled beyond words. It wasn't over-crowded at all, but people perched on the side of the Court and on the steps and walked in the galleries. Mozart K575, Debussy, Ravel. When the Gallery is crowded the sound carries magnificently. We had people there who'd never heard the Quartet before. Someone asked an old bird how he liked it, and he wrinkled up his owlish old face and growled "Never heard anything like it in my whole life!"

Monday—staff meeting with Lismer who is up to do the lecture to-morrow. He's in very good form and full of ideas. By the way, Eric Brown died last Thursday. I suppose McCurry will go in as director for next year, but you can't tell who will be given the job, what with all the politics around here and there.[5] A.L. [Arthur Lismer] thinks Baldwin will try for it and that they may put Gagnon in. Or try to get W.G. Constable or Alford. Norah [McCullough] is pretty definitely staying until next February at least—her salary has been arranged until then. A.L. tells me of various things working behind the scenes. Baldwin may not be there too long, he evidently isn't as completely secure as I thought. And I know of course that he has been working against Lismer. But A.L. won't be back unless a miracle happens,—however, I'm not surprised at anything anymore.

Oh, I nearly forgot to tell you one of the best jokes. I had lunch with Magda [Arnold] yesterday in a horrid little lunch joint that's opened up on Harbord Street right opposite Roy's [Roy Kemp's] place. Radio and Nickelodeon etc. She has been turned down by the American colleges she applied to,—that's not the joke. But Bert [Arnold] has *bought* a 90 acre farm near Oakville with no buildings on it and run-down soil,— and he is going to put up a house in the spring and farm it himself. He has arranged with a woman and her daughter to keep house and the house plan includes two rooms for these people but none for Magda. She heard about the whole thing indirectly a week or so after the plans were made. He expects to live there and put the children into county schools. Commuting will be necessary, and expensive. Magda doesn't know how she'll finance next year and thinks of living here and going there for weekends. The housekeeper is to have the use of the family living room,—and Magda had no word in the selection of the house-keeper! I haven't heard Bert's side of it but this way it does look pretty hair-brained. By Jove, I do hope you and I will always be on friendly terms, an existence like that seems to be unbearable. And yet they do stay in the same house.

Norrie, my dearest, I hope your work is going well, and I'm glad you're enjoying Blackpool. I've gotten over the Easter holiday now and that is a relief. I'm not miserable, not at all, but I am getting so impatient, sometimes I think I'll burst soon with excitement. If I were told, for instance, that you weren't coming here for six months instead of four—the four that it is at the most—I don't know what I should do. There is so much for us to do, to see, I want to kiss you and hold you tight and not let you go. When I finally do come to you I shall probably hold onto you so fast that we'll have a terrible time in buses and undergrounds, knocking people over and looking too newly-wed for anything. I want always to feel young and excited about you. I think I always shall. We'll always be busy and there'll always be so much to tell each other when we have a little quiet space to stop in. I've written all these pages without mention of the Polish border.[6] Damn the Polish border—I hope they hold off until you finish Oxford, and then you come home. I will not think of anything else. Good-night dearest.

 H.

1 A 1939 Paramount release, directed by Mitchell Leisen and starring, in addition to Claudette Colbert, Don Ameche.
2 The Imperial Order Daughters of the Empire (IODE); see Letter 86, n. 4, and Letter 177, n. 3, above.
3 After their return from Europe the Fryes moved into an apartment at 1574 Bathurst St., where they lived until they bought their house at 127 Clifton Rd. in 1945.
4 A story by M.R. James, published in his Collected Ghost Stories (London: Edward Arnold, 1931).
5 Brown died suddenly on 6 April 1939. By the end of the month H.O. McCurry had been named his replacement.
6 Nine days after the Germans entered Prague, Hitler issued ultimatums to Poland: on 24 March 1939, he demanded, among other things, the city of Danzig. The German invasion of Poland came on 1 September 1939.

257. NF to HKF   London

Postmarked 13 April 1939; addressed to HKF c/o Art Gallery of Toronto, Toronto, Ontario, Canada.

Sweet:

Somehow or other I keep thinking of you, of how much I want to see you and how little I want to do these asinine exams. You seem to me to be getting pretty close, and the closer you get the more restive and impatient I get. April's half over: that just leaves one full month. And if you're really coming across the Atlantic while I'm writing a lot of silly exams it will spread a glow of anticipation over them which perhaps my examiners will mistake for enthusiasm for their questions. June 15 is the day after I finish, so either that or the 16th will be all right. There's a Bodley Club dinner sometime that week I shall have to try to get out of: I'm secretary next term, worse luck.

As soon as Victoria gets around to hiring me they'll presumably start paying me in July, as they did last year, so if you bring all that money over I shan't have to ask for an advance. John Robins tells me I haven't written to Ned [Pratt], which surprises me: I was sure I had. The rape of Albania has changed Mike's [Mike Joseph's] mind about travelling to Germany and Italy,[1] but he'll go anywhere in France with us we want him to, and I may persuade him to take the rest of the trip.

Thanks for the New Yorkers: the cartoons are a bit feebler, but the stories have more variety: fewer reminiscences about eccentric Aunt Emmas. I've just bought George Moore's *Confessions* in the Penguins.[2] He can't write—lived too long in France to learn English, maybe. The world he lived in, with everybody talking endlessly about Ott and life,[3] is more remote from me than Beowulf: it really is. *Why* do people like Henry [Noyes] waste their time on people like that? By the way, if you send any more New Yorkers over, ask for the big stamps, will you? I'm besieged with collectors in Merton.

Mike [Joseph] and I went to Canterbury yesterday. Huge barn of a cathedral: central tower I thought was lovely. I was even more interested in tiny little St. Martin's Church, with its Roman and Saxon and Norman layers.[4] I don't know if you saw it or not: it has a leper squint in the west wall, where they could see the altar, and an excommunicate's squint on the side, where they couldn't. I'm still pretty suspicious of Tristram, but I liked his Canterbury things better.[5]

A news reel is advertising a March of Time film called *Europe in Review* as "the best gangster film since *Scarface*."[6] I met a friend of mine[7] at the B.M. today who is lecturing at Glasgow: he was at Merton two years ago. Said he was just back from France and had no watch because he got home from a party one night and wound his place-card and threw his wrist-watch in the fire. It gets you that way. He's tied up with a French girl but is rather leery of her because she's Royalist and pro-Nazi. I don't know why men bother with women like that: I certainly wouldn't marry anybody unless she were beautiful and intelligent and accomplished and sensible and virtuous and—what else are you darling?

Norrie.

1 The Italian Fascist government, in violation of its repeated assurances not to interfere with Albania's sovereignty, invaded that country on 7 April 1939, and quickly crushed the Albanian forces.
2 Moore's *Confessions of a Young Man* (1888) was first issued as a Penguin paperback in 1939.
3 "Art and life": NF is affecting a British accent.
4 Canterbury cathedral, constructed over the course of four centuries, is 514 ft. in length; its great central tower, the Bell Harry Tower, was erected in 1495. The quaint little Church of St. Martin, which dates from pre-Saxon times, lies on a hill three-quarters of a mile to the east of the cathedral.
5 NF is referring to the art historian Ernest William Tristram, whose speciality was medieval wall paintings. His study of Canterbury was published as *The Paintings of Canterbury Cathedral* (Canterbury: Friends of Canterbury Cathedral, 1935), a small booklet issued in numerous subsequent editions.
6 *The March of Time* was a newsreel series. *Scarface* was a 1932 Universal film, directed by Howard Hawks, about the life and death of a Chicago gangster in the 1920s.
7 Jim Arnott.

258. NF to HKF   Paddington

Postmarked 17 April 1939; addressed to HKF c/o Art Gallery of Toronto, Toronto, Ontario Canada.

Dearest:

I sent Miss Whinney a note, and a card came from "A. Duddington" to say she'd gone on her vacation. Apparently A. Duddington didn't recognize my name, as the card was addressed to Miss H.N. Frye. I don't seem to have any luck with that woman. I went to see the Burnetts last night. I can't seem to talk to them on anything but politics these days, and as I don't know anything about politics I doubtless sound pretty green to them. Amy's left them and they have a refugee maid— nice little girl: well, she's a married woman, but she acts a bit kiddish and nearly drives the immaculate Edith crazy with her slack down-at- the-heels Austrian *laissez faire.* Did I tell you about meeting Jim Arnott, the Merton man now at Glasgow? He told me about a friend of his who had a job during the last war I want for the next one: typing out fancy imaginary menus for the British Army and then releasing them in the trenches when a strong west wind was blowing. I guffawed and said I thought even a German could see through a trick like that, whereupon two Jewish refugees at the next table glared at me.

Don't keep looking at newspapers to see whether it's safe to come to Europe this summer or you'll never get here. It's the newspaper's business to scare you into buying copies. If I have the situation at all figured out, there isn't any danger of war unless somebody loses their head and blunders into it. That may happen, but in the meantime the ruling class of Europe knows that war means revolution. There are national rivalries all right, but the big shots behind the dictatorial and democratic dummies are an international unit and know exactly what they want. And I don't think they want a war: they can sell armaments all right by pretending it's around the corner. Of course eventually it will come, unless Japan collapses in a few months, but not for a bit.

Then I went to see Elizabeth [Fraser] and had quite a good time with her, for once, although as usual I stayed about fifteen minutes too long. We went to see a Rouault show at Zwemmer's: she's much more interested in contemporary painting now than she used to be—and then we went to her room and she showed me two sets of drawings: one to Marvell and one to Plato's Phaedrus. Grand stuff they were, too: I'm quite right about her ability, and she's come a long way from the swans.[1] She has an uncanny sense of colour and rhythm, and when she brings off a facial expression it's just about perfect. She'd just come from Paris, where she'd spent a couple of days calmly wandering into various people's offices, without appointment, and showing them her drawings. One was Ambroise Vollard.[2] Just like that. Vollard said "but these are very good," quite enthusiastically, the others said very interesting. The trouble was she hadn't any clear idea why she was showing them to them. But she had a good time, and if she can find an intelligent beautiful-book publisher she may land something.

I went to see Mrs. Sirnis, Henry's [Henry Noyes's] mother-in-law, & Gertrude tonight. Gertrude is a very cheerful & pleasant girl—the large watery type that looks T.B.ish. I shouldn't have expected her as Henry's wife, quite, but I think she's intelligent enough to hold up her job and single-minded enough to help him get along with people. Her mother is a very cultured and intelligent woman, with an enormous library of piano music I spent the evening exploring. Far more sophisticated in her tastes than her daughter. I liked them very much, and would have liked them even if Mrs. Sirnis hadn't given me three volumes of Elizabethan music.

Well, it's next morning, and I must catch an Oxford train. I love you.

Norrie.

1 Elizabeth Fraser had developed a swan motif throughout her illustrations for Pan. Aristophron's *Plato's Academy*. See Letter 162, n. 3, above.
2 A French art dealer and publisher (1865–1939); he championed the avant-garde (Cézanne, Matisse, Picasso, and others) in the late nineteenth and early twentieth centuries.

259. HKF to NF   [*Toronto*]
                                                                April 18th 1939.

My dearest: Two letters came from you to-day—April 4th and 8th. Also a long one from Lismer who went to Ottawa after leaving us and ran into Alford and all his students who went there to be lectured at in front of the pictures. A.L. [Arthur Lismer] is definitely in the dumps: he knows Baldwin doesn't want him back, and I know it. I thought there might be hope but Baldwin sat and lied to me yesterday—or was it this morning? (I've had such a long day I can't remember, being almost completely exhausted.) He told me how unfair it was to New York for us to ask Lismer to come back etc. He *is* such a yellow-livered cur that sometimes I nearly wonder why I consider staying with the job. I wish you were here to read this letter from A.L. and tell me not to get in a stew. To-day has come all in a rush. In the first place it poured as hard as it possibly could. There were your two letters waiting for me at the Gallery and I was jubilant. Then I had to go to the Faculty Women's luncheon at Wymilwood. Magda [Arnold] wrapped herself around my shoulders,—threw herself around my neck is putting it mildly—when she heard I'd had a letter from you, and had to hear what was in it. Do give me bits of quotable news for Magda, will you? Mrs Lane and Mrs Line and Mrs [Walter T.] Brown and Miss Rowell all asked for you, and so on. Mrs Brown said it would be so nice having you back next year—and I asked her whether Dr Brown had written to you, but of course she didn't know. Perhaps I was wrong to do that but I'm sure it didn't matter much. Kay Riddell sat next to me—she hasn't got acquainted with Do Fisher and is a bit dubious. Do Fisher is very friendly with Mrs Trethewey who looks a perfect hick— really, some of the new people on the staff this year *are* a queer lot. The people in the Oriental languages department for instance. Mrs Young is a large sized horse and she brought a larger one to lunch who spoke Persian. Kay [Riddell] tells me that Bert [Arnold] was in to see them one night lately and told Jerry [Riddell] all his troubles, and Jerry did not pass them on to Kay, but Magda assumed that she knew. Magda is quite evidently looking for a room for next year, so they seem to have decided to separate.[1] Kay is a little annoyed at the way they both separately make cynical remarks about the Riddell state of bliss. I haven't seen Bert for ages to talk to, so all I've heard is Magda's story, which I told you.

Here is a really cheerful piece of news for you. Next year Don Masters is going to Manitoba and Ernie Gould will be here to finish his thesis. He will be here in the spring when term's over I think.

Peggy Roseborough's address is 408 Elm Street, Greencastle, Indiana.

Norrie, your trip sounds wonderful and somewhat impossible, unless the war racket dies down. You wrote that last letter the day before Easter—the day after Albania was seized. I don't know where we shall be in two months' time, but Italy doesn't sound as if it would be very hospitable to English tourists. With America taking an active part, perhaps Hitler will back down. We evidently have to wait a week for his pleasure. And the Star is full of talk of gas masks and the fact that food tickets are all ready in England. And the IODE have rushed in and listed what they could do in the way of running ambulances.

Norrie, a while ago I sent your mother a handkerchief which we meant to send long ago—the one you bought at the University Settlement. And I got to talking the way I do, and told her what a great deal I think of you, and the students too,—I was feeling a little lonely and the way I love you sort of crept into it. I thought she wouldn't mind—and then I didn't know whether she would. I haven't heard from her lately and wondered whether she had been sick. After all, it wouldn't annoy a mother—your mother—to have me tell her how wonderful I think her son is, would it?

Underhill has just returned from a holiday to find all this fuss happened in his absence.[2] No news yet. Eric Havelock brought an uncle of Ellen's to see the Gallery this afternoon, a prosperous Harley Street doctor, very nice.

Daddy goes to Winnipeg to-night to the lip-reading conference. I love your letters so, do write when you can.

Helen.

1 Magda and Bert Arnold did separate in 1940, and soon after getting her Ph.D. in psychology, Magda accepted an appointment at Wellesley College (Magda B. Arnold to RDD, 12 March 1994).
2 See Letter 262, n. 1, below.

260. HKF to NF   [*Toronto*]
                                                                April 31. 1939.

My dear: Sunday night in Oaklawn with several cases of jitters and I'm trying to keep the bloody house quiet while someone is entertaining some goddam woman with a crying baby in her room, and the girl on duty is sulky about being on duty etc.

NB! Look here, will you please send back my passport as soon as possible, registered? I have to turn it in when I get another, which I am trying to do right away. I think there is time if you hurry.

Here are the alternatives re boats:

New York Queen Mary sailing June 7th arriving June 12th at Southampton, or a German boat the New York—which sails on the 8th. Others get me there June 19th.

Montreal The best is the Empress of Britain sailing 10th arriving 16th. There are no end of boats arriving June 19th, which is too late for the party: I wish you'd make up your mind about that party—I suppose I'd better bring along clothes for it in case.

The snag just now is that I'd like to visit the Lismers before I go, then that means New York which means arriving June 12th—too early. If you didn't care about that and didn't mind if I spent a couple of days in London by myself then that would be all right I suppose. On the whole the 16th is much better, and if I find the Lismers are going away or anything then I'll come on the Empress via Montreal. Don't worry anyway, just send along that passport and I'll turn up. I've got some extra time off from the Gallery in August. Counting roughly $200 off for return fare I'll come with around $250. Let me know whether I should borrow more—you'd better figure it out for both of us because I don't know how you stand. I can borrow on an insurance policy of mother's if necessary $50 or more—but I'd rather not. I can stay away until the last week in August, and I'm sure I could borrow from the Gallery if we need more. But I want to do it before I go.

These long distance arrangements are such a nuisance, but I think that's all I want to know just now. I'm going to get out of this house with Rièse to have some supper—I'm hungry.

This is a lousy letter.

I've now eaten and discussed the evils of residence life at this time of year with Rièse who feels more strongly about it than I do. So we both feel better.

I'm still looking for a place to live in, but if I don't find anything extraordinary then we'll get an apartment like what we had before.

Pratt had a party on Saturday for Henry Noyes. It was awfully nice. Robins asked about you and I said I'm coming over to get you. I sat next to Maclean, whom I don't like a great deal, but perhaps I just haven't seen enough of him. Rièse says her students have complained about him too. Did I tell you that Rièse tore the ligaments of her legs— busted up both knees, skiing in February, and spent about seven weeks in the Infirmary? She still limps, and the other day she banged a knee again and put something wrong. The doctor says she'll never be able to ski again.

I hope your work is going well, and I'm feeling most apologetic about this cranky note I'm sending—it's just spring exasperation. And I love you like anything and will write again in a day or so.

H.

261. HKF to NF   [*Toronto*]
                                                                   May 12 1939.

The postal telegram (PLT) mentioned in the first sentence is missing.

My dear: I sent you a PLT because yesterday I discovered that the Georgic was sailing from New York on the 10th and would fit into my plans very well. I'll just wait for your answer and the passport, and if all is well I'll come on the Georgic. I don't really want to hang around London waiting for you, although if you want me to come earlier,—on the Queen Mary on the 12th, so as not to hold up your plans for getting to the continent as soon as possible—send me a PLT to that effect and I'll switch to the Queen Mary. I'll have enough work to do to keep me busy in London for two days anyway: I'm ordering a lot of lantern slides from the Courtauld Institute and I'll have to see Miss Whinney about that, probably. I haven't written much because I'm working like the dickens trying to get away in time. At that, I'm scared that something may turn up to prevent my going—however, I shall get away. A matter of planning next year's programme ready for the printer earlier than it's ever been done before—it is to be ready before I leave, complete with lectures and class plans etc. It's crazy really, because the Educational Committee just does not seem to meet, and we're just as we were.

However, I expect to see Lismer in New York for several days—I'll probably go on the bus or drive down with Elizabeth Eedy. I haven't made any arrangements about a flat yet but we may have to leave that until we get back. And I haven't sent you any money, hoping that you could borrow enough until I get there and that the college will do something or other. I said in the PLT to let me know about that—I should hear from you in a few days. Do you think you will need your summer suit? I rather doubt it myself but you let me know if you want me to bring it.

I want to come to Southampton and I'd love you to meet me there. But it would be too bad for you to miss the Bodley Club dinner: that's why I thought the 18th might hit it right.

I am in a state of feverishly counting money and trying to get together three issues of *The Forum* before I go. June is done and I've got some more drawings coming along.

The newspapers are feeding us stuff these days about the royal family, enough to sicken anyone. They'll go past here May 22nd and the term is over early on that account.[1] I'll probably go home for a week then: if you say COME ON THE 12TH I'll be over like a shot. It is whichever is best for you. I can stay away until the end of August nearly and I suppose I might as well get over as soon as I can. The Queen Mary is more expensive but it means I'd have six days more there.

My letters seem to be one long series of travel bulletins these days. It is the winding up of a season for me too. I hope your work is not making you miss the spring—it has been glorious here, suddenly.

If I come on the Queen Mary it will be just one month from to-day. Or else five days later. Which shall it be? We'll have to get our heads together in earnest about France and Germany because I haven't got round to thinking about that part of it.

I hope you simply mop them up at examination time. It sounds like a horrible grind from what I hear. Anyhow, I'm hoping for you, and I'm terribly much in love with you.

Helen.

1   In May and June of 1939, George VI, the first reigning sovereign to visit Canada, toured
the country with Queen Elizabeth, their purpose being primarily to secure Canadian
support for Britain at a time when war in Europe loomed on the horizon; on 19 May he
gave royal assent to several Canadian bills in the Senate chamber, including the signing
of a trade agreement with the United States; an index of the king and queen's success in
invoking pro-British sentiment was the enthusiasm of the large crowds that poured
forth to greet them. On 22 May, the king and queen were welcomed at the U of T's Hart
House by Warden J.B. Bickersteth and H.J. Cody, president of the university.

262. NF to HKF   Oxford

Postmarked 15 May 1939; addressed to HKF c/o Art Gallery of Toronto,
Toronto, Ontario, Canada.

Sweetheart:

This is Monday morning, and I still haven't heard. Perhaps you'd better drop in and see Robins before you leave, but I think everything will
be all right. We could probably live quietly in Paris, seeing what we
liked, quite easily on your money alone (I'm quite shameless about living off you, but I always was) until my Viva, even if I couldn't raise any
more for a trip later. I'm beginning to wonder if [Walter T.] Brown isn't
being a subtle statesman and waiting to see whether I pass my exams or
not. I think we'd better stay close to Oxford until the viva and remain
either in England or France: I've grown a little more apprehensive about
war scares lately. After that, we can collect all the money we can and
take the big trip I planned. Of course I'll cable the minute I hear from the
College. Your passport should be there now. I think you've got enough
money for a month. We're not going to the party: none of my friends are
going: only poisonous public-school snobs I've barely spoken to. I admit
I don't sound very efficient, but with the College ignoring me my hands
are a bit tied. I shall finish this term owing Rodney [Baine] £20. That's
how I stand at present.

I think I did the right thing in writing to Robins rather than Brown,
but I shall have to write Brown if I don't hear soon.

Jack Garrett is getting hysterical, the way Roy [Kemp] was, and has
put off Schools a year. It must be something in the Canadian temperament. He's been worried over a complicated manoeuvre with two
women he rather messed up, and has got the wind up over schools. He
should go right away to Paris: I'm a great believer in Paris.

The Warden asked some men to dinner and with them went a man called Meredith, who was drunk, and, when he was served port, lifted his glass and shouted "Save you, sir!" After dinner, still drunk, he started embracing Lady Miles, which I don't believe the Warden himself could do if he were sober. When the other men rose to leave, Alan whimpered "Please can't I stay a little longer?" and stayed for one minute and 45 seconds longer.

What can I say about your coming over? Just a month and I'll be seeing you again. I suspect that those few days between schools and June 18 I'll be climbing telegraph poles and barking like a dog.

Let me know how that Grube–Underhill fracas turned out.[1] I suppose that with everybody booming imperial loyalties and so on they thought a few displays of terrorism would be a good move. Darling, I want to get a novel written and published. I've got the stuff of an unusually good writer in me, and the sooner I get established as one the sooner I can start defending people like Grube and making fools of people like Drew. I know how to make fools of people, and I don't want to be absolutely dependent on a sycophantic college and a Chancellor with brown stains on his arse for my living, or my reputation.

Oh, darling, I want to see you so much.

Norrie.

1 Prof. George Grube of the classics department at Trinity College was reported as having said that money allotted to Canadian defence was "a waste of public funds in the interests of British imperialism" at a CCF Convention on 7 April 1939, and Prof. Frank Underhill of the history department at the U of T was found to have made the statement in his published writings that "the poppies blooming in Flanders field have no further interest for us," with the result was that there were calls in the legislature for both of them to be fired. Neither of them was.

263. HKF to NF   [*Toronto*]
                                                                          May 16. 1939.

My dear: I have been expecting an answer all week to my PLT but it hasn't come: just your letter written May 4th came, but you evidently had not got my last then—asking for the passport. If you can't find it then I have to swear in front of a lawyer that I had one which has been mis-laid but will be returned when found etc. I do hope you find it. As for the rest of my message, I expect you haven't had any news yourself. But tonight I 'phoned Jerry [Riddell] about dropping in to see them, and as Kay was out I didn't go, but I had a very cheering conversation with him. He says that once a week he lays his ear to [Walter T.] Brown's keyhole and hears a few things. At any rate, to-day he overheard a conversation between Brown and Robins where Johnnie put it up to the Principal in words of one syllable the dilemma you are in about the appointment. I don't know what you wrote him but I gather that your poor wife is debating whether or not she can possibly afford to get over to be with you and it all depends on your appointment. So Brown said of course it was understood that you were coming back but that he couldn't put anything definite yet until a Board meeting[1] or something but on no account was I to hesitate in going to meet you because all would be well. Jerry says that J.D. [Robins] is likely to tell me himself and in that case I'm to look very surprised! There are times when I think I shall have to have twins to keep you right with the Principal!

Jerry also says that the Commemoration Ball is a marvellous spectacle and well worth going to if you can forget all the other things you might be doing with two guineas apiece. But once you get busy on the champagne you don't worry about that anymore. On the whole, I rather think it would be fun—if some of your friends are going too, and I'm sure I'd flirt with you most happily until morning. Of course if I arrive on the 18th and dance 'till dawn on the 19th I'll look like the devil afterwards: you'll have to take that chance.

It's getting late and *The Forum* is being made up a little early this time. Lou Morris trots around bringing me cuts and proofs and stray letters answering all the ones I sent out, and I get some pretty queer drawings sometimes. Jackson gave us one which Lou seems to feel rather wary about—he's bringing it up now.[2]

Preparations for the King and Queen: In Quebec they had elaborate meals all prepared but the boat is late and the food had to be eaten so the reporters are dining off the food of kings. Victoria College is issuing tickets to the staff etc for window space in the Vic buildings and they are issuing invitations to married couples to move into Gandier House for the night before so they won't have to worry about getting in in the morning. The college grounds will be closed at 10.30 and the procession isn't until 2.30! So we all have to picnic on the premises. The thing that worries us most just now is that perhaps the Americans will design hats like the Queen's and try to make us all wear them.

I love you!

Helen.

1   After the board of regents met on 20 June, Chancellor Edward W. Wallace wrote to NF,
    appointing him to the permanent staff of VC. NF received the letter when he was in
    London, and he replied to Wallace from Paris on 22 July, saying "I shall look forward to
    going home in the autumn. I have always enjoyed teaching at Victoria: I know the staff,
    I know what sort of students go there, I know something of the religious and historical
    traditions of the College, and would rather work there than anywhere else." E.W. Wal-
    lace's General Correspondence (89.130V, box 26, file 297) in the UCC/VUA.
2   A.Y. Jackson's drawing, *Arctic Lake*, appeared in the *Canadian Forum*, 19 (June 1939), 85.

264. NF to HKF   Oxford
                                                                    1939 May 16

Telegram; addressed to HKF at Art Gallery Toronto.

I THINK EVERYTHING ALL RIGHT YOUVE ENOUGH MONEY
PASSPORT DOUBTLESS THERE NOW LOVE

NORRIE

265. HKF to NF   [*New York*]
                                                     Wednesday. [*7 June 1939*]

NF's letter of 24 May, which HK mentions in the first sentence of the present
letter, is missing; HKF may have left it in New York or taken it to England
with her. Lismer, who paid HKF's expenses for the week, and A.Y. Jackson met
her at the train on 5 June; they looked for the Rivera murals without success,
visited the Associated American Artists on Fifth Avenue, the Metropolitan and
Frick Museums, the Museum of Modern Art, and took in other New York
sights.

My dear: Your letter of May 24 was sent on to me here yesterday: the
Queen Mary goes out to-day and I'll try to get a money order or something off to you. My money is all in sterling travellers checks—I'll send
you about 10 pounds if they'll do it at the post-office, otherwise I'll just
have to send you half that out of the American money I have now. I
have a little over forty-five pounds altogether. I 'phoned Robins before I
left and he said that Board meeting is this month and the year begins in
July—we'll just hang on—but I'll get mother to cash in that insurance
policy and we'll pay it back in the fall one of the first things we do.

I'm staying with Marjorie [Lismer] in the graduate house at Columbia and A.L. [Arthur Lismer] is showing me around New York like streak lightning. Jackson is here and Marius Barbeau. We ran into Baldwin at Bignoni's but we didn't want to. Have got to go to the post-office.

I love you

Helen.

266. NF to HKF   Waterloo Station, London
                                                            17 June 39

Telegram; addressed to HKF on the SS Georgic, *to await her arrival at the* Southampton *Docks.*

WELCOME TO ENGLAND I LOVE YOU WAITING IMPATIENTLY FOR YOU AT WATERLOO STATION = NORRIE

Appendix

Directory of People Mentioned in the Correspondence

For abbreviations used in the directory see pages vii–ix, this volume.

Abbott, E. Bea. Lecturer in French, VC, 1933–36: 616

Abercrombie, Lascelles (1881–1938). Goldsmith's reader in English at Merton College: 611

Aberhart, William. Radio evangelist, known as "Bible Bill"; premier of Alberta, 1935–43; headed the world's first Social Credit governing body: 622

Adair, Gladys. Friend of Vera Frye: 834

Adam, Alex. VC 3T3; dropped out in first year; married Dorothy Midgley: 219

Adam, W.P. Chairman of the Swift Current presbytery and supervisor of student ministers during NF's time on the mission field: 322

Adaskin, Frances. Wife of Harry Adaskin: 219

Adaskin, Harry. Violinist in the Hart House String Quartet; taught at the TCM in the early 1940s: 219

Addams, Jane (1860–1935). Social reformer and feminist; in 1899 founded Hull House in Chicago: 546–7

Addison, Margaret. Dean of residence, Annesley Hall, VC, 1903–32; dean of women, 1920–32: 69, 642, 643

Addy, P.C. Exchange student in residence at EC, 1933–35: 438

Adeney, Christopher. Marcus and Jeanne Adeney's son: 219

Adeney, Jeanne. Wife of Marcus Adeney: 34, 61, 109, 218–19

Adeney, Marcus. Cellist in the TSO, 1928–48; teacher at the TCM: 34, 41, 46, 61, 67, 75, 109, 218–19, 351, 601, 709, 802, 814, 844

Affleck, George A. VC 3T5: 868

Alexander, Howard. VC 3T3: 174

Alford, John. Professor of fine arts, U of T: 474, 475n. 3, 491, 616, 617, 619, 638, 639–40, 669, 670, 671, 685, 694, 707, 716, 807, 834, 888

Allen, Thomas John. Merton College, 1938–40; from Peterborough, Ont.: 780, 797, 805

ing their student days; taught NF ballroom dancing during their freshman
year: 19, 25, 40, 173, 175, 209, 219–20, 619

Comfort, Charles (1900–94). Portrait, landscape, and mural painter; director of
the department of mural painting at the OCA; taught at the U of T, 1938–60,
when he became director of the NGC in Ottawa: 75, 82, 704, 786, 787, 788, 844

Comfort, Louise. Wife of Charles Comfort: 807

Conklin, Nora. Sister of Bill Conklin; studied at the Julliard School of Music: 202,
209

Conklin, William T. (Bill). VC 3T3; married Ida May Clare: 30, 76, 158, 167, 198,
209, 272, 356, 461, 749, 760

Constable, William G. Assistant director of the National Gallery, London,
and director of the Courtauld Institute of Art; made a lecture tour across
Canada in 1933: 234, 304, 330, 383, 390, 391, 408, 419, 474, 602, 611, 694, 806,
807, 888

Constantine, Maud. Young woman HK meets aboard the *Ausonia* in September
1934: 337, 240

Cook, Alta Lind. VC 1T3; member of the French department at VC: 585, 704

Copp, John (Johnny). EC 3E5; B.A., Mount Allison University; married Jean
Evans: 179, 304, 315, 322, 323, 462

Cormier, Mr. Neighbour of NF in Moncton; an anticlerical rationalist: 521–2, 532,
547

Couratin, Rev. Arthur Hubert. Junior chaplain, Merton College, 1936–39:
825–6

Courtice, Rody. Toronto artist; graduate of OCA, where she taught, 1922–26;
worked with HK at the AGT: 552–3

Cowan, Jean. Membership secretary at the AGT: 583

Cowan, Tillie. Instructor for children's work at the AGT: 607, 819, 866

Cox, Lucy. Musician; friend of HK and Roy Kemp: 35, 61, 626

Cragg, Arthur Richard (Art). VC 3T3 and EC 3E7; married Florence Clare; performed NF and HK's wedding ceremony; brother of Laurence H. Cragg: 11,
19, 21, 24, 29–30, 50, 51, 66, 76, 84, 99, 121, 166, 169, 198, 199, 209–10, 219, 221,
225, 266, 272, 279, 286, 298, 299, 303, 356, 364, 367, 385, 386, 394, 396, 424, 426–7,
439, 459, 461, 462, 476–7, 594, 596, 617, 749, 760, 808, 811–12, 861–2, 871, 877

Cragg, Laurence H. (Laurie). VC 3T4; taught at McMaster University; later
became president of Mount Allison University; brother of Art Cragg: 176

Craig, Eleanor. Peggy Craig's younger sister: 123, 124, 136

Craig, Peggy (Peg). Vera Frye's roommate during her years in Chicago: 100, 105,
135, 136, 139–40, 834

Crawford, Thomas James (Tommy) (1877–1955). Choirmaster, teacher, and composer; conductor of the VC Music Club, 1927–42: 323, 600, 602

Crawford, Tom. Schoolmate of NF: 721

385, 426, 435, 443, 468, 495, 607, 624, 625, 691, 695, 698, 705, 707, 739, 747, 751, 754, 760, 765, 854

Davis, Ken. Wealthy neighbour of the Kemps at their Gordon Bay summer cottage: 128, 129, 144

Davis, Robert Tyler. Director of education at the Albright Art Gallery, Buffalo, N.Y.: 617, 640, 872–3

Davison, Earl. VC 3T2: 151, 175

Davison, Margaret (Marg). VC 3T3: 33, 117, 118, 175

Deakin, Lucy. Friend of HK; they were roommates at the Universal Exhibition in Brussels in 1935: 456, 470

de Kresz, Geza (1882–1959). Hungarian-Canadian violinist for the Hart House String Quartet, 1923–35; husband of Norah de Kresz: 362, 432

de Kresz, Norah Drewett (1882–1960). Anglo-Canadian pianist; taught at the TCM, 1928–35; wife of Geza de Kresz, with whom she often gave concerts: 219, 356, 362, 432

de la Roche, Mazo (1885–1961). Canadian novelist: 501

Dennison, Ruby. Violinist and cellist; taught at the Danard Conservatory; played violin with HK and Marcus Adeney in a 1929 recital at the HCM; Harold Kemp's cello teacher: 35, 46, 61, 129, 753

Denton, Frank. Member of the council of the AGT: 720

Devon, Dan. New Zealand student at Merton College; friend of Mike Joseph and roommate of Guy Nunn: 804–5, 840, 882

DeWitt, N.W. Professor of Latin at VC: 353, 377

Dickinson. One of the boarders at 90 Guilford St., London, where NF stayed in September 1936; attaché to the British consulate in Beruit: 567, 568, 570, 576, 577, 578, 590, 677

Dillon, Eleanor. VC 4T1; married Donald Ewing: 802

Dingman, Frank. Brother of Ruth Dingman: 107

Dingman, Ruth Gordon. VC 3T3; married Andrew Hebb in 1934: 21, 66, 107, 179, 204, 236, 270, 272, 283, 298, 371, 698, 712, 749

Dodgson, Campbell (1867–1948). Keeper of the prints and drawings at the BM; an Albrecht Dürer scholar and connoisseur of early prints: 406

Downard, William J. Building superintendent at the AGT: 853, 857

Draper, Ruth (1884–1956). American actress and monologist: 644

Drever, Dorothy (Dot). VC 3T3: 158, 272, 317, 320, 345, 355, 360, 373, 385, 386, 393, 394, 399, 426, 429, 444, 446, 450, 461, 462, 478–9, 487, 497, 534, 537, 540, 541, 552, 556, 557, 558, 563, 577, 580, 584, 592, 595, 596, 626, 644, 660, 667, 673–4, 685, 697, 710, 732, 739, 749, 759–60, 813

Drever, William and Lillie. Members of the Carnagh community in southwestern Sask. when NF was a student minister there: 321

Drew, George A. (1894–1973). Lawyer, ardent Conservative politician, and premier of Ontario, 1943–48; married Fiorenza Johnson: 559, 899

Fair, Harold. VC 3T4; editor, *Acta Victoriana*, 1933–34: 173

Fairley, Barker (1887–1986). Member of German department, U of T, 1915–57; cofounder of the *Canadian Forum* and an early friend of the Group of Seven; a painter himself and an authority on Goethe: 559, 600, 601, 685, 705, 795, 796, 814, 820, 854, 865, 872

Fairley, Joan. Staff lecturer in the Saturday morning classes at the AGT; daughter of Barker Fairley: 626, 672, 684, 685, 751, 754

Fairley, Tom, Son of Barker Fairley: 626

Fenwick, Kathleen (1901–73). Curator of prints and drawings at the NGC: 191, 194, 196, 204, 205, 212, 228–9, 247, 248, 254, 349

Fidler, Frank. EC 3E4; tutor in Gate House, VC, 1933–34: 292

Finch, Robert D.C. Scholar, artist, and modernist poet; taught French at the U of T, 1928–68: 379, 690–1

Fisher, Do. Wife of Joe Fisher: 893

Fisher, Joseph (Joe). Member of the English department at VC; appointed in 1937, and after a stint in the military, became chair of the department in 1945: 852, 871, 877, 883, 885

Flavelle, Sir Joseph Wesley (1858–1939). Canadian meatpacker, financier, and philanthropist: 873

Fletcher, Rev. Ronald F.W.H. Tutor in English at St. Edmund Hall, Oxford: 789, 790

Forbes, Elizabeth (Lib). VC 3T3; married Earl Lautenslager: 217

Forbes, Jessie. An "occasional student" at VC during HK and NF's fourth year: 318

Forbes, Kenneth (b. 1892). Canadian figure and portrait painter: 796

Ford, Norma H.C. Acting dean of woman, VC, 1933–34: 304, 802

Foreman, Phyllis. VC 3T3: 106, 651

Forward, Dorothy. Don in the women's residences at VC: 627, 642, 656, 667, 668

Fosbery, Ernest G. (1874–1960). Portrait painter; studied in Paris, and lived in Ottawa after 1911: 204

Fosdick, Harry Emerson (1878–1969). U.S. preacher and author: 203

Fowler, Daniel (1810–94). British artist who came to Canada in 1843 and painted natural subjects and landscapes after the manner of the French Impressionists and Cézanne: 707

Fraser, Elizabeth. Canadian book designer living in London; friend of Norah McCullough; befriended NF when he was at Oxford: 604, 610, 616, 619, 622–3, 632, 635–6, 645, 646, 652–3, 656, 658–9, 662, 664, 667, 675, 680–1, 688, 692–3, 699–700, 701, 708, 712–13, 739, 743, 756–7, 762, 769, 790, 796, 827–8, 842, 870, 879, 892

Freeland, Esther Margaret (Joby). VC 3T3; married Daniel Chittenden; friend of Lois Hampson: 174, 175, 263, 496

Fretz, Anna. U of T 3T3; graduated in household science: 118

Freyhan, Robert. Young German scholar who emigrated to England in the 1930s; later published on medieval art: 348, 383

Frye, Catharine Mary Maud Howard (Cassie). NF's mother; the fourth child of Eratus Seth Howard, a Methodist minister, and Harriet Hersey; born near Kingston, Ont., on 30 August 1870 (the same day NF's father was born); died in Moncton, N.B., 24 November 1940: 25, 30, 39–40, 42, 51–2, 112, 154, 170, 198, 268, 375, 522, 525, 526–7, 528–9, 531, 533, 547, 566, 666, 743, 744, 821, 822, 871, 894

Frye, Elizabeth. *See* Eedy, Elizabeth

Frye, Eratus Howard. NF's older brother, born on 29 March 1899; killed on 18 August 1918 by artillery fire near Amiens, France: 522, 837

Frye, Herman Edward. NF's father; hardware salesman; born at Windsor Mills, Que., on 30 August 1870 (the same day NF's mother was born), and died on 15 December 1959, at Evergreen Park, Ill.: 68, 154, 160, 169–70, 268, 361–2, 375, 522, 526

Frye, Vera. NF's sister; born in Lowell, Mass., 25 December 1900; taught school in Chicago most of her life; died in Los Angeles, California, on Good Friday, 1966: xvii, 29, 95n. 2, 101, 105, 119, 123, 124, 127, 135, 136, 139, 142, 147, 148, 167, 361, 375, 377, 468, 546–7, 714–15, 744, 833–4, 844

Fuchs, Albert. German friend whom Roy Kemp met at Camp Franklin; they played music together and studied with Norah Drewett de Kresz: 642, 733

Gabrilowitsch, Ossip (1878–1936). Conductor of the Detroit Symphony Orchestra and distinguished pianist: 201

Gagnon, Clarence A. (1881–1942). Canadian painter, etcher, and illustrator: 888

Gandier, Alfred. Principal of EC, 1928–32: 25

Garratt, Gloria. Adopted daughter of Elthea (Dolly) Howard, the older sister of NF's mother, and Rufus Garratt; after Elthea Howard's death, raised by NF's Aunt Hatty Layhew: 533, 552, 682, 722

Garrett, John C. (Jack). Rhodes scholar from Alberta; Merton College, 1937–40; B.A., Oxford, 1940; M.A., 1943; taught at the University of Alberta, the U of T, and Canterbury College in New Zealand: 829, 898

Gee, Eric. Fiancé of Marg Torrance: 557

Gibbon, John Murray (1875–1952). Publicity manager for the CPR and founding president of the Canadian Authors Association: 176

Gibson, Georgina. Friend of Harold Kemp: 666–7

Gillespie, Elizabeth. VC 3T3: 565, 596

Glaves, Emily. Stenographer in the VU library: 106

Glover, T.R. SCM official: 480

Godlonton, Charles and Jean. Members of the Carnagh parish in southwestern Sask. when NF was a student minister there; Charles was a cousin of Margaret Neely; Jean played the piano for church services at the Carnagh school: 253

Goodier, Marina. Ontario painter and watercolourist; studied in Philadelphia and Paris, taught art in Michigan, and immigrated to Canada in 1931: 691

Gordon, Doug. VC 3T3: 29

Gould, Ernie. VC 3T3: 30, 66, 84, 107, 131, 173, 192, 199, 218, 272, 279, 345, 351, 356, 359, 366, 379, 396, 444, 445, 450, 462, 894

Gould, Margaret. Toronto journalist: 847

Gould, Sydney (Sid). VC 2T9; older brother of Ernie Gould; returned to VC to teach classics in 1935: 684

Govan, Betty. Sister of Robin Govan: 304

Govan, Margaret (Robin). Extramural student at EC, 1933–34; head counselor at Camp Onawaw in the mid-1930s; later became director, and eventually owner, of the camp: 142, 247, 304, 311, 324, 338

Grant, William Carroll (Bill). VC 3T3: 284

Green, Gertrude Huntley. Canadian pianist: 11, 47

Green, Laura Georgina Frances (Georgie). Graduate in household sciences, U of T, 3T3: 48, 54, 74, 107, 118, 615

Gregory, Wilfred Palmer (Wilf). VC 3T3: 371

Grier, Sir Wyly (1862–1957). Canadian portrait painter; knighted in 1935 for his contributions to Canadian arts and letters: 707, 796

Grimthorpe, Edmund B.G. (1816–1905). English lawyer and authority on architecture: 492

Group of Seven. Canadian art movement that drew its inspiration from northern Ontario landscapes; its seven members were Frank Carmichael, Lawren Harris, A.Y. Jackson, Frank Johnston, Arthur Lismer, J.E.H. MacDonald, and F.H. Varley: 75, 450, 796

Grube, George M.A. Classical scholar; book review editor and managing editor of the *Canadian Forum*: 815, 818, 899

Guerrero, Alberto. Renowned piano teacher at the RCM; his students included Glenn Gould: 379

Gunther, Ruth. Art student; grew up in Brantford, Ont., next door to the house where Elizabeth Eedy Brown, NF's second wife, lived: 665

Haeckel, Ernst (1834–1919). German naturalist: 521

Hahn, Elizabeth Wyn Wood (Betty) (1903–66). Canadian sculptor, muralist, monumentalist, and medallist; married Emanuel Hahn; taught at the Central Technical School in Toronto: 460, 796

Hahn, Emanuel Otto (Mannie) (1881–1957). Canadian sculptor and teacher; well known for his realistic commemorative sculptures in the Toronto area and native subjects; married Elizabeth (Betty) Wyn Wood: 460, 796

Haines, Frederick S. (Fred) (1879–1960). Canadian landscape painter; served as curator of the AGT, 1927–32; principal of the OCA, 1932–51: 815

Justice, Rev. A.C. One of NF's supervisory pastors when he was a student minister in southwestern Sask.; served the church in Tompkins, Sask., 1934–42: 302

Kane, Paul (1810–71). Most famous of the Canadian artist-explorers; best known for his paintings of western scenery and native people: 796
Keith, Alexander Murdock. VC 3T4: 151, 159
Kelly, Nan. Communist friend of Maurice Ridgion: 576
Kemp, Clara. HK's paternal aunt from Forest, Ont.: 12, 13, 14, 557
Kemp, Daniel. HK's paternal grandfather: 14, 15n. 3
Kemp, Gertrude Maidement. HK's mother: xviii, 76, 107, 108, 129, 131, 150, 170–1, 176, 180, 524, 534, 543, 615, 656, 690, 695, 698, 733, 753, 843, 883
Kemp, Harold. HK's younger brother; killed in a bombing raid over Germany, February 1944: xviii, 13, 108, 116, 119, 157, 290, 356, 522, 523, 524, 525, 535, 537, 538, 541, 542, 543, 549, 558, 583, 601, 615, 642, 661, 666, 679, 683, 690, 695, 709, 722, 760, 814, 817–18, 819–20, 843, 844, 861, 868
Kemp, Helen. See Frye, Helen Kemp
Kemp, Hubert R. Professor of political economy, U of T; got undergraduates interested in making bamboo pipes, which they used in a 1939 concert at Hart House: 207, 214, 234, 247
Kemp, Ken. HK's first cousin, the son of her Uncle Ab and Aunt Minnie Kemp: 107
Kemp, Marion. HK's younger sister; went to South Africa in 1936 to marry Ernie Harrison, the first of her three husbands; died in Rhodesia on 2 February 1977: xviii, 82, 108, 119, 131, 149, 157, 159, 233, 236, 271, 325, 356, 464, 466n. 12, 525, 531, 538, 653, 656, 709, 733
Kemp, Rebecca Sarah Cronin. HK's paternal grandmother: 14, 15n. 3
Kemp, Roy. VC 3T8; HK's younger brother: xviii, 32, 33, 34, 36, 46, 47, 57, 73, 109, 118, 127, 149, 166, 172, 173, 195, 210, 218, 233, 236, 267, 271, 283, 320, 327, 338, 379, 382, 389, 456, 461–2, 465nn. 4–5, 534–5, 537, 538, 542, 549–50, 556, 584, 600, 608, 615, 624, 642, 650, 653, 656, 660, 661, 666, 672, 676, 682, 698, 708, 709, 733, 746–7, 748–9, 754, 759, 760, 763, 764–5, 792, 800, 816, 818, 819, 820, 843, 844, 847, 849–50, 853, 857, 861, 888, 898
Kemp, Stanley Herbert Franklin (S.H.F.). HK's father; VC 0T6; abandoned his intention to enter the ministry because of deafness; became a commercial artist for Grip Ltd., where early in his career he worked with Arthur Lismer and Tom Thomson; was the chief designer for the Crown Cork and Seal Co.: xvii, 5, 32, 76, 108, 129, 130, 132, 150, 170, 172, 176, 180, 197, 233, 303, 320, 339, 388, 389, 402, 419, 428, 449, 451, 486, 524, 525, 534, 541, 556, 615, 656, 683, 686, 694, 733, 753, 759, 850, 894
Kemp, W.W. (Well). HK's paternal uncle from Forest, Ont.: 12, 14, 107, 557
Keppel, F.P. President of the Carnegie corporation: 235, 260
Kerley, Annie. Music teacher; daughter of H.H. Kerley: 296

Kerley, Rev. H.H. Minister in Tompkins, Sask., 1924–34; supervisory pastor of the Stone mission field when NF was a student minister there: 223

Kermode, F. Director of the Provincial Museum, Victoria, B.C., and member of the Carnegie committee that studied the problems of museums in Canada: 260, 265

Kettle, H. Garnard (Rik). Founding member of the PLS, Canada's first art rental; member of the Canadian Society of Painters in Watercolour: 669, 691, 819, 843, 847, 857, 861

Keynes, Sir Geoffrey. Blake editor and scholar: 711, 750, 765, 789

Kidd, Gwendolyn M. (Gwen). Secretary of the children's art centre and public relations secretary at the AGT: 593, 686, 690, 817, 853, 865, 867, 874

Kidder, Margaret (Peggy). Education secretary at the AGT: 650, 670, 671, 682, 721, 732, 813, 817

King, Harold (1904–49). Toronto artist; taught at the NorthernVocational School: 818, 819

King, Marjory. Wife of Harold King: 787, 813

Kirby, Fred. Childhood friend of NF: 170, 529

Knight, G. Wilson. Professor of English at Trinity College, U of T, in the 1930s; taught at the University of Leeds, 1941–62; his main interest was Shakespeare, many of whose plays he produced and acted in; brother of W.F. Jackson Knight: 435, 536, 540, 567, 588, 625–6, 638, 657, 807–8

Knight, Norm. VC 3T4: 51, 67–8, 91, 107, 127, 149, 198, 279, 289, 292, 295, 367, 533, 679

Knight, W.F. Jackson. Professor of classics at Exeter University; brother of G. Wilson Knight: 579–80, 588–9, 638

Knights, L.C. Lived in the same boarding house as HK when she studied at the Courtauld Institute; editor, along with F.R. Leavis, of *Scrutiny*: 405, 412, 601

Koetse, Stien. Friend of HK; studied at the Courtauld Institute in London when HK was enrolled there; they met in Paris in September 1935: 454, 472, 490, 499, 748

Koldofsky, Adolph (1905–51). Violinist who succeeded Harry Adaskin as a member of the Hart House String Quartet in 1938: 747, 754

Kortright, Nell. Membership secretary of the AGT: 552, 564, 583

Kresz. *See* de Kresz

Krieghoff, Cornelius (1915–72). Canadian artist; best known for his genre paintings of *habitants* and Indians, most of which were produced for the tourist market: 230, 796

Krug, Charlie. Don of Gate House at VC during NF and HK's student days; UC 2T6 and EC 2E9; became professor of philosophy and psychology at Mount Allison University in 1932: 10, 83

Laing, Blair. VC 3T5: 53, 706, 722

Lambert, George. Canadian baritone; gave frequent public performances,

Lincke, Hans. Friend of Roy Kemp; played cello and studied at the TCM: 35, 46–7, 57, 61, 75, 82

Lindsay, A.D. English philosopher; vice-chancellor of Oxford University: 796, 806

Line, John. Professor of philosophy and history of religion at EC: 166, 167, 353, 490, 853

Line, William. Member of the psychology department, U of T: 858, 859, 860

Lipsett, Pat. VC 3T2; married Kingsley Joblin: 33

Lismer, Arthur (1885–1969). Painter, art teacher, and member of the Group of Seven; educational supervisor at the AGT, 1927–38; friend of HK's father: 4, 75, 129, 165, 176, 178, 185, 212, 215, 234, 235, 256, 258, 260, 261, 265, 338, 381, 382, 410, 419, 433, 443, 450, 474, 487, 490, 491, 559, 586, 607, 672, 676, 683, 710, 720, 794, 802, 806, 815, 820, 823, 854, 865–7, 868, 883, 888, 893, 895, 897, 902

Lismer, Marjorie. Daughter of Arthur Lismer; VC 3T5; a student at Columbia University when HK stayed with her in 1939: 165, 902

Listowel, William Frances Hare, Earl of. Lecturer on aesthetics at the Courtauld Institute: 351

Little, W.J. Bursar and senior tutor at VC during HK and NF's student days: 10, 221, 267, 298, 377, 491, 851, 852, 853

Livingston, Doris. VC 3T3; later, Doris Moggridge: 106, 107, 675, 676, 677, 698

Locke, George H. Chief librarian of the Public Library of Toronto; instructor at the library school, U of T: 116, 119, 165, 213, 235, 382, 428, 683

Locke, Malhon W. Canadian physician; claimed to heal numerous ailments by correcting foot posture: 521, 522n. 1

Longley, Beatrice Bond (Bea). VC 3T4: 304, 324

Loring, Frances Norma (1887–1968). Canadian sculptor and monumentalist; for 50 years she shared a studio with fellow sculptor Florence Wyle: 796

Lorraway, Marie. VC 3T2: 210, 216–17, 291, 298

Lowenthal, Helen. Student at the Courtauld Institute when HK studied there; later, guide lecturer at the V & A; travelled with HK in Italy in April 1935: 430, 432, 449, 552

Lyall, Laura Muntz (1860–1930). Toronto artist, best known for her paintings of children: 668

Lyall, Ruby. Friend of Vera Frye: 124, 139

Lyle, John M. Member of the board of the AGT: 807

Lyly, John (ca. 1554–1606). English dramatist: 688

Lytle, Dorothy. Student at the Courtauld Institute when HK studied there: 431, 456

MacAgy, Douglas. Friend of HK; worked at the Barnes Collection in Merion, Pa., and later at museums in Cleveland, San Francisco, and New York: 576, 641–2, 670, 672, 682, 690, 710, 716, 722, 733, 752, 754, 786–7, 817, 834

often participated in the intellectual discussions at Bertram Brooker's house: 460

Munro, Thomas. Curator at the Cleveland Art Museum; earlier, associate education director of the Barnes Foundation and professor of philosophy at Rutgers: 585, 642, 786

Murray, Gilbert (1866–1957). Australian classical scholar and translator of Greek drama; became Regius professor of Greek at Oxford; six times he stood as an unsuccessful Liberal candidate for Parliament: 638

Murray, Walter C. President of the University of Saskatchewan: 343

Nazimova, Alla (1879–1945). Russian actress who performed in the U.S.: 697

Neely, Donald and Margaret. Family with whom NF stayed in Carnagh when he was a student minister in Sask. during the summer of 1934; Donald Neely was the postmaster at Carnagh, 1930–68; their two children—during the time NF roomed and boarded with them—were Kathleen and Donald, Jr.: 253, 267, 302

Neil, John. Minister of Westminster Presbyterian Church, Toronto: 56

Newton, Eric. Art critic for the *Manchester Guardian*: 695, 813, 815, 825, 830; "Canadian Art through English Eyes," 843, 845n. 2, 850

Nichols, Beverley (1899–1983). English essayist, novelist, playwright, and gossip columnist; a number of his books were best sellers: 878

Nickle, M.I. Don in the women's residences at VC: 627, 642, 662

Nicol, Pegi (1904–49). Canadian artist; later, Pegi Nicol MacLeod; member of the PLS; helped create the first surge of Canadian modernism: 553, 557, 578, 669, 732, 796, 854

Noble, Eunice M. VC 3T2: 720

Norman, Egerton Herbert (Herb). VC 3T2; later a distinguished historian and diplomat: 295, 352, 389

Nott, Herb. U of T 3T8; one of Roy Kemp's partners, along with Christina Huidekoper, in a portrait photography studio at 24 Harbord St. in Toronto: 818

Noyes, Gertrude. Wife of Henry Noyes: 854, 864, 892

Noyes, Henry. UC 3T3; M.A., U of T, 1936; Ph.D., University of London, 1938; taught at VC in 1938–39: 663, 676, 677, 699, 791, 792, 798, 814, 846, 847, 851, 852, 853, 863, 871–2, 879, 883, 885, 886, 890, 896

Nunn, Guy T. Rhodes Scholar from California; B.A., Merton College, 1939; M.A., 1943: 840

Ogilvie, Will (1901–89). Canadian painter; the first official Canadian war artist; painted murals for the chapel at Hart House: 81–2, 559, 669, 796

Oldfield, Mildred (Millie). VC 3T3; married Graham Millar: 144, 396, 444, 594, 698, 749

Oram, Betty. VC 3T3; sister of Helen Oram: 157

Oram, Helen. VC 3T3; sister of Betty Oram: 157

Orchard, Bob. Poet whose work appeared in the *Canadian Forum* and the *Canadian Poetry Magazine* among other places: 657

Oughton, Jack. Close friend of HK; lived around the corner from the Kemps at 882 Carlaw St.; assistant in biology at the U of T, 1934–35; became an associate in zoology at the ROM, 1936; later taught at the Ontario Agricultural College and worked for twenty years for the World Health Organization at the United Nations: 157, 172, 249, 265–6, 338, 847

Oughton, Phyllis. Wife of Jack Oughton; studied biology at UC: 802, 847

Owen, Derwyn Trevor. Elected bishop of Niagara in 1925 and bishop of Toronto in 1932; became archbishop of Toronto and primate of the Church of England for all of Canada in 1934: 166, 290–1, 706

Palmer, Elizabeth. Chemist HK met at her rooming house in London, when she was at the Courtauld Institute: 381–2, 383, 386, 392, 393, 408

Palmer, Lou. American student, studying at Exeter College when NF was at Merton in 1936–37; during part of NF's trip to Italy, they travelled together: 738, 745n. 17, 834

Panton, Lawrence Arthur Colley (1894–1954). Canadian landscape painter; principal of the OCA, 1951–54; president of the Arts and Letters Club, 1953: 709, 857

Paul, James and Minnie. Members of the Carnagh community in southwestern Sask. when NF was a student minister there: 296, 302

Pellatt, Sir Henry Mill. Canadian capitalist involved in hydroelectric and transportation projects; his eccentric stone mansion, Casa Loma, became a Toronto landmark: 873

Pepper, Freda. Lecturer at the AGT; in charge of the Children's Art Centre, 1936–37: 628, 666

Perold, J.G. Lecturer in the department of political economy at the U of T: 347

Phillips, Lois. VC exchange student from Manitoba: 601

Pidgeon, Helen C. (Bunny). VC 3T4; married Cameron Caesar: 690

Pike, Bill. Friend of Roy Kemp: 32, 34, 82, 320

Pike, Ruth. Friend of HK: 57, 66

Pratt, E.J. (1882–1964). Member of the English department at VC and well-known Canadian poet: 116, 294, 375, 377, 378, 386, 394, 625, 691, 693, 760, 890, 896

Price, (Frank) Percival. Carillonneur, campanologist, and composer; helped design the carillon for the Peace Tower for the Parliament Buildings in Ottawa; brother of Marjorie Price: 236, 255, 261–2, 362–3, 365, 395

Price, Marjorie. VC 3T1; sister of Percival Price and friend of HK: 236, 261, 365

Proctor, David. VC 3T8 and EC 4E1: 802

Proctor, Elizabeth M. Sister of David Proctor; entered VC in 1938: 802

Pye, Yascha. Violinist who taught master classes at the HCM; replaced John Langley in the Hambourg Trio: 219

Rae, Saul F. UC 3T6: 660, 663, 864

Raeburn, Sir Henry (1756–1823). Scottish portrait painter: 125

Ray, Margaret V. (Peggy). VC 2T2; assistant to the librarian at VC; associate librarian, 1935; librarian, 1952; close friend and confidante of HK: 17–18, 35, 36, 107, 119, 120, 132, 158, 165, 172, 176, 178, 195, 206, 231, 235, 266, 270–1, 272, 280, 324, 339, 360, 382, 407, 428–9, 462, 487, 489, 500, 594, 655, 767

Raymer, Lorna. VC 3T5: 58

Redmond, Mildred. VC 3T4: 255, 807

Reid, George A. (1860–1947) Canadian painter and muralist; taught at the OCA, 1891–1928: 796

Reid, Hannah. Toronto physician: 543

Reid, Joseph B. Canadian Rhodes scholar at Merton College; B.A. in math, 1937; B.Sc., 1939; M.A., 1941: 598, 604, 612, 614, 621, 646, 664, 701, 811–12

Rennie, Almon Secord. Stepfather of Mackay Hewer, the boyfriend and, later, the husband of Mary Carman: 217, 263

Renwick, W.L. British scholar: 714

Ricker, Isabel. VC 3T3: 661, 697, 720

Riddell, Jerry. Senior tutor at VC; later joined the Canadian department of external affairs: 438, 445, 446, 480, 497, 558, 594, 624, 628, 642, 643, 651, 679, 685, 747, 791, 843, 852, 860, 894, 899–900

Riddell, John H. Father of Jerry Riddell; principal of Wesley College: 464

Riddell, Kay. Wife of Jerry Riddell: 616, 624, 628, 643, 667, 679, 685, 791, 799, 816, 843, 859, 860, 893, 894, 900

Ridgion, Maurice. Friend of Dickinson; NF met Ridgion in London in September 1936, went to a play with him and to his house on several occasions to listen to music: 567, 568, 576, 577, 590

Ridley, M.R. Member of the English faculty at Balliol College: 789–90

Rièse, Laure. VC 3T3 and longtime member of the French department at VC: 792, 799, 802, 806–7, 829, 865, 886, 896

Roberts, Charles G.D. (1860–1943). Canadian writer and naturalist: 449

Roberts, Richard. Minister at Sherbourne United Church, Toronto, 1926–38; moderator of the United Church of Canada, 1934–36; part-time lecturer at EC, 1933–34: 290, 353

Robertson, Elizabeth (Bessie) Chant. Distinguished medical doctor; wife of H. Grant Robertson: 799

Robertson, H. Grant. Member of the classics department at VC; son of J.C. Robertson, professor emeritus of the classics department: 801n. 10

Robertson, Mrs. J.C. Wife of J.C. Robertson, mother of H. Grant Robertson, and mother-in-law of Elizabeth Chant Robertson: 799

Robins, John D. Professor of English at VC: 166, 439, 462, 760, 843, 852, 863, 881, 883, 890, 896, 898, 900, 901

Robson, Albert H. Vice-president of the council of the AGT, 1927–39: 574, 872

Roger, Mary Isabel Martha (Maysie). VC 3T4: 108, 304, 315, 341, 402, 450, 469, 501, 710, 748, 807, 844, 865

Rogers, Evelyn. NF's ex-girlfriend in Moncton, N.B.; her father was a railway trade union organizer and active in the CCF: 9n. 2, 76, 99, 160, 529, 535, 539–40, 544

Rogers, Helen. VC 3T5: 717

Romans, Robert Gordon (Gordie). VC 3T3; married Lois Hampson: 10, 17, 20, 24, 89, 169, 253, 717

Rose, Millicent. Student at the Courtauld Institute when HK was studying there; a committed Communist; they travelled to Italy together: 369, 398, 399, 408–10, 412–13, 417–18, 420, 426, 429–31, 449, 451, 454, 475, 486, 533, 616, 710, 858

Roseborough, Margaret (Peggy). Member of H.J. Davis's graduate seminar on Blake that NF enrolled in during his first year at EC: 239, 355, 385, 393, 394, 401, 426, 439, 552, 672, 685, 693, 786, 883, 894

Ross, Earl. One of the guards at the AGT: 857

Rourke, Robert E.K. Master of Pickering College in Newmarket, Ont.; married Alice Strong: 133

Rowell, Mary C. Member of the French department at VC, 1919–35: 893

Rowell, Newton Wesley. Lawyer, politician, and churchman; helped to develop the work of the League of Nations and was a leading layman in the founding of the United Church of Canada; appointed chief justice of Ontario, 1936: 656

Rowland, Henry Edgar (Hank). VC 3T3: 92

Russell, Dora. Bertrand Russell's second wife; early feminist advocate of more liberal attitudes toward premarital sex, birth control, and planned parenthood: 106–7, 134, 141

Russell, Frances. VC 3T5; lived with Barbara Sturgis in 1936, taking HK's place in the apartment they had rented after HK became a don in the women's residences at VC: 289, 584, 650, 807

Russell, John Wentworth. Canadian artist and portrait painter: 81

Russell, Kathleen M. (Kay). VC 3T2: 720–1

Rutherford, Ewart. VC 3T3: 52

Rutherford, Gertrude. VC 2T1; associate general secretary of the SCM, 1923–34; principal of the United Church Training School in Toronto, which was affiliated with EC: 158, 159, 174, 315

Rutherford, J.F. Radio preacher and leader of the International Bible Students' Association and the Watch Tower Bible and Tract Society (Jehovah's Witnesses): 97

Rutherford, Phyllis. VC student, 1937–39: 872

Ryder, Lady Francis. Oxford resident who befriended a number of scholars and
  students from Canada and other Commonwealth countries: 409, 663

Sadler, Sir Michael (1861–1943). Helped develop the modern English educa-
  tional system; art collector: 795–6, 808, 814, 819
Sadlier, Helen. VC 3T3: 26
Sanders, Byrne. Editor of *Chatelaine*, 1929–51: 672
Sanderson, C.R. Deputy chief librarian at the Toronto Public Library and
  instructor in the library school, U of T: 198
Sarg, Tony (1882–1942). Illustrator of children's books and humorous stories for
  the *Saturday Evening Post* and other magazines and proprietor of his own marionette company: 137
Saunders, Doris. Member of the English department and assistant dean of
  women, University of Winnipeg: 450, 452n. 9
Schaefer, Carl (b. 1903). Ontario landscape artist; developed rural and social
  themes in his paintings in the 1930s: 497, 669, 787
Sclater, John Robert Patterson. Minister of Old St. Andrew's Church at Carlton
  and Jarvis Sts. in Toronto; father of Molly Sclater: 872
Sclater, Mary Lindsay (Molly). VC 3T6; ATCM, 1938; B. Mus., U of T, 1938;
  became a teacher, author, and organist-choirmaster; daughter of John Robert
  Patterson Sclater: 304, 305, 309, 310, 311, 318, 338, 388
Scott, Duncan Campbell (1862–1947). Canadian poet and short story writer and
  federal civil servant: 194, 204, 684; sister of, 196, 254
Sedgwick, Al. Former boyfriend of HK: 197, 231, 320, 327, 535
Sedgwick, Is. Brother of Al Sedgwick: 214
Shore, Taylor C. Member of the German department at VC: 731
Silvester, Betty. Riding instructor at Camp Onawaw: 319
Sim, Isobel. VC 3T5: 686
Sinclair, Isabelle. VC 3T3: 106
Sinclair, Kenneth and Mina. Members of the Stonepile community in southwest-
  ern Sask. when NF was a student minister there; immigrated from Scotland;
  one of the earliest settlers in the Garden Head district; raised nine children:
  277
Sissons, C.B. Professor of ancient history at VC: 165
Skitch, F.B. (Fred). VC 3T6; music, film, and drama editor for *Acta Victoriana*,
  1935–36: 174, 179
Sly, Allan. Organized the men's glee club at Hart House and directed the club in
  1933–34: 247
Smith, Audrey. Friend of HK; taught at the AGT in 1933 and studied at the Central School of Arts and Crafts in London the next year: 341, 371
Smith, David Nichol. Merton professor of English literature at Oxford: 596, 600,
  610, 693, 794
Smith, Florence A. (Smitty). Don in the women's residences at VC and a reader

in the English department: 574, 596, 618, 627, 628, 634, 642, 654, 667, 668, 669, 683, 733, 752, 846

Smith, Fred. Neighbour of the Kemps; spent time at their cottage at Gordon Bay: 129, 143, 542

Smith, Goldwin (1823–1910). Regius Professor of modern history at Oxford; taught for three years at Cornell University; settled permanently in Canada in 1871 and wrote on Canadian and international affairs: 695

Smith, Home. Architect known for a number of projects in the western end of Toronto: 34

Smith, Leo. Composer, writer, and teacher; principal cellist for the TSO, 1932–40; taught at the TCM; professor in the faculty of music, U of T, 1927–50: 356, 362, 695, 847

Smith, Lillian H. (1887–1983). Children's librarian: 371

Smith, Olive Irene. VC 3T2: 116

Smith, Thorne (1893–1934). American humorist: 438

Smith, Winifred. Proprietor of HK's boarding house in Ottawa: 191

Snelgrove, Gordon. Art student who studied at the NGC and the Courtauld Institute when HK was at both places; from Moose Jaw, Sask.; B.A., University of Saskatchewan; M.A., University of Chicago: 248, 252n. 7, 265, 330–1, 341–3, 358, 360, 381, 390–2, 400, 401, 405, 406, 408–9, 451, 473, 487, 625

Southam, H.S. Publisher of the *Ottawa Citizen*; became chairman of the board of the NGC in 1929; supported the gallery financially and gave it several paintings from his own extensive collection: 265, 707, 716

Sparling, Ruth. VC 3T2: 402

Spry, Graham (1909–83). Rhodes Scholar; publisher of the *Canadian Forum*; helped form the LSR: 873

Stacey, Harold. Designer in metal; shared a studio with Douglas Duncan at the PLS: 690

Stannard, Miss. NF's grade four teacher: 163

Steel, W.A. (1890–1968). Radio pioneer; member of the Canadian Broadcasting Commission: 251

Stephenson, Frederick C. (1864–1941). Secretary of the Young People's Forward Movement, 1906–25, and of Young People's Missionary Education, United Church of Canada, 1925–36: 868

Sterne, Beatrice (Bea). VC 3T3: 245

Stevens, Dorothy (1888–1966). Canadian etcher and portrait and figure painter: 796

Stevens, Helen. VC 3T3: 196n. 5, 676, 701

Stewart, Chester and Martha. Members of the Stonepile community in southwestern Sask. when NF was a student minister there: 238, 252–3

Stewart, Evelyn H. (Ev). VC 3T5: 534, 537, 541, 542, 563, 580, 595, 667, 673, 685, 692

instigation, S.H.F. Kemp joined the Commercial Artists Guild: 45, 47, 57, 87, 88, 753, 754

Toll, Ellsworth. Second-year student at VC, 1932–33: 651

Torrance, Margaret M. (Marg). VC 3T3: 557, 666

Trenka, Stephen. Hungarian sculptor who came to Canada in 1929; exhibited at the 1939 Canadian show at the Tate Gallery in London, taught at the OCA, and later received awards for his coin designs: 796

Tretheway, Mrs. William H. Wife of a member of the French department at VC: 893

Tristram, Ernest William (1882–1952). British art historian whose specialty was medieval wall paintings: 708, 712

Tuero, Edith. VC 3T3: 426

Turkington, Mrs. Owner-director of Camp Onawaw, a summer camp for teen-age girls on a peninsula in the south corner of Lake Vernon, near Huntsville, Ont.: 132, 142, 232, 235, 247, 266, 271, 313–14, 323

Turner, Walter James (W.J.). Music critic for the *New Statesman* and drama critic for the *London Mercury*: 17

Tweedell, W. Donald. VC 3T7: 731

Tweedsmuir. *See* Buchan, John

Uncle Rate. *See* Howard, Eratus

Uncle Well. *See* Kemp, W.W.

Underhill, Frank (1889–1971). Historian and political journalist; taught at the U of T, 1927–55; helped found the *Canadian Forum* and the LSR: 894, 899

Van Allen, Blanche. Sister of M.M. Van Allen: 615, 668

Van Allen, M.M. Dietitian at Wymilwood, VU: 615

Van Vetchen, Laura. The fiancée of Ken Davis, a neighbour of the Kemps at their Gordon Bay summer cottage: 128–9, 131, 143

Varley, F.H. (1881–1969). Canadian portrait and landscape painter; member of the Group of Seven; taught at art schools in Toronto, Vancouver, and Ottawa: 796

Vipond, Les. VC 3T8; editor of the *Varsity* during his fourth year; later became general secretary of the YMCA of Canada: 529, 535, 540, 731

Wace, A.J.B. Professor of archaeology at Cambridge: 845, 849n. 1

Waddington, Geoffrey (1904–66). Musical conductor and administrator; joined the faculty of the TCM and began career as radio musician in 1922; founded the CBC Symphony Orchestra in 1952: 46

Wagstaff, Doris. VC 3T7: 731, 734n. 3

Wainright, Eleanor C. VC 3T7: 720

Wright, Margaret B. (Marg). VC 3T3: 371, 428

Wright, Sherman. Art student on scholarship at the NGC during the time that HK was there in 1934; B.A. in architecture, University of Manitoba; postgraduate work in architecture, Columbia University: 192, 194, 200, 205, 235, 287, 390, 601

Wright, Victoria. Library employee, VC: 36

Wyle, Florence (1881–1936). Canadian sculptor; first woman to be accorded full membership in the Royal Canadian Academy of Arts; shared a studio with fellow sculptor Frances Loring for more than fifty years: 796

Young, George. Long-distance swimmer; named the Canadian swimmer of the half century in 1950: 56

Young, Mrs. T.C. Wife of T.C. Young, a lecturer in Oriental languages at the U of T: 799

Index

For abbreviations used in the index see pages vii–ix, this volume.

198; thesis on, 198, 286, 307, 321,
426, 468; lecture on, 400, 410; plans
to publish book on, 198, 711, 752,
762–3, 763–4, 766; papers and talks
on, 186, 194, 198, 353, 363–4, 436–7;
study of, 182, 183, 197–8, 203, 286,
307, 356, 375, 377, 384, 386, 414–16,
426, 434–5, 458, 467–8, 562, 689, 693,
762, 770
– Blake group, meeting with, 353,
355, 363, 385
– Blunden, Edmund, relationship
with, 599, 610–11, 623, 678, 681,
688–9, 692–3, 699, 794, 809, 825, 855
– Bodley club: dinner, 890, 897;
elected to membership in, 646;
meetings of, 653, 712, 714, 810; presents paper at, 700–1, 810, 822, 825;
secretary of, 890
– bookshops, visits to in London:
Foyle's, 570; New Atlantis, 573
– books read, 25, 26–8, 41, 62–3, 66,
52, 99, 148, 297, 526, 532, 540,
780
– Bryson, J.N., opinion of, 599,
– *Canadian Forum*, writing for, 769–70
– Canterbury, trip to, 890
– on the CCF, 140, 155–6, 168–9
– on Christianity, 62–4, 199, 242–3,
279
– church services, descriptions of,
42–3, 163–4, 182, 530
– on cities: Chicago, 101; Toronto, 84,
597
– Clare, Ida, relationship with, 198,
202, 209, 221, 239
– class standing, 24, 26
– on Coburn, Kay, 377, 395–6, 446,
498
– on Communism, 67–8, 416, 426,
564–5, 577, 739
– concerts and recitals attended, 199–

200, 201, 209, 219, 362–3, 378, 401,
481, 567, 576, 581, 654, 687, 713, 781,
805, 831, 838, 856, 881. *See also*
music, below
– Couchiching conference, attends,
497
– on criticism, 435
– Daniells, Roy, relationship with,
353–4, 364, 375, 378, 424, 435, 439,
446, 692
– debate team, 366
– dreams, 66, 466
– Duns Scotus, on the ghost of, 612,
632
– Emmanuel College: on his theology course, 354–5, 375, 376, 384,
415; first-class honours in theology,
198; church history scholarship,
199, 423
– England, impressions of, 560,
566–7, 570, 572, 575–6, 579, 611
– exams: at EC, 378–9, 384, 423–4,
434; on HK's failing, 482–3, 484; at
Oxford, 652, 659, 677, 680, 877, 889
– failure in religious knowledge
course, 22, 26, 38–9, 51
– Fascism encountered in England,
588–9, 622, 632, 638, 757, 789, 881
– on his father, 68, 153–4, 160, 169–
70, 268, 361–2, 375, 526
– favourite writers, 84
– films seen, 136, 375, 438, 444, 445,
467, 637, 645, 664–5, 742, 804, 828,
832, 864, 881, 885, 890
– financial difficulties at Oxford, 590,
604, 620, 649, 652, 653, 678, 712
– on fine arts training, 79
– Fraser, Elizabeth: attends plays
and films with, 664–5; meets, 604;
meals with, 610, 658, 664; observations about, 632, 636, 646, 653, 680–
1, 688, 692–3, 743, 756, 790, 827–8,